Praise for
PLAYING FOR THEIR LIVES

"This is an amazing story that has meaning for all of us in education. Plus, there's a blueprint for how your own school can duplicate the remarkable success of El Sistema. You'll love the book!"
      —**Eric Jensen, author of** *Teaching with the Brain in Mind*

"Tunstall and Booth provide a beautifully textured exploration of the intersection of child development, social justice, and the orchestral experience. Their book should eliminate any doubt about the global relevance of the orchestral canon and its transformative powers."
            —**Jesse Rosen, President and CEO,**
                  League of American Orchestras

"Tricia Tunstall and Eric Booth are writers I admire and respect. I am very enthusiastic that they share the story of the international growth of El Sistema in such an accurate and engaging way for readers across the world who care about helping children in need."
      —**Dr. José Antonio Abreu, founder of El Sistema**

"El Sistema is the most incredible arts education program in the world today."

                  —**Frank Gehry, architect**

"Tricia Tunstall and Eric Booth have thrillingly brought to life the transformative power of youth orchestras to generate meaningful social change in disadvantaged communities. Their global report would have gladdened the heart of my father, Leonard Bernstein—the original Citizen Artist."

            —**Jamie Bernstein, writer, filmmaker**

*Playing for
Their Lives*

Playing for Their Lives

THE GLOBAL EL SISTEMA MOVEMENT
FOR SOCIAL CHANGE
THROUGH MUSIC

Tricia Tunstall
and
Eric Booth

W. W. NORTON & COMPANY

Independent Publishers Since 1923

New York • London

For information about permission to reproduce selections from this book,
write to Permissions, W. W. Norton & Company, Inc.,
500 Fifth Avenue, New York, NY 10110

For information about special discounts for bulk purchases, please contact
W. W. Norton Special Sales at specialsales@wwnorton.com or 800-233-4830

Manufacturing by Quad Graphics Fairfield
Book design by BTDnyc
Production manager: Anna Oler

Library of Congress Cataloging-in-Publication Data

Names: Tunstall, Tricia. | Booth, Eric.
Title: Playing for their lives : the global El sistema movement for social
change through music / Tricia Tunstall and Eric Booth.
Description: First edition. | New York : W. W. Norton & Company, [2016] |
Includes bibliographical references and index.
Identifiers: LCCN 2016013663 | ISBN 9780393245646 (hardcover)
Subjects: LCSH: Music—Instruction and study—Social aspects. |
Music—Instruction and study—Venezuela—Social aspects. | Fundación
Musical Simón Bolívar.
Classification: LCC MT1 .T88 2016 | DDC 780.71—dc23 LC record available at
https://lccn.loc.gov/2016013663

W. W. Norton & Company, Inc.
500 Fifth Avenue, New York, N.Y. 10110
www.wwnorton.com

W. W. Norton & Company Ltd.
Castle House, 75/76 Wells Street, London W1T 3QT

1 2 3 4 5 6 7 8 9 0

We dedicate this book to

JOSÉ ANTONIO ABREU,

*founder of El Sistema, a citizen artist whose visionary leadership
has inspired a world community to bring art and social justice
together with unprecedented power and love.*

Contents

Introduction

I magine this. You have been hired to lead a large international agency charged with disrupting entrenched patterns of poverty around the world. You recognize that countless well-intentioned efforts by smart people over decades—government and NGO initiatives, economic reforms, education programs, aid of many kinds—have largely failed to reduce the percentage of the world's population (over 70 percent) who live in poverty. Few of these initiatives have made a sustainable change at more than a local level. The sixty nations supporting you have begun to wonder whether anything can make a substantial difference.

You have called an international press conference to announce your plan. You step to the microphone and raise two fingers to indicate that you have two big ideas. "Youth orchestras," you say. And, "Venezuela."

The scattered laughter that greets this announcement subsides as the reporters realize you are serious about proposing two of the least probable ideas on earth for the successful disruption of entrenched poverty: a country plagued by economic troubles and social turmoil, and an arts institution that is often seen, at best, as marginal, at worst as an anachronism.

You say, "It's already underway. And it's working."

AN ELLIPSIS OF TREE STUMPS punctuates the dirt road entry to Baleeira, a gang-controlled favela in the depressed interior Brazilian city of Campos dos Goytacazes. At night an armed man sits on guard, as much to dissuade the police from entering as to intimidate rival gangs. In the daylight there are no men visible; young girls cradling babies stand in doorways with no doors, and children wander in the rutted dirt streets. The half-abandoned dwellings have broken walls and patchy electricity and plumbing. There are lame dogs, blind dogs, rooting in piles of garbage. Roosters square off in pairs; they know the moves. In a room above a decrepit evangelical church, eight small children sit on the floor, singing and clapping with their teacher. The walls above their heads are covered with pictures of a youth orchestra and chorus; the children recognize many of the faces in the photos as their older siblings or cousins.

A mile or so away, in a large bare room off a sunny courtyard, those siblings and cousins are taking part in a rehearsal of Mozart's *Missa Brevis*. The members of the orchestra and chorus are mostly teenagers from Baleeira and similar favelas—although the youngest member, who plays piccolo, is only ten. A high trumpet line arcs above the strings and winds as the chorus sings "Osanna in excelsis!"

HAMMARKULLEN, SWEDEN, IS a section of the port city of Gothenburg where immigrants from many countries live in conditions of poverty, marginalization, and hair-trigger violence. Every afternoon, in a community center in the midst of these dangerous streets, children of Hammarkullen gather to sing, dance, and play orchestral instruments. Though ethnic hostilities run deep among their parents and families, the children have learned to play together so well that they are sometimes invited to play with the Gothenburg Symphony Orchestra, sitting side by side at music stands with the professional musicians in the fancy downtown concert hall. Some of their parents have been so impressed by what the children are accomplishing that they have crossed rigidly maintained ethnic lines and formed a parent chorus. At concerts, the chorus often sings the "Ode to Joy"—in Swedish.

FOR THE FIRST TIME, students from the intensive music program in Karonhianonhnha and Kateri elementary schools, in the Kahnawake Mohawk Territory of Quebec, Canada, were asked to take part in the 25th Annual Powwow "Echoes of a Proud Nation." To celebrate the occasion and to honor their music program, the students and their parents designed a T-shirt emblazoned with a name they gave themselves, along with a logo of crossed violins. Their Mohawk name is Ratirennenhá:wi, which means, "They carry the music with them."[1]

SOUTH CENTRAL LOS ANGELES is the community where the Rodney King riots erupted a generation ago, a ghetto neighborhood still ravaged by poverty, crime, gang wars, and chronic unemployment. In a municipal recreation facility called the Expo Center, on the fourth floor, a full symphony orchestra made up of children born and raised in South Central L.A. is playing Rossini's *William Tell* Overture. After a concentrated two-hour rehearsal, they are discovering that they can play it faster, and they sound better, than they did the week before. Many of the children are Latino, and call the piece *Guillermo Tell*. The smaller children hear it differently: when the conductor says rehearsal is over, they call out, "Please, please, can we play *The Deer Motel* one more time?"

SOMETHING UNPRECEDENTED IS HAPPENING in some of the bleakest and least hopeful corners of the world. A steadily growing number of people are specializing in a new way to take on intractable social challenges: they are teaching children to play orchestral music and sing choral music, together. The children don't know they have joined a worldwide movement to combat the ravages of poverty; they only know that making music is hard and fun, and they and their friends are getting better at it.

This is a new way to think about fighting poverty and exclusion. It's not, on the face of it, the most likely way; youth orchestras may in fact be exactly the last place one would normally think to look for a practicable answer to social ills. Yet an increasing number of people, in five dozen countries around the world, believe in this new idea, and are advocating for it, experimenting with it, and committing their lives to it.

The idea is simply this: the experience of inclusion in collective striving toward musical beauty can be a powerful force for positive change in the life of a child, a family, and a community. Across the world, musicians with strong social consciences are teaching young people suffering from poverty, marginality, and trauma to work and play in intensive ensemble music-making, in an atmosphere of rigor and joy.

They are doing this in big-city ghettos and remote farming towns, in jungles and on mountains, in many countries and on every continent except Antarctica (but including Greenland). They launch programs of initially modest scope and large aspiration. They find sometimes-precarious financing from unlikely sources. They place musical instruments in the hands of children who are more likely to be handed weapons or recruited into drug dealing—whose peers and friends *are* being handed weapons and drugs—and lead these children into the arduous collective pursuit of beauty and excellence.

And they are succeeding. The results, increasingly affirmed through qualitative and quantitative research, substantiate the hopeful claims. These programs are accomplishing what many social welfare programs have not been able to achieve. They improve school attendance, academic achievement, and behavior; they build social skills; and they strengthen the confidence and self-assurance of children who will need these qualities in order to beat the odds that poverty stacks against them and to make choices that, in their communities, have never been available to make.

The musicians and social activists leading these programs think of themselves as part of a growing worldwide network of people who share the simple but compelling assumption that if children spend several hours a day, for many weeks and years, learning to make music together and to create and communicate beauty, they can overcome difficult circumstances and become productive, empathic citizens. These children and young people can make life choices that others in their circumstances are unable to make. In the process, they can make a lasting difference to their communities.

We think of the leaders and teachers of these programs as "citizen artists," because they share an understanding of what it means to be an artist in today's world. They are convinced that artistry is a fundamental dimension of the human spirit, and that it is their responsibility to contribute, through both art-making and teaching, to social welfare and civic life. There have always been citizen artists, from cave painters to Pete Seeger, but the El Sistema youth orchestra movement— the international movement we describe in these pages—has been embraced by an unusually widespread new generation of artists who see their work in the context of a vision for social change.

The catalyst for this vision is an extraordinary program in Venezuela called El Sistema, which began over forty years ago as a youth symphony in Caracas and spread in the ensuing years throughout the country's barrios. El Sistema's founder, José Antonio Abreu, is an economist, former government minister, and accomplished musician—and a classic exemplar of the citizen artist. Under his leadership, El Sistema has blossomed into a vast network of children's musical ensembles throughout Venezuela, now involving 780,000 children.

Maestro Abreu's seminal insight is that bringing children and young people together in musical ensembles can provide social and emotional growth as well as musical learning. The El Sistema mission is not only to help children but often, literally, to rescue them—and, in the process, to effect real and lasting changes in the lives of their families and communities. "The orchestra and choir are much more than artistic studies," Abreu has said. "They are examples and schools of social life. From the minute a child is taught how to play an instrument, he is no longer poor. He becomes a child in progress, who will become a citizen."

The El Sistema idea began to spread from Venezuela to countries across Latin America almost three decades ago. The past decade has seen an explosion of interest in El Sistema throughout the world. In the United States, there are now Sistema-inspired programs in over a hundred cities and towns, a development accelerated by the Los Angeles Philharmonic Orchestra's appointment of Venezuelan conductor Gustavo Dudamel as music director. Dudamel, who was educated in El Sistema and has rapidly become one of the world's most celebrated conductors, is a high-visibility advocate for El Sistema in the United States. Across the world, there are Sistema-inspired programs in over 60 countries, including 26 European countries, a number of Asian and African countries, and Australia. The global Sistema now includes over 370 different programs, over 1,000 núcleos (the Venezuelan term for a Sistema community music center), over 1500 choruses, over 2,000 youth orchestras, and almost 1 million children. These are the numbers as this book goes to print; by the time you read it, they will be higher.

Since this book is an expression of our personal dedication as much as of our professional commitment, we feel it's important to share with readers our pathways to writing it. We came from different starting points, and joined forces in 2009.

ERIC'S JOURNEY

Conservatory-trained as an actor, I was working all the time in New York and around the country, mostly doing classical plays, but also popping up in soap operas on television and new plays on Broadway. But it didn't feel like enough; I felt underutilized by a New York actor's life, so I explored around the edges. I did a lot of volunteer work (including seven years as a New York City Auxiliary Police

Officer and cultural assimilation work with Russian emigré scientists) to try to contribute to the life of my hometown.

When I tried working as a "teaching artist" at Lincoln Center, in 1979, I immediately felt I had found an answer to my dissatisfactions with a professional actor's life. A teaching artist is a practicing artist who develops the complementary skills of an educator to accomplish a wide variety of learning goals. (El Sistema is rich in teaching artists.) I have pursued this vocation, working with learners from many corners of society, from inner-city kindergarten classrooms to Fortune 500 corporate boardrooms, from museums to prisons, and for the last thirty-five years have helped develop teaching artistry into a profession. For this work, I have been the first teaching artist to be awarded an honorary doctorate and, in 2015, to win the nation's highest award in arts education.

By developing the teaching artist program at Juilliard in the 1990s, I came into the classical music world, even though I have no musical background. Being an outsider-on-the-inside proved useful to the field and led to my consulting with many major orchestras, working with ensembles, and training musicians. But by 2005, I was frustrated. I wrote; I made speeches; I consulted; I did countless workshops and projects . . . but orchestras and artist training programs were slow to change. They weren't connecting to their wider communities, weren't growing with the times and needs (at least not fast enough for me), and weren't making as much difference in the world as I knew they could and should. Arts education in schools remained peripheral and stuck, and my advocacy efforts helped locally, but only to a modest degree. Neither policy nor practice was focusing on the social damages of children growing up in poverty and social stress—which I believed the arts could redress. The arts organizations themselves were flailing just to stay alive. I realized I was continually bashing my head against the same walls.

So I stopped. I took a sabbatical in 2007—a fancy and expensive term for a freelancer who takes a break. I promised myself I would live modestly on my savings and not come back to projects until I knew for gut-sure what my next chapter could be. This sabbatical was full of solitude, study, and learning adventures, such as working with teenagers in rural Tanzania to help them write a play about their lives, as part of the International Theatre and Literacy Project.

And in 2008, I piggybacked on my friend Jamie Bernstein's first trip to Venezuela to see El Sistema. I boarded the plane as a skeptic. I had heard gushy reports about El Sistema, with too many superlatives for my pragmatic mind, so I was sure it had to be hype. The hagiographic stories about José Antonio Abreu sounded a little syrupy-worshipful for my taste.

What I encountered was the single most astonishing social-artistic accomplishment I had ever seen—and I have worked with a lot of good programs. El Sistema exceeded what I had allowed myself to dream might be possible in our world; and there it was, joyfully growing before my eyes. Maestro Abreu was the savviest and most inspirational leader I had ever met. I knew immediately that I would dedicate much of the rest of my life to supporting the growth of this great project to help struggling children find empowerment through beauty, in my own country and around the world.

Since then, working in every possible way to advance the movement has enabled me to experience it from many angles—as investigator of how it works, as consultant to many developing programs, as project initiator, as teacher and coach, as fundraiser, and as reporter-writer and newsletter publisher. After the success of Tricia's book *Changing Lives*, which tells the story of El Sistema's growth in Venezuela and the United States, and after several trips to experience Sistema work in other countries, she and I realized there was another big story to be told: the story of the unprecedented international growth of El Sistema.

TRICIA'S JOURNEY

My piano lessons as a child and teenager were a serious and joyful business—and so, in a quieter way, was writing poetry and prose. I planned, vaguely, to make a vocation of either the piano or the writing. But my college years coincided with the early 1970s era of social protest, and I found the new social and political imperatives irresistibly compelling; I stopped playing the piano, studied political philosophy, and spent a few years engaged in activism for various causes.

Since that time, I've never found a way to be both artist and activist; my artistic proclivities won out, and my activist voice went quiet. As a writer, I have published short stories and freelance journalism and a musical memoir, and have been a lyricist in the worlds of musical theater, jazz, and children's video. As a musician, I've been an accompanist, an elementary school music teacher, a keyboard player in a band, a college lecturer in music history and appreciation, and, most happily and enduringly, a piano teacher. I've earned a master's degree in historical musicology and pursued years of advanced graduate work in music education. But for most of those years, my social conscience and political convictions went publically unexpressed.

Like Eric, I was lucky enough to go to Venezuela with that generous adventurer Jamie Bernstein—my trip was in 2009, a year after his—and, like him, I found El Sistema in Venezuela to be a revelation, the most powerful intersection of art and social engagement I had ever experienced. I was inspired to bring my literary and musical vocations together with my activist impulse, and to do my best to bring the story of El Sistema to the attention of the world.

I felt, and still feel, that the world is in acute need of El Sistema's central vision. To a global community riven by ethnic antagonisms and cultural marginalization, El Sistema brings a message of inclusion and cooperation. To an international classical music culture that risks irrelevance, and even obsolescence, in the face of the commercial pop juggernaut, El Sistema brings new life, re-creating symphonic ensembles as spheres of dynamism and exuberance. And in a context of decades of failed or compromised programs targeted to helping children in poverty, El Sistema introduces an imaginative reach into the realm of arts education as a place where children can grow whole.

As I began research for *Changing Lives,* a book about El Sistema, I was repeatedly advised to interview Eric Booth, who was said to be the foremost U.S. expert on El Sistema. This advice turned out to be auspicious. We have become partners both personally and professionally, and have worked together in exploring the world of El Sistema and advocating for the spread of its vision.

OUR RESEARCH JOURNEY

Before launching into writing, we traveled extensively in twenty-five countries, studying over a hundred Sistema-inspired sites and interviewing many dozens of directors, teachers, students, and parents involved with the programs. In city after city, country after country, we would land at the airport and go directly to one of its most struggling areas. In some places, we saw poverty so brutal that it overwhelmed our senses and jolted our understandings of what societies tolerate and what humans can survive. But the particular exhilaration of our travels was that in these bleak communities, we consistently found El Sistema programs that were oases of safety, energy, and beauty.

This juxtaposition haunts and inspires us, as we hope it will affect you. In every El Sistema program, the wall of the music center separates an environment of robust, often joyful learning from the harsh conditions that surround it. From Kabul to Rio, from Bethlehem to Soweto, from Manila to Manhattan, we have seen both sides of this wall, and sometimes the outer side is literally pocked with bullet holes. We have been touched by the way these small (and sometimes not so small) centers of promise find purchase in the grimmest settings. We have seen how the power of Sistema work can turn that wall into a semipermeable membrane that allows positive energy to flow into the surround even while filtering the inward flow of neighborhood and community stress.

In our interviews with Maestro Abreu during the past two years, we have experienced his depth of vision and single-minded determination. He articulates the power of music in children's lives with a kind of clarity unique in our experience; for him, music is the secular sacrament that can help young people lift themselves out of the suffering of poverty, discrimination, or trauma of many kinds. Like Mahatma Gandhi, like Martin Luther King, Jr., he has shown the world new ways to think about social transformation.

In every country, El Sistema-inspired work evolves its own specific characteristics, rooted in locality and social history. Yet all programs exemplify the same central principles and are clearly connected to a worldwide movement. This book reports our explorations of this movement. We hope it will activate our readers' interest to learn more. Ideally, we would have liked to write a thousand pages, properly honoring all the skilled work we have seen and the extraordinary people we have met around the world; we distill our observations here for the sake of readability, hopefully with the understanding and forgiveness of those whose stories we cannot adequately include.

A DISCLAIMER AND A CLARIFICATION

As the international El Sistema movement expands, there is growing interest from many quarters in assessing and evaluating the work of Sistema programs through formal research studies. The Latin American programs that are decades in the lead have not done substantive research, because their funding has not required it and because they have been busy focusing on program growth. Elsewhere, most Sistema programs are still new, and good research takes time and money. Hard data on the impact of El Sistema programs will therefore be slow to emerge.

There are some observers of the field who believe that there is not yet enough research to say anything authoritative, or indeed to make any positive claims, about the value of El Sistema work. At the other extreme are enthusiasts who consistently make claims that cannot be substantiated by research and may be inflated. And there are practitioners who say that given the urgency of the program's mission and the wealth of circumstantial but compelling evidence of its value, doing research to gather data is not a priority: "We know we're saving kids' lives; let's just get on with it!"

In these pages, we aim to adopt a stand somewhat apart from all of these. We think research is crucial to the long-term viability of the movement, and we welcome the growing number of research endeavors. Researchers are helping the El Sistema movement to learn as it grows, through careful investigation of its practice and the many aspects of its impact.

But this book is not a research report. We don't feel it makes sense to wait until a mass of hard data has been accumulated before we write about what we see as the value and positive impact of Sistema-inspired work. We make many statements that have not yet been affirmed by authoritative research, but we do not inflate our claims beyond what our observations, and those of experienced colleagues, can reasonably support.

Our book is also not a sales pitch. Like all human endeavors, El Sistema is not perfect, and we have endeavored to describe some of its challenges and difficulties, and to depict the struggles as well as the triumphs. Clearly, however, we are advocates for the power of El Sistema; we are deeply moved by what we have seen, and are dedicated to helping this work to grow. The stories we tell skew to the positive—because our experiences of El Sistema skew overwhelmingly to the positive. We know from experience that El Sistema is not too good to be true.

One final clarification. In our years of experience in the arts education world, we have seen many programs built around ideals and assumptions that are similar to those of El Sistema. In the course of this research, we encountered many more such programs. There is, in fact, an expanding universe of initiatives built on a belief in the potential of arts education to change lives, and a determination to bring that potential to children and young people who have had little or no access to it.

We have chosen to focus our book on programs explicitly inspired by the El Sistema vision, because we find this vision such a developed and clear distillation of the transformative potential of music education. But we are also impressed by the work of the wider sphere. We wish we could include all programs that manifest the more general perspective that is gaining slow but steady momentum across the world—that intensive participatory arts education is a fertile crucible for personal and social change.

Advocacy is not about changing what people think; advocacy is about changing what people do. People base their actions not on what they think but on what they believe. That is why we revert, in these pages, to the etymological meaning of "advocate": "to call toward." In calling you toward the phenomenon of El Sistema's worldwide growth, we hope not only to influence your thinking but also, possibly, to unsettle established beliefs, to open a crack of interest and to call you toward new beliefs.

Ultimately, we hope to move you to action. There is probably an El Sistema-inspired program in your country, your state or province, perhaps even your city. We hope you will go and visit. Perhaps you can help that program grow and thrive. We hope you will find it, and act.

PART I

What Is El Sistema?

El Sistema's way of making music has overwhelmed
our traditional world of classical music as a breath of fresh air;
and after 40 years this vision has convinced millions of people
around the world about the importance of music in our lives.

—CECILIA BARTOLI, MEZZO-SOPRANO

*Rehearsal of Ghetto Classics, in the open shed stage of St. John's School in
Korogocho slum, Nairobi, Kenya.*

PHOTOGRAPH: ERIC BOOTH

CHAPTER 1

To Play and to Struggle:
El Sistema in Venezuela

Eduardo Galeano wrote in *The Book of Embraces* that a
man could go to heaven and from there view a sea of little fires.
Each person shines with his or her own light among others and no
two are alike. There are large fires and small fires. Well, if that's true,
I have no doubt that the light of Abreu, viewed from above, is not a
little fire but a huge fire that has illuminated the Earth by lighting,
one by one, hundreds of thousands of little fires.
—ALEJANDRO GONZÁLEZ IÑÁRRITU,
MEXICAN FILMMAKER

BEGINNINGS

Great world movements usually have a founding myth;
sometimes the story is even true. So it is with El Sistema.
Its beginning can be traced to a specific night in February
1975, in Caracas, Venezuela—and to a specific person with an
urgent case of righteous indignation. José Antonio Abreu, a thirty-
six-year-old government official and conservatory-trained musician,
found it unconscionable that jobs in the country's few professional
orchestras went almost exclusively to Europeans or North Americans, meaning that most Venezuelan musicians could not get work.
Abreu knew many other young musicians who shared his frustration about this.

On the night of February 12, Abreu managed to procure fifty
music stands and set them up in an empty parking garage in down-

town Caracas, with some borrowed music parts on the stands. He had put out a word-of-mouth invitation among local musicians and music students, asking them to come by and play. Only eleven showed up. Somehow undaunted, Abreu explained to these young people—some of them long-haired and sandal-wearing, like many of their contemporaries across the world—that if they committed themselves to growing in number and working hard together, he would help them become one of the world's great orchestras.

"I can see us now," Fiorentino Mendoza recounted many years later, "counter-cultural musician types, standing in front of this dapper, elegant man. I remember thinking, 'Either he is an inspired visionary or he is a crazy person.' Actually, he was both. I guess the crazy part was believing in us."

At some point during the Maestro's pep talk, the youngest of the eleven decided to take his violin out of its case. Others followed suit. On Abreu's downbeat, they began to play. "When the exhaust in the parking garage got too bad," said Fiorentino, "we stopped and reconvened in a hallway."

They came back the next night and the next; their friends came too, and the numbers grew fast. Rehearsal venues kept changing, as Abreu struggled to find spaces that would accommodate his suddenly-seventy-piece orchestra; when he found an unused factory warehouse, they all cleaned it up and then rehearsed together amid the pieces of old machinery. Some played well, while others were relative novices. The more advanced players realized that the playing level of the ensemble would not improve unless they coached the less experienced ones, so teaching one another became the norm. As new players arrived, Abreu introduced them to every orchestra member by name, and they were each given a round of applause as they took their seats in the orchestra.

"If there was ever a perfect example of comradeship," pianist David Ascanio has said, "this was it." Abreu was devoted to the musical development of each member, but in addition, said Ascanio, "he taught us something vitally important in life: to cheerfully apply ourselves to a rehearsal . . . with enthusiasm and openness of mind and spirit."[2] In the heady feel of those days, there seems to have been an element of the international "we can change the world" youth movement of the 1960s and '70s.

Using his government connections, Abreu set up a first public performance date of April 30, 1975, at the Foreign Affairs Ministry. Rehearsals stretched to marathon length. The process was grueling, but it was also invigorating; the players could hear and feel themselves improving daily. After the rehearsals, they talked; there were continual conversations "about art, music, literature, philosophy, and life . . . always fed by José Antonio's wisdom." The rehearsals were thus a rich education, not only musically but also in many other dimensions of culture. "That was quite simply wonderful," said Ascanio. "They were . . . the kind of conversations you don't want ever to end."[3]

At their inaugural concert, the new ensemble played Vivaldi, Mozart, Handel, and Bach, and closed with the Venezuelan national anthem. The large audience of friends, musicians, and government officials, including the foreign minister, responded enthusiastically. "We were literally shouting with happiness," cellist Domingo Sanchez Bor has written. "It was then that we knew this was for real . . . the chances of work, our careers as musicians; all that was possible, it was all true."[4]

The great wonder of El Sistema's founding myth is that it is true. What could have turned into a pipe dream instead became a vibrant, unprecedented force for musical change in Venezuela. That impetus for change, and for prevailing in the face of long odds, only strengthened over the ensuing decades, as the unlikely youth orchestra evolved into the vast national music education network that is El Sistema today.

Gaining the respect and support of the Venezuelan musical establishment was the first hurdle; the prevailing consensus was that an all-Venezuelan youth orchestra—especially one with no sponsor, no budget, and (most alarming of all) no auditions—would never succeed. "You could count the people who supported us on the fingers of one hand," Beatriz Abreu, an organist and sister of the Maestro, has said.[5] It was within this reality that the El Sistema motto *Tocar y Luchar* (To Play and to Struggle) was born, a motto that continues to inform the spirit of the project in Venezuela and around the world. The motto has recently been amended to *Tocar, Cantar y Luchar*, in recognition of the seminal importance of singing in the youth development process.

Abreu's strategic weapon in this fight was to seek plaudits outside the country. He took his fledgling orchestra to perform in Mexico City, where they won the admiration of Carlos Chávez, Mexico's revered composer and conductor, and to Aberdeen, Scotland, where they were an unlikely sensation at a youth orchestra festival. These successes caught the attention of Venezuelan President Carlos Andrés Pérez, who was presiding over an economic boom from petroleum exports; he asked Abreu how the government could help the orchestra. Abreu responded with the caveat that support must come in the form of social welfare funds rather than from the Ministry of Culture. He knew from his experience in both government and music that funding for social projects would be more sustainable than cultural funding, which comes and goes as regimes change. In 1977, a federal government foundation called Fundación del Estado para el Sistema Nacional de las Orquestas Juveniles e Infantiles de Venezuela (FESNOJIV) was established to provide support for the orchestra as a youth development project.

THE EVOLVING VISION

On the night of their first concert in April 1975, Abreu had told his players, "You are the founding members of the Venezuelan System of Youth and Children's Orchestras. You are the pioneers of a great undertaking."

Within a very few years, his prophesy was already being realized to an extent the musicians could never have imagined. But something else, something unanticipated even by Abreu, was happening too. The players themselves were changing. They were becoming more self-confident, better and more empathic communicators, stronger leaders. The intensity of rehearsals, the communal accomplishment against considerable odds, the thrill of delving together into great works of musical art—all these things were having ripple effects. Their intensive ensemble endeavor was doing more than producing good music; it was beginning to change their lives.

Abreu has said that when he arrived at this seminal realization, he "wanted this possibility for every child in Venezuela." Thus his vision of an all-Venezuelan youth orchestra expanded and evolved into a broader vision of a continually transformative educational process for an entire society, one that would reach not only the most talented musical youth but also, and even more important, the vast numbers of at-risk children in the struggling barrio communities of his country.

With government support on his side, it was the right moment to pursue this vision. "I had all the necessary tools to build a great institution, a grand enterprise," he has said. "The project had to be structural; it was essentially a project for a new style of music education in Venezuela."[6] It was at this moment that Abreu's endeavor evolved from an orchestra to a true "Sistema."

Even as they continued to rehearse and perform together, the members of the now officially named Simón Bolívar Youth Orchestra of Venezuela took on the challenge of establishing musical ensembles for children and youth across Venezuela. Igor Lanz, who has been involved in developing El Sistema for decades, described the process this way: "The national youth orchestra was like a fertilized embryo that first divided into two and then into four and then kept multiplying. That is how the Sistema was born."[7] The young musicians who were creating and multiplying El Sistema didn't start with a carefully planned curriculum or organizational infrastructure; rather, they relied on the same intuitive drive that was propelling their success as an orchestra. Over the next several decades, they and their successors launched "núcleos" (the Venezuelan term for El Sistema music centers) across the country that drew students, teachers, and supporters by the hundreds and eventually thousands.

During those same decades, the Simón Bolívar Orchestra continued to grow in musical and expressive virtuosity, and as the musicians matured, new iterations of the orchestra formed, each more virtuosic than the last. The new millennium brought an escalating series of international tours under the baton of conducting prodigy Gustavo Dudamel. In recent years, a number of El Sistema's newer orchestras and ensembles have become international touring sensations as well. But the heart and soul of El Sistema remain the núcleos—the dynamic, multilayered music learning environments that bring children of all ages together in orchestral and choral ensembles at various levels of skill. The great majority of the children in these núcleos are poor. There are Sistema núcleos in 80 percent of the 128 municipalities categorized by the government as "very high risk" because of rampant crime and poverty. As of this writing, there are a total of 423 núcleos in Venezuela; they are in all of the country's 23 states, and collectively they sponsor 1,305 orchestras and 1,121 youth choirs. Five hundred thousand children and young people attend these núcleos. Another 280,000 participate in El Sistema initiatives within schools.

Altogether, El Sistema now serves approximately 780,000 Venezuelan children and young people every day—more children than are involved in sports, in a sports-mad country. Its current goal is to have 1 million children and young people actively participating by 2019. Said Alejandro Carreño, the concertmaster of the Simón Bolívar Symphony Orchestra, "El Sistema is everywhere in my country. In any town, you will see people with cases—oboes, violins, contrabasses—walking around. The only thing you have to do, to be part of El Sistema, is be there. And practice."

For many years, Maestro Abreu has continued to travel across the country, visiting new núcleos and revisiting established ones, as well as across the world with the touring orchestras. Some of his administrative duties have recently been passed to Eduardo Méndez, a former Simón Bolívar Orchestra violinist and now the executive director of Fundamusical (short for Fundación Musical Simón Bolívar, as the administering foundation has been renamed). But the Maestro's vision is still crucial in guiding the future of El Sistema.

CREATING MUSICIANS, CREATING CITIZENS

In El Sistema Venezuela, belonging to a núcleo means coming every day. Five days a week, children and young people attend núcleos for three or four hours after school, and they often come on weekends as well. Many programs start with children as young as two years old, who come for an hour once or twice a week with parents or relatives to learn the playful rudiments of rhythm and ensemble. As students grow and develop musically, they proceed through a sequential series of orchestras and choruses that provide growing levels of musical challenge and opportunity. This gives every participant both the assurance of belonging to an ensemble and the opportunity to continually reach higher, from their early years into their teens and even sometimes their twenties.

Virtually all the people we spoke to at the núcleos we visited—directors, teachers, children and parents—said, at some point and in their own words, a version of this sentence: "El Sistema's goal is not to create musicians. It is to create successful, happy, and good citizens." This is a crucial point: the vast majority of graduates of this uniquely immersive musical education go on to nonmusical careers. While many Sistema graduates find work within the growing system as teachers and administrators, most continue to play music but become welders, nurses, teachers, accountants, journalists, chemists, architects, or politicians. That is precisely the business of El Sistema.

But of course there are many children who want to become musicians and have the talent and drive to do so, and for them, El Sistema offers a rich pathway of training and experience. Violist Norma Núñez

Loaiza, who began playing her instrument in a Caracas núcleo at the age of nine and immediately demonstrated strong talent and interest, went from the top orchestra of her núcleo to a city-wide children's orchestra. She honed her playing through twice-weekly private lessons within the Viola Academy (not an actual place, but a network of master teachers; there's an Academy for every instrument) and the Simón Bolívar Conservatory. She auditioned for the national children's orchestra, and made it on her second try, at the age of fourteen. Her next half-decade was spent in the intensive atmosphere of near-constant rehearsals and international tours. "Great times," she told us. "And we began, collectively, to understand the true impact of what we were doing." Norma eventually took her musical career in the direction of international cultural management, and is currently the director of El Sistema Lehigh Valley, in Pennsylvania.

There are now so many Venezuelan children and young people playing at the highest levels of musical accomplishment that the number of international touring ensembles has multiplied. The Teresa Carreño Youth Orchestra, under the leadership of Christian Vásquez, is every bit as good, many say, as the Simón Bolívar. (There is some friendly rivalry around this point.) The Youth Orchestra of Caracas, with Dietrich Paredes at the helm, has a slightly younger membership. There is a national choral ensemble, a national brass ensemble, and a national jazz big band. The National Children's Orchestra, the youngest and newest national ensemble, with members as young as eight (including a twelve-year-old violinist, Rayson David Tercero Cumares Sequera, who sometimes conducts), is regarded by Sistema veterans as a group of the most precocious virtuosi El Sistema has ever seen.

The Simón Bolívar Symphony Orchestra of Venezuela remains at the apex of the structure, an exemplar and inspiration to the entire worldwide El Sistema community. Although they are no longer a youth orchestra, they were still officially "Youth" back in 2008, when the veteran British music critic Richard Morrison, writing in *The Times*, came up with a ranking of the best orchestras in the world—a kind of "Orchestral World Cup," as he called it.[8] His Five Best were the Berlin Philharmonic, the Amsterdam Concertgebouw, Claudio Abbado's Lucerne Festival Orchestra—and in fourth place, before the London Symphony Orchestra, the Simón Bolívar Youth Orchestra of Venezuela. "It stunned me with its spirit," he wrote of the Venezuelan ensemble.

El Sistema's top ensembles represent its highest artistic achievements; they are the Sistema's worldwide musical ambassadors. And there is another cadre of ambassadors rapidly gaining in global prominence: the young conductors who have followed Dudamel's path, coming up through the ranks of El Sistema and now sought after by prestigious orchestras around the world. Christian Vásquez, chief conductor of the Stavanger Symphony Orchestra in Norway, and Diego Matheuz, principal conductor of Teatro la Fenice in Venice, are both from Venezuela, as are Rafael Payare, the chief conductor of Ireland's Ulster Orchestra, and frequent international guest conductors Manuel López-Gómez and Dietrich Paredes.

Forty years later, the fulfillment of Maestro Abreu's promise has been realized on a scale vaster than even the Maestro had dared to imagine. "Wherever we went in the world," said Norma Núñez about her orchestra tours, "we found that people were moved by witnessing a young people's orchestra that worked so perfectly and naturally together. It was then that we understood that the relevance of what we did transcended the repertoire. The exceptional part was how truly together we were."

EVALUATING RESULTS

El Sistema's steady growth in Venezuela has not been accompanied by a commensurate wealth of data on its results; Latin American cultures tend to be less oriented toward formal evaluation and assessment of program results than are North American and European cultures. However, two significant research efforts during the last decade have focused on El Sistema in Venezuela, both carried out by the Inter-

American Development Bank (IDB). Among the important findings of the 2008 study: comparing Sistema students with non-Sistema demographic peers, the school dropout rate is 7 percent vs. 26 percent; the percentage of students who have behavior problem incidents in school is 12 percent vs. 23 percent; and the percentage who find a formal job after graduating is 41 percent vs. 13 percent. The percentage of students who participate in community events after graduating is 60 percent vs. 40 percent.[9] The IDB has more research underway.

In the meantime, longtime El Sistema teachers and leaders have amassed a lode of experiential knowledge about other dimensions of El Sistema effectiveness. All say that the program has strong retention rates, although there tends to be some drop-off in participation around age twelve, and again around the end of the high school years—two important transitional times in families' lives when sending children to work is often felt as an economic necessity. Among young people who stay with the program into their twenties, some evolve into part-time or full-time teachers, and many into part-time volunteers. Most important, say Sistema leaders and observers, the children of El Sistema carry the social and emotional learning from their núcleos into full lives in other fields.

Many graduates of Sistema programs continue playing music as they follow other life paths. At the núcleo in Barquisimeto (the childhood home of both Abreu and Dudamel), Coordinator Gary Núñez told us that about 70 percent of the young people who have completed the program play music for the rest of their lives, although most of them not professionally. "They join amateur orchestras around town; they play in different kinds of bands. Some just play at home for themselves. The important thing is that they never want to stop."

ENCOUNTERING CONTROVERSY

Ever since El Sistema's beginning, Maestro Abreu has enlisted financial support from the government through eight changes of administration ranging from conservative to leftist, without the program's becoming identified as a project of any specific political party or interest group. His diplomatic genius has been to maintain El Sistema as a vital social project above and beyond the tides of politics, enabling it to survive and grow steadily throughout forty years of political fluctuation.

Since the death of left-wing president Hugo Chávez in 2013, Venezuela has suffered a drastic increase in political and economic turbulence under Chávez's anointed successor, Nicolas Maduro. Demonstrations against the regime have sometimes turned violent; the Maduro regime has responded with repressive measures, including the arrest and imprisonment not only of demonstrators but also of elected officials and influential leaders. As this book goes to press, the sociopolitical crisis caused by drastically reduced oil revenues, triple-digit inflation, and political instability has worsened. Stores are empty of many life essentials, and the country struggles with endemic corruption, escalating violent crime, and one of the world's worst homicide rates.

Abreu and his colleagues have striven to handle this crisis as they have handled every other upheaval of the past four decades, by working with the government to sustain the Sistema program without publicly engaging at a political level. Fundamusical tries to keep its focus on continuing to create musical havens amid social turmoil. Some Sistema observers, however, believe that El Sistema has allowed itself to become too identified with the Chávez/Maduro regime. The size of the government's contribution to El Sistema during a time of scarcity; the frequency with which the government calls for El Sistema ensembles on public occasions; the government's recent replacement of some Sistema personnel with politicized figures—all this makes it difficult for Fundamusical to maintain its mission-driven identity completely independent of politics.

There are those in the classical music world, including Venezuelan piano virtuoso Gabriela Montero (not a Sistema alumna, but a onetime friend of El Sistema), who have taken an oppositional position, asserting that Fundamusical and Dudamel should speak out against the Maduro regime. The leaders of Fundamusical have not answered this criticism publicly, beyond saying that their priority is to continue the focus on serving the children of El Sistema. Dudamel, like Abreu, prefers to support the work of El Sistema through non-political actions in place of pronouncements. Even as he builds a stellar international career (leading the Los Angeles Philharmonic, guest-conducting many of the world's greatest orchestras, composing a critically acclaimed film score), he devotes a substantial amount of time to El Sistema, traveling to núcleos in remote areas to show support for the students and teachers, and continuing, without fees, to direct and tour with the Simón Bolívar Symphony of Venezuela. In September 2015, Dudamel formally expressed his position in an editorial in the Los Angeles Times:

> Everything that I am and everything that I have achieved is a direct result of my participation in El Sistema and the steadfast mentoring of Maestro Abreu. El Sistema instilled in me what I stand for today: equality, fairness and opportunity.
>
> In El Sistema's orchestras, the son of an opposition leader and the daughter of a government minister may sit next to each other creating beautiful music. In that moment, they know no politics. They are not defined by their differences; they are defined by what they share—a passion for great music.
>
> If I aligned myself with one political philosophy or another, then, by extension, I could also politicize El Sistema. That might turn a revered and successful program into a political punching bag and make it much more vulnerable to political whims. El Sistema is far too important to subject to everyday political discourse and battles. It must remain above the fray.[10]

Given Venezuela's profoundly complex politics and the intricacies of Fundamusical's relationship to the government, El Sistema is in a difficult position. The stakes are clearly high. But the country-wide interpersonal networks of dedication, commitment, history, and practice are vast and deep, and the strong likelihood is that El Sistema in Venezuela will survive and flourish. Whether it will ever grow so large, and produce so many mature, socially competent graduates, that it can contribute to a tipping point in the country's fortunes—this is a question impossible to answer, given the magnitude of the country's crises. We do know that the El Sistema leaders, teachers, and students we have spoken to are profoundly distressed by the current troubles, but their visceral love for their country is undaunted and unanimous, and they are sustained by a long-term hope that peace and prosperity will eventually prevail, with youth orchestras as their proud banner across the world.

Furthermore, the accelerating expansion of El Sistema across the world guarantees that the legacy of El Sistema Venezuela is secure, as new leaders and practices emerge and illuminating research evolves. Venezuelan Sistema leaders often say, in response to the many requests they receive from would-be visitors, "You are welcome here! But you can also visit Scotland; visit Sweden; visit Colombia; visit Los Angeles; there are many exemplary Sistema-inspired programs around the world to learn from."

In the midst of its political challenges, there have also been more general criticisms leveled at El Sistema in Venezuela by several observers. Any organization as large and long-lived as is Fundamusical is bound to develop flaws. And any phenomenon as revered and celebrated as El Sistema has been in recent years can become idealized, inviting skeptics to call out and magnify its flaws. We are confident that the leaders of El Sistema in Venezuela will strive to address its flaws and to amplify its strengths. And we are confident that as idealization subsides, the fanfare around criticisms will diminish, and El Sistema in Venezuela will come to be generally understood as a valuable institution that contends with organizational and human frailties just as do all educational programs and human institutions.

PLANS FOR THE FUTURE

El Sistema is never complete; much of its vitality emanates from the foundational belief in continual growth and evolution. Within the last several years alone, there have been new initiatives in a number of directions, including the development of Sistema programs among pediatric hospital inpatients; the New Members Program for prenatal to age-three children and their parents, to bring whole families into musical exploration; the extension of El Sistema into the school day, in public schools; and the expansion of the Sistema's longtime practice of including children and young people with special needs.

One particularly promising initiative is the Penitentiary Academic Program, launched in 2007 with the dual purpose of rehabilitation and enhanced reintegration upon release. These are prime concerns for prison systems around the world, and most countries admit to failure at accomplishing either goal. In the Venezuelan prison system, known for particularly violent, anarchic prison environments, a network of eight orchestras and choirs has been instituted, founded and directed by musician Kleiberth Lenin Mora. In its first eight years, some 8,000 prisoners have participated in the program, giving close to 1,000 concerts. A research study found dramatically positive results for this program in terms of behavioral and emotional change, self-evaluation, and social interdependence.[11]

Nathan Schram, a U.S. violist and music educator, visited several of these programs in 2014, including a women's prison at Los Tequesa occupied by inmates with short sentences. The Sistema orchestra there includes almost 50 percent of the inmates, and has a dedicated building. Nathan was struck by the difference in feel between the general population of inmates and those in the music building. "Dull stares in the general population turn to smiles in the orchestra building," he wrote to us. "Whispering becomes laughter, and the great silence gets filled with music." Many inmates intend to move directly into núcleo orchestras when they get out.

Nathan also told us about a public concert performed by all the prison Sistema programs, brought together in Venezuela's most prestigious concert venue. "Prison management bussed inmate musicians from each of the prison núcleos to Venezuela's national concert hall in Caracas," he wrote. "For security, two prison guards accompanied each musician. This meant that the hall was filled to the brim with a combination of prison guards and inmates' family members. A logistical operation of this magnitude for a prison population is unimaginable for most countries in the world. Yet for me, that is not the most remarkable aspect of the event. By including the security guards in the audience, El Sistema broke down the oppositional, authoritative system of incarceration, even if just for the length of the concert. Security guards became supporters, cheering for these new musicians to show the world what they could accomplish with music, and offering them a sense of pride many of them have never known."

∞

WHENEVER MAESTRO ABREU is congratulated on a new Sistema milestone, he receives the plaudits graciously. But it is when he's asked about future plans that his face really comes alive. He is always living toward the next project, and seems to experience the completion of a mission as a mandate to move on to new ones. Speaking about the culmination of a series of projects, he said, "I felt as if I was back to zero, as though I was starting something new and already behind in my homework."

When we asked him in July 2014 what he sees as the most important areas of growth and change in El Sistema, he immediately described three current priorities. The first is continuing to grow the numbers of participants—to serve 1 million Venezuelan young people by 2019. This growth may also branch out into other art forms.

Second, the varieties of music embraced by El Sistema are proliferating. While the great orchestral works of the Western canon continue to hold a prominent place in the national repertoire as an optimal training ground for technical, aesthetic, and social excellence, many other genres are being widely pursued. There is now a professional choral track, with the internationally touring Simón Bolívar National Youth Choir of Venezuela at the top. Jazz is also flourishing, including Latin, big band, and bebop styles, with an internationally touring Big Band ensemble.

In addition, there is an emphasis on forming ensembles that specialize in Venezuela's rich variety of folk traditions—Latin rhythms, Afro-Venezuelan, Caribbean, and plains music. A national project called *Alma Llanera* (Soul of the Plains, named after a famous Venezuelan folk song) engages musicologists around the country in capturing and notating regional and local folk music traditions, some of which are identified with just one small town. Over forty of these previously undocumented works have already been transcribed and sent to núcleos throughout the country, and El Sistema students are learning to play them on traditional Venezuelan folk instruments like the cuatro, bandola, and Creole harp, so that vernacular music will be kept alive and shared across different traditions. These scores will also be made available on the Internet for musicians around the world to play.

There is a Baroque orchestra created by Marshall Marcus, a longtime contributor in Venezuela who is the founding leader of Sistema Europe. There is a special orchestra created for the purpose of performing new works by El Sistema students who have been inspired to compose through a partnership with Very Young Composers, a project led by Jon Deak of the New York Philharmonic. Chamber music ensembles are multiplying. There are ensembles that specialize in world music, rock, and more cutting-edge sounds like urban fusion.

As musical genres proliferate, Sistema musicians take delight in mixing and juxtaposing them. Saxophonist Pablo Yang, who spent time traveling and volunteering in Venezuela and has founded a small núcleo in Vietnam, offered this description of a concert in Barquisimeto: "Where else but in El Sistema will you find one of the country's finest percussionists staging a concert hall performance of Yngwie

Malmsteen's Concerto for Electric Guitar in between his other duties? The concerto was preceded by a forty-minute set involving full orchestra, and also a heavy metal band in latex and black lace. Talk about programming! There is an immense freedom of expression and exploration there."

In addition, the number of Venezuelan composers is growing; El Sistema has supported Latin American composers for decades by performing their works and commissioning new ones, and is now beginning to include compositional training in núcleo curricula. Finally, a growing network of lutheries around the country brings hundreds of young people the opportunity to be trained by masters of instrument-making and repair.

The third overall priority emphasized by Maestro Abreu was infrastructure: Fundamusical is building major new structures to honor and support the expansion of musical activity. While El Sistema has a durable tradition of using any and all kinds of space for music learning and rehearsing, from repurposed warehouses and derelict buildings to tree-shaded courtyards, the Maestro believes that creating beautiful new spaces specifically for Sistema activities is important both practically and symbolically. Such buildings give students' families and communities a sense of belonging to the kind of magnificent musical space that used to be the exclusive preserve of the affluent. In 2008, for example, a new national center for El Sistema activities, the Center for Social Action Through Music, opened its doors in downtown Caracas and established a new paradigm of imaginative beauty for Sistema buildings. Designed by Venezuelan architect Tomás Lugo, the building includes over a hundred usable spaces, including two concert halls, rehearsal and practice rooms, a library and tech center, open-air hallways with views of the city's main park, and artworks by Venezuela's most prominent public artists. There is a band shell for free concerts on the park side of the building.

At all hours of the day and night, this building is swarming with young people and filled with their music. The playful elegance of its design gives them a strong message about the worth of their endeavors. The building has no administrative offices; it was deliberately conceived as a space for music-making.

As of this writing, the city blocks adjacent to the Center are now construction sites for companion buildings, most prominently a huge academic structure that will become a center for Sistema teaching and learning. At the same time, Fundamusical is planning to build new buildings and complexes in six other cities. The first one will be in Barquisimeto, with a design by one of the world's most famous architects, Frank Gehry—who is also the architect of Disney Hall in Los Angeles, where Dudamel regularly leads the L.A. Philharmonic.

These three goals of massive growth—in numbers of children served, kinds of repertoire played, and quality of infrastructure—will take years to accomplish. But even beyond these, Maestro Abreu and his colleagues have a more radical and fundamental mission. "What's needed," he has said, "is for all states to adopt this as an intrinsic part of their education systems. The day our public schools include teaching the arts to every single student, from two-year-olds to university students, as part of their basic curriculum—that day, our country will become a different country."

CHAPTER 2

The Global Spread of the El Sistema Vision

El Sistema deepens and expands. It has grown into the
most extraordinary musical and educational movement I have ever seen,
because of the standards of musicianship it has achieved, the extent of
the lives that are directly saved and enriched, and the vast scale on
which El Sistema now works—in Venezuela and now
with an influence across the world.

—SIR SIMON RATTLE

GROWTH ACROSS LATIN AMERICA

Fiorella Solares was a professional cellist in Rio de Janeiro in the 1980s when she married Brazilian conductor David Machado. At the time, Machado was developing a lively interest in the El Sistema project of his friend José Antonio Abreu, who often invited him to come to Venezuela to teach conducting classes and to lead the Simón Bolívar Youth Orchestra in some of its earliest performances of Strauss and Mahler. Every visit strengthened Machado's conviction that Brazil needed an El Sistema program, and he and his wife worked together for years to set up a Brazilian foundation, Ação Social pela Música, dedicated to realizing this goal.

Fiorella, a short, vigorous woman with fashionably spiked hair, told us her story on a day of pelting summer rain in Rio. "In 1995, just before our 'Ação Social' program was to begin," she said, "David was conducting the Simón Bolívar Orchestra in Caracas. They were supposed to play Mahler's Third, but at the last moment David switched it to Beethoven's Third, which has the Funeral March in it. I believe he made that switch because he had a premonition. That was the last music he ever conducted. Days later, he had a heart attack and died instantly. He was fifty-two. I was six weeks pregnant with our only child.

"Of course, Maestro Abreu called me and said, 'Fiorella, there are no words strong enough to express my grief about your loss.' And then . . . then he said, 'And now, my dear Fiorella, you need to do this work in his place.'"

Fiorella smiled slightly and shrugged. "He knows what each of us is capable of, and he has such a visionary quality that when he says something needs to be done, there is no doubt in anybody's mind that it needs to be done. And we do it."

During most of her pregnancy, Fiorella worked closely with Abreu to set up the framework for launching Ação Social pela Música. "The Brazilian government was interested in starting the program in the rural areas of Brazil as well as in the cities," she said, "so I was flying into the interior on small planes, to meet local government officials and musicians. Because I no longer had David, Maestro Abreu came with me every time." She recalled that late in her pregnancy, on a trip to the Amazon jungle city of Manaus, the maternity dress she was wearing had become too tight and the buttons down its back were coming undone. "Pop-pop-pop, they all came out. And Maestro just stood behind me, as I talked to the mayor about El Sistema, and buttoned them back up."

In the city of Campos dos Goytacazes, Fiorella found a kindred spirit in the person of Jony William, a violinist who had studied at the conservatory in Rio and then started a small music school in Campos. Under his leadership, the first El Sistema program in Brazil began in a Campos favela, soon after Fiorella's daughter was born. In 1996, a delegation of Venezuelan leaders and teachers came to Campos—where, according to Luis Mauricio Carneiro, a cofounder of the program, "no one had ever heard an orchestra"—and worked to help Jony and his colleagues to create an El Sistema learning environment.

Ever since that time, Fiorella Solares has devoted her life to launching and developing El Sistema programs. She told us that she thinks of her life in two parts. The first part was lived within the elite international classical music world. "When my husband was a conductor in Rome, in Sicily," she said, "our lives were full of artistic privilege and luxury. There were many concerts, many parties." But it is the second half, dedicated to building El Sistema in Brazil, that she most values. "I will never quit on this dream," she told us. "The only thing that will stop me is death."

She thought about that. "Maybe not even death," she added. "After all, death did not stop David."

Fiorella's Sistema-founding story is a particularly dramatic one. But in almost every Latin American country, word spread fast about El Sistema, even as it remained largely unknown for decades in the rest of the world. In countries connected to Venezuela by geographical proximity, cultural affinity, or both, musicians began to get wind of El Sistema almost from its inception, and throughout the 1980s, 1990s and early 2000s, El Sistema programs began to spring up across Latin America. Maestro Abreu's high renown as a musician was key to this development in many countries, as it was in Brazil. He had credibility and connections with eminent performers and teachers across the continent, and he missed no chance to cultivate these connections, inviting them to come to Venezuela and work with the children and young people of El Sistema. The visitors were often amazed by the young Venezuelans' musicality, moved by the social dimension of the work, and inspired to bring the Sistema vision home to their own countries.

The first seeds of the process were sown as early as 1976, when the youth orchestra's Mexico City performance of Carlos Chávez's Toccata for Percussion so electrified the composer, who happened to be in the audience, that he came to Caracas and worked with them for months, and then decided to bring El Sistema home to Mexico. Chávez was a figure of international stature, having appeared as guest conductor for many of the world's leading orchestras and given the 1958–59 Norton Lectures at Harvard. "Carlos Chávez was a giant of Mexican music, and really a universal figure," we were told by José Luis Hernández-Estrada, a Mexican conductor, educator, and writer who heads Sistema Tulsa, in Oklahoma. "From early on, he spoke of the socializing, civilizing function of music. He believed that the socializing impact was intimately connected to its beauty and artistic value."

The coming together in 1976 of this great elder statesman of Mexican music and the young Venezuelan just beginning his own crusade for Latin American musical potency was a lucky confluence of ideals and genius. Both Chávez and Abreu believed in the capacity of Latin Americans to become leaders in the international world of art music. Both were engaged in the exploration of what music learning might mean for the empowerment of young people. Chávez, who was seventy-seven and ailing, saw in Abreu the possibility that his dreams could be carried forward and eventually realized. And for Abreu, Chávez was an inspirational guide. The man who perpetually mentored every one of his orchestra members had found his own mentor.

In 1977, Chávez founded an El Sistema program in Mexico. But his health was steadily worsening, and he died in 1978, before the program could ignite. It would take another decade for the Sistema vision to come alive in Mexico.

Elsewhere, however, the vision began to gain traction. In 1982, the Organization of American States (OAS) passed a resolution in favor of a "Multinational Project for Extending the Simón Bolívar Foundation Music Education Model" throughout Latin America and the Caribbean. The presidents of a number of countries contacted FESNOJIV and asked for help in creating Sistema programs in their countries. Abreu and his colleagues said yes to every request, and delegations of Venezuelan Sistema teachers began to crisscross the continent, bearing their novel idea of orchestral education as social transformation.

They were not always met with open arms on the part of local music teachers, just as Abreu's youth orchestra had not been universally welcomed in his own country when it began. Local teachers sometimes insisted that what the Venezuelans were trying to do was simply not possible; children couldn't play Beethoven and Tchaikovsky in such a short rehearsal period, and children couldn't rehearse more than a couple of hours a day. The Venezuelan musical ambassadors had to prove their point fast.

Ulyses Ascanio, one of the original eleven Sistema founding members and now an honored senior maestro in Venezuela, told us about his first trip to Paraguay in 1980. After seventeen hours of flights, his team of twelve arrived in the middle of the night, looking so bedraggled that no one believed these were the visiting maestros. They were taken to a dilapidated military barracks and served a questionable breakfast—"to this day, we cannot figure out what it was; we still argue about it"—and were finally rescued by the ambassador and taken to a cheap hotel for a quick sleep before starting work the next morning.

"They had exactly three students waiting for us," Ulyses recalled. "They wanted us to somehow create El Sistema out of those three students, and they had scheduled a concert in five days."

The Venezuelans went out to the parks and alleyways of Asuncíon and found kids who could play instruments—or who wanted to play instruments—and rehearsed them like mad. Five days later, the Paraguayan president and other dignitaries heard the brand-new orchestra of 150 young people play Beethoven's Fifth Symphony . . . perhaps not brilliantly, but together. Ulyses told us proudly that one of those kids, who first received a violin from his hands, is now the leading violinist in the country.

In Mexico, meanwhile, the Sistema vision made a dramatic reappearance in 1987 in the person of Eduardo Mata, a conductor who had been Carlos Chávez's protégé and had spent the first two decades of his career leading the symphony orchestras of Phoenix and Dallas. At Abreu's invitation, Mata began to conduct the Simón Bolívar Youth Symphony in the late 1980s and became the first official conductor of the ensemble after Maestro Abreu himself.

Back in Mexico, Mata proclaimed that he had discovered the best orchestra in the world. Like Carlos Chávez before him, he was determined to create an El Sistema program in Mexico. In an eloquent letter to the secretary of education, he wrote, "If we don't do what the Venezuelans have done for music in their country, we won't have God's forgiveness. . . . They have proven that it is possible to disseminate the great symphonic music even in the most remote of places, and to teach youngsters to master a musical instrument through play and festivity." The government took him seriously, and El Sistema Mexico was launched in 1990.

A Sistema program also began around that time in Colombia, where civil war was escalating between guerrilla rebels, paramilitary armies, and the national militia—in essence, a war against and between the powerful drug cartels that held Colombian society hostage. Refugee tent camps were overflowing with the largest displaced population in the world at that time, many of them children and youth. It was to alleviate the misery of these young people that the Colombian government launched an El Sistema program called Batuta (conductor's "baton" in English), and funded it through the Department of Social Prosperity.

During its early years, Batuta was more focused on bringing younger children into musical ensembles, to provide creative activity and socialization in their stressful displaced settings, than on creating high-level orchestras of teenagers. Orchestral instruments were unobtainable in refugee camps, so Batuta children grew up playing Orff and rhythm instruments, singing and playing musical games. But the basic ethos was the same: young people growing and healing through intensive communal music-making.

To reflect upon the various El Sistema founding stories in Latin

America is to realize that while each Sistema-inspired program developed in its own particular way, driven by the convictions of its own guiding lights, José Antonio Abreu was a personally supportive force in every story. All the program leaders we have met in Latin America seem secure in the knowledge that to this day, they can call upon the Maestro if they need him. And some, like Fiorella, have had the experience of bending to the inevitability of a directive from Abreu. The late Bolivia Bottome, one of Abreu's closest colleagues, once put it this way: "When the Maestro makes a clear request, there is no such thing as 'no.' He knows what we are capable of, sometimes better than we know ourselves."

During these same years, Abreu was also deeply engaged in guiding El Sistema in Venezuela toward both greater reach and greater depth. Even as more and more núcleos were being created across the country, and the numbers of children involved were multiplying rapidly, the Sistema's attention to the quality of the music-making was building in every núcleo, every orchestra and choir.

Abreu's pursuit of musical excellence was most dramatically evident in his decision to hand over the baton of the Simón Bolívar Youth Orchestra to Eduardo Mata. For the young Bolivarians, the Mexican conductor brought new levels of musical consciousness. "He was an empowerer of creativity and imagination," said José Luis Hernández-Estrada. "He had the pulse of a truly Latin American sound."

For Mata, the Simón Bolívar was what he had been seeking all his professional life but had not been able to find, even in prominent U.S. ensembles: an orchestra capable of rendering the spirit and rhythms of Latin American classical music with virtuosity and passion. "Eduardo Mata chose the Simón Bolívar Youth Orchestra," Abreu has said, "to head up a vast movement aimed at the reconstruction and rescue of Latin American symphonic repertoire, and gaining it international recognition."[12] This was the Latin American ideal Abreu had long envisioned—the entrance of Latin America, as a full and equal contributor, into the world of international art music.

Describing the playing of the Simón Bolívar, Mata wrote, "They make Beethoven sound as though he belongs to us all . . . and our Latin composers sound as though they had left us their souls."[13] He worked with the orchestra for nearly eight years. The essence of their collaboration has been preserved in the form of an indelible set of recordings on the Dorian label, featuring the music of great Latin American and Spanish composers including Heitor Villa-Lobos, Alberto Ginastera, Carlos Chávez, Silvestre Revueltas, and Manuel de Falla. This fertile alliance between orchestra and conductor came to an unfortunate early end in 1995, when Mata died in the crash near Mexico City of a small plane he was piloting.

In the meantime, Abreu had been working to create a new ensemble, the National Children's Orchestra, that brought together a new crop of gifted young musicians from Sistema programs across the country—mostly young teenagers, some as young as ten. Quickly, a teenager from Barquisimeto named Gustavo Dudamel emerged from the violin section to become its leader. With the steady mentorship of Maestro Abreu, Dudamel's wealth of musical and communicative talents evolved rapidly.

As the El Sistema model spread across Latin America in the 1990s, it won the attention of the United Nations as a new and potent force for social welfare and even international peace. In 1995, UNESCO approved the creation of the "World Movement of Youth and Children's Orchestras and Choirs for Promoting World Peace." Meanwhile, Abreu's vision of a unified Latin American musical culture resonated strongly with organizations promoting continent-wide cooperation. For example, the Andean Development Corporation (CAF) created the Andean Countries' Youth Symphony Orchestra, which debuted in Caracas and went on to tour the Andean countries; this was a forerunner of the still-robust Youth Orchestra of the Americas, created in 2000 by the OAS.

This intracontinental focus infused the mission of El Sistema with new energy, and Sistema-inspired programs continued to grow across South and Central America and in the Caribbean Island countries as well. In some countries, programs have flourished; in others, they have suffered and even disappeared, as local governments have failed to provide sufficient support. But Ulyses Ascanio and other lifelong traveling teachers are proud that almost every Latin American country now has Sistema-inspired projects.

Despite cultural differences between these countries, their Sistema programs are generally similar, because they evolved in the same basic social context: a wide gap between a small, wealthy upper class and an impoverished majority, and a correspondingly wide gap between an elite arts culture and a near-complete absence of arts education for poor children. Longtime Mexican Sistema administrator Armando Torres-Chibrás speaks of the unity of purpose among all these programs: "What we are all sharing is the idea of music as a tool to create good citizens and to rescue children from poverty and bad circumstances—to help them develop self-esteem and responsibility, and be inspired by the power of music. So we are all on the same page."

By the end of the twentieth century, then, Latin America was reverberating with the sound and light of El Sistema. For the first time, significant energy was being poured into youth development through classical music. Governments were recognizing the efficacy of this vision. The canon of Western classical masterworks, fast losing vitality in the countries where it was developed, was blooming with new life and urgency.

And yet, throughout the rest of the world, almost no one—no musicians, no music educators, no government officials or policy-makers—had ever heard of El Sistema.

THE MILLENNIUM DAWNS: EL SISTEMA GOES GLOBAL

An unlikely confluence of forces began to bring El Sistema to the attention of the world at large in the beginning years of the

SNAPSHOTS OF LATIN AMERICAN EL SISTEMA PROGRAMS

Since we couldn't visit every Latin American program, we focused most of our attention on the largest programs (Venezuela, Colombia, and Mexico) and the fast-growing programs of Brazil. Here are some snapshots of the evolving landscape of Sistema programs elsewhere in Latin America. The list is far from comprehensive; our apologies to programs we have inadvertently omitted.

South America

Argentina: SOIJAr (Sistema Orquestas Infantiles y Juveniles de Argentina) serves 6,000 children; María Valeria Atela is its founder and director. In addition, conductor Mario Benzecry has recently started a new initiative with the José de San Martín National Youth Symphony. **Bolivia:** The Instituto Academico de Urubicha, in the state of Santa Cruz, has 700 students and 30 music teachers (in a town of 5,000), supported by the Ministry of Culture. There is a long tradition of Sistema-inspired work, and a recent groundswell of interest in Baroque music among the tropical indigenous Chiquitano Indians, who have reconstructed thousands of pages of original musical scores left behind in Jesuit missions three hundred years ago. **Chile:** Founded in 2001, the Chilean program FOJI (Fundación Orquestas Juveniles e Infantiles) serves almost 12,000 children and youth in 190 municipalities. They have begun to tour internationally and to record. Chile is also home to the Escuela de Música Papageno, launched by retired Austrian opera singer Christian Boesch, which provides ensemble music learning for children in the scenic but remote region of Patagonia. **Peru:** The Sinfonía por el Perú, sponsored by the electricity company Endesa, serves children in thirteen núcleos in Lima and elsewhere, and is led by famed tenor Juan Diego Flóres. A smaller program in the Trujillo region, Arpegio, is directed by Tatjana Merzyn (Sistema Fellow '14), a German musician who recruits a dozen or so volunteer music teachers from Germany each year to work in the program. **Uruguay:** Fundacion Sistema de Orchestas Juveniles e Infantiles de Uruguay is another large and well-established program, with 900 children in 9 núcleos. Its director, Ariel Britos, trained in the Venezuelan Sistema.

Central America

Costa Rica: Since 2007, the national Sistema organization SINEM has launched núcleos in several areas of the country. **El Salvador:** The Female Orchestra of the Salvadorian Institute for Childhood and Youth, a project of the OAS, engages teenage girls from rival gangs in a common orchestra. **Guatemala:** Several decades of Sistema-inspired activities have waxed and waned in strength but have produced some of the international Sistema community's best ambassadors, including Alvaro Rodas, director of New York City's Corona Youth Music Project, in Queens; Bruno Campo, in Europe; and Samuel Matus, in Istanbul. **Honduras:** A Sistema-inspired program has recently begun in the rural area of Taulabé, sponsored by the humanitarian organization Honduras Croissance; through the interconnective LinkedIn site Sistema Global, attempts are being made to provide this fledgling but ambitious program with teachers and teacher training.

The Caribbean

Puerto Rico: The Music 100x35 program, modeled on Venezuela's El Sistema, was launched in 2009. It serves over 1,000 impoverished children in 5 núcleos across Puerto Rico. **Belize:** A nascent National Youth Orchestra and Choir of Belize (NYOCB) has received some support and training help from the Sistema-inspired People's Music School project YOURS in Chicago. **Dominican Republic:** There are four or more small programs, and the oil company Refidomsa is starting another. The Sally and Dick Roberts Coyote Foundation in the United States is funding a Sistema start-up in Santiago de los Caballeros. **Haiti:** Sponsored by the Petro-Caribe initiative, Venezuela's Fundamusical has sent teams of teachers to work with 1,000 students at the Hinche núcleo. The same initiative will open a new núcleo at Jacmel soon. In the rural town of Pandiassou, Hinche, the weekends-only INAMUH (National Institute of Music of Haiti) program of 650 students has formed a children's orchestra but struggles to find support. The longstanding (since 1956) École de Musique Sainte Trinité has a variety of choral and orchestral ensembles, with 600 students. **Jamaica:** The six-year-old National Youth Orchestra of Jamaica, based in Kingston, aligns closely with Sistema principles, and is supported by the OAS. **Santa Lucia:** The Santa Lucia School of Music (founded 1988) has eight music ensembles and many more for outreach concerts in the community.

twenty-first century. One major force was the creation of a second-generation incarnation of the Simón Bolívar Youth Orchestra of Venezuela and the beginning of this orchestra's extensive international touring under the baton of Gustavo Dudamel. By the early 2000s, these young virtuosi were performing regularly in Paris, Milan, Rome, Lucerne, Berlin, Vienna, New York, Tokyo, and many more cultural capitals.

What most astonished their audiences was the musicians' combination of musical brilliance with extreme youth and unabashed high spirits—as well as their unlikely provenance: never before had Venezuela been associated with symphonic greatness. "One wonders," wrote a German critic in 2001, "how Dudamel manages to bring these youngsters so close to the true symphonic essence of music." From Spain, in 2007: "Such richness of sound, such flexibility . . . the most extraordinary sounds we have ever heard in Seville." From England, the same year: "There are some great youth orchestras around today, but none is as exciting to behold as this." When they appeared at the famously highbrow Lucerne Festival, a reviewer marveled at the audience as well as the orchestra: "To no orchestra or director have our hearts been given so generously as they were to the Simón Bolívar Youth Orchestra of Venezuela and its conductor Gustavo Dudamel!"

The blaze of international attention shone upon Dudamel individually as well. In 2004, he entered the Gustav Mahler Conducting Competition in Bamburg, Germany, and won first prize over competitors from thirteen countries. That prize opened many doors; in the following year, he guest-conducted eight of the world's leading orchestras, including the London Philharmonia, the Camerata Salzburg, the Los Angeles Philharmonic, and the Berlin Philharmonic.

The ascendancy of Dudamel and the Simón Bolívar to international classical music stardom was accompanied by a second important phenomenon: the rise of the Internet. In particular, the popularization of YouTube coincided with a riotously successful concert by the Simón Bolívar Youth Orchestra at the BBC Proms in

August 2007, and a video from the concert "went viral" on YouTube at just the moment when people were beginning to understand the meaning of that term. The video was a three-minute clip of one of the encores, "Mambo" from Leonard Bernstein's *West Side Story Suite*, with the players twirling their instruments, shouting "*Mambo!*" and leaping to their feet to dance as they played. The clip went into feverish circulation, popping into the inboxes of musicians and music lovers around the globe, with subject lines like: "You won't believe this!" or "Who ARE these kids?!!!" or "Check this out: classical music LIVES!"

With the orchestra as El Sistema's virtual as well as live ambassador, many among the global classical music aristocracy became curious about what was going on in Venezuela. The world-famous conductors Simon Rattle, Claudio Abbado, Daniel Barenboim, and Zubin Mehta came to Caracas to learn about and work with the youth orchestras of El Sistema—and they returned again and again. Star performers, including Itzhak Perlman, Luciano Pavarotti, Placido Domingo, Cecilia Bartoli, Emanuel Ax, Lang Lang, Leonidas Kavakos, Tsuyoshi Tsutsumi, and many others, also went to Caracas to observe, admire, and play.

In the United States, after the dazzling dust of first encounters began to settle, attention shifted from the extraordinary youth orchestra to the less glamorous but equally extraordinary system that had produced it. Those inside the classical music establishment, and even some outside of it, began to realize that this remarkable orchestra didn't come out of nowhere, and that what it *did* grow out of was distinctly different from the machinery of traditional music education.

Two pivotal, game-changing events in 2009 accelerated this shift of attention: the award of a TED Prize to Maestro Abreu and the ascension of Dudamel to the conductorship of the Los Angeles Philharmonic. The first happened in February, when Abreu was awarded a prize by the TED organization. Abreu's videotaped acceptance speech, articulating his wish for support from TED, is an articulation of the El Sistema vision that remains unparalleled for its eloquence and clarity. Circulating on YouTube along with "Mambo," it continues to function across the world as a kind of "Sermon on the Mount" for El Sistema.

Abreu made the speech in Spanish (the video has English subtitles), but at the end, he switched to succinct, highly accented English to make his TED wish: "I wish that you would help create and document a special training program for at least fifty gifted young musicians, passionate for their art and for social justice, and dedicated to developing El Sistema in the United States and in other countries."

The TED community went into immediate action, helping Abreu to create a formal partnership with the distinguished New England Conservatory in Boston and to launch an "Abreu Fellowship" that would train ten musicians a year, for five years, in the principles and practice of El Sistema. Just nine months later, the first cohort of ten citizen artists had heard about it, applied, been selected, and moved to Boston to begin an immersive year-long learning experience that would include a six-week trip to Venezuela. The Fellowship, the first in-depth exploration of how the achievement in Venezuela might be adapted to serve non-Latin American communities, was an unusual move on the part of a prominent conservatory; training leaders to start orchestra programs in impoverished neighborhoods is not what conservatories generally do. Clearly, NEC's then president Tony Woodcock and Sistema Fellows Program founder Mark Churchill felt their own sense of "We must bring this here!" mission strongly enough to champion an unprecedented initiative in the heart of the Western classical music establishment.

At about the same time, on the country's other coast, a seminal event with a different feel was unfolding. Gustavo Dudamel, then twenty-seven, accepted the position of Los Angeles Philharmonic music director, and instantly became Los Angeles's newest celebrity. His name, face, and celebrated mane of curly dark hair were suddenly on buses and banners everywhere, paired with breathless Spanish words: *"RADIANTE!" "ELECTRICO!" "PASION!"* Behind this blaze of public fanfare, Dudamel and the Philharmonic were quietly committed to bringing El Sistema to Los Angeles. More than a year before his debut, the orchestra launched a Sistema-inspired program, Youth Orchestra Los Angeles (YOLA) in a South Central Los Angeles ghetto. For the L.A. Phil, this was a distinct departure from orchestral tradition; many orchestras sponsor youth orchestras, partly to nurture a next generation of players and audiences, but none had ever launched a major program for impoverished children in a locale that had no orchestral tradition. Buoyed by Dudamel's determination, L.A. Philharmonic president Deborah Borda planted a bold marker for the field in this high-profile experiment, without any certainty that El Sistema's successes in Latin America would work in the markedly different context of Los Angeles.

The experiment was dramatically front and center when Dudamel took the podium at the Hollywood Bowl for his first official appearance as music director of the Los Angeles Philharmonic— wearing not a tuxedo, but a YOLA tee shirt. The orchestra before him was not the L.A. Phil but the children's orchestra of YOLA, whom he led in a simplified version of the "Ode to Joy," a performance that made up in aspirational spirit what it lacked in musical finesse. Among the audience of 18,000, over a third were Latinos who had been provided free seats; many had never seen an orchestra perform. After the children played, the professional musicians in white tie and tails took the stage to perform the whole Ninth Symphony. But the unique and lasting image of that concert was the tee-shirted ensemble of young black and Latino children, some very small, taking ownership of the world's most famous classical anthem, in front of thousands of their community members, sitting beside thousands of the city's arts elite.

This confluence of events in 2009 seems to have been a tipping point. In the years since, the El Sistema vision has begun to spread more rapidly than anyone can keep track of, capturing the imagination of musicians and social activists alike. More than 117 Sistema-inspired programs have been launched across the United States, in some of the country's poorest communities. In some cases, the initiators were graduates of the Fellowship established at the New England Conservatory (initially called the Abreu Fellowship but later renamed the Sistema Fellowship, at Abreu's request; he was uncomfortable advocating for a project that bore his name). But many other programs began simply through the initiative of a single individual or a small group of people who saw the YouTube clips of the BBC Proms "Mambo" or Maestro Abreu's TED talk, or saw one of several documentary films and television features about El Sistema, and said, "We *must* bring this program to our city!"

Gustavo Dudamel's celebrity and his critically praised long run with the Los Angeles Philharmonic (his current contract has him there until 2022) have continued to turn up the heat around El Sistema. His charismatic podium presence, deepened by years of brilliant performances, has caught the interest of the classical music establishment and sparked the notice of a much wider public than is usually attentive to classical music.

Even as Sistema-inspired programs proliferated in the United States between 2009 and 2015, that same half-decade saw the explosion of El Sistema-inspired programs throughout the world. The social and cultural contexts for these programs vary widely from one country to another, and so do the programs; El Sistema in Japan looks different from El Sistema in Romania, which looks different from El Sistema in England—and they all look different from El Sistema in Kenya. Some programs are large and sponsored by state or federal governments; many others are small and funding-challenged. They differ in how they are organized and in when and where they take place.

More important than these differences, however, is the kinship in spirit among the programs. They are all guided by the determination to help children in difficult life circumstances redirect their life trajectories for the better, and by the conviction that making music together can tap reservoirs of personal and social possibility. They are connected by an ethos of inclusion. They are created and sustained by people who fuse artistic aspiration with the combustible fuel of social change—the people we have come to think of as "citizen artists."

It may not be a coincidence that the rise of the international Sistema movement came at a historical moment when the global human rights community was newly focused on the particular suffering of children in poverty and traumatic circumstances. The practice of child trafficking was first recognized as such by the United Nations Palermo Protocol of 2000. The World Health Organization has drawn attention to the magnitude of childhood malnutrition and estimates that it is the root cause of one-third of all child deaths internationally. In 2014, Pope Francis chose to focus on the plight of children in his annual Christmas address "Urbi et Orbi," speaking of "children displaced due to war and persecution, abused and taken advantage of before our very eyes and our complicit silence." He denounced "the globalization of indifference" and called for the world's attention to "so many abused children."

In the context of this increased global awareness of children's suffering, Maestro Abreu has received a multitude of international awards and tributes—including Sweden's Right Livelihood Award, often called the alternative Nobel Prize, for "outstanding vision and work on behalf of our planet and its people;" the Harvard School of Public Health's "Q Prize," for "extraordinary leadership on behalf of children"; and Spain's Prince of Asturias Award, for "having combined, within a single project, the highest artistic quality and a profound ethical conviction applied for the improvement of our social reality." (See endnote 14 for a more complete list of these awards and honors.)

The rapid ascendancy of El Sistema to global prominence represents several historical "firsts." Never before has an idea from the arts been embraced so widely and quickly as an answer to a social problem. Never has the symphony orchestra been taken seriously as an instrument of social change within marginalized parts of society. And seldom in modern history, if ever, has an idea for social transformation originating in Latin America been welcomed by countries around the world. Developing nations are rarely seen as the generators of game-changing ideas for the rest of the world. But with El Sistema, Latin America is the source of a big idea that other countries are learning from and embracing.

SALZBURG 2013: A MARKER OF CHANGE

An emblematic moment in the global development of El Sistema occurred in 2013 at the Salzburg Festival, an annual summer festival in Mozart's birthplace that is among the most venerable events of the classical music world. In 2013, the festival organizers programmed a complete cycle of the Mahler symphonies, and many regular festival subscribers from across Europe and Asia bought subscription tickets. What some didn't fully understand was that many of those hallowed nine symphonies were going to be played by orchestras of teenagers and young adults from Venezuela.

Led by the Austrian cultural impresario Alexander Pereira, who was the director of the Salzburg Festival from 2011 to 2014, the festival administrators had resolved not only to honor El Sistema at the festival but also to feature it in an authentically Sistema-esque outsized way—not just a performance by a single Sistema orchestra, but a high-visibility residency that would demonstrate the depth, breadth, and power of El Sistema. Pereira, an ardent Sistema enthusiast, believes that the world of European art music has something crucial to learn from El Sistema. "In Europe," he has said, "children study music alone in a room for years, only seeing their teacher, without ever seeing another child. The message that comes from El Sistema is to teach our children to make music together."

No fewer than seven full Sistema ensembles, the festival administrators decided, would do. So to Salzburg they came: the illustrious Simón Bolívar Orchestra; the younger Teresa Carreño Youth Orchestra; the decidedly teenaged Youth Orchestra of Caracas; the 300-member National Children's Orchestra, whose youngest players were eight; the Simón Bolívar National Youth Choir of Venezuela; the Venezuelan Brass Ensemble; and finally, and most improbably, the White Hands Choir of Venezuela, composed of children with disabilities of various kinds.

To Salzburg they came, with a large entourage of staff and chaperones—over 1,400 in total—with most of the young musicians under twenty-five. For two weeks, the cobbled streets of that surpassingly elegant city were filled with young Venezuelans splashing in the street fountains, sampling gelato, and occasionally coming to grief on rented bicycles, which for them were exotic novelties. (More than one player showed up to play Mahler with a bandage or a sling.)

And, of course, filling the concert halls with magnificent sound and communicative energy. These performances confronted festival audiences with something far outside of the usual concertgoing experience; they had come to hear Mahler in one of the world's most refined venues, and there on the stage were two hundred Latin American teenagers. In each concert, applause after the first piece was grudging. But as the performances went on, and the young players gave their wholehearted, often stunning accounts of these canonical pieces, audience members began to unfold their crossed arms and lean forward into the music. By the end of every concert, there was foot stomping and rhythmic clapping; there was even some waving of Tyrolean jackets.

Night after night at the festival, audiences of the cultural elite were moved to celebrate ensembles that grew from impoverished circumstances—ensembles whose very young members had learned through group endeavor rather than individualized training, and who lit up great works of European art music with their fresh, unbridled spirit.

As we left one performance, we asked an audience member if Salzburg audiences usually responded to concerts with such enthusiasm. He laughed and said, "I come to the Festival every year. I live in a town where Mahler composed symphonies. And I have never seen audiences react like this in my entire life."

One of the world's preeminent pianists, Austrian Alfred Brendel, attended a Festival performance of Mahler's First Symphony, conducted by Simon Rattle and performed by the nine-to-thirteen-year-old musicians of the National Children's Orchestra. Brendel described it as "one of the most affecting performances I have witnessed in Salzburg in half a century. . . . From my skeptical corner, I look at the Venezuelan miracle with amazement. Has the power of music ever generated such comprehensive social benefit?"[15]

As for the seventh ensemble—the White Hands Choir—that concert may be the one many festivalgoers will remember above all others. In this choir, created in the city of Barquisimeto, the children are arranged in two sections, one comprised of children with various disabilities including Down syndrome and autism, and the other made up of hearing-impaired children, many completely deaf, whose white-gloved hands convey the meaning of the songs in graceful gestures.

In their Salzburg performance, the White Hands Choir's singing was not as technically proficient as that of the National Youth Choir, nor was the White Hands choreography synchronized to water ballet perfection. But the children sang and "danced" with all their hearts. The audience's cheers and tears were simply about the expressive and communicative capacities of the human spirit.

The 2013 season of the Salzburg Festival had another novel dimension: it was the scene of the first gathering of children from Sistema programs across Europe, and their first public performance as a combined group. The gathering was hosted by Superar, a new multinational entity (the name is a nod to Venezuela, meaning "to overcome" in Spanish) that sponsors núcleos in central and eastern Europe. Nearly 300 children came from Sistema-inspired programs in Austria, Bosnia, Italy, Portugal, Romania, Slovakia, Switzerland, Turkey, and elsewhere to rehearse and perform together. The combined choir performed at an airplane hangar refurbished as a recreation center; they sang songs from each of their home countries and then sang along with the Simón Bolívar National Youth Choir. That concert concluded with a rousing "Oh Happy Day," performed by both of the choirs, all the audience members, and just about every person in the airplane hangar, security guards included.

Meanwhile, the members of the Superar combined orchestra had been in Vienna for a week, rehearsing in the largest space anyone could find—an empty swimming pool at the Vienna Boy's Choir School (strings and winds inside the pool, basses and percussion around the edge). They came to Salzburg on the last day of the Festival to play for and with the National Children's Orchestra of Venezuela. Many of the children had never left their hometowns and had been playing their instruments for less than a year. They came away from the encounter with a whole new idea of how fantastic—and fast—Rossini's *William Tell* Overture could actually sound, along with a transformed understanding of themselves as musicians who can contribute to international musical events, and who have kindred counterparts everywhere in the world.

As for the audiences of Salzburg 2013, they went home with a transformed understanding of what music can mean in the lives of young people, and what young people can mean for the world of classical music. "We took El Sistema to the artistic mountain peak," said Alexander Pereira, "to show the world what it has achieved and what it really means. The results are now visible worldwide. . . . At the festival we opened a new door. A new and fresh air has entered Europe."

CHAPTER 3

Understanding El Sistema:
A Few Key Ideas

If there is something to be changed in this world,
then it can only happen through music.
— JIMI HENDRIX

There is no textbook for El Sistema. There is no manual or official "how to"—a fact frequently observed with some frustration by Sistema practitioners around the world, many of whom would love to have a guidebook or at least a checklist to lead them through the complicated processes of starting and running a Sistema-inspired program. But El Sistema has never been about guidebooks. In Venezuela and across the world, El Sistema is not a program or a pedagogy; it is an inquiry—aspirational, passionate, and flexible.

The story of the global Sistema, therefore, is so rich with variety in response to cultural context that there is no simple way to tell it. Creative abundance is the nature of this global experiment. Since we can't offer a guidebook, we focus in Part II on the commonalities of philosophy and practice that seem crucial to creating the distinctive learning environments of El Sistema programs everywhere. It is the quality of the learning environment—more than the pedagogy, more than the curriculum—that gives Sistema programs their potential to transform lives.

Before we begin this endeavor, we offer a few key elements for readers to keep in mind throughout—elements we think of as El Sistema's open secrets, since these aspects of Sistema are not often explicitly identified, but appear so consistently as to be defining elements of the work. El Sistema did not invent these "secrets." Rather, they have the feel of durable human truths, rediscovered and reactivated to address modern problems—and not only by El Sistema, but also by many organizations working to effect social change. They are not even secrets in the literal sense, as El Sistema has never made any attempt to hide them; they merely tend to be taken for granted as background assumptions and conditions for nourishing the learning environment. They are, we believe, part of the elemental appeal of El Sistema in so many varying cultures and countries around the world.

THE CITIZEN ARTIST

Karis Crawford is about as midwestern American as it's possible to be; no one in her family has moved out of Michigan in generations. She studied violin at the University of Michigan, with an interest in Suzuki methodology, and then decided it was time for an adventure. When a prospective schoolteaching job in England fell through because of visa problems, she was referred to a job in the rural Rift Valley of Kenya, at a school with a population of wealthy international students. Several years into teaching there, she tired of the students' entitled attitudes and found ways to volunteer-teach in programs for impoverished communities in Nairobi. Soon she was driving many hours each weekend to teach at Ghetto Classics, a Sistema-inspired program in a Nairobi slum. In 2014, she moved to Nairobi to start her own Sistema program in the heart of the dangerous Kawangware ghetto.

There is a clear demarcation line, just past a gated and guarded private school, where the wealthier city ends and the slum begins.

Karis can't afford a car, so she walks about a mile into the ghetto every day on the main dirt road, lined with tin shack stalls and shanty huts. When she was completing negotiations with the Kawangware School about starting El Sistema Kenya there, she asked school administrators about her safety. They got back to her some days later: "It is okay; you will be safe." In the interim, the officials had had a covert conversation with the Mungiki, a mysterious ethnic-religious sect that functions like a local mafia gang and controls ghettos with terrifying force. Murders, disappearances, and beheadings are common enforcement practices by the Mungiki in the areas they control. Espousing an anticolonialist ethos and adhering to indigenous Kikuyu traditions, they impose a code of sexual modesty and abstinence from alcohol (although some enforcers exempt themselves from the rules) and are ruthless in their control.

The local Mungiki leaders okayed the school's question about a stringed instrument program and put out a directive that Karis was not to be harmed. So far, she has not had a single incident or scary moment, walking that mile to her school. Everyone knows who she is. School personnel have become her friends; some of the locals recognize her and wave. She was just three days into her program when we visited her. She plans to stay a long time; she has already opened a new program site in a different ghetto and is negotiating safety considerations for a third program site.

We live in an era when "high art" music (music variously defined as classical, symphonic, or art music) exists in a social and cultural universe almost completely separate from mainstream popular music, the music created for and listened to by the vast majority. The small percentage of people who inhabit this rarefied universe might be characterized as the high art "club." It's not an easy club to get into; membership requires considerable background and training in the languages of the arts, and the ability to reliably find personal meanings inside those languages. It's a club almost entirely disconnected from the reality of most people's lives.

Artists like Karis who start, lead, and teach in Sistema programs are usually experienced in the institutions of the high art club and are often products of its pipelines—conservatories, music departments, orchestras, private teaching. Many, although not all, are musicians who play or sing at professional levels. All are dedicated to teaching and to the belief that music enhances children's lives. But there is also a social dimension to their commitment. They are inspired by the idea that musical engagement can make a difference in the social conditions and opportunities of children, families, and communities. We think of them as citizen artists.

We choose the word "citizen" because it connotes dedication to community. When traditional orchestras or individual artists make forays into "the community" to do a performance in a public school or a meeting hall, such one-shot connections are more like acquiring a tourist visa to a foreign land—or, in more resource-invested projects, a work permit—than like applying for citizenship. Citizenship is a commitment of one's time, inquiries, and identity.

Artists with highly active social consciences have been present and effective throughout the history of the arts, and not only in music. The settlement houses of England and North America in the late nineteenth and early twentieth centuries, for example, were filled with musicians and other artists committed to ameliorating the lives of struggling urban populations, and aiding in their process of assimilation, by enabling them to engage with the arts. It's our impression that there is currently an especially strong surge of interest in citizen artistry among young artists around the world. El Sistema seems to have captivated imaginations worldwide because it embodies a buried but not extinguished belief within many people—and not just artists—that if given a sustained chance, the arts have the power to change feelings, attitudes, lives, and societies. El Sistema is fueled by the energy of this optimism, and is fueling citizen artistry, in turn, by giving it more visibility and collective power.

Ricardo Castro and Jovianney Emmanuel Cruz, the founders of thriving El Sistema programs in Brazil and the Philippines, respectively, are internationally touring concert pianists. Both achieved a high level of success in the classical music business: thriving careers, financial rewards, artistic mastery, and international renown. Hemispheres apart, and unknown to one another, they used almost exactly the same words to express how they felt at this career pinnacle. "It just didn't feel like enough," they both told us. "Something was missing." Jovianney said, "I asked myself what really matters in society, and the answer was not concerts." Ricardo's recollection: "I realized this way of doing music was not making me happy." Now, five years later, they are the founder-directors of rapidly expanding Sistema-inspired programs in their countries. They both continue to perform concerts, although less frequently.

Eunsuk Chae, the music director of the South Korean Orchestra of Dreams Bucheon Núcleo, has lived the conductor's version of this story. Chae pursued twelve years of perfection-focused training in Europe and returned to South Korea to become senior conductor of the Seoul National Symphony Orchestra. He soon added the directorship of a high-achieving youth orchestra to his duties. In 2010, when he heard about the Sistema-affiliated Orchestra of Dreams, he began volunteering his time to conduct the beginning orchestra of the núcleo in Bucheon, a city adjacent to Seoul.

The students learned fast, but were still far behind the quality of more established audition-only, pay-to-play youth orchestras. Many of Chae's friends told him he should not give so much time to this "social project" because those kids were never going to make great music. His wife worried that his attention to the Sistema work would damage his career by lowering his social and professional status. The board of his professional orchestra threatened to fire him because he gave so much time to this orchestra of poor children, when, according to them, "any music school recent graduate could do that job."

After a time, however, his wife noticed a change in him. "The only time you are really happy," she told him, "the only time you smile when you come home, is after you have been to the Orchestra of Dreams." She became a strong supporter of his increased commitment to the Sistema work. Chae is determined to make his Sistema orchestra the best youth orchestra in Korea—which, by the high standards of youth music in Korea, is quite an ambition. He told us, "I want them to feel what it is like being 'the best,' and I totally believe they can do that. In five or six years, these kids will become unbeatable."

Julian Lloyd Webber is the United Kingdom's most famous cellist (and the brother of musical theater composer Andrew Lloyd Webber). A world-renowned concert artist for many years, he has also been a longtime passionate advocate for universal music education in his country. In 2003, he formed a "Music Consortium" with percussionist Evelyn Glennie and flutist James Galway, and they visited the prime minister to protest drastic nationwide cuts in music education. Several years later, he helped bring El Sistema to the United Kingdom, and founded the charitable organization Sistema England to provide supplemental support for Sistema-inspired programs. When his performing career was sidelined in 2014 due to physical injuries, he announced publicly that while he would greatly miss playing, he was glad to be able to pour more energy into building Sistema England.

These are musicians with high international profiles, only somewhat less famous than the classical music superstars who have championed Venezuela's El Sistema. In the course of our travels, we encountered literally hundreds of equally dedicated citizen artists who are doing Sistema-inspired work, forging vivid and often idiosyncratic life paths in the service of strong commitment to their ideals. They could be found in every rehearsal room, in every small, cluttered office, on every escorted walk through a dangerous neighborhood. All are highly trained artists who found themselves yearning for something more, and who changed their life pathways to act on that yearning. "For me," South Korean conductor Chae told us, "this is not simply volunteerism to give to others, because I get so much in return. I learn from my students as much as I give."

GROUP INTRINSIC MOTIVATION

There is one essential thing a society must accomplish if it is to succeed.
It is to teach its young people to find pleasure in the right things.
—PLATO

Psychologists use the terms *intrinsic motivation* and *extrinsic motivation* to distinguish the two kinds of drive that influence the actions we take. The distinction is more concrete than such academic-sounding words might imply. Intrinsic motivation seeks internal, personal satisfactions; extrinsic motivation seeks external rewards or avoidance of punishment. When a piano student works hard to master a run of sixteenth notes in a Mozart sonata, feels the pleasure of accomplishment in mastering them, and enjoys their beauty, that's intrinsic motivation. When a piano student works on those sixteenth notes because if she plays them perfectly, she'll please her teacher or get an A in music class—that's extrinsic motivation.

Extrinsic motivators are common influencers of learning, habits, and beliefs, and can improve results for repetitive, mechanical, and algorithmic tasks. As most of us know from personal experience, extrinsic motivators, which include social pressure and anxiety about negative consequences, drive much of the work we do in schools and workplaces. However, a strong body of research affirms that the kind of learning that contributes to substantive personal growth, creative accomplishment, and sustained inquiry emanates only from intrinsic motivation. Reward-punishment approaches are proven to get certain kinds of short-term results; intrinsic-motivation approaches invest in the longer term. Intrinsic motivation often appears first as simple curiosity. When encouraged to evolve, curiosity becomes interest and exploration, and can eventually bloom into commitment and even into life change. Some researchers say that in the long run, intrinsic motivation *always* delivers the better results.

El Sistema is in the intrinsic-motivation business.

When El Sistema came to Japan in 2012, we asked Michiko Shimizu, a prominent businesswoman and founding supporter of El Sistema Japan, what Sistema had to offer her country, which is so rich in music education opportunities. She answered with one word: "Joy." We were later to learn that many in Japan refer to El Sistema as "a pedagogy of joy." El Sistema is a laboratory for experiments in combining the hard work of developing musical skills with the feelings of pleasure and joy that are among the most potent intrinsic motivators.

On the level most obvious to visitors, kids in Sistema programs have fun with their friends and with their instructors and conductors. We once asked Gustavo Dudamel what makes El Sistema so successful. His answer was immediate: "Two things. Every child feels like an asset. And we never forget fun." The spirit of play is strong in Sistema programs, and is modeled by teachers, who are often just recently past the teen age themselves. As children get older and more skilled, the business of pleasure becomes more complex. There is no way to develop musical skills without painstaking, disciplined, often repetitive practice—which is simply not, on the face of it, much fun. This is where Sistema environments become so intriguing: they provide learning environments that nourish the capacities of young people for intrinsic motivation through more subtle and complex kinds of pleasure.

Key to this learning environment is the strength of ensemble connection. Painstaking and repetitive practice, when done with a group of friends, can come to be associated with pride in collective accomplishment and satisfaction in making a contribution. When mastery is achieved, a whole new pathway of pleasure opens up, leading to the joy and awe of aesthetic experience. Throughout the entire process, motivation remains intrinsic.

These are profound arenas of learning to open for children whose daily environments may offer them, at best, only superficial kinds of instant gratification—a norm that becomes riskier as children get older. As Sistema programs support and accelerate experiences of satisfaction and joy, students discover a kind of personal reward system different from the world of instant gratification. They come to learn that disciplined practice produces more substantial satisfaction, and they develop the grit to work harder and longer. One might call this "self-discipline," but it can also be seen as more sophisticated pleasure-seeking and -attaining. The developmental journey through El Sistema years can be described as a steady expansion of the palette of pleasures a young person acquires a taste for and begins to seek regularly, even pleasures that don't seem so tasty on the first encounter.

In the process of observing many Sistema ensembles in rehearsal, we realized that these ensembles provide a particularly compelling blend of intrinsic motivators. We have sometimes seen these ensembles improve over the course of a few days, faster than our experience tells us is possible. It seems to be a group drive, mobilized and fueled by multiple kinds of intrinsic motivation, that makes this possible. In effect, the players in a Sistema ensemble seem to experience a kind of group intrinsic motivation, a drive toward expression and accomplishment on the part of the ensemble as a whole. As group motivation grows, the intrinsic motivation of each individual stays active but also opens wider to align with the motivation of others. The sheer force of such collective motivation is astonishingly potent. The kids playing and singing Mozart's *Missa Brevis* in that núcleo in Campos, Brazil, connect to and channel one another's motivational energies, fusing them into a group energy strong enough to lift them out of the world of the favela and into the shared virtual space of a musical masterwork.

The motivational power of group belonging is not unique to music; it's visible everywhere from sports teams and Girl Scouts to Parent-Teacher Associations and walkathons. But an El Sistema ensemble is an especially effective incubator for group motivation. Unlike a sports team, it is a team whose object is not to win, not to cause another team to lose, not to gain personal glory, but to make something together that has the power to move people. Further, it's a team whose less competent members don't get dropped or left to sit on the bench in hopes they get to play; they are consistently coached, assisted, and relied upon.

Juan Antonio Cuéllar, former director of Batuta, the national Sistema program of Colombia, told us a story that illustrates group motivation through shared joy in process. The Batuta Youth Orchestra of Bogotá (now known as the Batuta Metropolitan Symphony Orchestra) had the opportunity a few years ago to go to Caracas and play with the Youth Orchestra of Caracas, one of El Sistema Venezuela's top touring orchestras. The members of the Bogotá orchestra had long revered their Caracas counterparts, listening to their recordings and considering them heroes and role models, so excitement around the trip was high.

At the first rehearsal of this tremendous combined orchestra, with each of the ninety members of the Youth Orchestra of Bogotá sitting as stand mate next to one of the ninety members of the Youth Orchestra of Caracas, the conductor Manuel López-Gómez announced that they would first work on Tchaikovsky's Fifth Symphony. He lifted his baton; they began to play the first movement. He stopped them after a few measures, to work on the rhythm of the opening clarinet melody. Then they began again. And then—they just played, with a collective force so strong that the conductor couldn't bear to break it. They played the entire symphony from beginning to end. "It sounded like they had been playing this symphony together forever," Juan Antonio told us. "I completely lost track of who was Colombian and who was Venezuelan. It was an emotional experience. Maestro Abreu was there, and he was deeply moved as well."

There were also many flaws, of course, and the conductor and musicians got around to working on them. But that first coming together of two group-motivated orchestras had resulted in a group motivation of exponential intensity. "There was a sense of awe at the end," said Juan Antonio. "Something rare in life had just happened. They knew it, and they would never forget it."

HABITS OF MIND AND HEART

> We are what we repeatedly do.
> Excellence, then, is not an act, but a habit.
> — ARISTOTLE

Sixteen-year-old Özmen Genç spent most days walking around his poverty-stricken neighborhood in Istanbul carrying two knives, one in each jacket pocket. He had dropped out of school two years before; he couldn't find a paying job, and his chief daily occupation was trying to protect himself from gang members and drug dealers by looking as menacing as possible.

One day, as he passed by the Music for Peace building in the Edirnekapi district, he heard a drummer practicing; curious, he opened the unlocked door and walked in. Yeliz Yalin, one of the directors, greeted him and invited him to stay, even though "he looked kind of scary," she told us, "like the kind of guy most teachers would call a 'bad kid.' But I could see he was interested in the music."

When he showed up next, Özmen was carrying the two knives and his older brother's guitar. With the assistance of teachers at Music for Peace, he began to learn how to play it. He started coming every day, and learned so quickly that within a few months he was teaching younger kids how to play. Then he started learning the double bass, and began teaching that too, as he learned. It was around this time, said Yeliz, that Özmen started coming to the program without his knives. "He's like a big brother to the kids now," she told us. "He uses his connections with the drug dealers to negotiate with them to stay away from the Music for Peace children." Özmen is now the conductor of the Mozart Orchestra, one of the three orchestras at Music for Peace.

With years of practice, young learners in Sistema environments internalize the values of El Sistema. The values become more than ideas expressed and embodied by their teachers; they become habits of mind and heart that are alive within each child. Many of these habits transfer outside the language of music, giving young people psychic tools to which they otherwise have scarce access in their daily lives. For Özmen Genç, the life change stimulated by his Music for Peace encounter could be seen as a profound change of habit: when he got up each morning, his new routines—going to the music building, learning more about playing music, helping kids who looked up to him and depended on him—trumped his old one of stalking the streets with a pocketful of knives.

Arthur Costa and Bena Kallick are the leading advocates in the United States for reforming education to prioritize the development of habits of mind rather than the mastery of information. They posit sixteen habits of mind that should be developed in the educational process; these include persisting, managing impulsivity, listening with understanding and empathy, thinking flexibly, and other cognitive and emotional skills essential to maturity and success. "A Habit of Mind is a composite of many skills, attitudes, cues, past experiences, and proclivities," they have written. "It means that we value one pattern of intellectual behaviors over another; therefore, it implies making choices about which patterns we should use at a certain time."

In more colloquial terms: habits of mind are the repertoire of strategies we have available to use when we encounter unfamiliar challenges. On one end of the repertoire spectrum stands the limited learner typified by Abraham Maslow's comment, "If the only tool you have is a hammer, everything comes to resemble a nail." If the only tool you have is a habit of walking the streets with a knife, everything resembles danger. On the other end of the spectrum is the creative problem-solver with adept access to a wide range of habits of mind.

El Sistema work is about developing new internal habits in children—an expanded repertoire of strategies for coping successfully with the countless challenges they will face in their lives.

INVERTING A PYRAMID

In forming his "Hierarchy of Needs" theory in the 1940s, Abraham Maslow distilled a range of research into a simple pyramid-shaped model of human growth through stages of need to full realization. He proposed that there are baseline needs of physiological survival and safety that people must fulfill before they can move up to addressing "higher" needs. When the "deficiency needs" of physical survival essentials and safety are met (and only if they are), an individual can proceed to the level of seeking love and belonging. When that need is met, she can move on to the need to experience self-worth, and then, finally, the need to experience self-actualization, which opens creativity (and, Maslow later added, encompasses self-transcendence). This model has been widely adopted, even without empirical proof, and absorbed into widespread understanding of how people develop.

Our own acceptance of Maslow's theory has been challenged by our observations of El Sistema programs, where we have repeatedly observed and interviewed children who seem to have inverted the hierarchical process. Although they live in chronic physical need, inadequately fed and housed in unsafe communities, they brim with feelings of belonging and self-confidence. They are confident and curious; some even show self-transcendence in their habits of mind and heart, helping others actualize themselves. These "higher" attainments often lead to a greater ability to meet the "lower" deficiency needs, for those children and for their families—not always, but frequently.

We are interested in exploring the possibility that Maslow's hierarchy of human needs can sometimes work backward. Perhaps the needs for belonging, self-esteem, and self-expression can be addressed and fulfilled even when one is hungry, cold, and unwell—and feeling loved and confident can energize the search for material sufficiency. Perhaps the experience of beauty and purpose, of efficacy and creativity, can be the *foundation* for growth, not just the result of it.

We want to make it clear that we do not believe that people are poor simply because they make bad choices. In our lifelong experience of the United States, at any rate, people are poor because poverty is endemic in the economic and social structures of a still-classist, still-racist society. Until those structures are addressed and altered at the levels of policy, poverty will be a fact of life here, and the children of poverty will continue to inherit a landscape of constricted choices. El Sistema cannot change this fact.

What El Sistema can do, however, is to offer an alternative to that inheritance: the forging of internal habits so robust and durable that young people are able to confront and overcome daunting odds. We think of these crucial habits as emotional and psychological as well as cognitive (hence "habits of mind *and heart*"); it takes more than thinking for a child living in poverty or a stressed environment to overcome institutionalized discrimination and to make the affirmative, constructive choices that are usually unavailable to her and her community. One of the consistent discoveries of social programs is how difficult it is to accomplish this goal of helping children develop new habits of mind and heart in the context of a larger society that relentlessly reinforces the status quo of old patterns, and how complex the internal struggles are for these children. Even within such thoughtfully designed programs as Head Start and the Harlem Children's Zone, teachers have found, through decades of investment and exploration, that the trajectory of youth development is more roller coaster than ladder; a new thought doesn't always lead directly to a new life choice—and a new life choice can't always be sustained against the gravitational weight of the discriminatory biases and institutions of the larger society. New beliefs, feelings, thoughts, and choices develop holistically, and, especially in societies with entrenched barriers of class and race, must develop to a point of confident resilience in order to prevail against nearly overwhelming odds.

PARADOX

> Any time you see seeming opposites,
> look for the greater truth that contains them both.
> —DAVID BOHM, PHYSICIST

In Sistema programs around the world, leaders struggle to introduce their work with an "elevator pitch"—a succinct description of a project designed to win the favor of a potential benefactor in the limited time of an elevator ride. It's particularly challenging to make an elevator pitch for El Sistema, because the Sistema is based on assumptions that can seem paradoxical—and these are hard to present succinctly in a context that favors uncomplicated truths. In descriptions of El Sistema, concepts usually understood as opposites are routinely linked: the learning process is "rigorous fun" that involves "the difficult and the joyful" and develops "discipline and delight." Even its most famous slogan, *Tocar y Luchar* (To Play and to Struggle), is a paradox.

Yet El Sistema at full strength creates a space where such polarities of modern life actually thrive together. Mass culture in modern society tends to equate work with drudgery and fun with the absence of work. El Sistema philosophy and practice illuminate a greater experiential truth that contains both hard work and joy.

El Sistema's most fundamental truth lives in another paradox: musical excellence and social inclusion. Logically and grammatically speaking, those look like two different goals—and goals, moreover, that tend to be mutually exclusive. It should stand to reason that the more socially inclusive a program is, the lower its level of musical excellence must be, since including children who have no musical background or talent, whose families have no financial resources, and who are behaviorally challenged would preclude the creation of an ensemble of high quality.

Yet for El Sistema, musical excellence and social inclusion are not two goals; they are one. We will further explore this confounding dimension of the Sistema in later chapters; it is one we saw and heard about almost everywhere we went. Obadias Cunha, pedagogical manager of the Brazilian Sistema program NEOJIBA, said: "In all our núcleos, we strive for excellence. We are trying to make it the best music possible. But actually, music is our way to reach the education of all the children. Of course, we value the ones who have musical potential, but we're never leaving behind all the other children."

Bjørg Lindvang, the head teacher in Aarhus, Denmark's Musik-Unik, told us that the concept was hard for her to understand at first. "I finally understand it," she told us. "Music as a goal, but also music as a tool for something larger."

What is difficult for a traditionally educated Dane comes more easily to those who have grown up within El Sistema in Venezuela: for a child with few preconceptions about paradox, it's as reasonable to associate hard work with joy as to associate it with drudgery. El Sistema offers us a bracing rethinking of our many preconceived notions about work and play, excellence and community, rigor and joy.

SOMETHING ABOUT MUSIC

> Music creates order out of chaos; for rhythm imposes unanimity
> upon the divergent, melody imposes continuity on the disjointed, and
> harmony imposes compatibility upon the incongruent.
> —YEHUDI MENUHIN, VIOLINIST

We have met enthusiasts in various countries who intend to start Sistema-like programs in theater, dance, and animation, and others who believe El Sistema's guiding principles will someday flourish in learning programs for mathematics and engineering. It's not hard to imagine engaging the intrinsic motivation of students in these extra-musical fields so that they strive for excellence in ensemble formats. Maestro Abreu himself would agree. "We at Fundamusical are convinced that our experiment can be extended in many ways," he has told us, "especially in other performing art forms, like ballet and theater."

There are living examples of such success, though they don't always call themselves Sistema-inspired. Dance, because it is so closely allied with music and involves group artistic performance, seems to be a particularly fertile area for Sistema practices. At the Renaissance Arts Academy, a Los Angeles charter school for middle and high school students, there are orchestral and modern dance ensembles practicing in parallel during and after every school day; the school has found that the overall benefits for dance students are identical to those for music students. (It's noteworthy that RenArts, a school that dedicates many hours to artistic ensembles and that accepts students by lottery, with no special allowance for talent or means, has become the highest academic-achieving high school in Los Angeles, with a 98-to-100 percent college matriculation rate.)

Another apt example is El Colegio del Cuerpo (The School of the Body), in Cartagena de Indias, Colombia. This unusual contemporary dance school provides children with both dance instruction and social education. In her study of the school, "Discipline and Happiness," Gabriella Windsor wrote that students "learn with and from the whole body, not only alone but also interacting directly with others. In turn, they develop personal and social values." The school works with youth from challenged neighborhoods in Cartegena, including shantytowns; its cofounders are motivated by "a need to help socially marginalized children through contemporary dance."[16]

There are Sistema-like initiatives in nonartistic fields as well. In Brooklyn's Intermediate School 318, a chess club with a strong team orientation and a focus on mastery has achieved a series of wins in national competitions, the only middle school ever to win the national high school trophy. There are many exceptional sports coaches who nurture teams that work as successful ensembles, while at the same time attending to individual development. There is every reason to believe that a Sistema-like learning environment and Sistema-like program priorities can produce good results in almost any rewarding medium of group endeavor.

However, we also believe that there is something special, something particularly powerful, about music-making and music-learning for children in challenging life circumstances. Many citizen artists working in Sistema-inspired and similar programs are intrigued by the question of how and why music-learning makes crucial differences in the lives of at-risk children. There is no single theory, and no conclusive evidence, as to why this might be true. The Belgian musician, scholar, and musical activist Lukas Pairon has undertaken a rigorous study of music learning in relation to violence; his research asks the question: "Can mastering a musical instrument and musical repertoire bring young people who are victims or perpetrators of violence to amend their position in society?" Pairon has spent two years studying street children involved with music in Kinshasa, the Democratic Republic of Congo; his research results, when they are available, will enrich the field's understanding.

Our conjectures about why music is such a potent catalyst arise from our own observation and experience. We have asked many young people in Venezuela why they spend the vast majority of their free time in their núcleos. We usually receive some version of the same two answers. The first is, "This is where my friends are." The second: "I love the *sound.*" There seems to be something uniquely satisfying about simply being inside the sound of a musical ensemble—especially the large, rich sound of an orchestra.

Within and beyond the sheer sound of ensemble is the immense range of feeling that music, and particularly classical music, can evoke. As Alejandro Carreño, the concertmaster of the Simón Bolívar Orchestra, said to us, about Beethoven's symphonies: "There is every human feeling in that music." For young people learning to process and understand their feelings as they grow, experiencing these feelings transmuted and distilled through the wordless eloquence of art can be profoundly satisfying and even comforting.

Further, it may be that playing an instrument and getting better as an ensemble are challenges scaled just right to maximize the development of intrinsic motivation. It also may be that the brain processes music in ways that produce distinctive patterns of pleasure and bonding, as neuroscientists are finding through brain-mapping research. The recent documentary film *Alive Inside* demonstrates that music taps deep recesses of identity; patients with advanced dementia and Alzheimer's disease are seen to "come alive" when they hear the music of their formative years. The distinctive power of music may have to do with its life in our brains.

In other words: there is something about music that makes it intricately bound up with memory, feeling, and the sense of selfhood. That hard-to-define something will appear in the ensuing chapters as an accelerant to the Sistema impact, and we will continue to explore the question of why it works so well.

There are many important kinds of self-knowledge and empathic connection that can arise from playing chess, or creating plays, or playing basketball. But music has an elemental power that goes back 40,000 years, when humans were making bone flutes. It took us another 30,000 years to get around to agriculture and 33,000 years to invent the wheel. There is something about music.

PART II

Key Elements of the El Sistema Learning Environment

You have to treat children like artists.
If you don't, the action of art doesn't work.
—GUSTAVO DUDAMEL

Younger student observes the Mariuccia Iacovino Orchestra rehearsing Mozart's
Missa Brevis *at the Orquestrando a Vida program in Campos, Brazil.*

PHOTOGRAPH: ERIC BOOTH

CHAPTER 4

Radical Inclusion

The most miserable and tragic thing about poverty is not
the lack of bread or roof, but the feeling of being no-one, the feeling
of not being anyone, the lack of identification, the lack of public esteem.
That's why the child's development in the orchestra and the
choir provides him with a noble identity and makes him
a role model for his family and community.

—JOSÉ ANTONIO ABREU

In the world's happiest country, we encountered one of the world's most challenging Sistema environments. The United Nations World Happiness Report has ranked Denmark the happiest nation on earth, using internationally agreed-upon measures—of wealth, health, social welfare, generosity, and freedom—to rate happiness in 150 countries. (In 2012, the top five were all in northern Europe). Spending time in Aarhus, Denmark's second-largest city and one of the most human-friendly as well as eco-friendly cities on the planet, we could believe the U.N. findings. The site of a major port on the east coast of the Jutland peninsula, the city combines Old-World provincial elegance with a modern public sector of parks and community arts projects, and it twinkles with turning bicycle wheels; many Aarhus citizens pedal through its vast network of bike lanes daily, leaving the automobile roadways eerily unclogged even at rush hour.

Just outside of Aarhus, the Gellerup district is the largest housing project and the poorest neighborhood in Denmark. Fully 88 percent of its population are immigrants and refugees from many countries; they are mostly Muslim. (In 2005, the local Aarhus newspaper *Jyllands-Posten* published cartoon images of the prophet Muhammad that sparked controversy and violence there and across the world.) The "new-Danes," as they are officially called, often do not integrate well with local Danish culture; they tend to live in a parallel society, turning inward to sustain their homeland cultures and to resist assimilation. Unemployment is over 70 percent; crime, tension, and poverty are high. The community resists government help and resents the necessity to accept it.

The Gellerup housing development, built in the late 1960s and early '70s, began as a solidly middle-class area but has declined in the last two decades. A recent government study identified poor housing as a major contributor to the stress in the Gellerup neighborhood, so the government, in a move typical of this quintessential social-welfare society, is building an entirely new housing district. Meanwhile, however, the cycle of alienation and exclusion continues. During the past few years, the neighborhood has seen over thirty teenage boys leave to join ISIS in Syria.

In one Gellerup elementary school where nearly all the children are from immigrant Muslim families, a Sistema-inspired program called MusikUnik (Unique Music) brings ensemble music-making to about fifty second- and third-graders three or four times a week during the school day. The children play flutes, clarinets, a few trombones and trumpets; they play at a rudimentary skill level, even after two years. The day we observed them, three little girls were learning a simple flute melody, while the other children learned even simpler harmony lines on their instruments. Bjørg Lindvang, the head teacher, told them: "I wrote this tune because these three flute players are working so hard, they inspired me." The children were fairly shy and withdrawn, but the teachers—all young, skillful and tirelessly sweet-tempered—coaxed the notes out of them.

After the session, Bjørg talked to us about the program's difficulty in cultivating relationships with the children's families. "The parents are hard to enroll," she said. "The kids will practice for weeks for a concert, and then the parents don't come. The kids cry. Or sometimes they arrive halfway through the concert, dragging their parents with them."

For some of the parents, she explained, music itself is a suspect activity because of religious beliefs. Others avoid anything connected to the school because they don't trust its native Danish administrators and teachers. Some parents refuse to answer calls or mail from the school, believing that any contact from a government entity can only be bad news of a child in trouble or a bureaucratic hassle of some kind.

Bjørg helped launch the MusikUnik project two years ago. Her background is as a schoolteacher, but she is also a conservatory-trained flutist and music educator—trained, that is, to teach middle-class kids for whom learning an instrument is part of family culture. But Bjørg has the citizen artist gene; she told us that her lifelong dream was to bring music to children who have little access to it, so she was excited by the opportunity to help create MusikUnik.

During the first year of the program, she told us, she cried every day. "The kids were so hard to reach; we felt like we were getting nowhere, no matter what we tried, and we tried everything we could think of. But we are beginning to have a little success now, so we know there is something to hope for."

Naadir, a nine-year-old trumpet player, was a case in point. (His name and the names of some of the other children depicted in this book have been changed, at the request of program directors.) He started coming to the program when it first began, but wouldn't sing, play, or join in any way. The teachers didn't know what to do, but because inclusion is a foundational priority of El Sistema programs, they made an agreement with him that he could attend as long as he didn't distract the others. He attended the entire first year of classes, often with his back to the action, sometimes having to leave when he began distracting others—but returning, day after day, week after week. The teachers treated him as someone who belonged, and never pressured him. After about a year and a half, Naadir casually picked up a trumpet and started trying to play along with the group. He had been paying attention, it turned out; he had a pretty clear idea of what to do, although he couldn't do it at first. A teacher sat down next to him immediately and started coaching him.

At every MusikUnik session since then, Naadir has played the trumpet. They don't let him take it home, but he clearly assumes it's his. He attends most days, has almost caught up musically, and is a full member of the ensemble. Naadir feels valuable. He feels included.

INCLUDING THE "UNINCLUDABLE"

Inclusion is the first principle of El Sistema. In visiting over a hundred núcleos around the world, we found that no matter how vastly different their cultural settings are, they share a profound dedication to this ideal. The citizen artists who launch and run these programs have chosen to work with children and families who are sidelined—by poverty, discrimination, or other kinds of adversity—from the flourishing centers of their societies. They commit themselves to bringing these children into a state of belonging. They encounter difficulties that are almost always greater than they had anticipated. In most cases, they keep going.

José Antonio Abreu has often said that of the manifold kinds of suffering caused by poverty, none is worse than the feeling of exclusion—of not belonging, of literally being "no one." This feeling can be a complex tangle of perceived and reinforced rejection. A child in circumstances of poverty or ethnic discrimination, for whom exclusion is a material fact of life, will internalize the feeling of not belonging, of being no one. That feeling will become a psychic certainty that persists regardless of circumstances. Naadir lives in a community that feels excluded even as its host city goes to serious lengths to make the new-Danes feel included. He re-created his deep feeling of exclusion even within a program that reached out to include him with every kindness it could devise. It took more than a year of daily, patient welcoming before Naadir could trust that, in fact, he belonged. By the end of the second year, he began to feel he was valuable.

The phenomenon of social exclusion has been increasingly recognized by social scientists as one of the most damaging threats to emotional wellbeing. In 1995, psychologists Roy Baumeister and Mark Leary argued that a sense of belonging is a fundamental human need, not simply a preference, and that the absence of this sense results in mental illness.[17] In more recent research, brain scans have shown that the feeling of being excluded registers in the brain as actual physical pain.

There is also increasing recognition that social exclusion is deeply connected to poverty, with research showing that poor children, whether in the absolute poverty of developing nations or the relative poverty of wealthier ones, often grow up with an abiding sense of exclusion. Some researchers have concluded that social exclusion is the single most damaging result of poverty. "We typically think of stress as being a risk factor for disease," scientist and professor Steve Cole has said. "And it is. But if you actually measure stress, using our best available instruments, it can't hold a candle to social isolation. Social isolation is the best-established, most robust social or psychological risk factor for disease out there. Nothing can compete."[18]

Research on gang membership around the world indicates that the psychological drive to belong in a group is one of the primary reasons for joining a gang. In Venezuela, a country rife with gangs, there's extensive observational evidence that early engagement in Sistema programs can effectively lower the risk that children will join gangs. Around the world, the anecdotal and early evaluative data suggests significantly lower gang involvement on the part of Sistema youth in comparison with their non-Sistema peers.

To date, research on the cognitive, psychological, and physical damages of chronic stress is rarely combined with the research on social isolation. But our observations suggest that the combination of stress and social isolation can be distinctively toxic to children's development.

"ONLY COMMUNITY TRUMPS GANGS"

Father Greg Boyle is the founder of Homeboy Industries in Los Angeles. He has dedicated two decades of his Jesuit ministry to helping young people involved with gangs turn their lives around, most famously by starting enterprises that hire young adults who have spent years inside gangs and prisons. He knows what it takes to redirect the lives of young people in gang neighborhoods, and what it might have taken to prevent their original involvement. He recognizes they need material and social support, but much more important, they need jobs. He knows their families and their stories. After two decades of work in the worst gang center in the United States, he has concluded: "Gangs are about an absence of hope. And community trumps gangs. It may be the only thing that trumps gangs."

Homeboy Industries is not a Sistema program, but it has many resonances with the Sistema vision. Like Maestro Abreu, Father Boyle does not want his model to become a franchise. "We don't want to airlift this Homeboy model into other communities," he has said. "We want other communities to determine their own needs and have ownership at a local level. We want each one to have its own character and nature, with an understanding that what can happen in Los Angeles, the gang capital of the world, sometimes does not translate to other places. We have a hyper-reverence for the dynamics of other communities rather than a need to import our model. We are not proposing a one-size-fits-all model, but a way of proceeding."

During the 1990s, "social exclusion" became a commonly used term in public and social discourse; in 2000, the European Union adopted an official policy to combat it. But combating so complex a phenomenon, in contexts ranging from ghettos and refugee camps within poor countries to immigrant enclaves within wealthy ones, is not simply a matter of policy change. Real change can occur only when individuals' internal psychic structures of "being no one, belonging nowhere" begin to change. Social remedies that do not invest in what it takes to change internal psychic structures, the habits of mind and heart, are going to achieve limited results at best, no matter how well intentioned or well funded they are.

This is the investment El Sistema attempts to make, by creating youth musical ensembles that include the conventionally unincludable. Through the sustained pleasurable experience of community inclusion in music-making, children are given a chance to re-create their sense of belonging in the world. In the most successful Sistema programs, each child experiences the wholeness of musical community and internally reconstructs it as psychic wholeness. The sense of inclusion within a larger human endeavor nurtures a sense of self-worth and intrinsic value.

This may sound abstract, but we encountered specific examples of it many times in the course of our travels. Arriving late at night in Bucharest to learn about the Sistema program in Romania, we were picked up at the airport by a young couple, Avram and Alina. As they drove us to their small town in the Transylvanian mountains, they told us that belonging to the Sistema program there is the best thing that has ever happened to their nine-year-old son. When we asked why, Alina said, "We are Roma. So the rest of society looks down on us and doesn't want to associate with us. But my son feels now that he is worth something, that he is valuable. He is much happier and more self-confident. Now he sings all the time."

In Turin, Italy, observing a Sistema program for preschoolers, we noticed a particularly tiny boy who could barely hold his one-eighth-sized violin but was completely on board with the rhythmic chants. *"Lun-a! Lun-a! Sol-e! Sol-e!"* he sang vigorously as he endeavored to pluck his open E string. His teacher, Ayben Soytuna, a music student from Turkey, told us that the boy, whose parents are immigrants from China, had been mute for the first four months of the program, clearly terrified to try to speak Italian. But when he found he could sing it, he felt a sense of inclusion that changed his demeanor. "We were all in tears when he began to sing," Ayben said. "It felt like he was being born all over again."

In Scotland, Nicola Killean, the founder and CEO of Sistema

Scotland, told us, "The most important factor in the learning environment is for kids to feel acceptance, and to feel they are connected to something. A child can have that feeling of being part of a learning community, in an orchestra or in a sectional—that crucial feeling of belonging and acceptance."

In the course of our travels, we have seen that "inclusion within a larger human endeavor" can mean several different kinds of inclusion. For the Venezuelan founders of El Sistema in the 1970s, the goal was to include an entire class (lower-class and poor Venezuelans) in a cultural practice traditionally reserved for a superior class (Europeans and upper-class, wealthy Venezuelans). The fact that classical music was an elitist practice made the ownership of it by lower-class Venezuelans an especially potent objective.

This definition of inclusion is still felt as a vital priority in the Venezuelan Sistema and in other Latin American Sistema programs. Rafael Elster, director of a núcleo in the notoriously poor and dangerous Caracas barrio of Sarria, told us emphatically, "No exclusion! Classical music for hundreds of years has been excluding people. We are about changing that. We are the opposite of that! We say to everyone, 'You too can play classical music!'"

INCLUSION ACROSS CLASSES AND ETHNICITIES

In other Sistema programs, an equally important aspect of "social inclusion" is class integration, the bringing together of children of different classes, and thus the breaking down of class barriers and prejudices among all. Ricardo Castro, founder of Brazil's NEOJIBA Sistema program in Salvador, feels that this is an important aspect of the Sistema principle of inclusion. "If we bring together kids from different social classes to play together," he told us, "before they are old enough to have learned prejudice, they will form friendships. Then they will never learn prejudice."

Fiorella Solares, in Rio de Janeiro, also believes this. "It's never been possible here to unite musicians of different classes in orchestral ensembles," she told us, "because there never were any classical musicians in the poorer classes. Now, because of our programs, it is actually possible for the first time in Rio's history to see a mix of really great musicians from all social classes—including Afro-Brazilians."

Sistema programs on other continents open up similar oppor-

OPENING UP THE BOYS' CHOIR

Since 2001, Gerald Wirth has been the artistic director of the Vienna Boys' Choir, founded in 1498 and one of the most famous youth choirs in the world. After a number of years, he said, he was feeling that the work of the Boys' Choir "was excellent, but wasn't enough. I wanted something else—I wanted to make a real difference. I became aware that we need to give children who don't already know how great music is, a chance to learn about it." In 2010, he worked with the social service foundation Caritas Vienna and a small team of influential leaders, all of whom shared his concerns about inequitable access to classical music, to launch Superar, an umbrella organization sponsoring Sistema programs in six central and eastern European countries. Many of the children in Superar programs, in Vienna and elsewhere, are the traditionally "unincludable"—children of immigrants and victims of marginalization.

Gerald had been inspired by working with children of poverty in India and in Native American tribes, where igniting interest and motivation was part of his task—unlike his work with Boys' Choir singers, who arrive in the choir with training and motivation. "I saw what self-esteem these poor children gained, even through a small project, and what different mindsets they had after the project," he told us. "This made me interested in becoming more personally involved with such endeavors. We have social difficulties here in Vienna that this might be able to help."

Within just a few years, Gerald was able to see his two very different choral projects come together. In May 2015, the Superar Chorus joined the Vienna Boys' Choir in singing for the televised opening of the Eurovision Song Contest. In Gerald's words: "Vienna is considered the world's capital of music. We have to make some changes in order to really *be* the capital of music, and to continue into the future."

tunities for class integration. Ian Burton, founder-director of the In Harmony project in Nottingham, England, told us that the city's youth orchestras have traditionally been composed of mostly white children. "Many children in Nottingham are from black and other minority backgrounds," he said, "but they were largely invisible in the youth orchestra world. We have been able to change this situation, and minority children are now well represented in our youth ensembles."

There is a third variety of social inclusion underway in the programs of Denmark, Sweden, Italy, Portugal, Spain, France, and other European countries where immigrant populations from North Africa, the Middle East, South Asia, and many other places have swelled in recent years. In these countries, the Sistema priority is often "ethnic integration," with the object of bringing the children of marginalized immigrant ethnicities into the mainstream of cultural and social life in their new countries.

As we have seen in Aarhus, the pursuit of this goal can be complicated. In immigrant communities that turn inward, sustaining their separateness as a source of comfort in alien circumstances, El Sistema can be perceived as an unwelcome intrusion. Even where this is not the case, immigrant children's lives are often desperately difficult.

In France, the Sistema-inspired program Passeurs d'Arts operates in the city of Cergy, on the outskirts of Paris. When we asked program founder-director Jean-Claude Decalonne about the children in the program, he said they are mostly from immigrant families from North Africa, Pakistan, India, and elsewhere. "These are children who have nothing. They are extremely poor. Some of them have parents in prisons. Some have parents who speak no French. These children have no opportunity to discover music, anywhere in their lives."

The Passeurs d'Arts program began in a public school in January 2014; it was so immediately successful that the next year the city government supported an expansion to 22 schools, involving 1,320 children. We asked Jean-Claude what had convinced city officials to fund such a large-scale expansion. "They heard the children play," he said. "That's it. To see these children who have no place in the society, in the culture, playing music together like that after just six or seven months of learning—it was electrifying."

Jean-Claude and his colleagues have plans to create similar Passeurs d'Arts programs in other cities, building on their successes and learning experiences in Cergy; they also sponsor a youth orchestra in the city of Fougères. There is another strong Sistema-inspired orga-

SMUGGLING MUSIC TO CHILDREN IN NEED

Jean-Claude is a citizen artist whose lifelong mission is to bring orchestral playing to French schoolchildren. A conservatory-trained trumpet player, he began an instrument sales and repair business in 1984, which supported his evolving quest to bring music education to more children in France. "Since forever," he told us, "I have been passionate about music pedagogy and children playing together. There was a kind of *tristesse* (sadness) about conservatory learning, because it was so much alone."

Years ago, inspired by the orchestral learning he saw on a visit to Japan, he returned home proclaiming that there must be an orchestra in every school in France. "Most people thought I was totally crazy because at the time there wasn't a single orchestra in any public school. But everyone just said, 'That's just the way it is *chez nous.*' "

"When I visited Venezuela and met Maestro Abreu," Jean-Claude added, "I asked him how it was possible that children from the poorest neighborhoods were so attentive and diligent. He answered, 'You know, for us, each child is a potential Nobel Prize winner.' "

Jean-Claude Decalonne chose the unusual name Passeurs d'Arts for his program. The word *passeur* means literally "boatman" or "ferryman," but it also can connote a smuggler, someone who manages to get something valuable transmitted secretly or outside of regular channels. Passeurs d'Arts "smuggles" musical experience to children who would never otherwise have it—children from whom the cultural status quo conspires, systematically if not deliberately, to withhold the treasure of music education.

nization, El Sistema France, that operates separately in the city of Gorges, in Normandy; other similar programs are emerging. France is slowly but steadily creating a lively presence in the global Sistema arena, as a force for ethnic integration.

The goal of ethnic integration is especially challenging in places where mutually hostile ethnic populations live in close proximity. In these Sistema programs, the overwhelming priority is to bring together the children of marginalized ethnic groups who mistrust and sometimes hate one another. In Turin and in Florence, we visited Sistema programs in which the ethnic diversity was vast; the children's families were Moroccan, Namibian, Peruvian, Chinese, Turkish, and many other nationalities. In Turin, fully 90 percent of the children are from immigrant families. These three- and four-year-olds don't speak one another's languages and have only a rudimentary command of Italian; from their parents, they sometimes learn mistrust of other ethnicities and nationalities.

"These kids are lost," Ayben, the teacher in Turin, told us. "They really don't feel they belong anywhere." Ayben and program director Nadia Bertuglia led this group of small, struggling children with constant smiles and positive encouragement, keeping them engaged in a well-constructed lesson plan that moved all the way from intoning a *"Ciao!"* welcome chant at each other to ensemble playing of "Twinkle, Twinkle, Little Star" on tiny violins and cellos.

"Bravi! Bravi!" Ayven and Nadia told them at the end. "Now caress your instruments before you put them away. Then turn and sing *'Ciao'* to your neighbor."

It is not always easy, or even possible, to make these children say hello to their neighbors of different ethnicities. Ayben says she gets discouraged sometimes. The greatest challenge of this work, she says, is that "every day you have to wear a big smile for the kids, and sometimes it's hard to summon that; sometimes you feel like crying instead. But . . . we can't abandon these kids."

The Romanian Superar program includes several sites near Braşov, deep in the mountains of Transylvania, where ethnic Hungarians and ethnic Romanians have lived in antagonistic proximity ever since Attila staked a Hun claim to Romanian territory 1,500 years ago. They are united only by their common animosity toward yet another ethnicity, the ghettoized Roma (gypsy) population. The three populations were forcibly integrated in schools and social institutions during the era of the Soviet Union, but they quickly re-isolated as soon as the U.S.S.R. fell apart. The program's ideal is to bring the children of these three polarized cultures together through music.

This ideal is still some distance away. The parents of some Romanian Sistema students will not allow their children to come to ethnically mixed music classes, so the program is still in the preliminary stage of running separate sessions for ethnic Romanians, ethnic Hungarians, and Roma children. But they are preparing the ground for integration: all the kids are learning how to play in ensembles, and all are being taught the same songs—in many languages, including Spanish, English, Chinese, Italian, and Swahili—so that when they come together they will have a shared repertoire.

"They will know the same songs, so they will be able to sing together," said Elana Andrews, the director of Superar Romania, "and we deliberately *don't* include songs in Romanian, Hungarian, or Roma, because their parents wouldn't allow them to sing in one another's languages. So we have these songs in many neutral languages. We are developing a language of songs they can all share."

Elana is an Australian singer and music teacher who first landed in Romania by doing a Google search for "volunteer for organizations in Europe" and connecting with a Christian charity. She fell in love with the rough beauty of the Transylvanian mountain region, learned the language, and found her way, a week before her visa expired, to piloting Sistema Romania with Superar. Teaching music here is immensely harder, she said, but immensely more rewarding, than it was in Australia. In action in the classrooms, she was a whirlwind, pedagogically deft and highly emotive. The clear favorite song everywhere was a lusty pop-gospel tune called "I've Got Music in My Soul."

In two of the towns we visited, Sfântu Gheorghe and Zizin, crossing the line from non-Roma to Roma neighborhoods was a vivid experience of the concrete meaning of radical exclusion. In both cases, the paved road lined with neat houses stopped abruptly. We were suddenly walking on paths of rocks and mud, lined with derelict shacks. There was horse manure everywhere; there were broken windows and broken roofs, basins of dirty water for plumbing, an occasional dead animal. We were instructed not to make eye contact with residents; Elana is known and trusted, but strangers who are clearly "other" can ignite emotional tinder. In Zizin, this scenario of destitution was all the more vivid because it was set against the backdrop of picturesque mountains, with golden fields and purple peaks—as though a Roma ghetto had somehow sprung up in *The Sound of Music*.

We could see these mountains through the small crooked window of the low-ceilinged Pentecostal church room where Elana set up her electric piano to work with her Roma students in Zizin. A gaggle of eager children, including teenaged mothers with babies and older siblings with toddlers in tow, waited outside the room until they were allowed entry in a formal, one-by-one protocol of introduction and shaking our hands. (The purpose of this, Elana explained later, was to give the children practice in making direct contact with outsiders.) Then they sat in a big circle on the floor; their clothes were ragged but colorful, and all the girls wore headscarves. Elana led them briskly through the same songs and musical games we had seen her teach the non-Roma kids. "Five little ducks went out to play," they sang, and "Adio Mama," and "J'entends le moulin . . ." They sang imperfectly but heartily, a little wildly. Here, too, "I've Got Music in My Soul" was the clear favorite.

There was some wailing when she told them it was the last music program of the summer. (The parents need their children at home full-time in the summer, to work with them in the fields.) One girl composed herself, saying, "It's okay, music lady, the songs will stay in my head."

The music lady is determined to create occasions when these children will sing with the ethnic Hungarian and Romanian children who live in the neat houses on the paved roads. She believes they will become friends. She even has hope that their parents may, in time, begin speaking to one another. When we mentioned Sistema parent choruses of mixed ethnicities in Sweden, her sigh was a clear acknowledgment of how much patience is required to bridge these boundaries.

Superar is the first formal multinational Sistema program (in Austria, Bosnia-Herzegovina, Liechtenstein, Romania, Slovakia, and Switzerland), and this is one of its overarching goals throughout all countries: to integrate ethnic groups who live in the same place and mistrust or hate one another. It is an especially quixotic goal in Bosnia, where the genocidal massacre of thousands of Bosnian Muslims by Serbs is still a life-defining traumatic memory for all who remain. But Ismar Poric, a Muslim music student at the University of Sarajevo, decided a few years ago that a Sistema program of radical inclusion, integrating Bosnian Muslims and Bosnian Serbs, was not only possible but also necessary. "The only way to move a society out of ethnic hatred," Ismar told us, "is to get to the children, apart from their families, and teach them to sing together."

The Bosnian War (1992–95, with a death toll of 100,000) exploded in the wake of the breakup of Yugoslavia. Its defining genocidal event, in which more than 8,000 people died in two days, occurred in July 1995 in the mountain town of Srebrenica, where Muslims and Serbs still live as neighbors in silent tension. It is exactly there, in this still rubble-strewn town, that the Bosnian Superar program began. Ismar and two fellow conservatory graduates and kindred spirits, Kenan Glavinić and Riad Music, make the two-and-a-half-hour drive from Sarajevo and back several times a week, to teach the children of Srebrenica songs about love and harmony in languages other than their own. We asked Ismar why they make this considerable effort. "Because—why not?" was his answer. "The kids in Srebrenica are traumatized. They weren't alive when it happened, but they are living it every day. There is so much need. As a musician and as a person, I feel a responsibility to help out."

One Saturday in June, Kenan and Riad took us with them on the drive from Sarajevo to Srebrenica. (Ismar was in a studio that day with Bosnian pop stars, who were laying down solo tracks over a recording of his students singing a song called "Love People" that he had just written for a charity.) Riad is fair, with hip, spiky light brown hair; he is the guitar teacher. Kenan, who teaches accordion and piano, is thin-faced, with an aquiline nose, a dark beard and mustache, and a mane of curly black hair. Wedged in the back of Riad's tiny car, we set forth in a driving rain and were immediately in steep mountains. The narrow two-lane road barely clung to the switchbacks; trucks and tankers barreled past us in the other direction, throwing torrents of water at our windshield. We didn't mind when Riad undid his ponytail and his hair spread out, effectively blocking the somewhat alarming view from the back seat.

Kenan talked about how they teach the kids songs in many languages, as Elana does in Romania. "We just sing about love, love, love. There's so much hate and vitriol in the world, and they know about that anyway. We want them to know something else exists, something positive." He told us he has a theory that it is essential for children's musical study to be based in "the classics—music that has stood the test of time." We asked for some examples, and he said, "You know. Deep Purple, Pink Floyd, Led Zeppelin, jazz. Excellence of any kind."

The program in Srebrenica is so popular with the children that it has grown within two years from 8 to 150 students; however, not many come in the summer when school is out. We were greeted upon our arrival by a group of 40 or so shy children, ages eight to fourteen or so, who sang for us in unison: "Imagine" and "I Like the Flowers" in English; a Latin American song, "Leo Leo"; an African song, "Henne Henne"; all with Kenan's bluesy piano accompaniments. The program's instrumental component consisted of one accordion, one electric piano, and eight guitars; the children took turns playing and being coached, while the other children listened quietly. They didn't laugh often; they were mostly serious, with a kind of ingrained wariness. One wore a tee shirt with "New York Unbreakable" on it—the slogan of recovery from 9/11. On the blackboard there were sharps, flats, quarter notes—and hearts—written in chalk. "I Love You" was written under the hearts, in English.

The students sang "Imagine" for us one more time as an encore, and with that ringing in our ears, we were driven to the genocide memorial, which is utterly simple: rolling green fields with 8,000 slim white markers stretching to the horizon. The fields surround a circular flagstone courtyard with sloping marble walls where the names and ages of the dead are engraved—alphabetically, so it's easy to see that there are many family groupings of ten or fifteen or twenty, of different ages, who were all massacred together.

Riad and Kenan drove us back through the rain-soaked mountains to Sarajevo. We congratulated them on their students' strong singing and on the way they are learning to play even with such a shortage of instruments. Riad replied, "I'm just trying for one thing: that they all play as one."

"As one"—that is a lyric in Ismar's new song, "Love People," which he was recording that day and is now available on YouTube (findable as Superar Bosnia "Love People"). Bosnian pop stars sing the verses in Bosnian, but the chorus is sung in English by the children of Superar Srebrenica, who are shown in a field together, clapping and swaying. "Well, the time has come," they sing, "to stand together as one/Carry each other to a better life./We are all the same, a brotherhood of man/Strong, free and ready, we can win this fight." The song begins and ends with a chant sung in the children's high voices: "Love people, love people . . . Love people, love people." They often sing to raise money, not for their own needs or for their program, but for other regions of their country that suffer catastrophic natural disasters. When Pope Francis visited

Sarajevo in June 2015, the children of Superar Srebrenica were there to welcome him with "Love People."

INCLUSION AS THE SINE QUA NON

Whether Sistema programs focus their efforts on including children in a formerly inaccessible cultural practice, integrating them with children of other social classes, or bringing them together in ethnically or socially mixed groups, the essential remedial effect of "inclusion" remains the same: children become part of a community that offers them a sense of identity and value. They are welcomed into a group endeavor in which their efforts matter. They begin, gradually, to internalize a sense of belonging and to develop new ways of thinking and feeling that eventually become the way they meet the world.

In referring to Sistema-supported inclusion as "radical," we use the word more in its etymological sense than in its current denotative meaning of "extreme." According to its Latin derivation, the word refers to roots, and connotes "going to the essentials." Bjørg Lindvang and her colleagues in the Danish Sistema program held firmly to their radical view that Naadir belonged inside the program orchestra. Based on their understanding of inclusion as an essential root of well-being and a cornerstone of El Sistema philosophy and practice, they maintained this view for a long time, even though his actions didn't confirm it. They could see that Naadir was drawn to join the musical ensemble and yet held back by the sense of being "apart" and "outside" that he had internalized from his family and community. His teachers persistently communicated a different message, until he came to believe, in his own time, that he belonged in the ensemble.

As a simple but absolute priority, the principle of inclusion is embodied in El Sistema practice first and foremost as an admissions policy: entry is open to all, with no auditions and no fees (a few have very modest fees), and targeted at underincluded communities. When compared to the procedures of most non-Sistema youth ensembles across the world, this is a policy radical in every sense of the word. Ever since the beginning of El Sistema, when José Antonio Abreu shocked the musical establishment of Caracas in 1975 by eliminating auditions for his new orchestra, many longtime musicians and music educators have been skeptical about the musical efficacy of its all-inclusion policy. To welcome all comers, including those who demonstrate no musical aptitude at all, into an endeavor that aims at the complex goal of ensemble mastery is to challenge most of classical music's received wisdom about both talent and mastery. Orchestral excellence is difficult to achieve under any circumstances. How can an orchestra possibly aim high and become great, if the untalented kids are welcomed and kept in the ensemble? El Sistema's inclusivity mandate caused many to conclude that El Sistema work was doomed to musical mediocrity—until the evidence from Venezuela began to undermine that verdict.

Ricardo Castro of Brazil's NEOJIBA program described to us his difficulty in finding good conductors who were willing to accept the Sistema approach. "I tried hiring a prominent conductor, but it lasted a half-hour. He wasn't good with the kids; he was so impatient with them. He couldn't trust that they would get better." Ricardo, a concert pianist, solved the problem by learning to conduct. "These kids were abandoned, and a good conductor would never conduct them. So I had to do it. I'm not a good conductor, but I knew what they needed. I trusted their potential. That's probably the main point in El Sistema: to trust the kids—to know that they will improve, and to be patient enough to wait for it."

How does this trust evolve within a Sistema program? In visiting sites across the world, one of our primary questions has been how the principle of inclusion manifests in the daily practice of El Sistema learning environments. We discovered that it shows up in ways both obvious and subtle. Typically, every child is included in singing and musicianship activities, and every child is given an instrument and included in one or more ensembles—a section, an orchestra, a chorus, or a folk ensemble. Within orchestras, students are sometimes rotated among seats so that each has a chance to experience being a sectional first chair. Sometimes even the leadership position of concertmaster/concertmistress is rotated throughout the violin section.

In conventional, meritocracy-based youth orchestras, this kind of seat-swapping would be seen as a waste of time at best, and at worst a motivation killer for the more talented students. Such orchestras usually emulate the hierarchical sectional system of professional orchestras, in which the best musicians sit closest to the conductor and the players in the back of the sections vie periodically to unseat them. For youth orchestras and professional orchestras alike, this is accepted as the most efficient way to get as good as possible.

In El Sistema ensembles, however, there is a compound goal: to get as good as possible, *and* to bring every single player along in the process. The two are seen as inseparable; the emphasis is as much on empowerment of each member, and cooperation between members, as it is on musical improvement. Competitive feelings exist in El Sistema orchestras, of course—they are inevitable, especially when students begin auditioning for spots in higher-level regional and national orchestras. But our experience, in Venezuela especially, was that students' competitiveness is tempered by the supportive communal attitudes they have learned through being in Sistema for years. Norma Núñez Loaiza told us that when she and her friends auditioned for the national orchestra for the first time, she was the only one who didn't get in. "I felt terrible!" she said. "So I decided to make an extra effort and try again, and with the help of my friend Antonio (who had gotten in), I studied Tchaikovsky's Fourth Symphony as hard as possible. And the next time I auditioned, I got in." That is competitive auditioning, El Sistema-style.

The Sistema programs most successful in holding both goals simultaneously are those in Latin America—particularly, and unsurprisingly, in Venezuela. Because of their relatively long experience in working within this paradox, Latin American Sistema teachers and directors tend to assume that radical inclusion need not compromise high quality. They are convinced that every individual has some musi-

INCLUSION MEETS TRADITION

A 2014 concert at the United Nations provided a poignant example of the difference between these two kinds of youth orchestra culture. The concert, produced by a charitable foundation of the Chinese pianist superstar Lang Lang, brought teenaged musicians from Sistema programs in Venezuela, Colombia, Brazil, Peru, and Kenya to New York, to play with conservatory students from the Manhattan School of Music, who filled in with the instruments that are harder to bring on airplanes. When we asked the Kenyan students (whom we had met in Nairobi just a few weeks before) how rehearsals were going, they said that they were working hard but felt keenly that they weren't as good as the conservatory students or the other Sistema players.

Alexandra Mukiri, called Noni, a seventeen-year-old violinist, said that she had expected this to be the case. "They sat me so far back in the violin section that I am almost off the stage," she said with a laugh. She added: "Some of the Manhattan School kids won't talk to us, and we heard one of them saying we don't belong here because we're not good enough. But the kids from the other Sistema programs were always helping us. In each pause, they would help us with things we were having trouble with. It was fun to hang out with them."

We heard later that after the performance in the United Nations General Assembly Hall, the Kenyan students hosted a party at the Harlem YMCA, where they were staying. They pooled their tiny stash of U.S. dollars to buy potato chips and soda, and they invited all the musicians; Noni even invited a young man from the Manhattan School who had been openly mean about their playing. The Manhattan School student came, and had a great time.

cal ability, and that everyone's ability can be developed in a way that contributes to a high-achieving ensemble. They believe that everyone is an asset and everyone belongs; no exceptions.

INCLUSION ACROSS SKILL LEVELS

Another of El Sistema's most important inclusive practices is the convention of enabling children of different skill levels to play together. Children with limited skills often play alongside more skilled children in orchestral ensembles. Such experiences enrich children's feeling of inclusion. There are musical benefits as well. For less skilled children, the development of musical skills is accelerated—because in this setting, there is nothing abstract about getting better; "better" is sitting right next to you, playing in your ear and hearing you play. For more skilled children, the opportunity to help and teach their less advanced friends deepens their musical intelligence and maturity; it is a basic Sistema premise that to teach something is to know it in a more masterful way.

This kind of mixed-ensemble inclusion is possible thanks to a Sistema tradition of creating orchestral arrangements that allow children of differing skill levels to play big, sophisticated masterworks together. For beginning and intermediate players, simplified parts are written that are the same length as the full-scale works, and thus can be played alongside more advanced students playing the original orchestral score—so that every single member of a núcleo can join together in playing, say, Beethoven's Fifth Symphony or Tchaikovsky's *1812 Overture*. This practice has been developed over decades in Venezuela, where we heard many such renditions of great symphonic works, with small players executing vigorous downbeats and then counting the in-between beats like crazy, while advanced-level teenagers were dashing off the showy sixteenth notes and complex rhythms of the original scores.

The inclusive advantages of such multitiered arrangements are obvious; programs can use various combinations of parts, depending on available players' skills, and still achieve fairly complete-sounding performances. When this arranging technique is applied to great masterworks, the arrangements provide children with consistent through-lines of learning over years.

Inclusiveness as pedagogical practice is often raised to still another level among Sistema programs through a ritual known in Venezuela as the "seminario," a gathering of several núcleos for a joint performance. The Venezuelan Sistema thrives on seminarios; doubling an ensemble's size, or expanding it to five hundred or six hundred—or more—is a surefire way to generate greater excitement and enjoyment, in Venezuela and in Latin American Sistema programs in general. Seminarios are becoming regular occurrences in the United States, where programs of one or another geographical region sometimes combine forces. In 2015, there were a number of large regional seminarios in the U.S., Canada, and Europe. Sistema Korea holds weeklong summer seminarios, with hundreds of students from all around the country—a practice so popular that it grew to 850 students in 2014, and has been scaled back slightly to be more manageable. (As we go to print, we hear that a three-day seminario with over 1,200 children is happening in the city of Pyeongchang.) Seminarios pop up wherever geography puts programs into accessible proximity. We have heard more than a few tales of children and chaperoning parents staggering onto or off of buses at four in the morning. But for the kids and teachers—and maybe even for the parents—the discomforts of travel seem to be outweighed by the novelty and excitement of the adventure.

A seminario is a good example of the educational concept of "enabling constraints," imposed limitations that create extra application in the learner. Seminarios usually offer children challenging repertoire and an accelerated timetable toward a culminating concert. The vigor of a seminario is all about concentrated accomplishment: "We are going to pull off this miracle together!" The time constraint in a seminario quickens the learning and provides an incentive for kids who don't know one another to suddenly begin playing together. Advanced students become teacher-helpers, refining what they know. Less advanced students learn at warp speed, to keep up with their mentors. When there is no time to waste on shyness, friendships grow quickly.

A seminario of any significant size often has the quality of an amazing stunt; but for the children participating, and often for the audience, it holds more substantial meaning. Children experience being a part of a bigger sound—often, a huge sound—and they take that sonic impression back home in their heads and try to replicate it, with increased confidence in their playing. In addition, the extensive mix of musicians in a seminario says "we" on every level. Exclusion isn't even an option; it is "all hands needed on deck" from the first moment through the final bows. As a teacher from In Harmony Telford and Stoke-on-Trent, in England, remarked at the end of a 2015 seminario hosted by El Sistema Sweden in Gothenburg: "Our kids have matured by three years in one week."

In recent years there have even been a number of international seminarios, such as the Sistema Europe Summercamp, a Scottish trip to Venezuela, some reciprocal visits between Canadian and Sistema Europe students, and the Youth Orchestra Los Angeles's trip to Japan. The logistics and costs of these make them out of reach for most programs, but they serve as a kind of ideal. Few things deepen the impact of Sistema learning in children more surely than visiting another country, working side by side with peers who look different and speak different languages, and bonding more deeply with their own program peers. The students go home feeling included in a much larger and more diverse community.

Sistema Europe's annual summer camp is probably the world's most colorful seminario. The second annual camp seminario, held in Istanbul in August 2014, brought together 200 young musicians from nine different countries. The repertoire included Tchaikovsky's *Slavonic March*, Arturo Marquez's *Danzón No. 2*, Rossini's *William Tell* Overture, Elgar's "Nimrod," and Mozart's *A Little Night Music*. All the children learned all the music in a week.

The organizers added another layer of opportunity by including

THE DISCOVERY OF BELONGING

In March 2015, fifteen students of YOLA (Youth Orchestra of Los Angeles, the Sistema program led by the L.A. Philharmonic) were invited along on an international L.A. Phil tour to Japan, to visit, play, and sing with students of Sistema Japan. The YOLA students toured the area where these children live in Fukushima, where the devastation and toxic after-effects of the 2011 tsunami are still apparent. The language barrier was high, so they became friends mostly through music-making. They learned one another's childhood songs and sang them on the bus; they worked hard together in rehearsal. Their musical partnership culminated in a joint rehearsal conducted by Dudamel in Tokyo's Suntory Hall.

On the last day of the trip, the YOLA students, who are from tough neighborhoods in Los Angeles, were shown around parts of old Tokyo, including famous Buddhist shrines, by a Japanese-American master taiko drummer, Chris Holland. He took them back to his studio and gave them a lesson that required each to perform the mentally and physically demanding skills of taiko. As a group, the students followed Holland's lead as he played sounds and rhythms, but he sensed their energy wasn't full-out. "You have to do this with total commitment," he said, "or it has no power." He pushed them to go beyond comfort, beyond their sense of their limits. Surprising themselves, they rose to his demanding standard.

At the end of the workshop, he said to them, "Now you are musicians. When you come to Tokyo, you will call me, and we will make music together. I will help you find work or help you solve your musical problems. That is what being a musician is about." The students had entered a worldwide professional community, an ancient one, and they knew they belonged.

52 teachers from 14 countries (including Iran) and leading a simultaneous teacher professional development conference. The teachers watched one another work, collaborated constantly, and exchanged tips about negotiating the sometimes elusive complex of Sistema principles. On the spot, they constructed a new "we"—the multinational,

multiethnic, multiage potpourri of campers and teachers—and propelled it toward the goal of a joint concert.

Margaret Gonzalez, a product of Venezuela's El Sistema and now a Sistema leader in California, was on the seminario faculty in Istanbul. She described the atmosphere: "The daily schedule was rigorous, with sectionals and rehearsals until 8 P.M. every night. There were lots of déjà vu moments for me as I thought of the many hours I spent during my childhood in rehearsals and sectionals. It may sound a little insane that these European kids could play so many hours and stay focused! But they did. They were all so motivated towards a common goal. In fact, they were having fun."

This leads us to one final, essential point about ensemble music as a vehicle for inclusion. A choral or orchestra concert is in many ways like a big team-sports event; it represents the culmination of teamwork and cooperation, intensively practiced. But there is one crucial difference: in a musical event, no one loses. In any sports game, fully half of the players always lose. And no matter how enlightened the coaching, showing up as losers can color the young players' sense of self. In addition, there are usually players on both teams who sit on the bench, just hoping for a chance to play—in effect, visibly announcing they are not so good, and thus feeling only half-included and less important.

When a Sistema orchestra team takes the field, everyone—every single one—wins. Every single player is necessary and equally responsible. This is the singular potency of musical ensemble inclusion. Children learn that team triumph doesn't necessitate someone else's loss.

In this sense, Sistema revives the original meaning behind the word "competition," which derives from Latin words for striving *with* others, not striving *against* them, as current usage has it. In the ancient Olympics, races were held not so much to determine who would win as to motivate everyone to run faster. Although a winner did emerge, that was not the purpose of the exercise. The purpose was to advance everyone's performance.

INCLUDING THE DISRUPTIVE CHILD

Sooner or later, most Sistema programs come up against the inevitable problem of radical inclusion: the radically disruptive child. Program teachers and leaders are forced to consider to what lengths they should go to continue including children whose behavior repeatedly hijacks the productive flow of the group. In simplest terms: when should a child be kicked out of a program?

For many Sistema programs in Europe and North American countries, particularly during their first few years, the issue of how to manage disruptive behaviors is a troubling concern, one that can dominate conversation when program leaders and teachers get together. Different programs navigate this ethical dilemma in different ways. In Venezuela, forty years of experience have led Sistema practitioners to a fairly pragmatic conclusion: it's important to make a concerted effort to help behaviorally challenged children learn less disruptive behaviors, but there's a point at which it's legitimate to kick them out, in the interests of the other children. All the students know there are limits, and few test them.

In Europe and the United States, on the other hand, some programs are dedicated to continuing to include every child, no matter how arduous a task this represents. Sistema Scotland, for example, has a policy of doing whatever it takes to keep every child involved.

At the Soundscapes program in Newport News, Virginia, teachers struggle with the same mandate. "The most disruptive children are often the neediest, the ones we are most committed to reaching," said Soundscapes cofounder and director Rey Ramirez. He described students whose manic, distracting behavior seems uncontrollable. "But honestly, we don't know what to do."

We encountered several programs that require kids to sign behavior agreements (at a program in Cali, Colombia, we were told that "punishment" was a forbidden word), and one program, the YOLA at HOLA site in Los Angeles, where the behavioral agreements posted on the wall are written by students. Many programs address the behavior problem by seeking to bring students in at earlier ages. Imagine, for example, that Naadir in Aarhus had been included in ensemble musical play from the age of two, as he might have been in Venezuela or Scotland; it might not have taken him a hundred hours to break out of his feeling of isolation. Imagine further what might have been different if some of the teenaged ISIS volunteers from Naadir's neighborhood had been in daily MusikUnik sessions from the age of two on. The appeal of jihad among Muslim youth is a complicated phenomenon; still, it's possible to speculate that inclusion from an early age in the common pursuit of musical play, where they would have experienced pleasure, success, inclusion, and self-worth on a daily basis, might have gone far to vitiate that appeal.

As programs mature and begin to add younger children, they're also growing a cadre of musically and socially competent young people at the advanced level. This causes the inclusive spirit to strengthen; it becomes like a fast current in a river, pulling along everyone who steps into the water. As programs find this maturity, behavior problems become less severe, because the inclusive atmosphere of the learning environment has become attractive enough to reduce the liminal period during which kids are likeliest to defy or test behavioral boundaries. To take the simile further: as the current is strengthened, the amount of still water at the edges lessens, and anyone who enters is swept up more quickly. The slipstream of inclusion can become so strong as to bypass awareness; even as visitors, we found ourselves beginning to set up chairs or music stands before we even had the conscious thought, "It might be helpful if we set up chairs and stands."

INCLUDING THE SPECIAL NEEDS CHILD

In the mid-1990s, a young núcleo director in Barquisimeto, Venezuela, began to experiment with extending the Sistema ideal of inclusion to a population even more radically excluded than children of poverty. Jhonny Gómez and his colleagues undertook the painstaking creation of a pilot program for including children with special needs. "I was formed in El Sistema in Barquisimeto," Jhonny told us, "and when I was a teenager, I began to ask the question, is there a way that children with special needs could be part of our musical ensembles?"

Jhonny's initial inspiration was a video he had seen when he was sixteen, of Itzhak Perlman in a wheelchair playing a violin concerto with a symphony orchestra. But his goal was not to help young people with special needs become concert artists or even professional musicians. "I realized that these kids who are so completely isolated from society—if they could be integrated into musical ensembles with other kids, they could develop the capacity to be integrated into the social lives of their communities."

The Barquisimeto núcleo has been a thriving enterprise since the early 1980s. When the special-needs pilot program began in 1995 with 16 learning-disabled children and 12 vision-impaired children, the new students were welcomed fully into the life of the núcleo, playing in the existing ensembles as well as in special-needs groups. In the ensuing two decades, as the program expanded, more and more ways have been found to include special-needs children in núcleo life. When hearing-impaired children began to attend, all the students in the núcleo learned rudimentary signing skills. As vision-impaired attendees increased in number, Jhonny and others developed a pioneering technique for translating written music into Braille and printing it, so that students could take home Braille versions of their orchestral parts to study and memorize.

Barquisimeto's special-needs program, now in its twentieth year, serves 2,800 children with specific or multiple special needs, including hearing, sight, cognitive, motor, and learning disabilities; autism; and Down syndrome. There is a bell orchestra ensemble for children with only one functional arm. There are percussion ensembles for hearing-impaired children. There are many ensembles in which special-needs children play side by side with their non-special-needs peers. "In the beginning, we thought these things were not possible," Jhonny said. "But the children have shown us what is possible."

The program serves as inspiration and guide for a rapidly growing network of special-needs programs in El Sistema núcleos across Venezuela. Its Braille Research and Printing Center is a model for such initiatives. A meticulously developed Functional Diversity Teacher Training program produces hundreds of teachers each year who are equipped to lead this work across the country, and increasingly across the world.

Jhonny's vision for El Sistema special-needs programs remains both ambitious and unsentimental. "This is not music therapy," he told us. "This is education. This is formation. For a long time, people with disabilities were taken care of from a therapy point of view. But a handicap is irreversible. So what we try to do is work with the young person's potential—what he *can* do—and develop that. The handicap is put aside, and we work with the rest of the child. Every single child has potential."

The most internationally famous feature of the Barquisimeto program is the White Hands Choir, the ensemble that so captivated sophisticated audiences at the 2013 Salzburg Festival. Developed by Jhonny and his wife Naybeth García, the structure of this choir—part special-needs children who sing, part hearing-impaired children whose white-gloved hands perform choreographic movements—has been replicated throughout Venezuela, and more recently in several other parts of the world.

We encountered many other programs that prioritize the inclusion of special-needs children and young people. One dramatic example was a program run by Batuta in a Bogotá barrio called Ciudad Bolívar. Here we saw children and young people with a wide range of disabilities gathered in a kind of circle and playing various kinds of percussion instruments. Some were ambulatory but vision-impaired or hearing-impaired; some had Down syndrome; some were autistic. The children in wheelchairs had little motor control. The lead teacher, Eva Calderón, played guitar and led the group in playing percussion and singing; the ones who could sing sang lustily, and the ones who could not sometimes cried out in pleasure. "We're very emotional," Eva told us.

There was a small audience of mostly older people; we thought at first that they were parents or relatives, but it turned out that they were simply people from the community. They tapped their feet and clapped along when the students played and sang a tune with a brisk Latin rhythm, a rhythm that most of the kids could effectively play; even a boy whose motor skills were challenged was able to mark the rhythm with a shaker. The marimba parts were extremely simple, and the students concentrated extremely hard.

"That was so nice!" several audience members said at the end to the program's creator, María Cristina Rivera, who is now the music director for Batuta. María Cristina is a music therapist by training and a force of energy by nature. She told us that the special-needs program employs several social workers who visit the students' families, to learn about each student's circumstances and to work with families to help them better support their children.

"Five years ago, when I began to work here, I used to cry every day on the streetcar home," she said. "These children live in a place of such palpable need. This program is the only experience in their lives of being in a place that feels nice, that feels welcoming." Her main goal, she told us, is "for the children to have a good feeling: a feeling of being skillful, and a feeling of being together."

In Campos, Brazil, the staff social worker, Mariana Andrade, told us that when children who are "diagnosed with something" (meaning a cognitive, physical, or psychological disorder) join the núcleo, she often doesn't make the diagnosis known to anyone but the child's primary teachers and ensemble leaders. "And sometimes," she said, "the disorder that was reported to us simply never shows up in this environment. If and when it does, we deal with it. But the child is never singled out or labeled. Eventually, these children become part of the group, just kids in the program."

At England's In Harmony program site in the Lambeth neighborhood of London, special-needs children are "just kids in the program" too. "We have children with special education needs who don't have the ability to read music," program director Gerry Sterling told us, "but they are right in there with everyone else, playing in the ensembles, doing everything by ear. It's tremendously exciting."

The NEOJIBA program of Salvador, Brazil, includes twenty students, mostly teenagers, with a variety of mental impairments. In their own ensemble, they master the difficult rhythmic patterns of parts written especially for them to play with the Itapagipe núcleo's top orchestra in rehearsals and performances. The parts are crafted to enhance the orchestral scores, so that mainstreaming (combining special-needs students with those who do not have special needs) becomes both progressive social policy and enriched artistic experience for all. The musicians with special needs learn that they don't just "fit in"; they are a valuable addition.

This practice thrives as well in Milan, Italy, where the Allegro Moderato program of Sistema Lombardy includes ninety "special musicians" who have autism, Down syndrome, visual or auditory impairments, or other special needs. "We want every one of our students to develop autonomy on an instrument, to be able to play it alone as well as playing together," we were told by program director Luca Baldan.

As in NEOJIBA and in Venezuela, "playing together" means that Allegro Moderato students play in their own ensembles and also join with non-special-needs ensembles. "Our way of playing is special," said Luca. "More percussion, more pauses. It means a lot of adjustments for our arrangers and conductors." He showed us a video of a combined orchestra playing *Pomp and Circumstance* in which the many prominent percussion parts played by the special-needs students made for such a high degree of pomp and circumstance that the standard arrangement paled by comparison. Luca pointed out that his students were contributing more than enthusiastic drum playing. "Watch the glockenspiel player—he's playing the melody!" he said.

Students also play in their own jazz and pop bands, Luca told us; the more relaxed and improvisatory nature of these ensembles works better for some of the students. " 'Hey Jude' is their favorite song," he said.

The students of Allegro Moderato range in age from twelve all the way to sixty. Luca explained that because these students usually can't move on to other ensembles in their adult lives, they are allowed to stay in the program indefinitely. He described a new program initiative: each week, several students and teachers visit chronically ill children in Milan's San Carlo Hospital to play for them and also to teach them rudimentary instrumental skills, so that they can play along. "This is a great occasion for our special musicians," said Luca. "For a few hours, they become teachers. Many of them have never in their lives felt capable of teaching anyone."

Allegro Moderato was not in session when we were in Milan, but when Luca met with us, he brought along Davide, one of his students. Davide has Down syndrome and speaks with great difficulty, but he was eager to try to communicate, and Luca translated. When we asked Davide about his favorite piece of music, his answer was "The Ode to Joy." He plays percussion because that's what Luca plays, he said, and more than anything else, he wants Luca to be his teacher. He added that his second-favorite music is a reggaeton piece, "because I get to show off."

We asked him how old he was, and before Luca could translate, Davide answered in fairly clear English, "Twenty-five." Luca, who has known him for ten years, was astonished. "I never knew he spoke any English," he said.

Davide returned to Italian to say one more thing he wanted us to know: "Playing music is the most important thing in my life."

With 9,000 students throughout the country, Sistema Italia is the largest Sistema-inspired program in Europe, and also one of the programs most focused on the inclusion of special-needs children. An Italian documentary film released in 2009 brought Allegro Moderato a degree of prominence throughout Italy. There are now at least seven

Sistema-launched special-needs programs across the country, in Piedmont, Lombardy, Veneto, Friuli, Tuscany, Rome, and Puglia; some of these include White Hands choirs.

The citizen artist responsible for the birth of the Italian Sistema was the world-renowned conductor Claudio Abbado, who learned of El Sistema through his long friendship with Maestro Abreu. For nearly a decade, Abbado made regular trips to Venezuela to work intensively with its advanced youth orchestras. In Italy, he used his considerable prestige to push for the creation of an Italian El Sistema, and he remained a strong Sistema advocate until his death in 2013.

The Italian Sistema, a loosely affiliated federation of programs that are funded and administered at the provincial level, is at the forefront of widening the meaning of "inclusion" as a Sistema foundational principle. When we met in Rome with Roberto Grossi, the director of Sistema Italia, he spoke about this expansion. "We want Sistema to be everywhere there is need! In Puglia and in Bari, we collaborate with the ministries of health on Sistema programs in the prisons, for prisoners. In Foggia, we have a program for chronically ill people in hospitals."

Under Roberto Grossi's lead, Sistema Italia has opened núcleos in southern Italy for the children of workers in Mafia-controlled factories. "In Bari, we petitioned the state to clear out a discotheque controlled by the Mafia and give it to us. There is a núcleo there now."

Roberto's vision encompasses the need for inclusion even on the part of middle-class children, whom he sees as isolated by the very social media they use to try to maintain connection. "Middle-class children have another kind of hunger," he said. "They have spiritual and ethical poverty. So many of them are tied to their cell phones. So they have no capacity for silence. Without silence, there can be no music."

Roberto spoke of Italy's central legacy to the world of music. "Italy doesn't invest enough in keeping culture alive," he said. "We seem to have forgotten that the past is still valuable for the living. El Sistema can remind us." This view that Sistema is essential for revitalizing the relevance and vitality of traditional artistic capitals echoes the urgent declarations we heard from Gerald Wirth in Vienna and Julian Lloyd Webber in England.

"Our aim," added Roberto, "is not to create musical geniuses. It's to offer the feeling of community for those who have none. Music can do that, where nothing else can succeed."

INCLUSION: HABITS OF MIND AND HEART

In Chapter 3, we suggested that the essential attributes of the Sistema learning environment help children and young people to develop certain habits of mind and heart that can be usefully extended to the rest of their lives. Let's consider three habits that radical inclusiveness can help to build.

A positive inclination toward differentness. Humans, indeed all animals, are cautious about unfamiliar things. It's a survival instinct. For some individuals and in some cultures, different means dangerous, and can provoke a dangerous response. Given the alarms of terrorist violence, and the fear-mongering of much popular media, a day-to-day fear of differentness may be more prevalent than ever.

Radical inclusiveness as a practice, reinforced every day over years, loosens innate and learned distrust, slowly giving way to a positive inclination toward differentness. Living in a learning community where everyone is seen as an essential asset, children learn that attitude of positive inclination even toward those who look different, speak differently, or are less skillful.

Empathy. We sometimes hear the phrase "a crisis of empathy" used to describe the self-absorption that, according to some pundits, characterizes the current young generation in the United States and other wealthy countries. Whether that is true or not, the phrase expresses a concern that children who are raised in material plenty, whose feelings and desires are frequently indulged, and who invest free time in electronic rather than in-person connections, grow up to be more self-centered than previous generations were, and will have fewer occasions to exercise the capacity for understanding how others feel. In self-help books, parenting classes, and op-ed articles, concerned leaders ask: how can families and communities raise empathic children?

Like creativity, empathy cannot be required; it arises from a disposition, a habit of mind and heart. Empathic capacity takes social imagination, the ability to enter the world of another and experience what it's like in there. In a healthy person, both creativity and empathy arise often. We can mandate compliance with behavioral requirements, but we can only nurture empathy, teach it by authentic example, honor and enjoy its appearance, and try to build learning environments in which it is a natural and satisfying choice.

Strong ensemble music programs cultivate the capacity for empathic connection. For hours each week, an ensemble player or singer strives to find musical consonance with her peers. Since musical expression is rooted in feeling, she can only succeed if she is alert to the currents of emotion that charge the playing and singing of others. To accomplish a coordinated diminuendo, an accented chord, or a plangent melody together, musicians must be attuned to the feelings of their fellow players. In a good ensemble music program, the *pp* of pianissimo doesn't mean "play very quietly"; it means "find the right quietness with your peers." The music doesn't make emotional sense unless these attunements are strong.

When the circle of musical communicators widens to include children with special needs, the potential for the exercise of empathy is even greater. Maestro Eunsuk Chae, music director of South Korea's Orchestra-of-Dreams Bucheon Núcleo, told us that his students and teachers are learning sign language so that they can better communicate with their deaf peers and audience members. "We take an hour every week to learn, and we practice in between. It makes us better, more sensitive people. At the end of this year we will perform for an audience with special hearing needs, and we will be able to connect with them directly."

There is also an extent to which playing great music requires reaching into the emotional world of the composer. This is a different dimension of empathy—we might call it aesthetic empathy—and it can actually add new elements to a student's emotional palette. Young people playing Mahler's Symphony No. 1, for example, find themselves suspended at the very outset in a musical landscape of quiet unease, a stillness filled with premonition—and there's a good chance they have never encountered precisely this feeling in their emotional lives before. Thus empathic connection with the music of a great composer allows players to learn new kinds of sensibility, new ways of feeling, to which they would otherwise have no access.

This pathway to new kinds of feeling, and to the specific experience of aesthetic delight, is one of the great virtues of learning in the performing arts. Pablo Neruda wrote: "To feel the affection that comes from those whom we do not know . . . widens out the boundaries of our being, and unites all living things." The original meaning of "empathy" is "in passion," which is exactly how students connect in Sistema; they feel the same passions inside the music. This bond connects them to others across time and culture; they join a human community larger than they have known before. Through performing, they discover that their families and their neighbors can understand these passions as well.

Sense of abundance. Growing up in material poverty can generate a habitual mindset of scarcity. The habit of identifying oneself as poor, and as having little of value, usually generates low expectations that can undermine success over a lifetime.

Maestro Abreu has said, "The huge spiritual world that music produces in itself ends up overcoming material poverty." It's a profound but fairly abstract idea. However, we have seen its manifestation in concrete practice. We have seen how children who live in severe poverty begin to feel self-confident and valued as their feelings of belonging deepen. In Rio de Janeiro, in Bogotá, in Baltimore and Nairobi and Istanbul, we've seen children carrying their violin and clarinet cases through dangerous neighborhoods and across gang lines with composure and pride. We have heard countless children in núcleos say, "My favorite thing is playing with my friends in the orchestra." Or "I love hearing the sound around me when I am inside the choir." And even, "When I play music, I feel strong."

We sense the inner feeling of sufficiency, even plenty, in these children, and it stems from the fact of belonging. They may not have nice clothes or reliable electricity at home, but they have a choir, and it's theirs. They may not even have enough to eat. But they have an orchestra.

THE CHALLENGES OF RADICAL INCLUSION

It must be said that the pursuit of radical inclusion in Sistema programs is not always entirely successful, and that many programs struggle with the challenge of balancing the principle of radical inclusion with the goal of musical excellence. The MusikUnik program in Aarhus is a case in point; while Naadir and children like him are learning to feel included, the level of musical skill in the program remains quite limited. Bjørg Lindvang described to us her mixed feelings about her students' initial performance in the impressive city concert hall in downtown Aarhus. "I had worked so hard to make that concert happen so the kids could have the experience of performing in such a place, and could feel they belonged there. But the only thing they were able to perform all together was a simple five-note pattern: 'SOL-FA-MI-RE-DO.' I felt bad, almost embarrassed, that this was the best they could do."

In Florence, the Sistema-inspired program in the Le Piagge neighborhood works with very young children, aged six to ten, whose families are immigrants from across the world—North Africa, Asia, the Middle East, and Latin America—and who struggle with manifold social and personal challenges. The program's way of responding to their needs is imaginative and touching: each child has a small version of an orchestral instrument (including not only strings but clarinets, oboes, trumpets, and one very small French horn), and they play extremely simple music. The teachers encourage them to sway as they play, and also to take turns soloing while the others play down-beats to the beat. The feel of the ensemble is playful and utterly accepting. When a seven-year-old girl soloed with her three trumpet notes as the others swayed and tooted around her, it was clear she had no inkling that her accompanists weren't sounding so good. It was simply the sound of ensemble, and she was inside it.

In Nottingham, England, where many of the Sistema students deal with family dysfunction or ethnic exclusion (and sometimes both), we stopped in on a sectional of fifth-grade brass players in the In Harmony Sistema program. They had been playing for over a year, and yet some could barely make a sound on their shiny instruments. "They haven't quite got their embouchures developed yet," the teacher told us with true British understatement. But his priorities were clear: instead of spending the session on embouchure development—the traditional imperative to get things right before you can move on—he was teaching them how to improvise over the changes of a blues in F, using just three of the few notes they knew: C, E-flat, and F. They took turns playing short solos, all of them, again and again. Skills were minimal but engagement was high. Inclusion was rampant. Accomplishment would come later.

Reality-tempered musical goals also characterize some of the Superar programs of eastern and central Europe, where the goal of achieving integration between antagonistic ethnic groups is so her-culean that musical standards tend to become a distant second pri-ority. In the countries where ethnic tension is high, Sistema programs often don't advance musically as quickly as do programs elsewhere. Superar children in Romania, for example, have been singing for two years but have not begun playing instruments. In Bosnia, one teacher told us that his students sing only in unison because "they're not ready to sing in harmony"; we guessed that this was less a musical assess-ment (kids between nine and fourteen, as these were, are quite capa-ble of singing in parts) than a nod of recognition for the social struggle inherent in simply bringing these children together in song. In both Bosnia and Romania, when a roomful of children whose parents don't speak to each other can sing a Native American folksong or a Chinese New Year's anthem together, teachers acknowledge that, as Bjørg put it, this is "the best they can do," and feel it is success enough.

Actually, it is success, period. The success becomes qualified only when value judgments from outside the Sistema worldview are imposed. The etymological sense of the word "success" is *to have a follow-through*, as in the succession of queens and kings. When Bjørg's students managed those few notes under the pressure of performance, in an imposing and unfamiliar downtown setting, it was a genuine success for them, because they grew more invested in their follow-through; the long journey toward internal self-worth and social integration had begun. In time, they will learn to make music that earns respect on its own terms. But success begins with those first few notes in public.

"LET'S MAKE A PROJECT TOGETHER!"

For a final snapshot of inclusion as practiced in an El Sistema environment, we return to another Scandinavian port city. El Sistema Sweden was born in Gothenburg, where Dudamel was for six years the principal conductor of Sweden's national orchestra, the Gothenburg Symphony Orchestra. During his tenure, the symphony orchestra went to the immigrant enclave of Hammarkullen to give a concert—a rare event for the orchestra, and thus big news across the city—and the response was so enthusiastic that the director of a local community arts school, Camilla Sarner, went to talk to Dudamel. "I was nervous," she told us, "because I knew he was very famous. But I asked him, 'From your experience in Venezuela, how would you advise us to create music education in a place like Hammarkullen?'

"He immediately said, 'Let's make a project together!' We remember that phrase as the beginning of El Sistema in Sweden."

Helena Wessman, then the president of the orchestra, was immediately on board. Helena and her colleagues felt strongly that the Gothenburg Symphony Orchestra should commit to substantial long-term support for an El Sistema program. In the words of Petra Kloo Vik, the orchestra's director of education, "The great ship that is the Gothenburg Symphony Orchestra got a necessary push in a new direction, with the arrival of Gustavo Dudamel." Petra told us that the dynamism of Gustavo and the example of El Sistema in Venezuela has inspired the orchestra to "dream bigger than we ever have before."

The launch of the Gothenburg program was the beginning of El Sistema Sweden, which now thrives in 20 cities, with 30 program sites and 6,120 students. The ten núcleos in Gothenburg (1,580 children) are located in impoverished immigrant districts, riven by ethnic tensions that sometimes erupt into violence. The Gothenburg Symphony Orchestra is a committed partner; for the Swedish government, the predominant funder, the program is an investment in fostering community and easing ethnic tensions.

Whatever preconceptions we may have harbored about the Swedes as a cool, cerebral people were dispelled within minutes of meeting the Sistema community in Hammarkullen: this was an environment all about play and dynamic connection. We heard the word "love" spoken here more times than we have heard it anywhere. There was no question that inclusion meant everyone, including us.

The heart-centric spirit of El Sistema Sweden is a reflection of its teachers and leaders. Development Manager Malin Aghed, one of the key founders, is a vivid, exuberant woman with bright blue eyes and ever-evolving shades of red hair, prone to wearing a long feather earring in one ear and bright red canvas sneaker-boots that lace up to the knee. Although not a trained musician, she organizes the environment of the program around songs, chants, and physical movement. The children at the Gothenburg sites learn many of the same songs, including the bluesy, student-composed "Home in Gambia" and an "El Sistema" song with a kind of pop-rock beat. This was the only time in our travels that we heard the words "El Sistema" used as lyrics in a children's song—not to mention "El Sistema yeah!" The students in the program are taught about the Sistema in Venezuela and feel strongly connected to Venezuelan children.

Malin sometimes writes songs for the program, and one in particular may be her best-known contribution not only to El Sistema Sweden but also to worldwide Sistema. A simple tune with nonsense syllables, "Babumba" was conceived several years before El Sistema Sweden began. As Malin tells it, "I was on a rooftop in Ramallah, Palestine, in 2011, with a group of special-needs kids who didn't really have the ability to talk. The sun was setting but the heat was still intense, and they were restless. So I started singing and clapping, just any silly thing I could think of . . . 'Hey-ey-ey/Hey-ey-ey/Ba-bum-ba, ba-bum-ba, ba-bum-ba hey-ey.' And it worked. They sang it and clapped it, and they calmed down."

It works in Sweden too. Every child in the Sistema knows it, and so does any adult who comes near the program for any length of time. It's instantly learnable. The chorus ends with a shout. It can be sung in rounds. When El Sistema Sweden teachers come to international conferences, they tend to sing "Babumba" as a wake-up call in the morning and during breaks throughout the day. Beware the inclusional power of this song; it's impossible *not* to sing along.

In Gothenburg's modern, blond-wood concert hall, we heard "Babumba" played in an arrangement for full orchestra by the Gothenburg Symphony, with the singing children of Sistema Gothenburg surrounding the symphony players. In this performance, the bouncy little tune became unaccountably moving. It was part of a "Side-by-Side" concert, meaning that the orchestra members were literally side by side with the Sistema children, often paired with them at music stands. The concert included music from *Pirates of the Caribbean*, with the children who could play instruments—a little—sitting among the professional players, and also the Coldplay song "Fix You," with rewritten Swedish lyrics about being "side by side," during which there was much waving of colored scarves by the smallest children, who weren't yet ready to play instruments. Completing the overwhelming Sistema aura of the concert was the Venezuelan guest conductor Manuel López-Gómez.

One of the most notable aspects of Sistema Gothenburg is the strength of its support from this orchestra, which is one of the most respected symphonic ensembles in Europe. In addition to its central role in the founding of El Sistema Sweden, which reserves a chair on its board for the orchestra president, the orchestra partners on a variety of projects. We were told that despite Dudamel's long association with the orchestra, not all musicians were initially enthusiastic about the Sistema idea. But in the concert we saw, they seemed to have come around—even those who occasionally got poked in the shoulder by an errant bow, or had a singer's scarf wave across their music scores. Some of the musicians are now deeply involved with the program, playing regular side-by-side concerts of the kind we saw and working with the children in the núcleos. Several told us that the work has not only changed them personally but has also changed the feel of the orchestra, making it "more cheerful and open," in the words of one musician.

Helena Wessman played an important role in this process; throughout her tenure, she was unequivocal about making the program a priority for the orchestra. "We want to open up this house to everybody," she said. "We want people here who have never been here in their lives. It's their home too."

In the everyday life of the núcleos, Malin and her colleagues work hard to make ethnically divided families feel at home in the places where their children make music together. Every Wednesday, all the Gothenburg sites hold a one-hour late-afternoon party (called Vänstay, a Swedish word which connotes both friendship and the day of the week) for the children and their families. Vänstays always include food, and there is a different theme for every Wednesday of the month: children's performances, a guest performance, a food festival focusing on one of the ethnic cuisines represented in the program, or a surprise.

Malin told us that when the Vänstay ritual was first introduced, very few parents showed up. She persisted. "We'll have a potluck dinner," she told them, "so bring your favorite food to share with us." Or, "Your child is going to perform this Wednesday! Come and hear!" She also learned to say (and mean it), "It will only last an hour." She found that if parents knew the event would be short, they were likelier to come.

After a few months, one mother approached her in private. "She said to me, 'Malin, I know what you are trying to do. You are trying to get me to talk to *those people.*'" The mother was referring to an ethnic group from another country. "'You know what, Malin—I will probably do it, someday. But you're going too fast. You have to give me time.'"

For Malin and her staff, this was an important thing to learn. "We understand that we have to be patient," she said. More parents are coming to Vänstays now. At the one we attended, during a group performance of a song about love, several parents undertook to teach us how to form a half-heart shape with thumb and forefinger, and join it to someone else's offered thumb and finger, to create the shape of a whole heart. Some parents were even singing and dancing along with the kids. Still, says Malin, there are many parents who don't come.

The learning environment of El Sistema Sweden strongly encourages children to become teachers as well as learners. In one playful Macarena-like dance, the children were scattered strategically among the adults, to help teach us the dance. An Armenian eight-year-old helped a Somali mom with her moves; crossing ethnic lines didn't seem so problematic when it was initiated by a child. From the children's perspective, it seemed, this was just a room full of short instructors helping clumsier tall learners, who finally, after many mistakes, got it—sort of.

The teachers in the program, many of whom come from classical music backgrounds, sometimes worry that the children are not developing musical skills fast enough. They know they are teaching profound habits of inclusion, the primary goal of the program. But they are concerned that they're not setting the musical bar high enough. They worry that if they aim higher they will lose some of the students they've worked so hard to include, but if they don't aim higher they won't activate the transformative potential of their most excited students.

The dynamic balance of pursuing both excellence and inclusion will continue to be a complicated one for Sistema-inspired programs. The El Sistema movement provides a laboratory for this inquiry, on an unprecedented scale. Introducing radical inclusion into the realm of artistic achievement represents a challenge to all kinds of received wisdom and high arts industry belief. But the willingness to take on this challenge is at the heart of El Sistema's distinctive vision.

CHAPTER 5

Ensemble Learning

The orchestras and choirs are much more than artistic studies.
They are schools of social life.
To sing and play together is to intimately coexist.
—JOSÉ ANTONIO ABREU

W hen you stand in the large sun-baked courtyard of the old Spanish-style house where Orquestrando a Vida ("Orchestrating Life") runs an El Sistema program in Campos, Brazil, you can hear everything going on in the program at that moment. There is a rehearsal of the beginners' orchestra, an ensemble of various ages led by a young teenager, under the shade of an ancient tree. Seven or eight children are involved in a violin sectional rehearsal in another corner of the courtyard, practicing the Portuguese equivalent of a "Mississippi Hot Dog" rhythm. Several smaller ones are running around in the sunny patches between the trees. In one of the rooms off the courtyard, a singing teacher from Venezuela leads a choral rehearsal. In a larger room directly across from that, the program's advanced orchestra—the Mariuccia Iacovino Symphony Orchestra, named for a great Brazilian violinist who is in *Guinness World Records* for the world's longest violin career—practices for hours, as it does just about every afternoon and evening.

In the midst of this amicable cacophony one afternoon in July 2014, a small boy named Ciao agreed to step out of rehearsal for an interview. He wore his baseball cap backward and clutched his piccolo. At ten, he is the youngest player in the Mariuccia Iacovino Orchestra. He has been playing piccolo since he was six, and was just moved up to the top orchestra because he was progressing so well (and the top orchestra needed a piccolo player).

"When you first came to this place," we asked him, "what did you think?" When the question was translated for him, he squinted his eyes, trying to conjure a memory about a thought—then just shook his head.

We tried again: "What did you see?"

He squinted again and then said matter-of-factly, "I saw a place that could give me a future."

He loves his piccolo more than anything, he told us. He wants to earn a degree in music. He said he's finally found a place in the street behind his home in the favela where he can practice and his mother won't yell at him that she can't hear her cell phone. His favorite composer is Rossini. He was relieved when we asked him to play instead of talk; up came the piccolo, and he whipped through a tune from Tchaikovsky's *1812* Overture. We applauded and then asked, "What do you like best about coming here?"

This answer was instantaneous: "Playing with my friends in the orchestra."

We asked him one last question. "Are there ever times when you are playing in the orchestra, and you think to yourself, 'We sound really good!'" Ciao nodded. "When was the last time that happened?"

"Five minutes ago," he said. We got it: interview over, please. He ran back to his orchestra.

Playing with my friends. That single, simple phrase defines the experiential core of El Sistema. We have heard children in Venezuela and across the world say it more times than we could possibly count. Here it was again, in a dusty courtyard in Brazil.

Ensemble learning is at the heart—no, it *is* the heart—of Orquestrando a Vida. It is the heart of every El Sistema program, because it is the Sistema's pedagogical first principle. In ensemble, children learn how to play rhythms. In ensemble, they learn how to read notes, how to play melodies, how to render *forte* and *piano, legato* and *pizzicato*, *presto* and *largo*. In ensemble, they also learn to listen to one another, to emulate and to teach, to cooperate, to keep trying even when it's hard or tedious. They learn how to stay confident even when they fear something is too hard, and to improve more than they might have imagined possible. They learn how to help others succeed, and how to receive help when they need it. In ensemble, they learn collegiality as an incubator for selfhood within community. To spend time in that courtyard in Campos was to understand how ensemble learning as practiced by this program—daily, with concentration, and with constant positivity—can, in fact, encompass all these kinds of learning.

It was also to understand one often-overlooked but crucial point about El Sistema: "ensemble" doesn't necessarily mean "orchestra." During our visits to Sistema programs, we observed many large orchestra and choir rehearsals, but many more small-ensemble rehearsals—in particular, sectional rehearsals, which involve the players in a single instrumental section—i.e., the second violins, or the violas, or the clarinets. Sectionals often take place with players sitting in a circle; they are variously led by the section leader, a teacher's aide, or a teacher, and they tend to be participatory, with contributions welcomed from all players. Sometimes the feel of a sectional is playfully competitive; nearly always, it is mutually supportive. We came to think of sectionals as the backbone of the El Sistema experience. It's every bit as important as the full orchestra as a seminal opportunity for ensemble learning, both musically and socially.

Of course, the full orchestra experience can be more exciting. The beginning orchestra under the tree on that sunny afternoon was working on the *William Tell* Overture, and they were definitely excited. Some of the players had been playing for less than a year, and the others for two or three years; the sound was rough around the edges. But the kids were going for broke. The young conductor, who was also a student in the advanced orchestra, was pushing them to a faster tempo and crisper articulation, as intent as if he were dribbling a soccer ball down an open field with a defender just behind. When the music fell apart, they all burst out laughing and then started up again. On the fourth or fifth try, it held together. Near the end of the piece, during the big brass fanfare, the violinists and violists swiveled around in their seats as they played, to watch the trombonists during their big moment.

We noticed that in many instances there was just one instrument per stand, and stand mates were taking turns playing. Luis Mauricio Carneiro, one of the leaders of Orquestrando a Vida, told us there's a chronic shortage of instruments in the program. But they keep accepting all new students who want to come, even if there are not instruments available for them yet. "Jony always says, when you are making soup and there are more hungry people, you just have to add water to the beans," he said, referring to Jony William, the program's director. "So we just rotate the instruments we have. In fact, it's a learning experience for the kids—they learn to take turns, to share, and to pay attention to the music in another way when they're not playing."

Since new students enter at various times throughout the year, Mauricio said, they are always dealing with the challenge of integrating new students. "Our practice is to put them in orchestras and ensembles right away. Sometimes it's not easy . . . sometimes it's really difficult, because these children have a lot of problems in their lives, so it takes them a couple of months to develop concentration and self-confidence. But in the ambience of the orchestra, they develop so quickly!"

We asked him how and why that happens. "We are always teaching our kids to help the new ones," he responded. "We teach the philosophy that anything we know, we share."

In Orquestrando a Vida, the use of musical ensemble as a vehicle for learning social behavior and individual self-worth is a conscious one, a message that is often articulated. "We talk with them every day about this; it's part of the learning process, to talk about it. I'm always asking them, 'What do you want to do with your life? You have to dream big; you can do it! But you can only do it if everyone is working together, helping everyone else. All the time.'"

Mauricio was our semiofficial guide on our visit to Orquestrando a Vida. He had met us at the Campos airport early that morning and driven us along the narrow potholed road to the city during rush-hour traffic, amid growling mopeds, fume-belching buses, schoolchildren on foot, and chickens everywhere. When we got to Campos, he gave us a quick tour of his hometown—a flourishing city in the nineteenth century, but now a blighted and mostly impoverished place. The requisite cathedral and an oddly yellow city hall are all that distinguish the downtown, and its favelas stretch for miles.

Mauricio has gray hair, but there is a boyishness about him; he was cheerful and unflappable even when his English failed him, which was fairly frequently. As he drove us around, he related the story of how Orquestrando a Vida began. Twenty years ago, when he returned here after graduating from music school in Rio de Janeiro, he had joined forces with Jony William, another Campos violinist a few years his elder, to build a small music school where kids could learn to play orchestral instruments. "Jony is the visionary here, and he has always been my mentor. I am a violin teacher today because of him; I am a conductor today because of him."

In 1996, they were visited by Fiorella Solares, who was on her quest to find a city in the Brazilian interior where El Sistema could take root. "At that time, we didn't know anything about El Sistema in Venezuela," says Mauricio. "But Fiorella knew Jony from attending music festivals with him in the past. She could sense right away that he was the right person for this project."

At first, Jony and Mauricio based the new El Sistema program in their music school. "In the beginning, we simply changed the structure of our lessons there," said Mauricio. "We began to develop the pedagogy of El Sistema; we started meeting with the students every day instead of once or twice a week, and encouraging them to help and teach each other."

But a visit to Venezuela the following year, he said, really made the essence of El Sistema clear to them. "We returned with a consciousness that we must change our work—we must have a symphony orchestra of children. Because learning all together, they will learn more than learning one by one. This is the real beginning of our history."

Orquestrando a Vida moved several years ago from the music school, which still continues as a conventional fee-charging institution, to its current building a mile or so from the favelas where most of its students live. Bright flags and banners decorate the entrance. The building was used for decades as a warehouse for contraband goods and automobiles confiscated by municipal authorities, and the city agreed to let the orchestra program use it for ten years. The entire staff worked on the place for days, moving out broken cars and rusted farm equipment and boxes of files; family members and friends pitched in to help with cleaning and painting and fixing the plumbing.

The advanced players who have been with the program for years think of not only the advanced orchestra but also the whole program as "their" ensemble. Many of these students function simultaneously both as lynchpin players in the advanced orchestra and as teachers, conductors, and sectional leaders for the younger students. Sometimes they leave for several years to study music or other subjects in Rio de Janeiro or São Paolo; often, they return to teach in the program part-time or full-time.

Twenty-five-year-old Marcos Rangel, whom Mauricio introduced as "my right arm," plays French horn in the Mariuccia Iacovino Orchestra and also teaches and conducts the intermediate orchestra; he has been with the program since he was nine. "My life has been completely different from my siblings' lives," he told us. "I have had the dream of El Sistema to lead me."

He said that this dream crystallized when he visited Venezuela at sixteen with other students in the program, to observe El Sistema núcleos there. "I thought to myself, I need this, not only for my life but for my country." It's interesting to note that in nearly all Sistema programs around the world, the most committed and advanced students describe their participation with an element of civic pride. In some countries the pride seems more nationally focused, in others it tends toward the local; but in either case, El Sistema's dual goals of social and musical advancement are manifest in these students' sense of civic as well as artistic identity.

Marcos spoke of how the ethos of ensemble extends beyond the sphere of music and permeates every aspect of life at Orquestrando a Vida: "The Sistema way is that everyone pitches in on everything. You don't say, 'Oh, that's his job, I don't do that.' If it needs to be done, you just do it." He introduced us to twenty-one-year-old Luis-Felipe, a violin teacher, by saying, "He's my right arm."

Luis-Felipe, who remembers almost nothing of his life before age twelve, when he entered the program, spoke about the rapid pace of learning in an ensemble context. "It's amazing to go in just a few years from knowing nothing to knowing Brahms and Mahler, classical and Baroque style. But that's what happens here." He added that the most important thing about ensemble learning is "when minds change—when thought patterns change, when people see new goals and new possibilities for themselves."

Eighteen-year-old Derekson, who began teaching at fourteen, seems to function as Luis-Felipe's right arm. "This learning can transform life," he said simply. "It's a different reality. So many of these children, everything in their lives is so ugly . . . and then there's this."

Catarina, who is ten, wanted to tell us "a funny story" about walking home with her friends to their favela a few nights ago. They heard gunshots nearby, she said; they all hit the dirt and then went home with mud on their clothes. "But they weren't shooting at us, just at somebody else," she assured us. "And my friends looked funny with dirt all over them."

She told us she loves the program, even though her friends in the neighborhood don't get why she likes to play the violin all the time. We asked her what she likes about it. She likes the way it sounds, she answered, and the way the orchestra sounds around her. "It makes me feel safe," she said.

Orquestrando a Vida is one of the few programs we visited

that employs a social worker to help oversee and guide the social aspects of learning. Mariana Andrade, a social psychologist trained in family therapy, described her job as being "the mediator, the bridge between the program and the kids' life experiences." She spoke of the strenuous personal challenges these students face, and the difficulty some of them have in finding their way to full participation in ensemble, given the home and school backgrounds they come from. She has worked in many contexts, she said, but this program feels more effective than any of the others in delivering the change that social workers wish to provide. She adds that it isn't easy for anyone involved—but it works.

The motivational power of ensemble learning is an essential element of her work. "When children misbehave, we don't send them away or call their parents," she said. "We pull them out of the ensemble, and they sit apart and listen. When they are ready to go back in and join, they do." Sometimes, with kids who have particular difficulty focusing, she provides an alternative "ensemble" experience. "I say to these kids, 'You don't want to play music today? Okay, but you are here, you are part of this community; you have to contribute in some way. Here's a broom! If you're not going to be an artist, you'll have to learn another way to contribute.'"

Jony William, who imagined Orquestrando a Vida into being seventeen years ago, still leads the program and shapes the vision. Jony is in his fifties now; he has blue eyes and a pallor that suggests sleepless nights. He has been to Venezuela many times and, like Fiorella, feels a strong personal connection to Maestro Abreu. His words about the orchestra as a metaphor were very similar to those of the Maestro. "Orchestral music is a great envelope," he said. "It is not only beautiful, but it can also transmit other kinds of values, like collective responsibility."

Jony doesn't speak English, but Daniel Soren, an opera singer who is one of the program's choral directors, had attended Roanoke College in Virginia and was able to offer his fluent translation skills. When we asked Jony how he came to dedicate his life to this work, he recounted his early experience as a naïve, well-intentioned musician working with young people in a São Paolo favela. "For some of them, violence was all they knew about. I started going to visit them and meeting their families, trying to understand what they were going through. I came to see that, aggressive as they might be, these kids were actually not tough. They were vulnerable." He said that when he began to teach the young people to play music in ensemble, he saw a dramatic change. "I always knew in theory that music could affect people, but working in this project, I could see it happening before my eyes. That transformed my whole perception of music. And transformed my life."

Jony pointed out that Orquestrando a Vida has no cleaning staff—with their bare-bones budget, he can't justify spending on that—so he turns this job into part of the ensemble learning experience. "We all take responsibility for making sure that everything is clean. Everyone, absolutely everyone, is part of taking care of this place. Every day." His parents and sisters pitch in to take care of the núcleo; when the aging building has an electrical or plumbing problem, Jony's dad is the one they call, even in the middle of the night. "The students see them helping, and they help too, and they all feel they have something to contribute to the whole. Since we have daily contact with the children, it's almost like living together, and this provides the opportunity to break out of the cycles that have them trapped in the other parts of their lives."

He told us that in many of the public schools, there is a behavior crisis. "There is graffiti all over the walls, people are throwing paper and trash on the ground—there is little respect for the teachers, and no sense of belonging to something valuable. Sometimes the classroom teachers from the public schools visit us, to see what we are doing. They see how their students behave here, focused and responsible, and they say 'How is it possible?' It's possible because of the ethic of collective responsibility that we create here."

Jony has a palpable sense of urgency about the program's mission. "I don't want to turn anyone away—even if we don't have enough space or instruments for them all. We must take in everyone who wants to come. Because if we don't—while we wait, and ponder, and plan, the drug dealers just get the kids. They are not pondering and planning, they are acting. When they act, the kids are lost. For good. So how can we not act? Sometimes we cannot choose *not* to do it." He paused a moment, then said, "Maybe you would like to visit the neighborhood where our children live?"

That afternoon Mauricio drove us with Jony and Daniel to the Baleeira favela. We had to park just outside the ghetto; there were big tree stumps in the road at the border of the neighborhood, put there by gang members demarcating their turf from other gangs and signaling a defiant message to the police. Every day at dusk, an armed man assumes his position on one of these stumps.

We got out of the car and were welcomed by Maria, the "unofficial mayor" of Baleeira. With both of her sons lost to gang violence, one dead and one in jail, Maria uses her moral suasion to take a lead in bringing Orquestrando a Vida into this favela and enrolling as many children as possible. "We are safe walking here," said Jony, "as long as Maria is with us."

With Maria, we walked through the unpaved streets. There were partially standing shacks and corrugated lean-tos, many with no electricity and with barrels on the roof to collect rain for drinking water. "This is where one of our viola players lives," said Jony, pointing through a dark opening with no door. "Over there, brothers who play trumpet. Here"—he reached down to greet a toddler—"is the little sister of one of our cellists. Do you want to come play in our orchestra, little one?"

We passed children playing with the parts of cars and bicycles that littered the streets. "That one is my grandchild," Maria told us as we walked, "and that one too, and that one is my great-grandchild. . . ." She hugged them all. She knew everyone, and Jony did too.

Maria led us up the stairs of a tiny Pentecostal church to show us the room where the smallest children of the program join their first ensemble, singing together and beginning to play instruments, before graduating to the Orquestrando compound a mile away. There are inspirational quotes on the walls, intermingled with musical posters; there is a photo of José Antonio Abreu and a photo of the top Orquestrando orchestra. As the children sit on the floor, holding and playing their first musical instruments, that's what they look up at: a picture of a full symphony orchestra made up of their older siblings and cousins and friends.

Maria is a kind of Sistema archetype, a local nonmusician who holds the trust of the neighborhood. She is the moral compass for the community, and her decision to support the orchestra program—to assure gang leaders and families living in acute poverty that an orchestra is good for everyone—has made all the difference in community acceptance and participation, simply by virtue of her personal authority and credibility. Perhaps we could call this archetype the "authorizer;" she's the trusted insider who defuses distrust and danger by declaring her personal support of the outsiders' ideas. We have met similar authorizers in gang neighborhoods around the world; their role in the global Sistema movement is invisible to all but a few, but proves to be crucial to the lives of thousands.

When Maria walked back to the car with us, we asked her what she thought classical music ensemble learning could bring to this neighborhood and its children. "It changes their behavior," she answered. "It makes them more courteous, more responsible. They socialize better. The family starts to be together more, because they attend concerts together. This builds up their strength to persist, so they won't give up. Respect and working together: that is what we need here. That is what children learn in orchestras."

In the car, driving away from the favela, Jony said to us, "Whenever times are hard, and I think about perhaps giving up, I come here. Then I know there is no giving up, no turning away from this mission."

Back at Orquestrando a Vida, we walked past the banners and flags, through the entrance hall and into the interior courtyard—and there it was, the bright jumbled medley of sounds from many ensembles rehearsing, ensembles of kids who lived in the streets where we had just walked. The advanced orchestra was playing a Mozart mass; the beginning orchestra was pounding away at *William Tell*; the chorus was rehearsing the rhythmic and harmonic complexities of a Brazilian folk song. A sectional rehearsal of violists in a corner of the courtyard played a scale together, in varying rhythms. Elisamara, a seventeen-year-old advanced student, was crossing the courtyard on her way to rehearsal, and stopped to talk with us. She told us that her ambition was to be a conductor, and we asked why. "Because I love to hear the mass of sound coming at me," she said. "And I know what to do with it."

A GANG FOR MUSIC

Eight hundred miles to the north, in the Brazilian coastal city of Salvador, the capital of the state of Bahia, the Sistema-inspired program NEOJIBA (Núcleos Estaduais de Orquestras Juvenis e Infantis da Bahia) serves approximately a thousand children and young people who play and sing together daily in a multitiered system of orchestras and choirs similar to that of Orquestrando a Vida. "We are making a gang for music," said Obadias Cunha, the program's pedagogical director. "What builds kids' motivation here is the pleasure of making beauty with their friends— and that's the critical part: with their friends."

Obadias observed that one of the attractions of gang membership is the sharing of an insider language, a special code that others don't understand. "Of course, classical music has a vast language of its own," he pointed out. "So, think about it: right here in this núcleo, we have two hundred eighty kids talking 'classical music' with their friends. And they love doing it. It is the language of their 'gang.'" Obadias recalled that within three months of NEOJIBA's formation five years ago, there was a Facebook group for NEOJIBA oboe players.

We saw this musical gang spirit in action on our first visit to a NEOJIBA program in Itapagipe, an impoverished neighborhood of Salvador. The program is housed in a restored colonial mansion, a donation from a board member; it was brimming with kids of different ages playing in string, brass, and wind sectionals, in addition to a beginner orchestra rehearsing Ravel's *Bolero*. In a front room, teenagers from the núcleo's advanced orchestra were taking a rehearsal break—and their break activity of choice, even with open courtyards and a soccer ball right outside the door, was watching a video of the city-wide NEOJIBA touring orchestra on a large-screen TV. As the orchestra onscreen launched into "Tico Tico," a well-known Brazilian pop tune, the kids reached for their instrument cases, pulled out their instruments and started to play along. Their satisfaction in being part of this "gang" and sharing intricate skills and understandings together could not have been clearer.

A couple of continents away, in an impoverished area of London, the director of the Sistema-inspired program In Harmony Lambeth uses a different metaphor. "The orchestra, the choir, and the sectional are really the family for our kids," said Gerry Sterling, "and they provide a healthy family, not a dysfunctional one. The ensemble is where we live, learn, know each other, have arguments sometimes and learn to compromise . . . it's really the key to our whole program. It's at the heart of everything."

On still another continent, in Paterson, New Jersey, a city of persistent poverty and divided ethnicities, we heard the leaders and teachers of the Sistema-inspired Paterson Music Project, encourage their students to think of themselves as a team. Cello teacher Terrence Thornhill told his students: "This team isn't out to beat anyone else. We are a team that accomplishes great things because its members constantly support each other."

A good gang, a functional family, a noncombative team—all these ideas refer to the primal need of all people, and especially children and adolescents, to feel a part of something larger than themselves. Satisfying that need is a crucial element in the passage toward self-

A CITIZEN ARTIST ON THREE CONTINENTS

In Maputo, Mozambique, Eldevina (Kika) Materula started music school when she was seven; it was her after-school daycare, because her mother worked all day and her father was away working in South Africa. Kika loved choir more than anything, because "it was like magic to create all those harmonies so fast." At age thirteen, she moved to Portugal on her own, to study oboe; she went on to complete her studies in Sweden in 2007. Then she took a job as an oboist in the Bahia Symphony Orchestra in Salvador, Brazil, where she began to teach at NEOJIBA. Her initial plan to teach there for three months has stretched to eight years; she keeps coming back because of "the human connection" to her students and how much she gets back from them. One of her slogans, often repeated by her students: "Learn who teaches and teach who learns. We should always be ready to learn!"

NEOJIBA inspired Kika to start the Xiquitsi Project in her Mozambique hometown of Maputo. Friends called her crazy, she said, for starting a children's orchestra in a country with no orchestras at all (and not even performances by touring orchestras). When she persisted, finding instruments and interested students, they called her a fighter. Now that the program is thriving, the concerts are good, and the government education ministry is using the Xiquitsi model for learning projects in schools, her friends call her brave and visionary.

She's also highly itinerant; she travels between her program in Mozambique, her teaching job at NEOJIBA in Brazil, and her current "regular job" playing oboe in the Orquestra Sinfónica do Porto Casa da Música in Portugal. Asked how she manages a three-continent life, she says that each provides something different: in Portugal, she plays with a strong professional orchestra with a wide repertoire; in Brazil, she is helping to build a strong Sistema orchestra; and in her home country, she is building a future from scratch.

definition and self-esteem. In the growing body of scholarly literature on the psychology of gangs, findings consistently point to a need for community as the principal reason young people join gangs. According to psychology professor Robert T. Muller, "experts propose that young people join gangs because they act as a surrogate family, and provide a sense of belonging, power, control and prestige—all things that are commonly identified as absent in the childhoods of gang initiates."[19]

The musical ensembles of El Sistema, then, satisfy a deep psychosocial need. But can they really provide effective musical learning experiences? This is a question often asked by members of the classical music establishment. The centuries-old tradition of Western art music mandates many years of solitary instrumental learning in one-on-one lessons and daily private practice. It is a received belief that these pedagogical priorities are the only way to learn the discipline and technique essential for high-quality performance. From the point of view of this tradition, it's misguided or even insulting to propose that high-level instrumental and musical competence can be achieved through ensemble learning.

But to visit El Sistema programs in Venezuela or in other Latin American countries with strong Sistema traditions, such as Mexico, Colombia, and Brazil, is to witness a level of musical excellence, in ensembles of all age levels, that is generally very high. On our initial visit to Venezuela, we found ourselves saying, "Kids this age cannot play this well," even though the kids right in front of us were clearly that age and clearly playing that well. We would square our rational minds with our eyes and ears by deciding that we had seen the single showpiece orchestra—until we encountered the same sense of incredulity in the next room or at the next núcleo.

It is this consistently high level of musical skill that has won El Sistema the attention of the non-Latin American world; conductors and concert artists from around the world have come to visit Venezuela because they were astonished by the playing level of its touring youth orchestras, and then discovered the vast social program from which those orchestras grew. In the words of Daniel Barenboim, the internationally esteemed pianist, conductor, and composer: "El Sistema takes music from the ivory tower and makes it something essential to everyone, enriching the lives of both musicians and listeners all over the world."

It's important to note that even though ensemble learning is at the structural center of Sistema education, individual lessons do form a part. At nearly every núcleo we visited, we were told that young people who attain advanced skill levels take regular private lessons, and children of all ages and skill levels receive one-on-one lessons whenever the program's resources allow. Often, it happens whenever an accomplished foreign musician makes a visit; the visitor will find himself suddenly corralled into a string of private lessons. Sistema Fellow Dan Berkowitz tells the story of visiting a Caracas núcleo and being drafted into a lesson with a promising trombone player. After a half-hour went by, and then an hour, and then two hours, Dan asked the boy if he was supposed to be somewhere else. "Oh, yes," said the boy, "I was supposed to leave a long time ago, but I stayed because you were willing to keep teaching me."

Still, it was clear at every núcleo that the ensemble is the primary and fundamental context for music learning. It was also clear that teaching musical excellence in ensemble environments requires special skills that are often unfamiliar, and sometimes uncomfortable, for non-Sistema music teachers. We had an opportunity to talk with members of the Colombian Sistema program's top youth orchestra just as they were ending a month of training that included time with a team of top U.S. conservatory teachers and then with Venezuelan El Sistema teachers. The U.S. teachers, they told us, were generous and kind, and had remarkably helpful insights and "brilliant tricks" about issues of technique. But they weren't good at moving the whole group forward together; they dealt with players one by one, and they tended to tire pretty quickly. The Venezuelans, they said, didn't have as many technical tips and insights, and some didn't play as well as the U.S. faculty did; but they were urgent and tireless, and kept the whole group moving forward all the time. The young musicians concluded that they learned more from the Venezuelans.

The Sistema experience resonates in this regard with contemporary developments in theories of how children learn. In the field of education scholarship, there is a growing body of work on the effectiveness of cooperative learning through participatory group activities, in comparison with conventional teaching methods that rely on each student privately processing transmitted content. The authoritative study on cooperative learning, David and Roger Johnson's *Cooperation and Competition: Theory and Research* (a metaanalysis of over 750 research studies on the subject), finds that cooperative learning generates pronounced advantages for academic achievement, productivity, motivation, interpersonal skills, empathy, psychological and physical health, self-esteem, and lasting personal relationships. The study also includes the finding that "students who work in cooperative groups do better on tests, especially with regard to reasoning and critical thinking skills, than those that do not."[20]

Marshall Marcus, the president of Sistema Europe, who has worked closely with Venezuelan Sistema ensembles for over three decades, notes that Sistema practice is a healthy corrective to the highly individualized training conventions of music education in the Northern Hemisphere. "The way kids learn instruments in Venezuela is the way kids naturally learn anything—in relation with others, in practice," he told us. "The way we in Europe have created music learning acts as a brake on the natural tendencies of kids to play together."

Richard Holloway, who as head of the Scottish Arts Council led the initiative to bring El Sistema to his country, said, "What struck me in Venezuela was that these children were immediately introduced to what I call the communalism of the orchestra from the beginning. That was the complete reversal of the European classical music pedagogy where you slug away for years, and if you're lucky, you'll get into an ensemble."

Back in Campos, Jony William talked about being challenged by pedagogical traditionalists. "There are still people who say to me, 'This ensemble thing is not the right way; kids should study their instruments at home.' And I say—'You know what? They're not going to study at home. It's just not part of their daily reality. So we have to create a new reality.'"

A SCHOOL FOR SOCIAL LIFE

Historically and philosophically, the idea that music is key to mental and emotional development has a long lineage of antecedents. Ever since Plato, who famously wrote, "I would teach children music, physics, and philosophy; but most importantly music, for the patterns in music and all the arts are the keys to learning," thinkers and educators have theorized about the value of music education for its ennobling effect on individual development and its civilizing influence on social life.

El Sistema's contribution to this tradition is to emphasize ensemble learning in particular. At the core of El Sistema is the conviction that, as children and young people become part of instrumental and choral "teams" and experience the pleasure of making music, talking music and reaching for musical excellence with their friends, these teams provide an effective learning environment for social and emotional skills. Dudamel has said, "The orchestra is the most perfect example of how the world needs to work. Everyone in the orchestra has many differences from one another, but the music unites them all."

British academic Geoffrey Baker has challenged this notion, arguing that because orchestras are hierarchical and nondemocratic organizations, the primary social skills fostered by orchestral experience are obedience and submissiveness rather than cooperation, mutual responsibility, and self-esteem. It's true that in most orchestras, votes are not taken on artistic interpretations, and there is usually a single unelected conductor up front who teaches through "imposed" repertoire. And there are long-time professional orchestra players with whom Baker's observations may resonate. But they do not ring true with regard to the Sistema orchestras we observed, which were hothouses of multiple learning—occasions for learning from teachers, mentors, and one another, as well as from the conductor. On our núcleo visits, we often saw orchestras that rotated concertmasters, orchestras that rotated all chairs, and orchestral rehearsals that featured nearly constant interaction between students and their mentors and coaches, who sat or floated within every section.

Further, the orchestra offers opportunities for complex and often simultaneous communication, which makes it a valuable vehicle for communicative learning. The conductor's gestures, the often-subtle body language of the section principals, and the multilayered listening-and-responding habits that every player practices can produce highly effective results in short periods of time. If we define "elegance" as a maximal amount of beauty with a minimal expenditure of effort, the orchestra is an elegant communications system. (In fact, there has been a surge of interest within the corporate world in using orchestral models to improve intraorganizational communications.[21])

In every Sistema-inspired program we visited, leaders, teachers, students, and parents spoke unprompted about the ways students grow in ensemble environments large and small. Julio Saldaña, the director of Esperanza Azteca in the city of Puebla, Mexico, told us that he often begins rehearsals by giving each student one piece of a puzzle. "I say to them, 'Each piece is unique and necessary. When they are all put together they make something beautiful. That is what we can do if we work together well. We join together and make something beautiful, a musical marvel.'"

In France, Jean-Claude Decalonne of Passeurs d'Arts spoke of the efficacy of orchestral learning with something like reverence. "The orchestra: that's it. That's the most beautiful form of human association. This is the reason for everything I do. It's the reason that I and my colleagues work so hard: because we are absolutely convinced of this."

In Los Angeles, L.A. Phil president Deborah Borda spoke in similar terms of her organization's philosophical commitment to El Sistema. "Maestro Abreu's core vision, the principle that all Sistema programs are built upon, is the orchestra as a metaphor for humanity— for citizenship, kindness, passion. We believe in that assumption, and it's the philosophical basis for our Sistema work."

In Italy, where traditions of classical music education go deep and the language itself remains the lingua franca of classical music, we heard the word "*insieme!*" ("together!") many times during visits to núcleos in Milan, Turin, and Florence. "We have fifty-five conservatories in this country," we were told by Sistema Italia director Roberto Grossi, "and fifty-eight thousand kids studying in them—but their study is mostly individual. The great news of El Sistema is that we understand how working in a whole group, all working together, is different. It's about collaboration."

THE REHEARSAL IS THE POINT

Juan Antonio Cuéllar, former director of Batuta, Colombia's federal Sistema organization, made this point when he spoke of the value of group learning. "Children learn everything in orchestras," he said. "Values. Habits. It's really important that we work toward these things, not just toward technique. That's why the rehearsal itself is the point." It's an insight we often come back to. While the anticipation of performance often adds motivational energy to students' efforts, rehearsals are not just preparations for performance but also the homeland of musical and social learning.

In Aarhus, Denmark, we observed a youth orchestra rehearsing for the first time with a guest conductor, Guatemalan Bruno Campo, who studies conducting in Austria and co-leads the Sistema Europe Youth Orchestra, frequently working with developing Sistema programs in Europe. The Danish young people were rehearsing Dvořák's Ninth Symphony, and they began with a well-tuned but timid sound. Bruno stopped them at the seventh measure and said, "If any one of you is holding back at all, it won't work. Everybody has to be giving everything. When that happens, that is when we create an orchestra."

This was not a Sistema orchestra; it was a conventional middle-class youth orchestra, and they were encountering the unconventional values and drive of a Sistema rehearsal for the first time.

They played perfectly well together, but they were used to focusing their attention on playing their own parts well and not making mistakes. This was something different. "Your sound," said Bruno, addressing a girl in the viola section, "will help her sound." He pointed to a second violinist, and then to a clarinetist. "And her sound will help his sound."

Some minutes into the piece, as the music grew stormier and more multilayered, the playing began to disintegrate, with many different ideas of tempo and beat going on. Instead of spending ten minutes on the passage, drilling the beat into them with a stern baton, Bruno stopped conducting. "You all play it without me now and figure it out," he said. "Listen to each other!"

They did. The passage came together fast; beat was established, entrances were secure. The teenagers looked surprised but pleased. "That is what you are here to do," he told them. "You are here to find ways to agree with one another. That is the secret of making beautiful music."

It was Lars-Ole Vestergaard, the director of the Aarhus Music School, who created this ensemble, which includes many of the more advanced students at the school. Lars-Ole is also the founder of the Sistema program in Aarhus, MusikUnik, whose students live in the city's poorest immigrant district. He believes in the power of Sistema work there to foster amicability between this community and its host city; he also believes in its capacity to invigorate the middle-class youth orchestra, to move it from pleasurable after-school activity to the combustible thrill of true ensemble.

At the Nucleo Project in London, we got a fascinating glimpse of what teaching social development through musical ensemble can look like when very young children are involved. Founder/director Lucy Maguire's 200 students range in age from four to eleven, and many are beginners on their instruments. But even the youngest play together daily in a string ensemble. Lucy had them begin rehearsal by taking a deep breath, all at the same time, and then bowing to their stand mates. Then she worked with them on playing two simple songs. "Let's do it again!" she said repeatedly. "Let's see if we can *all* be in agreement!"

At the end of the final "Twinkle," Lucy said to the kids, "That was almost perfect!"

"Who was it that wasn't perfect?" asked a tiny cellist.

"What do you mean, 'who was it?'" she responded. "It was you guys! It was the orchestra."

RENEWABLE MUSICAL ENERGY

The phrase "a force of nature" rings differently in Denmark, the world's leader in wind power. Lars-Ole Vestergaard, the founder of Musik-Unik, is a renewable source of positive pushiness on behalf of children and music. A conservatory-trained classical musician, he directs a well-established community music school in Aarhus; he has expanded the genres of music taught at the school and broadened the range of instruments played beyond the traditional orchestral ones.

When Lars-Ole saw the Sistema documentary *Tocar y Luchar* in 2007, he was struck by the realization that Aarhus's immigrant population did not have the same opportunities as did the children of his school, and he pushed the city government and the public schools to fund the launch of MusikUnik in 2012. When he took us to see the program, some flute and clarinet students began to work their way through *C-Jam Blues*, and he sat down at the piano to give them a fluently bluesy accompaniment.

Lars-Ole told us that when he heard about the Sistema-like Afghanistan National Institute of Music and learned that some advanced students there were showing real promise, he arranged to bring four of the students to his music school on scholarship to help them along. They couldn't afford housing, so he invited them to stay at his home for three months, providing them with a home-stay living experience in addition to advanced musical training.

On our last evening in Campos, we listened to the Mariuccia Iacovino Orchestra rehearse Mozart's *Missa Brevis* with the núcleo's advanced chorus. Mauricio was conducting, and the sound, bouncing off the walls of the crowded, poorly lit concrete room, was glorious. The brass players aced every one of their high notes, as did the sopranos; the strings were spirited and the winds glowed; orchestra and chorus romped through the contrapuntal passages. The choral passages were short on vocal sheen but deeply integrated into the fabric of the orchestra. There is no other way to describe this rehearsal: they were having a party inside Mozart.

When the long rehearsal ended, sometime after 9 P.M., Jony William came to the podium and formally introduced the visiting writers from the United States. He asked us to say a few words. With the help of our opera singer/translator Daniel, we told the young musicians that we were researching and writing a book about the international El Sistema movement, and that there are Sistema-inspired programs in more than sixty countries—"which means that all over the world there are kids like you, who deal with many challenges in their lives, as you do, and who learn ensemble music together and find it changes their lives."

They listened to us intently, their arms wrapped around their instruments. They asked questions: "Why do you have El Sistema in the U.S.—why would you need it, since everybody's rich?" "Is El Sistema in Africa?" "What is El Sistema like in Japan?"

The final question came from a bass player in the back row. "Do you think it would ever be possible," he asked, "that there could be a world Sistema orchestra?"

We both answered at once, with Daniel chiming in: "*Sim!* (Yes!) It will happen, and musicians from your orchestra will be a part of it." At which point the whole orchestra broke into cheers, yelling and whistling and stomping, clapping on their cellos and basses, as though they had just won the World Cup.

Jony thanked us ceremoniously and hung green-and-yellow-beribboned "Orquestrando La Vida" medallions around our necks, and our departure turned abruptly into another party. An octet of violins serenaded our exit with a heart-melting rendition of "Over the Rainbow," escorting us across the dark courtyard. Then, as we passed through the little entrance hall and walked out into the night, a six-piece percussion band surrounded us and started cooking up a samba rhythm. (How had they managed to get from the rehearsal hall, where they had just been playing kettledrums and French horns, out here to the street with their percussion instruments and cocky white hats, in the time it took their friends to play "Over the Rainbow"?) They played and played, and everyone danced, including the parents who had come to pick up their kids at the end of the day and were waylaid by this impromptu celebration of El Sistema spreading across the world, the cosmos, the universe. The drumming got faster and more insistent. One dad was dancing with his little girl on his shoulders. The teenagers danced with each other, holding the corners of a large Brazilian flag. Even the visiting writers had to grab a corner of the flag and do some approximate dancing as they pulled us into the circle—because, after all, we were part of the ensemble.

When the samba party finally ended, the students dispersed into the Campos night, some with their parents but many unchaperoned. We caught a brief glimpse of Catarina and her little band of friends, heading out on foot through the dark in the direction of the Baleeira favela, their violin cases tucked under their arms. We could only hope that she and her musical gang would have no "funny stories" to tell of this night, as they crossed the borders of gangs who deal in drugs, rival vengeances, and death.

CHAPTER 6

Peer Learning

The orchestra gave me confidence and skills with my friends. I have
learned that in the absence of a teacher, I must take the lead in team
practice and care about those younger than me.

—ELEVEN-YEAR-OLD SEO HYO-JIN,
AN ORCHESTRA OF DREAMS STUDENT IN SOUTH KOREA,
AFTER SEVEN MONTHS IN THE PROGRAM

Music for Peace in Istanbul hit its low point in November 2013. Just a couple of months earlier, this slow-growing after-school orchestra program had been promised municipal funding for the first time. The program had made plans to expand into four local elementary schools, with new faculty, new instruments, and many more children. But suddenly, within a few weeks of the funding date, the municipality changed its collective mind for some never-explained reason and withdrew support.

Music for Peace had begun in 2005 as a voice of peace activism, and its first incarnation was as a youth accordion ensemble. It had always been funded out of the personal savings of its founders, Mehmet Baki, a retired architect, and his wife Yeliz Baki, who has a doctorate in French literature. Mehmet and Yeliz had poured their own resources into growing the program gradually and intuitively, with close attention to the students' needs. Mehmet designed and renovated a graceful three-row-house compound in Istanbul's Edirnekapi neighborhood to serve as the núcleo. In 2011, Maestro Abreu paid a visit. The local government's agreement to support the program's expansion was the breakthrough moment they had been waiting for; it would dramatically increase their impact on the local community. The in-school programs would awaken musical possibility in many children's lives and would multiply the number of students eager to join the orchestras that Music for Peace was developing at the núcleo. So when the government about-face occurred, and the funding was pulled, Mehmet and Yeliz were devastated. The entire faculty had to be fired, and there were no operating funds to continue.

When we arrived some months later, we heard about this crisis from everyone we spoke to. We were always offered one particular image, an image so maudlin that it was credible only because every single person, from students and administrators to Aysel Kızıltan and Serap Gökdeniz, two pink-uniformed ladies who cook and clean and serve as everyone's surrogate mothers, remembered it exactly the same way. "The worst moment," they all said, "was when the government people were forcibly pulling instruments from the hands of the weeping children."

Shortly after this traumatic day, the teenagers of the program's more advanced orchestra met together at the music center. Mehmet and Yeliz spoke to them about the economic realities that were forcing the end of the program, and the students expressed their shock and sadness. Yeliz recalls that fairly quickly, however, the conversation turned. "They said, 'Wait a minute, this is *our* orchestra.' They realized they could do it themselves; they could teach one another." The students decided that if Mehmet and Yeliz would let them use the building, they would continue. They would find new instruments somehow, and they would become a great orchestra by teaching and learning from one another.

The Edirnekapi district is filled with economically struggling families of moderately conservative Islamic beliefs; many of them are of Roma (Gypsy) lineage, the most widely discriminated-against ethnicity in Europe. Students walk to the Music for Peace núcleo through narrow, twisting streets next to the fourth-century Constantine Wall; sometimes they slide their hands along the wall as they walk to rehearsal. Next to the núcleo stands the eleventh-century Chora

Church, still in use, with some of the oldest mosaics in Christendom. Here in this ancient setting, a group of teenagers who were raised in an environment of ethnic bigotry toward Roma people, and in a cultural tradition of youth subservience and obedience, were taking charge of their situation and changing it.

Mehmet and Yeliz recall that from the moment the older students made this decision, a different energy infused their work. They spent more time at the music center than they had before. Their sectional work became more rigorous. Some students switched instruments because the orchestra was weak in one area or another; they told Yeliz it was fun to switch. They had adopted the same spirit, even the same determined words, that had inspired the original El Sistema orchestra back in that Caracas parking garage. Across time and geography, in utterly different cultural contexts, a similar moment of commitment changed everything.

The program had recently found a lead teacher/conductor in the person of Samuel Matus, a twenty-two-year-old cellist from Guatemala. Sammy, who looks younger than some of his students, began his musical studies during his teens by way of YouTube, that peculiarly peer learning-friendly modern phenomenon. He then entered the El Sistema program in Guatemala and became a strong cellist and dedicated teaching artist. Sammy's arrival at Music for Peace typifies the spontaneous and sometimes roundabout way in which the international Sistema movement seems to work. He moved from Guatemala City to Zurich to study and teach in Superar Suisse, the Sistema-inspired program there; on a visit to teach in the Istanbul program, however, he encountered sudden visa difficulties and couldn't return to Zurich. So he stayed on in Istanbul, learned Turkish, and worked with Music for Peace, as well as continuing his cello and conductor studies at a Turkish conservatory. Sammy was central in raising the musical standards and skills, as well as the spirits, of the Music for Peace orchestra. He helped to sustain their commitment during this transitional time by encouraging them to teach one another whenever they could.

It was easy to see that they were following his advice. Every-where we turned, students were helping other students. In the all-purpose room where endless glasses of tea and a hot lunch (for many, the only hot meal of the day) were served to students, they would gather in groups, pull out sheet music, and talk through difficult sections. They practiced together in the courtyard, in the hallway, in any corner they could find. We saw two violinists doing an impromptu performance for the program dog, Miço, an aged golden retriever who did not seem to mind when, in the middle of the performance, the older girl paused to correct the younger one.

Music for Peace now has three orchestras—the beginning string "Vivaldi," the intermediate "Mozart," and the advanced "Beethoven." They are integrated through a mentoring system that speeds the learning of all three orchestras. The Beethoven players teach the Mozart and Vivaldi players; Beethoven players from each instrumen-tal section regularly work with Mozart members of that section on a particular piece of challenging repertoire that eventually the two orchestras will play together. The mentors prepare the learners by having them play scales that ground the piece and then practicing the melodies and drilling the harder sections. The less advanced Mozart kids may not be able to play every part of the piece, but they catch more and more of it each time they work on it side-by-side with the slightly older musicians who can play it a little better.

We watched the Mozart and Beethoven orchestras play together in a side-by-side rehearsal of *Danzón No. 2* by Arturo Márquez, a signature piece of the Simón Bolívar Orchestra of Venezuela and a favorite of Sistema orchestras worldwide. Seated in the combined orchestra, Nihan, a teenaged violist, was surrounded by seven Mozart mentees. Throughout the rehearsal, as she performed her part and responded to the conductor, she also managed to watch her seven charges. During every break in the rehearsal process, even if it was just a few seconds, she connected with them, emphasizing an accent with one, correcting an error with another, reminding a third about instrument position. On the longer breaks, while conductor Sammy

Matus worked with specific sections on problem areas, Nihan worked with the two learners who were struggling the hardest. She encouraged them to laugh a little at how hard it was for them.

It was virtuosic teaching. Nihan was demonstrating a sophisticated capacity of attention, pedagogical awareness and guidance, and was able to combine performing well with teaching well. There were many habits of mind and heart at work here: empathy (sustaining awareness of what each of her mentees was struggling with); responsibility (keeping each one encouraged and enjoying the rehearsal); and creative problem-solving (managing the improvement of each mentee even as she managed her own part).

When we spoke with her after the rehearsal, she seemed surprised at our compliments. "I don't think of it as teaching," she said. "It is just what we do; it's nothing special. Teaching is something wonderful. I dream of being a teacher someday."

"What do you call what you were doing with those children?" we asked.

She thought for a few moments, and finally said, "I call it being helpful."

BUILDING THE HABIT OF INTERDEPENDENCE

In Venezuela, students are told from their earliest years: "You are not expected to be a teacher, but you are expected to help your friends." When the goal is clear and the learning environment is healthy, that is how peer instruction feels to those involved—no big deal, just helping. And everyone, the helper no less than the helped, gets better. This is the habit of mind and heart of interdependence. The goal is the ever-increasing excellence of the orchestra, and it can only be achieved through everyone's "helpfulness."

Peer-to-peer learning is one of the consistent features of Sistema-inspired work around the world. The practice was born in El Sistema's earliest days, not as a pedagogical ideal but as a necessity.

Among the first young musicians recruited by Abreu in 1975 to join a pickup ensemble "that will someday be a great orchestra," some recruits were conservatory-trained and some were not. They had limited access to strong teachers and instructional support materials. They had Abreu's inspirational leadership, of course, but during the many times he was unavailable, all they had was one another. They knew that the only way they could improve quickly was to teach each other what they knew—fast.

Thus the philosophical tenet was born in practice, as a creative solution to a substantial problem. In the words of David Ascanio, one of the orchestra's founding members: "If you know how to play four notes, it is your responsibility to teach your friend who only knows three. And in teaching your friend, you become better prepared to learn a fifth note."

To engage well in peer-to-peer learning, the key habit of mind and heart a child must internalize is more than simple helpfulness; it is empathy. In Chapter 5, we explored the ways that ensemble work cultivates this crucial habit. Peer learning develops and expands it even further. Primatologist Frans de Waal, who sees humans to be as innately empathetic as they are aggressive, proposes that empathy has three layers: "emotional contagion," in which people experience the rush of emotion flowing through a group; "feeling for others," the automatic experiencing of someone else's experience of a particular situation; and "targeted helping," a creative response to tailor a specific helping tool or effort to the needs of the other. Sistema practices develop all three levels of empathy consistently and profoundly over time.

How is this habit of the heart developed in El Sistema work? We have seen both formal and informal approaches. Many programs create explicit partnership pairs of more skilled and less skilled players for a particular period of time. In Rio de Janeiro, for example, in the Sistema-inspired program Ação Social pela Música, we heard an orchestra of young kids play a rendition of "Love Me Tender" (Sistema repertoire can go many places) with such nuance that when we spoke with their conductor, Julio Camargo, we marveled about their skill. Julio attributed it to peer learning. "That's our B orchestra, and they had a lot of trouble with that piece at first—they couldn't play it at all. So we had a joint rehearsal with our A orchestra, and we put each A kid next to a B kid as a stand mate. They played it and played it, the A's always helping the B's, sometimes by talking but often by just being there and playing it well, offering an example to model. So, quickly the B's became able to play it fine by themselves." Julio added that peer learning is a main feature of sectional rehearsals as well. "Sometimes, I will teach one kid in a section something, and then ask the kid to be a section leader that day and teach the others what I just taught her."

In Liverpool, at the Sistema-inspired program In Harmony, we watched a teacher, Laura McKinlay, ask her violin students to play a particularly challenging musical phrase one by one. A shy girl played it and then made a face.

"How d'ye think it sounded?" Laura asked her.

"Kind of . . . wonky," the girl answered.

Instead of seizing the pedagogical moment herself, Laura asked the other students, "What d'ye think might help our friend Caitlin?"

They offered suggestions, some helpful, some less so. Then one boy said, "Use more of your bow maybe?" The others agreed: "Yes! Use more bow!" Which the girl did, and the phrase sounded better.

Very frequently, more experienced players are asked to demonstrate a phrase or explain a musical concept to less experienced players. Some programs also seed the daily musical activity with peer instruction practice—i.e., "make sure you and your stand mate are both on top of this passage," or "look around and make sure everyone in your area has got this right." Or "raise your hand if you are still not confident about what we are working on, and someone who has learned it will come and work with you."

The distinguished El Sistema violinist Susan Siman, who now lives in the United States and travels internationally as a master teacher and consultant, once told us, "The whole secret to Sistema is seating. You seat the right student who plays better next to the student who doesn't play so well, and most of your problems are solved." Susan was oversimplifying for effect, but this Sistema practice—which in conventional youth orchestras might be considered a dubious idea— can be an efficient solution to multiple challenges.

In strong Sistema programs, teachers sometimes model peer-to-peer instruction. Students see their teachers working together to solve a problem, discussing and planning and making suggestions to one another. It can be as simple as a teacher asking a fellow teacher, "Do you have another way of explaining this?" or handing over the reins for a moment: "Why don't you take over here? You are so good at this." Again and again, students observe their teachers being open to the suggestions of their colleagues.

In a learning environment that encourages peer teaching, students are quick to internalize and practice it on their own. Julio Camargo, the teacher in Rio de Janeiro, told us that his students are always putting together impromptu chamber ensembles and finding things to play, without even telling him. "Like the other day, I was surprised to find four kids playing a quartet version of Pachelbel's Canon—they had taught themselves. I'd never heard them play that before."

At Soundscapes, in Newport News, Virginia, almost-beginner students recently started forming small "bands" of four or five players to rehearse (sometimes on weekends) and perform their own pieces. Although their playing is at a basic level, their small-group interpretation of "Hot Cross Buns" is entirely their own, and was a hit with their peers. We watched the Cool Tunes (naming a group is a big deal) rehearse, and the struggling viola and trumpet players received patient help from their usually impatient band mates. Joe Hamm, a Soundscapes teacher, encourages interdependence among his students by creating small bands that rehearse and audition for the right to perform for all the students in the program. Joe said that he's noticed students usually adopt a different set of rules and attitudes when they are responsible for their own performance. Watching one of the groups

LEADING FROM EVERY CHAIR

Citizen artists serve as leaders even when not in top leadership jobs—meet Joe Hamm, as one example among many. While working as a percussion teacher at Soundscapes in Newport News, Virginia, he has taken on an initiative to connect his colleagues across the country—peer teaching and learning on a national level.

A drummer since the age of fourteen, when he and some friends formed a punk band and made a recording, he studied jazz in college, played and recorded with a few bands, and has led a busy professional life as a local performer. When Soundscapes was launched, he was hired as a percussion instructor, and he learned to teach Sistema-style by observing and talking with peers. As he continued to learn and experiment, he came to love the kids and their families, and grew excited about their progress.

Joe and his boss, Soundscapes director Rey Ramirez, decided to make an advocacy film for the program. Joe produced, directed, wrote, shot, and edited the film—none of which he had ever done before. The Soundscapes film was one of the first advocacy films of any U.S. pro-

rehearse, he pointed out five or six ways in which students were behaving more interdependently than they do in regular rehearsals.

MENTORING

In the Sistema learning environment, peer learning shades seamlessly into mentor teaching, which involves older and more skilled young people providing consistent guidance for younger and less skilled children. It's impossible to imagine Sistema without mentoring; every child growing up within a Sistema program is mentored frequently and informally many times along the way, and every older, more advanced player considers mentoring younger students an integral part of musical development.

gram, and Joe is especially proud that he created it in such a way that other Sistema-inspired programs could use it for their own advocacy purposes as well.

Making the film led Joe to understand that the Sistema field needed a better understanding of the facts about their movement. "When I was making the film about Soundscapes," he said, "I wanted to cite the number of Sistema programs in the U.S., and I couldn't find a credible number or source. I figured it would be easy to do a census."

It wasn't. He gathered information, followed leads, searched online, called people, sent out surveys, figured out data collection software. People responded slowly and sporadically, but he kept pushing for several years. By early 2015 he was able to report the first reliable facts on the U.S. movement.

Meanwhile, Joe has continued to grow as a Sistema teacher, creating new performance opportunities and experimenting with ways to help his students compose because he finds it boosts their engagement. He meets with city officials, funders, and architects to discuss how his ideas can invigorate his home city of Norfolk and its artistic life—the citizen artist as citizen entrepreneur.

One kind of mentoring is simply modeling, setting an example. In Lambeth, for example, Gerry Sterling spoke of the pivotal moment when the youngest children in the program first heard the older children's orchestra play. "We sat the little ones down in front of our Holst Orchestra, and the orchestra played—and the expressions on those children's faces were incredible. They were seeing who they could become, what they could be capable of."

Núcleos are fueled by more active kinds of mentoring as well. Among our most indelible images of how this looks and feels in action is a Friday morning orchestra rehearsal at the Lomas del Paraiso program in Guadalajara, Mexico. On a large open-air platform adjacent to a town plaza, the seventy children of this núcleo's advanced orchestra were rehearsing. A blue canopy shaded the platform, but the children were surrounded by the bright morning light and warm breeze; on the plaza, some of their parents stood listening as their siblings ran and played.

What was most striking about this ensemble was its wide age range. There were kids from seven to seventeen, and they were completely intermingled: little next to big, proficient next to beginner. Anchoring the percussion section was a teenaged boy playing a busy snare drum part while at the same time guiding two small girls on a ride cymbal and an even smaller boy with a triangle. He managed to dispatch his snare duties expertly while at the same time nodding cues to the cymbal and triangle players. Elsewhere, an older flutist coached a younger one in fingerings; a young cellist showed a younger one how to bow a phrase. It's not an exaggeration to say that in that orchestra that morning, nearly every music stand was a mentoring site.

Just as peer learning shades into mentoring in Sistema programs, mentoring shades easily into teaching. Luis-Felipe, the young violinist-teacher in Campos, Brazil, said to us, "I soon got the idea here that everything I was learning, I should give to others. So right away I started to work informally as a mentor for my younger friends, and then, when I was sixteen, the director asked me if I would teach a violin class. I didn't feel ready to be a teacher, but it's never right to wait until one is ready, because that time never really comes. You just have to begin. You will find your way."

At twenty-one, Luis-Felipe has been teaching so long that now some of his students are teachers. "The second generation, already!" he said with the pride of a parent bragging about his adult children.

Jony William, the program director, spoke to us about how many of his strongest students go away to college or conservatory, but often come back to be part-time or full-time teachers in the program. "They keep this idea of sharing their knowledge. It stays with them all their lives. So even if they follow other professions, they often come here and teach."

Obadias Cunha, the curriculum director at NEOJIBA in Brazil, said to us, "All the teachers in our núcleos—they are the members of the Youth Orchestra of Bahia, our most advanced orchestra. Being a teacher is simply part of being in the orchestra. They are giving back to the kids who will be coming to the orchestra in the future."

Within this atmosphere, students improve fast. Josbel Pulce, the director of La Rinconada, one of the largest núcleos in Caracas, told us: "Our students improve quickly because they do not waste any time with mistakes. We correct them immediately. A teacher corrects them, or a friend corrects them. In other ways of teaching, a child gets a lesson, then makes the same mistakes for a week before it is corrected, and by then it has settled in."

EL SISTEMA JAPAN: "NO FIXED TEACHERS OR LEARNERS"

When the practice of peer and mentor learning permeates a program, students come to understand and live by a principle as radical as it is simple: everyone is a teacher, and everyone is a learner. A particularly notable example of a program that lives by this maxim is El Sistema Japan, which prioritizes peer learning in the context of an educational culture that does not traditionally emphasize interdependence. The principal conductor of this program, Yohei Asaoka, told us, "I say to them all: teach one another, just as I teach you. They love it; it's fun for them."

Program founder Yutaka Kikugawa and his colleagues consider peer learning so important that it has been at the center of the program's evaluation system since its inception in 2012. The results are already striking. The program's 2013 Evaluation Report states, "The new teaching system, in which beginners and experienced players are mixed together, enables children to have more opportunities to discuss with peers and friends. Moreover, children do not only give/take advice, but also practice difficult parts together. What is unique about the project is that an elder member with less musical experience naturally seeks assistance from a younger but more experienced player."

El Sistema Japan is unusual in that it includes not only young people but also adults of all ages who have never studied before but want to participate in an orchestra. "The peer teaching and learning regardless of age is a unique feature of this project," noted the evaluation report. "Ninety-four percent of participants have been taught by friends/peers. . . . To teach and to be taught are not mutually exclusive. . . . There are no fixed teachers or learners, and everyone can learn from others."

In a Sistema learning environment, children and young people learn to flexibly inhabit both roles, in relation to each other and even to the adults in their world. The feeling of having something valuable to teach others changes a child's sense of self; when this recurs over years, it can change that sense of self-worth for a lifetime. As Venezuelan master teacher Francisco Díaz has said: "Each student being a teacher is what fuels the system."

CHAPTER 7

Music as Passion and Expressivity

I had no room now for this fear, or any other fear,
because I was filled to the brim with music. And even when it was not
literally (audibly) music, there was the music of my muscle-orchestra
playing—"the silent music of the body." . . . The musicality of my
own motion, I myself became the music—you are the music while
the music lasts. . . . A creature of muscle, motion and music, all
inseparable and in unison with each other.
—OLIVER SACKS, PSYCHOLOGIST AND AUTHOR

In February 2014, Mexico was overrun by pirates. Somehow this managed to escape the attention of the major news media, but anyone making a tour of Mexican Sistema programs at that time couldn't have missed it. Rousing and even thunderous, if imperfect, renditions of the movie score for *Pirates of the Caribbean* turned up in Sistema programs from Guadalajara to Léon to Mexico City. Not many of the young musicians we spoke to had seen the movies; it was the music itself that had won their hearts. They played it with the urgency of the movies' dramatic storytelling—of adventure and excitement and lives at stake. "They have a lot of passion about music," said the director of the Lomas del Paraiso Sistema program in Guadalajara.

The director's name is José Antonio Herrera, but to everyone in the program, he is Pepetoño—a moniker that would seem to signify a paterfamilias, but he's far too young for that. Watching him conduct the orchestra in *Pirates of the Caribbean* on the sunlit open-air plaza that is the program's orchestra rehearsal space, we decided it's his kinetic focus, along with his beard and black-rimmed glasses, that has earned him the name. He was punctuating the accents with leaps and crouches, calling out dynamic changes, sparking the young players with the wild high spirits of the music.

Pepetoño and his wife, Verónica Soltero-Alatorre, who also teaches in the program, talked with us during a rehearsal break, while the kids ran around the plaza or strolled, playing their instruments. We asked Pepetoño where he studied conducting. "I didn't study conducting," he said. "I studied Gregorian chant in Mainz, Germany." When he returned to Mexico, it was during the recession and jobs in music were impossible to find, so he worked to become an industrial engineer. "But after several years of that, I said to myself, 'I'm a liar. I'm not being true to who I really am—which is a musician.'"

Pepetoño's epiphany came just at the time that a Sistema program was being launched in the Guadalajara barrio of Lomas del Paraiso. Pepetoño and Verónica were both hired, along with four other teachers. "It was hard at the beginning. This was something so different for these kids, and they learned slowly . . . it was just 'Twinkle Twinkle' for a long time. But now, five years later! They are"—he gestured toward the plaza—"well, you see what they are."

How, we asked him, did they get so good, so fast? "With passion," he answered. "I can't think of any other word for it. It's passion."

It's clear that passion drives the Lomas del Paraiso Sistema program—first and foremost, a passion to enter the expressive heart of the music and to communicate it through playing. Pepetoño models and evokes this in his students every time he conducts them. During their rehearsal, as they transitioned from their fiery *Pirates* rendition to a Baroque minuet, then an orchestral arrangement of a Mexican folk song, and finally a movement of a Mozart symphony, we heard them find, with each piece, the emotive through-line of the music, a feat particularly remarkable considering that at many of the music stands, sixteen-year-olds were sitting next to nine-year-olds. It wasn't that there was anything astonishing about their musical interpretations; it was just that all the kids seemed to have complete certainty as to what they were about: they were about feeling, and they cared about communicating the music.

"They learn to express themselves!" said one of the mothers, who was sitting in the sun and listening to the rehearsal. "I never knew they had so many feelings inside them."

It's also clear that at Lomas del Paraiso, passion propels more than musical communication; it drives everything. It has to. The program is short on funding, so it depends crucially on the personal devotion of the six young teachers and on plenty of volunteer help from dedicated parents. The núcleo itself, which is down the street from the open plaza where the full orchestra rehearses, is a former market; the rehearsal rooms are tiny, with white cement walls. There's little ventilation, so the kids have to rehearse in their sectionals with the doors open—which takes a serious level of concentration. The door of the room for the percussion sectional, of course, has to stay closed, so a group of parents raised funds for a ceiling fan.

The Lomas del Paraiso program is funded by the national Mexican Sistema organization, Sistema Nacional de Fomento Musical (National System of Musical Development). SNFM supports over 10,000 children across the country in ensembles including orchestras, bands, choruses, and a national youth orchestra, the Carlos Chávez Youth Orchestra of Mexico. Its funds come from the federal government's cultural budget. According to Alejandra Galindo, an SNFM administrator, the mission of SNFM is often grander than its finances. "SNFM is just a small part of our national cultural commitment," she told us. "The government supports many other projects in addition to us. So we often don't have sufficient resources." Stretched thin across so many núcleos, SNFM's budget is perennially strapped, and programs need to look for supplemental funding anywhere they can find it.

The Lomas del Paraiso program found it at the Guadalajara

Zoo. By what Pepetoño calls "cosmic coincidence," the zoo's chairman of the board happened to be in Japan when the Simón Bolívar Orchestra, with Dudamel conducting, was on tour there. The zoo magnate heard them play; "his mind was blown," and he came home and started looking for Sistema programs to support. When he found a program right in his own city, he offered immediate financial help.

Even with this welcome addition, the núcleo struggles. They don't have enough space for the 80 kids they currently have ("Here is my classroom!" Verónica told us, standing in a corner of the plaza), so they are constantly having to turn children away. Veronica said that there are days when as many as fifteen people come knocking at the program's door. "The demand is huge, and we have no more space, no more instruments. But we can dream . . . maybe three thousand kids one day? Maybe five thousand?"

Pepetoño and Verónica are available by cell phone to students and parents twenty-four hours a day, and they consider themselves part of every student's family. When any of the families has an emergency, they go to help, and bring along their two-year-old son, Mathias. It is a long way from the future that José Antonio Herrera imagined for himself when he was studying medieval plainsong in Germany.

Still: "This is the best job in the world," said Pepetoño. "Such an amazing opportunity for me—it was like a message from the universe. That I can be a musician, and that I can help kids have better lives through music."

A hundred and fifty miles away, in the industrial city of León, Óscar Argumedo similarly lives and breathes the work of the Sistema program Imagina. This program, like the one in Guadalajara, is located in a barrio with rutted dirt streets, empty shacks, and abandoned storefronts. In a shaded courtyard at the center of the núcleo, we were delighted to reencounter *Pirates of the Caribbean*. When the young musicians, conducted by Óscar, transitioned from *Pirates* to the "Ode to Joy" (with the chorus singing in German first, English next, and finally Spanish), there was no discernible shift in the fervor of their music-making. Óscar, like Pepetoño, physically conveyed the emotional contours of the music. The young musicians moved with him, dancing in their seats.

Óscar is a double bass player in the Guanajuanto professional orchestra, and he is also the coordinator of the statewide Sistema Bajio; he spends every other moment at the several Sistema programs in León. "The need is so great," he said. "Once I found myself in this work, I have never been able to stop." In the evening, driving us back to our hotel through the twisting streets, Óscar pointed out a park we were passing. "That is where the bad guys hang out and shoot people." After a pause he added, "Their kids are playing violins and cellos in my program."

For the Imagina program, extra financial support comes from a private foundation founded and headed by Señora Luz de Lourdes Arena de Orozco, the wife of a wealthy retired owner of a plastics factory in León. Lourdes, a frail, petite lady, was with us listening to *Pirates* and "Ode to Joy," and she was eager to speak with us about her mission. "My husband and I have eight children and thirty-three grandchildren," she said. "They have had so much in their lives that many children don't have. When I look at the children of León, I have always thought, 'I want an opportunity to help them live life in a different way.'"

She has that opportunity in the Imagina foundation, which also supports a health center with doctors and psychologists, a theater and ballet center, and two libraries. For the music program, she works closely with SNFM, the federal agency that funds Sistema Mexico, to provide whatever the agency cannot. "There is nothing more important than the children's orchestra," she said. "Playing music is a whole life. The kids can find passion right there in the orchestra. They don't need to go into the streets with guns."

On the other side of León, children at the Vicente Fox núcleo (named for a former Mexican president) greeted us with *Pirates of the Caribbean*. Then Armando Torres-Chibrás, who was serving as our tour guide, was asked to conduct the orchestra, and the young musicians delivered a short Baroque piece under his direction—with brio, although with more elegance than they had devoted to the pirates. *"Muy apasionado,"* said Armando, as he handed back the baton.

A VIRTUOSITY OF COMMUNICATION

"Passion" may be the word we have heard the most times, in the most number of languages, in our encounters with Sistema programs across the world (though the words "together" and "more" run a close second and third). It is used as the definitive explanation for what makes a great performance, a great núcleo director, a great teacher, a great funder, a great volunteer, and a great audience. It's also used to account for the children's connection to the music they are playing, the reason they learn to play so well so quickly, and the nature of their musical connections to one another, to their audiences, to their communities. In Sistema programs, music is never approached as primarily technical; at every level of proficiency, it is always approached first and foremost as something that stimulates, emanates from, and expresses feeling. We have come to describe the primacy of emotion in El Sistema with the phrase "passion provokes precision," meaning that the players' emotional investment in the music actually motivates them to play it as well as possible, hungry to improve their technique so their performance will more articulately convey what they feel. It's possible that the inverse priority, "precision prepares for passion"—the implicit bedrock of much traditional music instruction—doesn't feed motivation in quite the same way.

The belief that passion provokes precision has always been central in the Venezuelan Sistema. Marshall Marcus thinks of this as one of El Sistema's most important contributions. "The Venezuelans have given the world a whole new meaning for the word 'virtuosity,'" he has said. "What they most value is a virtuosity of *communication*. They certainly don't neglect technical virtuosity. But it is expressive virtuosity they most value. It's all about the kinds of feeling that can be expressed and communicated through music."

In an artistic medium where technical virtuosity tends to be the ultimate coin of the realm, it is this expressive virtuosity that first drew the musical world's attention to El Sistema. Long before anyone outside Latin America knew what a núcleo was, audiences knew that when they listened to the youth orchestras of Venezuela, they felt enlivened and moved in a way they rarely felt with other top world orchestras. They felt the currents of deep feeling that great music evokes when played by musicians committed to communication. Hence the cheering, foot-stomping, and jacket-waving that erupts across the world when these orchestras perform.

EXPRESSIVITY AND SOCIAL DEVELOPMENT

Why is expressivity such an essential part of El Sistema? In Venezuela, the ideals of musical affect and social development are so linked that it's impossible to think of them separately. "Music is tremendously important in the awakening of children's feelings and sensibilities," Abreu has said, and he ended that sentence by adding "—and in the training of young people to teach others." For him, the ideas of musical feeling and social empowerment are inseparable. Why? What is the connection between musical passion and social mission?

To our knowledge, there is no research that explicitly addresses this question. Our observations lead us to believe that playing great music can be a transformative exercise in the life of feeling, expanding the capacity to feel deeply and express feelings symbolically through the medium of art. Aesthetic philosophers have been exploring this dimension of human experience for centuries, and they often describe music as uniquely influential because it is the only art that is pure symbol, with no semantic meaning at all. The question inevitably arises: what, after all, does music mean?

Twentieth-century philosopher Suzanne Langer proposed an

answer to this question that makes intuitive as well as intellectual sense. Musical art is symbolic of "the dynamic structures of human feeling," she wrote. The symbols of music (pitches and melodies, rhythms, harmonic structures) represent not feelings per se, but the forms of feeling—the tensions, dynamics, and contrasts that permeate our emotional existence but cannot be adequately captured by words or images. "An artist expresses feeling," she wrote, "but not in the way a politician blows off steam or a baby laughs and cries. . . . What he expresses is not his own actual feelings, but what he knows about human feeling."[22]

This theory illuminates one of music's greatest mysteries, the question of why we love listening to sad music and why it doesn't make us sad. "It's so moving," we say. Music suggests and evokes feelings rather than causing them; we are moved to make a connection, rather than just receive a feeling. "Make a connection"—notice that the idiom is active, not passive; we meet the music halfway. Great music evokes emotions like love, grief, anger, and delight; we are stirred to feel, not those emotions directly, but an internal resonance, a kind of aesthetic quickening around them. "It gives me goose bumps," we say. Call it ecstasy, awe, euphoria; we are moved in a way different from simply feeling an emotion. To listen to great music is to experience our human emotions transmuted into the forms of beauty.

Think of the main theme of Tchaikovsky's *Romeo and Juliet* Overture, surely one of the most exquisite melodies ever created. It's as though Tchaikovsky has taken the feeling of nearly unbearable yearning and distilled it into musical form. When we hear it, it doesn't cause us to begin to yearn; rather, it presents us with the sheer essence of yearning (the F sharp that leans toward the G at the beginning, the A flat that lingers above G at the end), and those melodic gestures, transforming emotion into beauty, awaken in us a sense of visceral recognition and something akin to rapture.

That is the power of the aesthetic experience: the symbolic nature of the medium creates just enough distance from the direct experience of our feelings that we are able to contemplate, recognize, and cherish the strong emotions of human life without being at the mercy of them.

When children play or sing music together in an ensemble of friends, they are creating that symbolic and feelingful richness together; they are engaged in turning feeling into beauty through an endeavor that involves continuous connection with others. In El Sistema, children and young people have a daily opportunity to access that place of shared connection to resonant symbols and their affective meanings. They grow up within it, and it nourishes the growth of their habits of mind and heart, day after day, month after month, year after year. When they play *Romeo and Juliet* together, it doesn't make them sad; it gives them a way to share the thrill of expressing sadness through beauty—together. Their lives are often full of sadness; Sistema enables them to own beauty too. In the words of Bennett Reimer, another great twentieth-century aesthetic philosopher: "Music civilizes us, humanizes us, and harmonizes us with our world."[23]

Here, we believe, lies the answer to our question, "What's the connection between musical expressivity and social development?" We've taken a bit of a detour to get there, but the answer resonates with everything we've seen and heard in our research, as well as with our experience as music educators. To summarize: When a person actively engages with a musical masterpiece, she or he gains access to a new kind of participation in human feeling. When people co-create the world of a masterpiece with others, they begin to practice communicative complexity together. When *young* people co-create the world of a masterpiece, its emotional depth becomes a part of how they learn to experience life. And when young people do this *consistently*, their capacity for empathic connection widens, and together they can begin to co-create a new world for themselves.

For Sistema programs around the world, El Sistema Venezuela serves as a beacon and model for music as emotional communication. Ian Burton, director of the In Harmony Nottingham program, said of his experience in Venezuela, "They were never a bit bothered about having nine oboes in an orchestra, or things like that . . . but the playing is so full of feeling and understanding. I heard the *New World* Symphony finale in one of the núcleos—and there were police sirens going on outside—and it was just stunning! It wasn't completely in tune, maybe, but in terms of understanding what this music was about, the kids totally got it."

Ian spoke of how different this is from European orchestral conventions. "The British thing tends to be—'Okay, we'll learn the notes first. Then we'll add the expression later.' But actually, you know, it's the other way around. You can refine the technical stuff later. But you can't always go back later and get that expressive thing."

In Milan, we watched conductor Alessandro Cadario work on "that expressive thing" with the Sistema Lombardy chorus singing "O Fortuna!" from Carl Orff's *Carmina Burana*—a favorite among Sistema programs, and indeed all kinds of youth ensemble programs, because of its dark, chest-thumping drama, the mystifying Latin text, and the visceral clout of its sound. "Think of yourselves as part of a huge rock band, with rock-issimo energy!" he told them. "You have been singing like 'Oh, well, I'm in a chorus; it's boring.' We need you on the edge of your seats! With passion!"

Carlo Taffuri, conductor of the Pasquinelli Youth Orchestra of Lombardy, told us that he learned about the importance of expressivity from Sistema master violinist Susan Siman. "I first saw her in France," said Carlo, "where she was guest-conducting an orchestra of two hundred kids and making it look easy. I felt I had to learn what she knew. So I went to Miami, where she now works, and I spent a month just observing her. It opened my mind!"

He came back to Milan and helped to form the Sistema orchestra there. "I learned from her that this work is about passion, energy, and connection. That the first and most important goal is '*insieme*' (together). And that the orchestras can sound truly great, and that we must strive for that too."

In Korea, Eunsuk Chae, the music director of the Orchestra of Dreams Núcleo in Bucheon, described the program's emphasis on the development of musical feeling. "I always ask the kids how they feel about a piece they are playing. If they are young, they tend to say 'sad' about a slow piece and 'happy' about a fast one. But as they get older, they acquire more subtlety. They can find the joy inside a slow-paced piece and the sorrow in a fast one. They really live for these feelings. I had one student tell me he was going to memorize a piece right away, so that reading notes wouldn't get in the way of his feeling the music."

In the Orquestrando a Vida program in Campos, Brazil, the watchword among all the teachers is "Music first, then technique." Jony William spoke of how he sees this outlook as transformative not only for the kids but for their audiences in the community. "We're living in an era when classical music is performed in a cold manner, and audiences are shrinking and becoming indifferent. So the excitement of these kids, the vibrancy they bring—it has become a new experience for the audience, because they feel the aliveness."

In Barquisimeto, Venezuela, we heard the top núcleo orchestra, jammed into the cinder-block room where Dudamel first learned to play and conduct, play the first movement of Mahler's First Symphony. We have heard this movement performed many times, with more technical brilliance, by some of the world's most famous orchestras. But there was no question that this performance by Venezuelan teenagers made more emotional sense, and was more moving, than any we had ever heard.

"DOES IT HAVE TO BE CLASSICAL MUSIC?"

We are often asked this question when we talk about El Sistema with friends, interested audiences, and people hoping to create Sistema-inspired programs. In our experience, the answer is twofold. No, it doesn't have to be only classical music. And yes, classical music is integral to the long-term mission.

In El Sistema Venezuela and in programs across the world, students play a wide variety of genres in addition to classical. Folk and traditional songs, pop music, jazz, theater and movie music—all are considered rich and relevant kinds of music. We have heard national anthems and beloved folk songs; we have heard orchestral arrangements of the songs of *The Little Mermaid*, Coldplay, and the Beatles. In addition, the "classical" genre is becoming more widely and variably defined. Most Sistema teachers, students, and audiences would probably weigh in with the belief that if *Pirates of the Caribbean* isn't a fine example of modern classical music, then categorizing doesn't mean much.

In Venezuela, classical music is part of the repertoire for even the youngest children (their ensembles of three- and four-year-olds are often called Baby Mozart or Baby Vivaldi groups), but teachers in a number of other countries told us that they tend to start their beginners with folk or pop tunes, and then move to traditional classical repertoire later. In general, Sistema teachers and leaders choose music that will engage, challenge, and delight their students in multiple ways. Dan Trahey, the artistic director of OrchKids in Baltimore, sums it up: "We need to play music that inspires our community." As the orchestras grow in skill, and audiences grow in familiary, classical music becomes more and more intriguing. There comes a moment in the development of any Sistema program when the overture to *William Tell* is just the ticket; it challenges the students' abilities and quickens their blood, and it brings audiences to their feet. We have never encountered a culture in which Beethoven's "Ode to Joy" does not have an enduring appeal.

In El Sistema Venezuela, the masterworks of the Western canon are used as touchstones for students' musical development: children play Beethoven's Fifth, Vivaldi's "Spring," and other masterworks in simplified arrangements when they are young, and return to these pieces again and again, in increasingly complex forms, throughout their years at the núcleo. The emotional power of these works offers students recurring connections—to music, and to one another through music—that deepen with each revisiting. Conventional wisdom sometimes has it that "modern kids" or "teenagers" or "kids in barrios" have no interest in classical music. But we have seen that with some guidance, students in many different cultures move easily between the challenging fun of "The Theme from *Rocky*" and the deeper emotional currents of Copland's *Appalachian Spring.* Julio Camargo of Ação Social noted that kids move much faster than parents in their receptivity to classical repertoire. "The kids always love the hard stuff best," he said.

Often, programs emphasize the traditional music of their own cultures. "The Venezuelans have led the way in this, as in so much," said NEOJIBA director Ricardo Castro. "They include so many Venezuelan folk songs in Sistema repertoires. So we have to include songs in our own language, our own traditions." In Mexico, Colombia, the Philippines, and elsewhere, Sistema programs often build upon an already strong wind band tradition. "There are thousands of wind bands all around Mexico with old and illustrious traditions," we were told by Armando Torres-Chibrás, who was at one point the national coordinator of wind bands for the Mexican Sistema. "Every region has a distinctive band style. The bandas Norteñas don't sound exactly the same as the bandas from Sinaloa or in Oaxaca." Village bands are often called upon to perform for births, christenings, weddings, funerals, and saints' days.

Pedro Arpide, coordinator of Mexico's Unit of Community Musical Ensembles, told us that the clarinet is the common denominator among Mexican band traditions. "In the countryside, you will often see a symphonic wind band that has a full complement of brasses and maybe five flutes, one oboe—and twenty-two clarinets. The clarinet is the violin of Mexico." He added that SNFM, the federal Sistema program, sometimes commissions composers to write compositions specifically for these ensembles.

In Colombia, the Batuta program has constructed a thorough and extensive pedagogy for beginners around Colombian folk songs arranged for Orff ensembles and choirs. For more advanced ensembles, the organization has assembled repertoires for each of Colombia's many folkloric traditions. Marysabel Tolosa, who works in the music division of the Colombian Ministry of Culture, showed us thick books, each one used in a particular region (North Pacific Coast, South Pacific Coast, Caribbean, Andean, etc.), containing arrangements of traditional songs scored for traditional instruments. "Our folkloric musical traditions are very localized," Marysabel told us. "Sometimes people in one village won't know the music of the next village. So we try to work with all the folkloric traditions."

In the Philippines, we were told that the youth wind band tradition evolved as local military bands were phased out, and that youth wind bands are popular and sometimes highly competitive. Two old-timers told us that the tradition has degenerated in recent years, as bands became too driven by competition and even litigious behavior. Both of these older musicians were excited that Sistema programs were starting with wind ensembles and expanding from there; this will revive the honor of the wind bands, they said, and take them to new heights as full orchestras.

In many countries, Sistema repertoires include orchestral or choral arrangements of pop music. Children in Sweden play arrangements of Coldplay songs; children in New Jersey perform an arrangement of a Bob Marley song, "Three Little Birds," in a "mash-up" with the "Ode to Joy"; we heard an advanced percussion ensemble in Barquisimeto, Venezuela, play a hot jazz arrangement of the Disney song "Under the Sea." John Lennon's "Imagine," with its utterly simple tune and message of compassion, turns up across the globe, often with beginners singing in unison, and with simple hand gestures and body movements that trace the simplicity of the words.

In general, when Sistema educators discuss repertoire, the discussions are usually not about which genres to choose, but about which pieces accelerate what kinds of learning and which pieces stimulate the liveliest interest. The musical challenges need to be calibrated with students' skill levels, but not only that; the world of a piece has to speak to the inner world of the students in some visceral way. In Venezuela, in particular, teachers told us, "For us there is no classical, no pop, no jazz. There is only one thing, good music—music that is right for this group at this time." Gerry Sterling of the London

REMEMBERING THE MARCHING BAND

Regino Victorino, a Filipino man in his fifties who sports a scruffy beard, plaid shorts, and a baseball cap worn backward, may not look the part of the director of the Santolan núcleo (pictured in the photograph on the cover of this book) in the Philippines' Sistema-inspired Ang Misyon program. But he actually fits the part; he is a fine trumpet player and wind band leader and an astute musical thinker and teacher. His núcleo is wedged into a street of dingy shacks, up a steep concrete driveway leading to what was a tin-roofed car repair garage; there is now an open space where the orchestra rehearses and performs. A few shells of wrecked autos sit at the edges. The mothers of some of the students often hang out in a cooking area of pots over open fire pits.

Regino's drying laundry was hanging nearby, and he had to push away some shirts and underwear to show us a large framed photograph on a wall, an aging formal portrait of a marching band in full uniform regalia. He pointed out his childhood self on the paper so yellowed it was now brown, and also the brilliant teacher he remembers fondly. He spoke about the uniforms with the nostalgic longing of an older person recalling a first love; to him and his friends, he said, they meant the world. His dream is to provide some kind of uniforms for his núcleo orchestra members someday, so they can know that feeling of pride and belonging—although with more pressing needs like buying instruments, he knows it will be a while before this dream comes true.

Sistema program In Harmony Lambeth uses the same criterion: "What we try to do is choose *good* music," he said. Peter Garden of the In Harmony Liverpool program observed that his students "love the pop group One Direction and Brahms's First Symphony, the Beatles and *Carmina Burana*."

This lively eclecticism of repertoire gives Sistema students the clear message that good music lives in many genres. In this, it's a reflection of the wide breadth of interest of so many contemporary music lovers, who plumb the nearly limitless supply of music available through the Internet to find delight in many genres and create their own highly particular and wide-ranging musical universes. We live in a time of unprecedented access to musical options; Sistema program teachers and students enjoy and draw upon this wealth.

And yet there is no denying that classical music is essential to the El Sistema tradition, and it's hard to imagine a mature Sistema program entirely without it. This is partly lineage; the original motivation for founding El Sistema was to give young Venezuelan musicians access to playing and performing classical orchestral music. As the Sistema evolved, its strength and popularity derived from the fact that it put orchestral instruments, which were powerful symbols of prestige and high art, into the hands of poor and underserved children, and taught them to play these instruments well. A violin in a child's hands resonated louder than any number of words declaring, "You are as worthy as the wealthy kids."

One critic of El Sistema has alleged that its focus on classical music is a colonialist ploy to make Latin Americans hew to European cultural values. In response, we'll simply cite the words of Armando Torres-Chibrás, a longtime leader in the Mexican Sistema. "This music has been our music for many centuries," he said, "ever since the Franciscan monks arrived in 1522, singing madrigals and motets and teaching them to the Indians. It is *our* music now. It belongs to us just as authentically as it belongs to Europeans, or to the U.S., or Canada."

Armando pointed out that native Mexicans were adept at learning the techniques of plainchant and polyphony; the first European music school in the Americas was founded in Mexico, and the first book containing musical notation ever published in the New World was published in Mexico in 1556. "We were writing music in the style of Palestrina," he added, "before there was even a single European living in North America."

The orchestral ensemble is particularly useful for the purposes of El Sistema, because it is a flexible structure that can expand to accommodate a great many members, perhaps more than any other ensemble tradition. The string section can go as far back, the winds as far wide, as a rehearsal space can accommodate. So the orchestra serves the El Sistema goal of radical inclusion in an ingenious way.

But there's something more about the primacy of classical music within El Sistema—something related to the Sistema emphasis upon music as a medium for interpersonal connection. The Western classical music tradition, as it has developed over many centuries, has produced an especially eloquent musical language. Its highly varied instrumental timbres, its melodic sophistication and harmonic complexity, its structural plasticity, its ability to absorb and manipulate elements of other musical traditions—all these attributes mean that classical music has the capacity to communicate an exceptional range of emotive experience. The demonic exaltation of the "Witches' Sabbath" in Berlioz's *Symphonie Fantastique*, the hush of expectancy at the beginning of Ravel's *Daphnis and Chloe*, the celestial poignancy of a Beethoven slow movement—all this, and infinitely more, classical music can communicate. To be sure, every musical tradition has a range for expressivity. But throughout centuries of continuous development, the Western classical tradition provided composers such a fertile ground for experimentation that it has produced a body of music with an especially rich expressive range.

Arturo Márquez, one of Mexico's most famous living composers, put it this way: "I have a big respect for traditional popular music. But to be able to compose with the classical tools—melodic development, harmonic development, modulation, all the different timbres—it's amazing, it's wonderful. Those tools that you have, when you are composing in the classical tradition, are really big and powerful. They are really from the heart and to the heart. In that way—in that heart-to-heart way—classical music is a really, really big world."

From the heart and to the heart: this is the highest aspiration of every Sistema ensemble endeavor, and the strongest reason for the primacy of classical music in the enterprise of El Sistema. It's important for children to experience the rambunctious fun of pop music and the rhythmic and melodic dynamism of folkloric music. But for the fullest range of human emotional and aesthetic understanding, immersion in the classical canon is essential as well.

PERFORMANCE AND REHEARSAL— A CONTINUUM OF EXPRESSIVITY

Performance holds a special place in El Sistema programs. For one thing, it happens all the time. Every visit to a program by an interested guest, every opening of a new community venue or inauguration of a new public space—all these are performance opportunities. In our travels to núcleos across the world, there was never an instance when our appearance wasn't a cause for performance, whether planned or impromptu. "Let's play the Vivaldi," an intermediate-orchestra conductor would say when we appeared in the midst of a D-scale drill. The kids would get out their music and play the Vivaldi, in whatever state of relative mastery they could muster. Then they would go back to the D scale drill.

We came to understand that in the Sistema environment, going back and forth between performance and rehearsal didn't feel like an interruption; it felt like an organically connected flow. Moving from working on a scale to sharing a piece seemed to involve only a minor shift of focus. The performance was their way of saying "Hello"—it was what they had to give us by way of welcome and by way of identity.

In Venezuela this tradition is deep, stemming from Maestro Abreu's lifelong performance orientation, instilled by his beloved childhood piano teacher, Doralisa de Medina. Recounting the story of those early lessons, the Maestro said, "She used to hold performances because it was her cousin's birthday! Or, because it was spring! Or, because it was Friday!" Señora de Medina taught the children of Barquisimeto for free if they could not pay. She had seven pianos around a covered courtyard, and she created arrangements of major symphonies for seven pianists, with parts tailored to each student's technical capacities. It's an indelible image: José Antonio at the age of nine or ten, engaged with other children in creating the world of a Mozart symphony on seven weather-beaten pianos in a Venezuelan courtyard. The Maestro's life work evolved from that wholehearted ensemble engagement in beautiful music.

The essential feature of this performance tradition is that it creates a fluid continuum between the rehearsal process and the performance event. Performance is not a rare, terrifying mandate to display perfection or risk failure, but a recurring occasion for turning outward to include listeners in the mix of communicative pleasure. As students internalize this relationship between working hard in rehearsal and regularly sharing what they are working on, their fear of putting themselves on the line diminishes.

"Why would I be nervous?" said ten-year-old Ciao, in Campos, Brazil. "It's another chance to play music."

In the newer Sistema programs that have sprung up across the world in recent years, including those in the United States, it's not uncommon to have a performance within the first few months of beginning, and even within the first few weeks. Is the music "good"? Of course not. Is the event successful? Probably, because it introduces the idea that music is a communication, something to be shared with listeners. It celebrates accomplishment, even at a modest level. It asserts that a wider world than the rehearsal room cares about this process. Even very flawed performances are successful in the root sense of the word, which means "to have a follow-through." Through a performance, children often become more invested in making music together than they were before the event.

Another important benefit of performance is that it offers an opportunity to practice the habit of mind of marshaling focus under pressure. This is particularly important for children of poverty; the internalized habit of being able to stay calm and deliver well under pressure is essential for making choices that lead the way out of difficult circumstances.

All this is not to say that there's no difference between performance and rehearsal. In Sistema programs, as everywhere, performance is a heightened form of experience. When a public performance is planned ahead, and worked toward for weeks or months, heartbeats start to quicken. The stakes are raised; the risks and rewards are greater. Which can mean, of course, higher anxiety as well as more excitement.

El Sistema programs aren't exempt from performance anxiety. But the supportive ensemble ethos of El Sistema skews consistently in the direction of performances as positive learning experiences, even when there are mistakes—even when there are big mistakes. When a cellist misses an entrance, or a violist plays a note where the score calls for a rest, or a trumpet player just plain plays the wrong note, the important learning takes place after the concert, when the student wails, "I messed up!" and the teacher or conductor helps the student process the mistake and understand the meaning of success and failure.

"It's not about perfection," teachers will say. "Mistakes don't mean failure. They just happen sometimes. They are not a big deal; you survive the awful moment, and the music goes on. As long as your playing is communicating something, your performance is a success." Over time, the frequency of performance in this relaxed learning context helps to lessen the fear of failure that is so common and debilitating in traditional recitals and children's concerts. As the energy-depleting fear diminishes, new energy is released for fuller investment in performance situations.

It's also true that being part of an ensemble makes performing less stressful. When the performance entity is an ensemble and not an individual, it's easier to experience quickening heartbeats as excitement instead of stage fright. The learning environment of El Sistema can make for a team-spirit kind of fervor around performance events. Often, at the end of a piece, all the string players thrust their bows high in the air, brass and wind players hoist their instruments, and percussionists raise their sticks, in a "We did it!" move that happens everywhere from the Teresa Carreño concert hall in Caracas to per-formances by Maori beginners in Whangarei, New Zealand.

In Bogotá, the Youth Orchestra of Colombia gave a performance that exemplified this spirit. The concert took place in Bogotá's per-forming arts center, a huge modernist building of granite and brick, vaguely pyramidic on the outside and many-chandeliered on the inside. These several varieties of grandeur didn't affect the tone of the performance, which was pure exuberance, from the moment the young players burst onstage in multicolored Keds and started playing before they sat down (they had tuned up backstage) all the way to the samba-style encore, when, still playing, they came dancing down from the stage and into the audience. After the last encore, they didn't disappear into the wings; they stayed onstage and welcomed audience members to come up and chat with them. It was the beginning of the after-party, then and there.

"GROWING WITH EMOTIONS"

The music of Arturo Márquez is loved by orchestras and audiences around the world for its blend of lyricism and rhythmic vitality. Sistema orchestras especially love *Danzón No. 2*, which was inspired by the "danzón" tradition of Cuba and Mexico that fuses European, African, and Latin dance energies. Arturo lives with his wife, Laura Calderón de la Barca, in the picturesque village of Tepoztlán, about two hours south of Mexico City. "A few years ago, I decided I was ready to retire from teaching, and just relax and compose," he explained to us, sitting on the shaded veranda of the beautiful modern house he designed himself, in a neighborhood where the only sounds came from birds, roosters, and a full chorus of barking dogs. "But then Laura and I discovered there were no children's bands or orches-tras or choruses in this town! So, what could we do? A year ago, we decided to make a band here. Not a traditional band: we want to teach kids to read music and play more ambitious music in different genres, classical and popular both."

They began to work with the national Sistema program, and Laura is now the administrative coordinator for the district. Arturo has an official position too, "but I don't take any salary, because I have enough money." They started with a hundred children and thirty instruments, a ratio that seems about average for beginning Sistema programs in developing countries.

Arturo is in his mid-sixties, a gracious and gregarious man whose fluent American English derives from his high school experience in Los Angeles. "When I built this house, I thought I would have all these nice long afternoons to sit in my garden, and compose, and enjoy a cool drink," he told us. "But now we have . . . let's see . . . two children's bands and three children's orchestras, and I am with the children every afternoon, and I am writing arrangements for them all the time. The most exciting part is to hear the little kids play! I guess I'm not retired."

Arturo often composes specifically for Sistema ensembles. "I love doing that kind of multilayered arranging approach, so all the kids can play together," he said. One notable example is "Alas a Malala" (Wings for Malala), a piece he wrote for Sistema chorus and orchestra that honors Malala Yousafzai, a young Pakistani woman who was shot by Taliban gunmen at the age of fifteen for attempting to go to school, and went on to become the youngest-ever Nobel Peace Prize laureate for her activism on behalf of women's right to education.

"My daughter suggested the idea," Arturo told us, "and she wrote the text for it. There is a Mexican dance, you know, called the cumbia—you dance it with your hands like wings. So it all came together; I wrote a 'cumbia profana' for Malala, wishing her wings."

"Alas a Malala" was first performed in December 2013 by tremendous choral and orchestral ensembles of children from Sistema programs across Mexico. The piece epitomizes the Sistema spirit of passionate music-making, with a theme that connects children to a global message of equal education rights for girls. On the YouTube video of the Mexican Sistema orchestra performing the piece, there is a cameo introduction by Malala herself, who says, "*Gracias* to my friends! I'm really happy for your hope, your support, and your encouragement . . . it makes me really hopeful that we are going to make a great change in the world."

We asked Arturo why, at this late stage in a hugely successful career as a composer, conductor, and professor, he has become so devoted to the work of El Sistema. "Mexican society is very hurt, very ill," he answered. "There is so much sadness here, especially the last twenty or thirty years, and that's what children are growing up with. So—just imagine. When you give children three or four hours every day with music, they learn a different sense of society. They are growing with emotions, with being together."

Laura added, "We call our program Growing with Music. The children are growing in every way, socially and emotionally. It changes them. It gives them new kinds of happiness."

New kinds of happiness: there is no better description of the way El Sistema ensembles communicate musically with one another and with their audiences, families, and communities. In choosing to strive for a virtuosity of expressivity rather than merely of technique, El Sistema may be helping to guide the world of classical music back to its original role as a source of human connection and joy.

CHAPTER 8

Intensity

A writer—and, I believe, generally all persons—must think
that whatever happens to him or her is a resource. All things
have been given to us for a purpose, and an artist must feel this
more intensely. All that happens to us, including our humiliations,
our misfortunes, our embarrassments, all is given to us as
raw material, as clay, so that we may shape our art.
—JORGE LUIS BORGES, WRITER

The forty kids of Ghetto Classics started setting up for rehearsal
the moment the van full of instruments pulled into the courtyard of St. John's School, a walled Catholic school compound
in Nairobi's Korogocho slum. The van had been packed like a 3D
jigsaw puzzle, with instruments efficiently wedged in every possible
way, after the National Youth Orchestra of Kenya had used them that
morning. Every day, in fact, a different group uses them. Instruments
are scarce in the Nairobi region, so they have to be passed around.

Benjamin Wamocho, the head teacher of Ghetto Classics, drove
the instruments here today, with some visitors jammed in between
them. The snare drum and cymbals played random fills at every
bump in the pocked streets of the Korogocho neighborhood. The
name means "garbage" in Swahili, and when we arrived at the performance shed that is the program's rehearsal space, we could see the
largest garbage dump in Nairobi just beyond the outer wall. A hazy,
acrid stench from burning garbage hung in the air; there was a layer
of grime on every surface, including all the instruments, after about
twenty minutes of exposure. Benjamin said that the Ghetto Classics

students, mostly teens, live in this neighborhood, an enormous, densely populated slum with scarce water and electricity. They can't practice on Saturdays, because that is the best day for scavenging in the dump for things they can sell to help their families live.

But on Sundays, they gather on the concrete stage by the red dirt courtyard to play music together. We watched them set up seats and stands for rehearsal under murals of famous scenes in the Bible; the centerstage mural depicts an African-looking Jesus at a table in front of a village, with young and old Africans joining him, and a quotation from the Gospel of Matthew at the bottom: *"I am with you always, even to the end of the world. Amen."* Every few minutes, they paused to brush off the sediment accumulating on the instruments in the smoky air. The kids themselves were covered with dirt. They were teasing one another as they set up to play.

The rehearsal began with Benjamin conducting the group in their favorite piece, Elton John's "Can You Feel the Love Tonight?" To the right of the stage, on the concrete floor of the shed, another teacher, Celine, was introducing four little girls to the clarinet in front of murals of John baptizing Jesus and Jesus blessing a baby. Celine lives in Korogocho, and dresses stylishly; one little girl couldn't take her eyes off the teacher's shoes—until the teacher held out the shining clarinet. Celine explained its parts, its sounds, and how it works. Then she said, "Yes, you can touch it." The littlest girl reached out her index finger and ran it down a few inches of the wood. The other three took their turns touching, and the absolute focus broke into giggles only after the fourth withdrew her hand. Then each girl was invited to hold the clarinet for a few seconds. They passed it carefully to one another, cradling it as if it were a baby.

Vienna is marginally older, and already plays clarinet in the orchestra. It has been only four months since she first sat with Celine and reached out to touch the magical instrument, but her progress since then has been rapid. She told us that she chose clarinet because she heard Celine "play quavers" and knew instantly that she wanted to do that for the rest of her life. We asked her what she imagined herself doing in five years. Four months into her musical career, she didn't hesitate: "Playing *Finlandia* in the concert hall in the city."

Benjamin is not only the conductor of the orchestra; he does everything, from packing and transporting all the instruments to transcribing and photocopying scores and cleaning the rehearsal space. He grew up in the Kisii area of western Kenya, where he would be an animal herder if he had not discovered music. He now lives in an apartment in Nairobi, studies veterinary medicine at the University of Nairobi, and spends every spare minute with Ghetto Classics. We had been told by the program director that he is limiting his own musical advancement because he gives all his time to Ghetto Classics. But when we asked him about his career, he talked only about how well his students are doing.

He gets a tiny stipend for his work, much of which he gives to the students whenever they face some crisis expense—medicine, transportation, tampons. When players in his orchestra get good enough, they audition for one of the two or three higher-level youth orchestras in town, and some of them get in. Then they are on their way to actually realizing what has seemed to be a lunatic dream: leaving this ghetto by climbing a musical ladder. That ladder may or may not lead to a musical career; still, it is a ladder, the only one these young people have ever been offered. All the players who have made this big step, he told us, come back sometimes to help the orchestra that sits beside the smoldering dump in Korogocho.

Benjamin knows enough about each instrument to provide quick beginner lessons to students during rehearsal breaks, but violin is his own primary instrument. As the orchestra warmed up, he was able to fit in a two-minute violin lesson for a beginner. They stood on the side of the stage together, a tall man and a tiny boy silhouetted against a mural of the African continent surrounded by a blue ocean filled with portraits of African saints.

"This is your E string," Benjamin said to the boy, "can you pluck it?" The boy could, and did. "My E string," he said, and plucked it again.

⬅⬥➡

IT'S FREQUENTLY SAID that intensity is one of the signature attributes of El Sistema learning environments. We can state unequivocally that the experience of visiting a good El Sistema program *is* intense. But as we traveled, we were curious to explore exactly what this quality means, in theory, in practice, and in different cultures.

We found that it means many things. Most often, people use the word simply to describe the immersive quality of El Sistema, the number of hours per week that children attend the program. But the term is useful as well in describing other dimensions of the El Sistema learning environment.

"TODOS LOS DÍAS": INTENSITY OF IMMERSION

There's no doubt that programs' immersive hours are part of their effectiveness. In Venezuelan núcleos, students usually attend twenty hours a week or more, and many Latin American programs are close to that. At Esperanza Azteca, an El Sistema program in Puebla, Mexico, director Julio Sandana said, "Kids learn a lot of values here, because they are here with their instruments and their friends five days a week. Normally, music lessons mean one half-hour with a teacher and then 'See you next week.' The kid goes home, and out comes the cell phone or the X-box—but here, it's three hours and back the next day. That's the key."

At the Orquestrando a Vida program in Campos, Brazil, we were struck by the fact that people at every level of the program shared and could articulate this understanding. Derekson, a fourteen-year-old student and apprentice teacher in the program, said to us, "The reason this is so transformative is that we are here every day." The social worker in Campos, Mariana Andrade, told us that she has seen many children in the program develop the capacity to commit themselves to something. We asked how that learning happened here, and she answered, "It happens daily. *Todos los días.*" Jony William, the founder-director of the program, said, "It's because we have daily contact with the children that we have the opportunity to reach them in a different way, so that they can break out of some of the cycles that hold them back."

Programs outside of Latin America tend to involve fewer hours; many begin with seven or eight hours a week, but intend eventually to increase to more. Jean-Claude Decalonne, founder-director of Passeurs d'Arts in France, said, "The intensity of a Venezuelan núcleo—that's hard to replicate here. Currently, my students come twice a week for three hours. But in two years, when we build our own núcleo, we will be able to do three hours every day. That kind of intensity—that is our objective."

Richard Holloway, the Sistema Scotland founder-chair, spoke with conviction about why it's so important for Sistema programs to operate many hours a week. "The immersive nature of the experience is crucial," he said. "The fact that it is happening for them day after day after day after day. When I visited Venezuela, I could see that for a kid to be embedded in that creates a reality stronger than the reality that would otherwise kill him. And I thought, 'That might just do it in Scotland—to create a community for our kids that can become stronger than the one that's destroying them.'"

For many programs in North American and European cultures, in which the assumption is that kids need "exposure" to many activities rather than in-depth experience in one, it's a struggle to set the immersion bar this high. Lucy Maguire of the Nucleo Project in London said, "Everyone told me before I started, 'Four days a week? No kid is going to do that!' And I set up that schedule anyway, and every single kid does it."

At another London program, In Harmony Lambeth, director Gerry Sterling was initially one of those naysayers himself. "In the beginning, I really felt that getting kids to come four or five times a week wasn't possible. Now, after what we've seen here, I actually feel it is possible. If you immerse children sufficiently, it becomes simply their everyday lives. I think of it as immersive exposure."

At the Liverpool branch of In Harmony England, an unusual kind of immersive experience is being pioneered: all the children at one primary school in the working-class suburb of West Everton participate in music every day during the school day—along with all of their teachers. For these children, many of whose home lives are chaotic and difficult, the addition of their schoolteachers to the mix helps to reinforce the daily alternative reality provided by the music program. "The In Harmony program has transformed the whole school," we were told by Zoë Armfield, an administrator of the program. "It's a music space now."

A crucial dimension of El Sistema's time commitment is the continuity of the immersive experience. It takes years to achieve the goal of changing a life trajectory, and therefore good Sistema programs place a high priority on providing a continuity of programming, from the time students enter the program, no matter when that is, all the way through their high school years and often beyond. Many programs follow Venezuela's example of starting with children as young as possible, between two and seven years old (two-year-olds take just a thirty-minute class once or twice a week, accompanied by a family member), and then providing a series of higher-level orchestras that students can grow into as ages and skill levels increase. As immersive hours are extended across formative years, children's experience of this alternate world becomes more and more internalized. In Venezuela, one important reason for maintaining a core of common repertoire across all programs is that when families move from one region to another, their children can enter the new local núcleo confident that they will be familiar with some of the music being played, enabling them to be integrated and contributing quickly.

Continuity is a particularly knotty problem for programs that are located in primary schools. What happens when the children graduate and go off to middle school or secondary school? Programs address this challenge in different ways. "We can't desert these kids," says Gerry Sterling of In Harmony Lambeth. "But it's hard to say, 'Let's go to every single secondary school and get the principal enrolled in the idea of continuing the program through high school.' That's easier said than done."

Leaders and teachers of In Harmony Nottingham, which is school-based, feel the problem acutely. "Frankly, many secondary schools are reluctant to take on a program like this," we were told by administrator Beth Noble, "because they have so many other educational priorities to accommodate." Director Ian Burton said, "I sometimes get heartrending letters from parents, saying their kid played trumpet for three years and loved it, but now that he's gone to secondary school he's got nowhere to play. They can't afford private lessons."

The problem is particularly pressing because the passage between primary and secondary school is also the critical passage between childhood and young adulthood. The onset of adolescence is the time when most school music programs drop away, and Sistema programs are most likely to lose kids anyway. Even in Venezuela, more attrition happens during those years. The programs where we witnessed the most effective "intensity of continuity" were those in which children in that in-between age range, eleven to fourteen or so, were most engaged as helpers and mentors to younger ones, or where special program centers had been established for older children. In Medellín, Colombia, the robustly funded city program La Red, which is Sistema-like although not explicitly Sistema-affiliated, uses the city's modern, airy Casa de la Música facility for kids beginning in early adolescence, and busing is provided free.

However, beautiful new buildings are not required for creating an experience of long-term continuity. Luis-Felipe, the twenty-one-year-old teacher in Brazil's Orquestrando a Vida program, described how years of immersive experience in El Sistema opened the way for transformation in his own life. "I disliked the program at first," he said. "For the first few years, I didn't care so much about coming. But gradually that changed into a great passion. When I was twelve or thirteen, there was a big festival in the city, and we decided we were going to play a concert there. It was a big deal. We were all working together so hard, every single day, to play at that festival. I started to feel that it was really important, what we were doing. And suddenly, everything changed."

INTENSITY OF FOCUS

"Suddenly, everything changed." What leads a young person to open a doorway into complete personal commitment, a signal moment that changes a life path? As we investigated this question, we began to understand that "intensity" in Sistema programs isn't only about wealth of hours or number of years, although those are certainly important elements. Equally important is the concentration of other elements of the learning environment.

The intensity of attention and focus was one of the most striking aspects of Sistema learning environments everywhere. The etymological roots of the Latin-derived words "intense" and "attention" are the same, meaning "to stretch out," and this makes sense: intensity of experience brings an increase in focus. The word "intend" shares the same root, echoing the connection between motivation and sharpened observation. All good learning, of course, requires focused attention; our inquiry focused on how El Sistema practices create and sustain this quality in individuals and in groups.

First and foremost, this high-quality attention seems to be achieved through modeling on the part of teachers and teachers' assistants. Students continually get the unspoken message, from the examples set by their teachers, that focused attention is powerful, desirable, even "cool," and that it isn't incompatible with fun. Sometimes, particularly with younger students, the norm is articulated as an explicit rule about paying attention, with regular reminders about the rule. Often, too, there is a dynamic of trying hard to please the teacher. But because Sistema programs use few extrinsic motivators—there are no grades, rewards, stickers, or prizes, and individuals are seldom singled out for praise—the motivation becomes internalized fairly rapidly; students want to be in the flow as much as possible. More and more, focused attention becomes a habit of mind and heart acquired through modeling and practice.

In Barquisimeto, Venezuela, a setting where formal evaluation of such skill sets isn't part of regular núcleo operations, we observed a subtle example of expert executive functioning during a violin sectional rehearsal. Marisol was obviously smaller and younger than the other eighteen violin students in the group. We were told she had just been moved up to this more advanced orchestra, even though she's younger than the age at which that typically happens, because she is hardworking and a fast learner. (In Venezuela, teachers establish general norms for advancement but often break them for the benefit of particular students.) The section was rehearsing a difficult fast run of descending notes, with an asymmetrical rhythm, surprising accents, and a steady diminuendo. The teacher had them repeat it several times, and then broke the passage down to work on the variables layer by layer.

We could see that Marisol couldn't play all the notes fast enough to keep up with the others. As a result, she wasn't successfully managing the rhythms. Although she was struggling, she seemed to stay relaxed, and after just two repetitions, she began to adjust her approach to the challenge. She began playing only the accented notes and omitting the others, which allowed her to manage the rhythm and the decrescendo. It was an impressive coup of executive functioning; her efficient choices simplified the task enough to allow her to learn what was most important and to experience the feel of the passage in real time with the group.

Conventional wisdom among many music educators would hold that Marisol has been advanced beyond her capacities, and should be relocated back down a level. Conventional wisdom would further hold that Marisol is acquiring bad musical habits, like learning to skip whole handfuls of notes, and should be removed from the group and given individual practicing time to master those notes.

Conventional wisdom would have a point or two. It must be

BEING IN FLOW

The psychologist Mihaly Csikszentmihalyi called his concept of optimal attention "flow" because that was the term so many subjects used in describing how it feels. He reported that the human brain can process about 110 bits of information per second, and normal listening requires about 60 bits per second. In daily life, we do other things with those spare 50 bits of attentive capacity, a kind of minimultitasking. In the flow experience, we dedicate more of our 110-bit capacity to engagement with the task at hand. This is why people "in flow" lose track of time and release ego issues and daily concerns.

Csikszentmihalyi theorizes that this is also why humans find the experience of flow so pleasurable, so "other" than the quality of consciousness in daily life. Flow experience is more than simply delightful and addictive; it is productive. We learn much better in flow, and we retain our learning longer. Sistema environments are designed to incubate a feel for flow experience in learners, and increase it with group focus.

When students are really focused, they make myriad, continuous inner adjustments to help them keep learning at a maximum rate. Psychologists refer to this ability for self-management as "executive function." The Canadian psychologist Adele Diamond, whose research investigates and measures executive function, advocates for the primary importance of this capacity in youth development. She praises El Sistema programs as an excellent way for young people to develop these skills, and maintains that internal habits of smart self-management created during music learning are eminently transferable to other aspects of life.

In fact, some Sistema programs in the United States explicitly prioritize executive function as the key indicator of personal development, and they measure it in student evaluations. It's known that children of poverty and social stress tend to begin school with executive functioning capacities less mature than those of middle-class students, and the gap tends to widen as they get older, reinforcing patterns of lower achievement and limiting their potential for success. The first major research study on the U.S. Sistema movement, currently underway and led by a team from WolfBrown and The Longy School, recommends that U.S. sites use the development of executive function as one of their key measurements for success.

stressed that Marisol's choices make the most sense in a context where the primary goal is learning to play well within a group. If Marisol were training to become a soloist, these choices might not, in fact, have been the most effective ones. But since she is training to become a great ensemble musician and, more generally, to make responsible contributions within a structured community, her choices were appropriate and successful. Thanks to the supportive atmosphere of the learning environment, she managed to guide herself efficiently for this outcome without noticeable embarrassment or stress. Later, with extra practice on her own, she could learn all the notes. But now, she was making the choices that kept her with the ensemble.

Maybe it even felt like a game. Maybe it was even fun. Total focus doesn't mean "no fun"; it can often feel playful. For younger children, games and songs can in fact be the best way of teaching attention focus and nurturing the feel for flow, and Sistema programs, like all good music education programs, make plentiful use of them with preschool and elementary-age children.

With older children as well, fun can be used to concentrate focus. We have often cited a twenty-minute D-scale practice session we once observed in Caracas as the liveliest and longest practice of a single scale we've ever seen, with a series of challenging variations offered by the teacher to extend the practice. But that record may have been bested by a group of intermediate violinists in a sectional rehearsal we visited in Milan, Italy. This group of preteen children went at it for at least half an hour, and their attention never flagged, thanks to the imaginative coaching of their conductor, Carlo Taffuri. He began by asking each child in turn to assume the concertmaster chair and lead one full up-and-down scale by counting off a tempo and by choosing what body position to assume while playing (standing up or sitting down, feet together or apart, etc.). When one child, nervous about being in the spotlight, slurred his words as he counted off, Carlo turned it into a praiseworthy moment: "You are so brave to do it legato! Let's all play it that way."

Carlo then had them play the scale in a variety of articulation patterns, alternating legato and staccato. "Legato is like . . . Nutella," he told them, and no further explanation was needed. Then he had them stand up for the staccato parts of the scales and sit down for the legato parts. At the end of the sectional, the children may have had no idea that they had played nothing but one scale the entire time. They did know they had had fun. And they did play the D scale better, with more accurate intonation, at the end of the session than they had at the beginning. The games had increased their attentive focus. We tend to think flow experience is reserved for the richest kinds of challenges, but flow-prioritized environments can reap benefits even in pedestrian tasks like practicing musical scales.

INTENSITY OF TEACHER ENERGY AND COMMITMENT

"'The Pizzicato Effect" is the Sistema-inspired program of the Melbourne Symphony Orchestra, one of Australia's major cultural institutions. In the indigent, multiethnic Broadmeadows community, which the government is striving to turn around with a variety of new social programs, Pizzicato operates in the Meadows Primary School. Danielle Arcaro, a violist in the symphony, was the program's driving force for its first six years.

"My first year in this program felt like a disaster," Danielle told us. "I tried everything I knew from my experience as a teacher in middle-class settings—and I knew quite a lot—and it totally didn't work. We had chaos in the classroom. I cried a lot."

A clarification may be in order here: we did not end our research with the conclusion that weeping by staff members in the first year of a Sistema program is absolutely necessary. But we did learn not to be surprised by such reports. Danielle was not only an experienced teacher; she was also, atypically for Sistema program leaders, an active musician with the symphony. Although she was somehow finding the time and energy to continue developing the program, she was frustrated that for all her background, she didn't know how to solve the chaos problem, or how to create a dynamic Sistema learning environment. She redoubled her commitment, kept experimenting, and led her team in reexamining everything they thought they knew about working with kids.

Their partner in this endeavor has been Julie Lowerson, the principal of Meadows Primary School, who had transferred from an easier school setting to take on the challenge of turning this school around. "These Pizzicato teachers have come from privileged backgrounds, but their ethical purpose is so strong and genuine," she said. "The authenticity they provide is felt by the children. These teachers really care about them. The children know it, and respond. Most of the young musicians have become peer leaders in their in-school classrooms." An independent study done by a researcher at a local university has proven that there have been significant academic and social benefits for the children directly resulting from the Pizzicato Effect program.[24]

Sistema learning environments can only achieve a transformational impact on children when the alternative reality they offer includes an unwavering message of encouragement. While these messages can come from peers and mentors as well as teachers, the teachers are the ultimate role models; they embody for the students what it is to be a contributing member of a musical community, and they exemplify what positive messaging looks and feels like.

In fact, it looks remarkably similar across cultures and continents. Frank Biddulph, conductor of the Lambeth In Harmony program's "Sullivan Orchestra" (named for Arthur Sullivan, operetta composer of "Gilbert and Sullivan" fame), coaches his students to learn rhythms by chanting positive phrases. "Let's chant this rhythm," we heard him say. "We can learn it by using these words: 'We can get it right! We can get it right!'"

Alessandro Cadario in Milan, leading a choral rehearsal of twelve-year-olds singing Orff's *Carmina Burana*, exclaimed: "You have to startle your audience! You have to show them how much you love to sing this piece, and how great you are when you sing it together!" When they got to the Latin word *amor* in the text of the piece, he burst into impromptu song, in English: "Love is in the air," he sang, "quite clearly!" He was in constant movement, occasionally throwing in some beat boxing. He never broke his connection with them, and they responded in kind. *"Amor volat undique,"* they belted out, as though it were a pop song. "Cupid flies everywhere!"

In Istanbul, we heard about a particularly powerful instance of teacher commitment. Seçkin Özmutlu, the lead brass teacher at Music for Peace, was called away for military service. During his active duty, he continued to give lessons and guidance every day by Skyping into sectional rehearsals from his military base on the other side of the country. His students hung a countdown calendar on the wall of the rehearsal room, marking off with X's each day he was gone. When he returned, they celebrated with a rehearsal that lasted all day.

The importance of the teacher commitment factor in the success of Sistema programs was underscored by a finding reported in 2015 by researchers at the Glasgow Centre for Population Health, studying Scotland's Big Noise program. "We recognize the quality of relationship between Big Noise musician [teacher] and participant [student] as being vital to the reported impacts," they wrote.

The citizen artists we describe in this book, who teach in and lead Sistema programs across the world, are highly diverse in their talents, backgrounds, and personalities, but they all display this capacity for an unusually high quality of relatedness with their students. They understand that reaching children who are impoverished or traumatized in some way demands an extra level of empathic commitment, sustained over years. They have found in themselves the capacity to give their students 100 percent of their attention and somehow manage to sustain their own inner equilibrium. Inevitably, they feel depleted sometimes, and worry about burnout. But their inner reserves of determination and resilience seem limitless. They are at the heart of the Sistema endeavor.

Where do these teachers come from? In Latin American Sistema

THE LAW OF 80 PERCENT

Sistema teaching may be a particularly vivid example of one universal truth of teaching. We call it the Law of 80 Percent: "Eighty percent of what you teach is who you are." While the exact percentage is invented, it expresses a reliable truth: the thousands of natural ways a teacher listens, responds, gets excited, creates new ideas with students, and deals with challenges are the most important things the students will learn, far more important than the content the teacher delivers. This is why apprenticeship has always been an effective learning mode. Learners drink in those thousands of bits of subtle, intimate information.

Superb teachers of all disciplines and subjects, in all parts of the world, are exemplars of this law. Isn't it true that the teachers who influenced *your* life are most memorable for who they were as people, not for their curricula or handouts? Its truth is especially potent for those who commit to working with children in a holistic way, attending to their life circumstances as well as their classroom learning. That is why such a deep personal commitment is required of teachers who want to help students change their lives; partial or conditional commitment is inadequate when the goal is so great.

There's a powerful "gig mentality" among freelance musicians; this is a necessary mindset in a profession where there are few well-paid full-time jobs and where patching together a number of part-time jobs is the operative way to earn a living. But it can lead to a habitually conditional commitment—a reluctance to deeply invest time, energy, and self—that is counterproductive in an El Sistema setting, because it subtly undermines the intentionality of the whole endeavor. A teacher rationing her energy and attention, or half-thinking about her next gig, will not be a powerful "full commitment" role model for her students. The gig mentality remains a substantial challenge to building powerful Sistema faculties in the United States and elsewhere.

programs, they tend to be people who have grown up in the world of El Sistema and are following in their own teachers' footsteps. Daniela Das Dores, a Venezuelan violinist who was educated within El Sistema and came to London to teach in the In Harmony Lambeth program, reminded us that in the Venezuelan Sistema, the habits of mind and heart that make great teachers are learned in practice, through example. "It's simple," she said. "The students become teachers. The traditions are passed down through the generations." Essential to these traditions is veneration for the teaching profession. In Venezuela, it's common to hear children say they want to be teachers when they grow up. Students in Colombia told us that it would be exciting to be a musician, but the greatest accomplishment would be to become a great teacher.

In other countries, Sistema teachers are often recent conservatory graduates or career musicians or music educators. The transition into Sistema teaching can involve a steep learning curve, since Sistema learning environments often require them to teach somewhat differently from the way they were taught. Many are not used to working with beginners, not used to working with kids who live in impoverished circumstances, not used to prioritizing social development, not used to teaching groups rather than individuals. That's a lot to learn. Some can't manage it and bail out. Some make adjustments and are moderately effective. The most effective ones begin a long learning journey.

As of yet, there are few training programs specifically geared toward El Sistema teaching. The gold standard for such programs was the 2009–14 Sistema Fellowship at the New England Conservatory in Boston, which effectively jump-started the development of El Sistema in the United States. The fifty Fellows who graduated from that program (ten each year for five years) continue to be directly involved in Sistema or Sistema-like programs as founders, regional leaders, teachers, or consultants. In the United States, they are working in 37 communities across 17 states, in programs involving some 5,000 young people. Three work in Sistema programs in Colombia, Armenia, and Peru. A few have moved into related fields such as orchestra leadership, and five have returned to universities for advanced degrees that relate to Sistema work.

Another response to the need for Sistema-ready teachers is the

Take a Stand project, a collaboration of the Los Angeles Philharmonic, the Longy School of Music of Bard College, and Bard College.
In addition to producing symposia that have served as valuable national
gatherings for the U.S. Sistema field, Take a Stand offers a master's
degree program in El Sistema teaching, based in and working with
an El Sistema site (YOLA at HOLA) in Los Angeles. This is the
model training for the field at this point, and the demand for trained
teachers is so great that this program has a 100 percent success rate for
placing its graduates in paying jobs. In addition, academic courses in
El Sistema theory and practice are beginning to spring up at universities in the United States and several other countries, most prominently in Gothenburg, in conjunction with El Sistema Sweden. We
believe that the demand for training in social development-focused
music education—not limited to, but invigorated by, the global spread
of El Sistema—is such that in five years, there will be many ways and
places to develop the educational skills such programs need.

Around the world, program leaders consider hiring the right
teachers their highest priority and their greatest challenge; they mention it as readily as they state the need for more money. Julio Saldaña,
the music director of Esperanza Azteca in Mexico, said, "The teacher
has to be in the first place loving, a good listener, a good musician, a
good person, and needs to be motivating."

Eunsuk Chae in South Korea spoke of the challenge involved
in finding teachers with a feel for this work. "Of course I hire teachers
for their professionalism," he said, "but I am also listening for their
fervor, and their philosophy and goals for these kids. Can they develop
the capacity to love the kids?"

In Guadalajara, Mexico, Verónica Soltero-Alatorre summed it
up when she described her job interview for the Sistema program
there, Lomas del Paraiso. "They asked me, 'If you had a kid come in
the door of your program, and that kid was hungry and angry and
scared, how would you deal with him?' I didn't know what to say. So
I finally just said what sprang into my mind. 'First, I would give a big
smile,' I said. 'And then I would say: there is a place for you here.'"

INTENSITY OF MOTIVATION

The Ghetto Classics program in Nairobi is not intensive in terms of number of instructional hours. Yet there is no denying that the program has a palpable quality of intensity. We see it as an intensity of motivation. The motivational drive of the young students of Ghetto Classics is almost inconceivable given their life circumstances. It is personal and hungry and somehow, simultaneously, generous and supportive of others.

When Elizabeth Njoroge, founder of Ghetto Classics, grew concerned that some of its teenage graduates were floundering in their search for ways to translate their musical skills and drive into income, she made a connection with Junior Achievement (JA), a worldwide network of 435,000 volunteers in 121 countries helping to build entrepreneurship skills in the young. JA volunteers provided a three-month training for ten Ghetto Classics teenagers, who traveled hours to attend the sessions, tore into the learning, and emerged with a plan for how to create and market an ensemble. Less than six months later, the teenagers' new group, Rockers Ensemble, performed at a national prayer breakfast event with the Kenyan president as keynote speaker.

We encountered another example of unrelenting motivation in Drina, a teenaged Roma cellist in the Turkish program Music for Peace. Drina's father had announced that she would no longer be allowed to play in the orchestra—not an unusual decision, given the traditional roles of girls in her socially conservative Muslim Roma neighborhood. Drina's mother supported her wish to continue, but said they could not oppose her father's decision. Drina appealed to her father, but he held firm.

She did not give up. "If I give up music," she told her father, "I will become a cleaning lady until I die, just like every other woman we know. You will have done that to me. But if I have music, I can become something more. I don't know what—but something wonderful." Her certainty was so strong that her father decided to attend a few performances. He realized that the program was benefiting his daughter, and the risks were fewer than he had feared. He changed his mind and allowed her to continue. He trusts her now, and will let her go wherever she wants to go.

One of the places Drina wishes to go is music conservatory. By unspoken tradition, conservatories in Istanbul do not accept ethnic Roma students, and she knows this. She told us that this is simply another hurdle she will overcome. She has a plan: she would find ways to meet and play for influential people who might be willing to give her a free lesson or just advise her, and they would help influence the admissions process. "I will be the first Roma conservatory student," she told us. "I will blaze a trail."

Many months later, we learned that Drina had been accepted into and was attending the conservatory. In 2015 she won a prestigious international performance prize. She has blazed the trail.

What accounts for the strong motivation in El Sistema learners? Students at all levels, from beginners to kids with high skill levels— and even including kids at the intermediate preteen age, when boredom is often a badge of cool—often demonstrate a strong focus on the music-making, an absorption that goes beyond simple effort. The factors we have explored in previous chapters, such as the amplifying effect of the ensemble's ambition, the empowering experience of peer teaching and learning, and the crucial importance of feeling included, clearly help to account for this capacity for attention. But what accounts for the capacity for actual commitment?

The example set by their teachers is, again, a powerful factor. "It's about our young teachers!" said Edvan, the conductor at the Complexo do Alemão program in Rio de Janeiro. "They are not far away in age, and the kids can identify with them, and be inspired by them."

At NEOJIBA, in Salvador, Obadias Cunha said the same thing. "They see the passion in their teachers, and how well they play, and they think, 'I want to be like that.' Also, music is a beautiful art. When a child hears a beautiful tune and tries to repeat it and actually achieves it, he feels a pleasure that makes him want to do more and try harder. And it helps that the kids are among their friends. It builds the hunger for doing more, doing better."

In the book *Drive*, author and social analyst Daniel Pink distills the abundant research on motivation and identifies three key aspects that foster *intrinsic* motivation in workplaces, schools, and life: autonomy, purpose, and mastery. In good Sistema learning environments, children feel the autonomy of being in charge of their own improvement, making choices that work for them within the larger context of the orchestra. They feel purpose, in that their endeavors are connected to a larger goal and matter in some way to their families and communities. This seems to happen naturally; as we've noted, there is a consistent tendency for more advanced Sistema students to refer to themselves as representatives doing important work for their community or even their country.

And mastery. Children internalize the feeling that they are getting better; they have heard better orchestras than theirs, know what excellence sounds like, and feel that they and their orchestra are on the track to becoming like that. That gut feeling that excellence is achievable builds motivation.

In the course of visiting Sistema programs across the world, we were fascinated by a phenomenon we hadn't anticipated: motivation seemed consistently stronger in the Sistema programs within cultures of the deepest poverty. There seemed to be a difference between the way the program is received by children of *absolute* poverty (slums in poor countries) and the way it's received by children of *relative* poverty (ghettos within wealthier countries). Children of absolute poverty tend to grasp the offer of El Sistema with an immediate fullness of heart and unimpeded motivation. Children of relative poverty have a more complex response to Sistema's offer of learning an instrument and joining an ensemble. They have more doubts and layers of caution; many seem slower to embrace the opportunity and to become intrinsically motivated.

We have not found research that would explain this difference, and we don't have definitive explanations for it. We speculate that perhaps it's because in poor countries, children carry such low expectations of what life will give them that an orchestra program is seen as an unprecedented gift, and therefore sparks full investment. Children who live in pockets of poverty in wealthy countries are subject to a near-constant barrage of multimedia input about the world of abundance; even though their own lives are full of privation, they are bombarded, and often confused, by images of wealth and celebrity on television, on billboards, on the Internet, and in movies. Those images shape their sense of what's important and desirable. It may be harder for them, therefore, to grasp what kinds of pleasures and opportunities an orchestra program could bring to their lives. The unusual nature of the El Sistema offer makes them cautious, whereas in poor countries it seems to make children more interested.

Witnessing the breadth of this pattern across continents has deepened our admiration and respect for the citizen artists who commit to this work inside the relative poverty of wealthier nations. It takes extraordinary patience and persistence to guide students past the consumerist images that have colonized their imagination and sense of beauty, past the resulting expectations and behavioral challenges, past the caution about the strangeness of an orchestra, to open up the different kinds of motivation, commitment, and satisfaction that come with orchestral success.

There is no better example of blazing motivation in a Sistema-inspired program than a crowded núcleo within a church compound next to the squatters' shantytown of Lampara, in Manila, part of the Filipino program Ang Misyon. We visited the program with Jamie Bernstein, daughter of Leonard (Bernstein's music is revered in the Philippines), and with Jovianney Cruz, Ang Misyon's artistic director and founder, and his wife Cristina (Tinky) Cabanatan Cruz. Jovianney and Tinky invited us to walk with them into the squatters' colony before seeing the program. They led us across a narrow bridge of broken boards over a rain-filled trench, and then along dirt paths between tiny improvised shacks of corrugated tin, many with no plumbing, some with no electricity. The stench was powerful; there was trash everywhere, and children combing through it. We were told that over 3,000 families live in this place, which has sprung up over decades from the ruins of Tropical World, a resort built in the 1970s during the Marcos regime.

When we arrived back at the program compound, the children of Ang Misyon Lampara were all sitting in chairs with their instruments in their laps, waiting for us. "Good morning, Mum! Good morning, Sir!" they proclaimed in unison. "Welcome to our home!" We were shown to seats and given fruit drinks with crushed ice, and they played for us, one small group after another, first six little boys with violins and then groups increasing in age and size and proficiency. The room was baking hot and the electric fans clacked like factory machines, but the children listened to one another's performances as if receiving vital information. Several older teenagers who were members of Ang Misyon's flagship orchestra, the Orchestra of the Filipino Youth (OFY), and also assistant teachers for the younger ones, played solo pieces by Bach and Vivaldi; after each solo, everyone joined in on a Tagalog chant that means "I'll be the next one! I'll be the next one!" They weren't proposing they were all about to get up and play Bach; they were simply shouting out their feeling of ambition. Even as they were learning how hard it is to play an orchestral instrument, they didn't default to "I have such a long way to go," or "He is a million times better than me." They cut uproariously to "I can do that."

Roy Carandang, who runs the Lampara program with his wife Adora, is also a pastor, and also an architect. When we asked him how he managed this impossible career, he said, "I never sleep."

Throughout our visit to Ang Misyon programs, we encountered such relentless motivation among directors, teachers, and students alike that we began to wonder whether anybody ever slept. The teenagers who comprise the program's advanced orchestra, the Orchestra of the Filipino Youth, travel several times a week to rehearsal at Ang Misyon headquarters; given the vastness and the traffic jams of Metro Manila, this means a two-and-a-half-hour trip each way for many of them. They take two or three or four buses per trip, or they ride the rattletrap open-sided "jeepneys" that substitute for buses; one young woman told us she starts and ends every trip in a cart pulled by a water buffalo. Most are in high school and some in college, so they do their schoolwork during these long commutes, clutching their instrument cases between their legs. When they arrive home at night, they practice.

Jovianney told us that the second rehearsal the orchestra ever had happened to coincide with a typhoon. As he and Tinky drove to the rehearsal building through the flooded streets, Jovianney said, "Maybe we should turn around. This is pointless; there won't be anybody there."

Tinky responded, "I think we should just keep going." When they arrived, the orchestra members were all there in their chairs, tuning up, and soaking wet from the waist down; they had waded through the water carrying their instruments over their heads.

What accounts for the tenacity of their drive? Members of the OFY were usually surprised when we asked them this question, and said simply, "It is the chance of my life." For most of them, it wasn't the idea of becoming a professional musician that motivated them. Talking with four OFY musicians who had just started college or were about to start, we learned that only one, Vanette, is studying music; she wants to become a music teacher. Germain is studying broadcasting; Joshua is studying marine engineering; and Sophia, who is going to college next year, wants to be an accountant.

So it is "the chance of their lives" to do well, period, that keeps them galvanized—the chance to rise out of poverty, to do something the world values and rewards, to help their families and make them proud. Music becomes the vehicle for their personal growth. Jovianney and Tinky clearly make it part of their mission to support and encourage this growth. They seem to know every student personally, and they are continually reinforcing positive behavior in the "scholars," as they call the orchestra members, regarding everything from sitting up straight to applying for scholarships. Tinky regularly assigned members of the OFY to go along with us on outings and take care of us, and our caretakers were indefatigable, constantly at the ready with umbrellas if the sun was bright and fanning us throughout meals, to cool us and keep the flies away.

As cofounder and artistic director, Jovianney is a primary motivational force within Ang Misyon; he brings to his program all the energy that propelled his own career trajectory. Born in Manila, he was the tenth and last child of a piano teacher who was herself the daughter of the first female conductor in the Philippines. "She tried and failed to turn her first nine children into pianists," he told us. "With me, she hit the jackpot." Jovianney was a child prodigy who performed for Imelda Marcos at the age of five; he went to New York for high school so that he could begin studies at Manhattan School of Music, where he went on to earn his undergraduate degree. By the time he returned to his homeland, he was a virtuosic concert pianist. "I wanted to make a difference to my country," he told us, "and I thought I could do that by teaching piano students at the conservatory here. But after twenty years, it became clear to me that it didn't make the kind of difference I wanted to make."

When Jovianney began Ang Misyon, he knew he had found his life's work, where he could make the kind of difference he wanted to make. "My Manhattan School teacher doesn't understand it," he said with some sadness. "When I was a freshman, he told me to learn a Liszt piano concerto in two weeks—and memorize it. I did. I was his great experiment. Now he is disappointed in me."

Still, he has no regrets. Every time a student in the program learns to aim higher and strive harder, he knows he has succeeded. "I want to give a message to all Filipinos," he told us. "I want to say, 'You are a society of great creativity. What if this were really directed and cultivated? What couldn't we do?'"

The students of the Orchestra of the Filipino Youth also receive strong motivational pushes from Ang Misyon's manager of orchestras, Federico Frayna, and from its conductor, a young American-educated Frenchman named Olivier Ochanine. Olivier offers a constant stream

PARTNERS IN A SHARED MISSION

"I feel it's a gift, it's a privilege, to run Ang Misyon," says Tinky Cabana-tan Cruz, Jovianney's partner in life and work. Tinky's strengths are the perfect complement to her husband's: she is short on rhetoric and long on organization, budgetary planning, and quietly empathic communication. Every young musician in the Orchestra of the Filipino Youth and its junior orchestra, the Prep Club, and every teacher in the ten núcleos knows that Tinky is looking out for her or for him. She scolds them when they are careless and lends them money when they run short. Manners are big, for Tinky: "Look Mum Tricia in the eye when you speak to her," she says. "Introduce yourself. Ask her how she is doing today." She knows that training children to be good communicators and responsible citizens is as essential to Ang Misyon's mission as are scales and intonation. The kids love her, and call her "the boss." Jovianney calls her that too.

They love Jovianney for his pedagogical zeal and heart, though they also tease him. (When he speaks publicly about the power of music in young people's lives, they sometimes whisper to one another, "He's going to cry now." He always does.) They are in awe of his virtuosity. At a concert one night, we were standing in the wings with some of them when he played Leonard Bernstein's piano solo arrangement of Aaron Copland's "El Salon Mexico;" it was a rousing, muscular performance, with an ending chordal crash that propelled Jovianney all the way off the bench. Watching him, the kids literally jumped too.

Sitting in their small front yard one evening, as their four-year-old daughter Alexa danced around in her bare feet, Tinky and Jovianney talked about their experience of being part of a tiny middle class between a sea of brutal poverty and a fortress of immense wealth. "If we ever write a book," said Tinky, "we will call it *Broke Among the Billionaires*. Growing up here, we always knew about the poverty, but we were sheltered from it. Now, in this work, it is staring us in the face. We see what people have to go through."

of encouragement-plus-exhortation on the OFY Facebook page, challenging the kids to reflect upon music as well as to practice it. A recent sample: "Dear OFY, Please come to this Saturday's rehearsal prepared to answer the following questions. 1. What is good music? Is there such a thing? 2. Is music the universal language? And why or why not? I'm not after a particular answer, and it's likely some of you will answer in a manner I've myself not thought of before. Ponder it a while and let's talk about it on Saturday."

Finally, we can't underestimate the motivational importance of the young Filipinos' parents—which means, most often, their mothers. They are out in force at every rehearsal and concert, and they are role models of enterprise as well. Lanni, the mother of two violinists in the OFY, told us that when her husband left her and her daughters many years ago, she took on as much work as she could find. "I clean bathrooms in a hotel. I sell roasted corn at a street stall. I am studying to be a massage therapist." She flexed her biceps proudly. "I am *strong*!" she added.

IN HIS BOOK *Outliers*, Malcolm Gladwell explicates his theory of 10,000 hours, the time that must be invested in any kind of practice before one attains mastery enough to make significant contributions to the field. Gladwell proposes that this rule applies in a wide variety of fields, from ice hockey to computer programming. Though Gladwell doesn't mention this, those 10,000 hours must involve high-quality attention, not just going through the motions. So the learner must be driven by intrinsic motivation and practicing within a conducive environment. Venezuela's young Sistema musicians often reach 10,000 hours early in their teens. In Sistema programs around the world, teachers strive to create the best possible environment to nurture intrinsic motivation.

The Sistema movement is powerful because intense intrinsic motivation is part of the learning environment at all levels—from the gentle pleasures of beginning to the driving ambition of the top orchestra, from the personal investment of faculty and administrators to the generosity of private funders.

In Puebla, Mexico, Esperanza program director Julio Saldaña explained Sistema motivation this way: "The child learns a note; the next day, she comes wanting to learn, and learns another note. But another important thing is that very soon, during the first week, or the second week, she is already in an orchestra."

In Bosnia, Superar program director Ismar Porić spoke of the intensifying effect of expanding children's perspective by bringing them together with other children who make music together—in another city, another region, another country. "My students had never been out of their town, and really changed after we took them to Salzburg," he told us, speaking of the Sistema Europe gathering in 2013. We asked in what way they had changed.

He thought for a minute, then said: "They are hungry now."

That hunger—for challenge, for accomplishment, for beauty, and for inclusion—is what we saw in Sistema children across the world. "I see myself playing *Finlandia* in the concert hall," said ten-year-old Vienna, in Nairobi. She is hungry too.

CHAPTER 9

High Musical Aspiration

You'd be surprised what you can accomplish
if you're asked to do the impossible.
—ROLAND VAMOS,
INTERNATIONAL MASTER VIOLA TEACHER

When politicians of any country speak about poverty alleviation, they inevitably refer to raising the aspirations of the poor. However, the personal and social forces that keep people trapped in poverty are so potent that it's difficult for most to manage their way to new orbits.

The last quarter-century has seen some significant success in the reduction of extreme poverty (defined as living on less than $1.25 a day) around the world, cutting the percentage of the world's population in this category by half, to about 13 percent. This quietly remarkable change is due mostly to improved economies in China and India lifting large numbers of people over this statistical poverty line. However, 71 percent of the world's population still lives below the $10-a-day high end of poverty line. And there seems to be rising recognition of the obduracy of the cycles of generational poverty within that 71 percent. Social programs that seek to disrupt poverty cycles on a wide scale have had limited success, at best; fine programs have succeeded in many local settings, but larger initiatives have not succeeded across different kinds of poverty in different cultures.

Even in the United States, for so long a beacon of upward possibility, the likelihood of escaping poverty has become dismayingly low; current research shows that the U.S. is now ranked last among industrialized nations for upward mobility, on a par with India.[25] Little wonder that the phrase "to give hope" appears so often in the informal words of Sistema program leaders on every continent, in describing the purposes of their work.

In Latin, the word "confidence" means "with faith." How does a child of poverty or social stress learn to aim high with confidence? How does he gain faith in his ability to change the circumstances of his life when he has so few examples in his family and neighborhood of people who have accomplished this? There are, of course, no simple answers to these questions, but El Sistema is a promising laboratory for the inquiry.

A central tenet of El Sistema thinking is that children learn to aspire high in life by learning to aspire high in music. Tinky Cruz at Ang Misyon in the Philippines told us about a student there, Cathy Macalalad, who lived with a family of ten in a home of less than 200 square feet. In Ang Misyon, she began to play clarinet with the youth orchestra; she learned quickly, and when the need emerged for another oboist in the orchestra, she was asked to switch to oboe. She found oboe much more difficult. But her teachers believed she could handle it and kept their expectations high, and she began to internalize their confidence in her. Her steady advancement in the orchestra made it possible for her to experience her own capacity to succeed, and she began to be able to imagine herself succeeding elsewhere.

Now twenty-two, Cathy has completed accounting studies at a university and is launching a good career, with a job in the accounting department of an events planning company. From her musical experience, she has the tools she needs—confidence, self-discipline, focus, cooperative skills, and attention to detail—to reach high. "Her clients at the events place are ecstatic that someone in Accounting knows what a sound check is," Tinky said. "She wishes she could still play with the orchestra, but she can't right now because she has a mouthful of braces. She wants to look right so that she can achieve at a high level in the corporate world. And she will."

El Sistema has always maintained the centrality of the principle of high musical aspiration. Since the beginning of the Sistema in Venezuela, when Maestro Abreu told those eleven musicians that they could become a great orchestra, setting high musical standards has been part of the essence of Sistema practice. During the 1970s and '80s, when Venezuelans were helping to develop El Sistema programs in other Latin American countries, this kind of aspiration was one of their main contributions. "When the Venezuelans came to Guatemala," we were told by a longtime Sistema teacher, "and they told us we could learn Beethoven's Fifth Symphony in ten days—and we did—this was when we understood that in our own lives as well, anything was possible."

El Sistema's social goals can be achieved only if children and young people develop the habit of ambition. The more a child gains the courage and eagerness to reach high musically, the more she will be able to do so in the rest of her life. The more an ensemble strives toward ambitious goals rather than modest ones, and then succeeds, the more the ensemble members absorb the idea that ambitious goals are achievable.

As Venezuelan Sistema leader Francisco Díaz has said, "We are not simply about bringing children together in a room to keep them safe. We are not simply about bringing them together to play music. We are about bringing children together to play music *well*."

Felipe Martínez, conductor and director of the Notas De Paz Sistema program in Cali, Colombia, put it this way: "The work has to strive to be musically excellent, or it doesn't mean enough to the students. If we don't strive for excellence, they don't learn that aiming high is possible, and worth doing."

This certainty about the centrality of high musical intention is something that Latin American Sistema leaders have developed through decades of work, and they articulate it more clearly and consistently than those who have come recently to Sistema work. During a meeting of European Sistema leaders in 2014, in Birmingham, England, at which several Latin American Sistema leaders were in attendance, the discussion turned to the subject of musical goals at an upcoming Sistema Europe summer camp. Carmen Hiti, the founder-director of a just-launched Sistema program in Zagreb, Croatia, said, "In Croatia, what holds us back from aspiring high is our worry about failure—that the kids will aim for something they won't be able to achieve. How can we let go of that worry?"

Kathleen Turner and Katherine Barnecutt, from the Sistema program in Limerick, Ireland, seconded her concern. "We all live in cultures where failure is a terrible option," said Kathleen. "For us it can represent utter humiliation. How can we help kids learn not to fear failure but to see it as just a step in the process of achieving?"

Rey Trombetta, a Venezuelan who is an administrator of Sistema England, responded: "Of course you want to protect your kids; we all do. But what we have found in Venezuela is that when you push kids a little beyond what they think they can do, you help them grow."

Conductor Bruno Campo added: "No child will come to this summer camp and feel failure. We do push forward, but we don't want to break anyone. We always take care of the timid ones. We move everyone forward together. But we make it clear that we intend to move far in a short time."

THE WHY AND HOW OF HIGH ASPIRATION IN EL SISTEMA

This discussion illuminates a crucial point in Sistema practice: it's not simply ambition pursued by any means possible. It doesn't look much like high musical reach as practiced in most conservatories, where high-stakes, jury-adjudicated solo recitals and competitive auditions are the go-to routes; it's practiced in ways that are consonant with Sistema social goals. Building the habits of mind and heart that can help kids aspire beyond difficult life circumstances depends on *how* musical goals are pursued. Key to this "how" is the ensemble nature of the endeavor. Everyone moves forward together, including the superstars and the less able, and even including the extended ensembles of teachers and families.

The specifics of the "how" can vary widely across programs; there's no one franchisable method. In Medellín, students of La Red follow a specific preparatory curriculum of five classes that build the musical skills they need to succeed quickly and fully when they take up instruments. In the Manila ghetto of Santolin, small children sit cross-legged on the floor of a former car repair garage watching the multiage youth orchestra in rehearsal, imagining themselves among the players. In many núcleos in Venezuela, children are sometimes handed instruments on their first day at the núcleo and given a chair in the orchestra. In general, in Venezuela, the operating principle seems to be: identify what would be flat-out impossible, and then choose a goal just a fraction less difficult than that.

According to Carol Dweck, a psychology professor at Stanford University, aspiration depends on mindset.[26] In her research, which has increasing influence across the field of education, she has identified two basic kinds of mindsets, *fixed* and *growth*; most people fall somewhere in the middle on a continuum between these two polarities. The *fixed* mindset is the belief that one's abilities and potential are set, and that one's capacity for intelligence and creativity can't be altered. You are who you are, and that's basically that, although you can do a lot within what you were given. The *growth* mindset is the belief that you can get better in many ways through effort, training, and grit.

The fixed mindset leads to continual striving to affirm one's innate abilities; every challenge calls those abilities, and thus one's identity, into question, leading to an avoidance of risk-taking for fear of failure. The growth mindset relishes difficult challenges as opportunities, and experiences failure not as a pronouncement of inadequacy but as a natural part of learning and a spur to try harder. The fixed mindset is cautious and conditional; the growth mindset is playful and curious.

Since most of the children of El Sistema live in difficult circumstances, they tend to come into programs with fixed mindsets and
low standards about what they are capable of. This is a particularly
pernicious reality for children of poverty within wealthier countries,
who fall quickly behind their wealthier peers in academic achievement and continue to fall further and further behind as schooling
continues. They are bombarded with messages that underscore their
deficits and undermine their sense of potential; their teachers—in
school, at home, and around the community—tend to rely on strategies that unwittingly reinforce the fixed mindset.

Dweck's research focuses on ways that teachers can encourage
a growth mindset in young children. Adapting long-ingrained traditional teaching practices to align with Dweck's research can be painstaking, difficult work for teachers, and many are better at talking
about mindset pedagogy than actually delivering it. But we have seen
her precepts naturally in operation in good Sistema classrooms, even
though few Sistema teachers know of this research. One central issue
has to do with the problematic nature of praise. Praising children for
their achievements, she writes, moves them toward the fixed mindset,
whereas recognizing children for their efforts moves them toward the
growth mindset. The abundant positivity of good Sistema environments usually involves commending children for their effort, their
focus, the way they work together. Rarely does an ensemble teacher
or sectional leader single out one child with praise for an
accomplishment.

Another feature of the growth mindset Dweck describes is resilience in the face of failure. The Sistema learning environment inclines
powerfully in that direction; standards are set high, but failures to
meet them are an expected part of the process, and Sistema teachers
set an example of meeting failures with equanimity and redoubled
effort. Learning to play an instrument or sing in a chorus is funda-
mentally about working with frequent failures—hitting the wrong
note, missing the rhythm, holding your arm at the wrong angle. The

José Antonio Abreu rehearsing with the original Simón Bolívar Youth Orchestra, Caracas, Venezuela, 1975. PHOTOGRAPH: FUNDAMUSICAL ARCHIVE

Students rehearse in a percussion sectional at the Sarria núcleo in Caracas, Venezuela. (See page 70.) PHOTOGRAPH: TRICIA TUNSTALL

White Hands Choir in rehearsal, Barquisimeto, Venezuela. (See page 40.) PHOTOGRAPH: FRANK DI POLO

"Pepetoño" (José Antonio) Herrera
conducting the Lomas del Paraiso
Orchestra in Guadalajara, Mexico. (See
page 145.)

PHOTOGRAPH: TRICIA TUNSTALL

Composer Arturo Márquez
conducting at the launch of Sistema
Sonemos, at the Teatro Ocampo in
Cuernavaca, Mexico. (See page 165.)

PHOTOGRAPH: SECRETARÍA DE CULTURA/
RAMONA MIRANDA

Batuta children's
ensemble, Centro Musical
Lisboa, Suba, Colombia.
(See page 254.)

PHOTOGRAPH: ANDRÉS RINCÓN

Batuta Orquesta Sinfónica Libre de Quibdó, at Teatro Julio Mario Santo Domingo, Bogotá, Colombia.

PHOTOGRAPH: JONATHAN VELANDIA

Tuba section rehearsal in NEOJIBA's Bairro da Paz program near Salvador, Brazil. (See page 275.)

PHOTOGRAPH: ERIC BOOTH

Wind section rehearsal of the Mariuccia Iacovino Symphony Orchestra, at the Orquestrando a Vida program in Campos, Brazil. (See page 130.) PHOTOGRAPH: ERIC BOOTH

In the Gellerup district of Aarhus, Denmark, Bjørn Lindvang (foreground) and Signe Thorborg Addison (background) teach MusikUnik's emerging orchestra. (See page 63.) PHOTOGRAPH: ERIC BOOTH

Gustavo Dudamel with El Sistema Sweden
students at Gothenburg Concert House.
PHOTOGRAPH: ANNA HULT

A first encounter with a trumpet in
El Sistema Sweden program in
Stockholm, Sweden. PHOTOGRAPH:
ALEJANDRA FERNANDEZ DCZ COLOMBIA

Children's chorus in
Srebrenica, Bosnia,
part of the Superar
Bosnia program.
(See page 78.)
PHOTOGRAPH:
ERIC BOOTH

Children's chorus in the Superar program, Vienna, Austria. (See page 71.)
PHOTOGRAPH: ERIC BOOTH

Children's chorus in Roma neighborhood of Zizin, Romania, part of the Superar Romania program. (See page 76.)
PHOTOGRAPH: ERIC BOOTH

A preschool program of Sistema Italy in Turin, Italy. (See page 69.)
PHOTOGRAPH: TRICIA TUNSTALL

Carnival concert by Orquestra Geração at the House of Music in Oporto, Portugal. (See page 211.) PHOTOGRAPH: DIANA TINOCO

Double bass players in the Beethoven Orchestra at Music for Peace in Istanbul. Özmen Genç is second from right. (See page 52.) PHOTOGRAPH: COURTESY OF ERIC POLITZER PHOTOGRAPHY

Musicians of the Iranian Youth Orchestra at their first performance, in Tehran, Iran, 2015. (See page 315.) PHOTOGRAPH: TABAN ASKARI

The Sistema England Young Leaders Orchestra, composed of some of the most committed and experienced young musicians from In Harmony Lambeth, In Harmony Liverpool, Sistema in Norwich, and the Nucleo Project. (See page 324.) PHOTOGRAPH: IVÁN GONZÁLEZ / SISTEMA ENGLAND

Violinist at the In Harmony Lambeth program in London, England. (See page 230.)
PHOTOGRAPH: ERIC POLITZER PHOTOGRAPHY

Gustavo Dudamel conducting the Big Noise Raploch Symphony Orchestra of Sistema Scotland's program in Raploch, at the rainy "Big Concert" in 2012. (See page 224.) PHOTOGRAPH: FRANK DI POLO

Members of the Sistema Europe Youth Orchestra culminating their Summercamp 2015 in Milan, Italy. (See page 303.)
PHOTOGRAPH:
©MARCO CASELLI_NIRMAL

An ensemble of female students of the Afghanistan National Institute of Music practicing during lengthy security procedures before a performance celebrating International Women's Day in Kabul, Afghanistan. (See page 267.) PHOTOGRAPH: ERIC BOOTH

The ensembles of the Afghanistan National Institute of Music performing at Carnegie Hall in New York City in 2013, with Dr. Ahmad Sarmast, founder and director (standing at left), and William Harvey, conductor and arranger (right). (See page 272.)

Side-by-side performance of the Orchestra of Dreams and the Youth Orchestra of Caracas at the Deoksugung Palace, Seoul, South Korea, 2013. (See page 259.)

Part of the string section of the multiage orchestra of El Sistema Soma, Japan. (See page 248.)

Students of El Sistema Japan taking a selfie with visiting students of the Youth Orchestra of Los Angeles, 2015. (See page 87.)

Performance by beginning students of Sistema Whangarei, in Whangarei, New Zealand. (See page 233.)

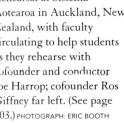

Rehearsal at Sistema Aotearoa in Auckland, New Zealand, with faculty circulating to help students as they rehearse with cofounder and conductor Joe Harrop; cofounder Ros Giffney far left. (See page 203.)

Esekia helping his stand partner in Sistema Aotearoa in Auckland, New Zealand, 2014. (See page 204.)

PHOTOGRAPH: MS. BLEAU BUSTENERA

Students of the Ang Misyon satellite program on Talim Island, the Philippines.

PHOTOGRAPH: RUBY RAYMUNDO

Performance by the wind ensemble of the Bulacan program of Ang Misyon in Manila, the Philippines. (See page 239.)

PHOTOGRAPH: ERIC BOOTH

Karis Crawford, founder of Sistema Kenya, in the first week with new violin students at the Kawangware School in the Kawangware ghetto of Nairobi, Kenya, 2014. (See page 43.) PHOTOGRAPH: ERIC BOOTH

A concert in the Bagamoyo neighborhood near Maputo, Mozambique, by the Xiquitsi Project of Kulungwana, an association for cultural development. (See page 121.)
PHOTOGRAPH: JOÃO COSTA

Malebo Motimele rehearsing for Music Enlightenment Project's "Celebration 2013" end-of-year concert, in Braamfontein, Johannesburg, South Africa. (See page 292.)
PHOTOGRAPH: YANA SEIDL

Students in the
Uummannaq Orchestra, a
project of the Children's
Home Uummannaq, in
Uummannaq, Greenland.
(See page 314.) PHOTOGRAPH:
COURTESY OF THE UUMMANNAQ
POLAR INSTITUTE

Traditional native drumming is incorporated into the music program of Sistema New
Brunswick (Canada) at its Tobique First Nation Centre. (See page 281.) PHOTOGRAPH: DAVE HAI PINE

Beginners with the OrKidstra program of the Leading Note Foundation in Ottawa,
Canada, perform with their more experienced peers. PHOTOGRAPH: ROBERT S. VIBERT, OTTAWA, CANADA

Juan Felipe Molano, conductor of the Youth Orchestra of Los Angeles (a project of the Los Angeles Philharmonic), rehearsing Dvořák's Symphony No. 8 at Walt Disney Concert Hall, with 400 YOLA students combined from its three program sites, 2015. (See page 213.) PHOTOGRAPH: CRAIG T. MATHEW/ MATHEW IMAGING

A member of the Simón Bolívar Symphony Orchestra mentors a student of the Youth Orchestra of Los Angeles in preparation for a joint concert in 2015.
PHOTOGRAPH: CRAIG T. MATHEW/ MATHEW IMAGING

First-grade student James Eldridge didn't let Halloween keep him from attending the after-school OrchKids class during which he received his trumpet for the first time, at Mary Ann Winterling Elementary School in Baltimore, Maryland. (See page 339.)
PHOTOGRAPH: RAFAELA DREISIN

First row of first violins at Fortieth Birthday Concert, Caracas, Venezuela, 2015 (foreground from left): twelve-year-old Rayson David Tercero Cumares Sequera, concertmaster; Gustavo Dudamel; Alejandro Carreño. (See page 349.) PHOTOGRAPH: FRANK DI POLO

José Antonio Abreu, Caracas, Venezuela, 2013.

PHOTOGRAPH: MERIDITH KOHUT

THE CONSEQUENCE OF MINDSETS

Stanford University psychology professor Carol Dweck reports an experiment involving hundreds of mostly adolescent students who were given ten challenging questions from an IQ test. Afterward, all the students were praised, but half were told, "Wow, you got a really good score. You must be smart at this," while the other half were told, "Wow, you got a really good score. You must have worked really hard."

They were then offered a choice between an easier next challenge and a harder one. Most of the students praised for being smart chose the easier challenge—i.e., moving toward a fixed mindset, characterized by caution about appearing less capable. Among the students praised for their effort, nine out of ten chose the harder new task—moving toward a growth mindset characterized by pleasure in grappling with hard problems.

In the next step, all were given a harder task, and predictably didn't do quite as well. The fixed mindset group reacted by describing themselves as less smart; the growth mindset group reported that they had to try harder. During the remainder of the experiment, the harder the questions got, the less fun the fixed-mindset kids reported having, and the more fun the growth mindset students reported.

Unsurprisingly, the effort-affirmed, growth-mindset adolescents improved in their abilities steadily throughout the experiment, while the ability-praised, fixed-mindset kids got worse and worse. After the experiment, 40 percent of the fixed-mindset group lied about how they had done to cover their embarrassment about their slipping scores.

growth mindset accepts imperfection and finds resonant satisfaction in improvement. In Latin American programs, we saw many instances of kids in orchestras lobbying to play harder music, because they wanted to challenge their abilities to the max and didn't fear that failure would cause harm.

Finally, Dweck believes that developing a growth mindset depends on an experiential certainty that one is getting better. In a

good Sistema learning environment, that certainty is built into the structure of the program. A child who enters a núcleo in Venezuela experiences an incremental step-by-step process that many others before her have followed. She often hears the intermediate and advanced orchestras play, even while she's in the beginner orchestra, and experiences herself making incremental progress, day by day, toward the next stages. The piece that seemed insurmountable ten days ago now sounds pretty good. Even if she is moving more slowly than others, the constant message is that she is doing well and can learn to do better.

Positivity directed at collective effort, renewed vigor in reaction to failure, step-by-step evidence of improvement—these practices build determination in children about the process of something genuinely hard to do: learning to play an instrument or sing well. They gain confidence that what seemed impossible is in fact possible, and they begin to bring that confidence to their lives outside the núcleo. Dweck has written: "As you begin to understand the fixed and growth mindsets, you will see exactly how one thing leads to another—how a belief that your qualities are carved in stone leads to a host of thoughts and actions, and how a belief that your qualities can be cultivated leads to a host of different thoughts and actions, taking you down an entirely different road."

For Sistema students, that "entirely different road" means a future they can shape and manage through practiced mind-and-heart habits of high aspiration. Every conductor who programs a Brahms symphony, every sectional leader who extends a rehearsal until the D-scale unisons are perfect, every choral director who holds a sung harmony until the last recalcitrant voice comes into tune, is working toward this end. Such moments can look like a tough teacher demanding too much, but we have come to recognize them as strong teaching that stretches students beyond the usual "good enough" to higher norms.

It must be noted that these teaching practices require considerable patience, understanding and clarity. Even in Venezuela, where

the potent maturity of the learning environment can vitiate pedagogical inadequacies, teachers can't always hit these high marks. In programs throughout the world, especially newer programs, teachers often struggle to find their way. It takes time and experience to create the kind of learning environment that nourishes the growth mindset. For music teachers—for any teachers—it can be hard to break long-held habits like praising achievement and avoiding failure. A Sistema teacher in a fairly new U.S. program, who attended a workshop about Dweck's research, responded as many teachers (and parents) do: "Oh Lord, I'm thinking of all the time I've spent praising everything my students did! Everything my own son did! Why didn't I know about this before?!"

One program that is conspicuously attentive to mindset issues and the practices that foster them is Sistema Aotearoa in Auckland, New Zealand, cofounded by Ros Giffney, a pediatric developmental therapist who knows a lot about Dweck's research. The program serves children mostly from Tongan and Samoan families who live in a complex and struggling immigrant community within wealthy New Zealand. Ros brings an unusually strong dimension of child development awareness to the program; her entire staff hews to Dweck's recommendation to give recognition (and not too much) about effort, rather than praise about ability.

With Ros as cofounder, Sistema Aotearoa has kneaded the most advanced youth development research into everyday practices. Every day before the students arrive, the teachers meet to coordinate their language, to clarify the key messages across all classes, along with the musical focus of the week and the particular lesson of the day. During an orchestra rehearsal we saw, children making mistakes of any kind were swiftly noticed and just as swiftly helped. Even more impressive, the teachers kept track of one another's interventions. Knowing that students can get confused and lose confidence if too many different instructions come their way, they try to limit the number of instructions each child gets during a rehearsal. If teachers spot a colleague adjusting a child's posture, for example, they let that child keep focused on posture, perhaps with further reminders, rather than asking her to attend to fingering as well. Fingering can wait for another day. The overall goal is to make sure each child feels successful every day.

The teachers told us about ten-year-old Esekia, who was the youngest in his cello group and couldn't keep up, so would act out and play the clown. He had a problem with fighting at school; he was "too quick with his hands." For one sectional rehearsal, they decided to give him the assignment of playing just one open string. "You, Esekia, are in charge of the A string," they told him.

Esekia took successful charge of the A string that day and beyond. He loved playing the A, because he was an expert on it. When the students attended a concert by the Auckland Philharmonia Orchestra, the parent organization of the program, Esekia listened to the musicians tune up and grabbed his teacher's arm. "That's the A! They're playing my note."

A year later, Esekia had become the best cellist in his lower orchestra. But the teachers didn't fast-track him to move up; maybe next year, they said. At the beginning of our visit, he was the student selected to present us with a gift at the formal welcoming ceremony, and he improvised a charming little speech in Tongan, thanking us for coming. When he learned we were writing a book, he asked us if he would be in it. He asked if he would be on the first page. He asked how many pages it would have. He had us write down his name so he could make sure that we spelled it right.

Our discussion of musical high ambition in Sistema programs must include an additional and more pragmatic reason for its prioritization: it's easier to attract financial support for Sistema programs if their orchestras and choirs sound great. From the beginnings of the Sistema in Venezuela, Maestro Abreu has consistently won large-scale support for the program by maintaining high standards of quality at every skill level—basically, by bowling over visitors and audiences with how good the music is. In Salvador, Brazil, Ricardo Castro had this precedent in mind when he decided to start NEOJIBA by building a great upper-level orchestra in order to have something remarkable to show government funders. "Maestro Abreu was my inspiration in this," he told us, "as in so many things."

We heard a similar statement from Esteban Moctezuma, the founder of the Sistema-inspired program Esperanza Azteca in Mexico. "One reason we are successful is that when our orchestra plays, the audience is always breath-taken. To make a social difference, you have to fight for quality and with quality." In the Philippines as well, the Sistema-inspired Ang Misyon program started with an advanced youth orchestra, the Orchestra of the Filipino Youth, in addition to programs for beginners. These three programs are exceptional in this regard; most new Sistema programs don't have the resources to build top-quality, knock-your-socks-off youth orchestras at the outset, but must build public support more slowly by nurturing children's orchestras from scratch, toward excellence that will be publicly compelling.

But almost all programs—and indeed, many students—understand this dimension of quality. As Darius, an African-American cellist in California, said to us, "If people see us play and say, 'That's so nice, black kids playing classical music,' we haven't succeeded yet. But if they see us play and say, 'Wow, those kids are amazing,' then we've succeeded."

When students from low-income families or challenging circumstances play with more privileged kids and experience themselves as competent, their habits of aiming high are not only affirmed but also intensified. In Braamfontein, South Africa, the first time students from the Sistema-inspired Music Enlightenment Project (MEP) visited a wealthy all-white private school to play with the school orchestra, everyone realized fairly quickly that the MEP students played much better. The visiting students stepped naturally, without even discussing it, into the role of helpful mentors, and their sense of themselves and of their ensemble changed that day. (The ingrained assumptions of parents and teachers from both schools changed that day as well.) A similar experience occurred for ten advanced players of the OrchKids program in Baltimore (from among the lowest-income families in the U.S. Sistema), when they were given scholarships to attend the prestigious Interlochen Summer Arts Camp in rural Michigan, where most of the other students were white or Asian, from families with means. OrchKids director Dan Trahey went with them. When we asked him how his kids had fared socially, he said, "There wasn't a problem. Our kids played as well as, or better than, the other kids, so there was a kind of attractiveness and specialness about them. Their musical skills wiped out the usual prejudices, and everyone had a great time. No tensions."

The percentage of Sistema students who translate the habit of high aspiration into ambition for a professional music career is usually small, perhaps 15 percent (and this varies among programs, countries, and cultures). For the great majority, the vision of Sistema programs is that consistently aiming at high goals, and often reaching them, nurtures the habit of mind and heart of taking on high goals throughout a productive, contributive life. Mature Sistema programs abound in anecdotal evidence that this works, although research about that other 85 percent is just beginning to emerge. A Mexican music teacher we met in Colorado, where he taught in a Sistema program, recalled his earlier days in El Sistema in Mexico City: "My four friends and I would have been in a gang if we hadn't been in the núcleo. Inside the núcleo, they were my posse, a musical gang of five. We grew up together in those orchestras."

We asked what had become of the other four. "Let me see," he said. "One is a priest. One is a lawyer. One works in a company, and one started his own business. We are all happy, and we all still play music." He was the only one who pursued a musical career, and was just completing his Ph.D. What are the odds that of five friends from a gang-controlled barrio, all five would manage their way around the powerful forces driving them toward failed lives and would imagine and create unlikely paths to satisfying ones?

HIGH MUSICAL ASPIRATION:
LEARNING FROM LATIN AMERICANS

This commitment to high aspiration is a distinctive habit of mind and heart. For many new programs, Sistema experts from Latin America have been mentors in this regard. There is an informal, fluid cadre of experienced Sistema practitioners from Venezuela, Colombia, Guatemala, Mexico, and elsewhere in Latin America who bring their years of experience and wisdom to newer Sistema programs the world over. Some live peripatetic lives, visiting Sistema programs to offer encouragement, guidance, and infusions of reach-extending energy. Others become leaders of núcleos on other continents, mentoring new generations of teachers. Wherever they go, these Latino and Latina mentors bring their conviction that excellence is not only compatible with inclusion but also essential to the success of El Sistema. Their generous willingness to share what they know about this is invaluable to the growth of the worldwide Sistema movement.

Nicola Killean, the CEO of Sistema Scotland, told us of visits by the Libertadores String Quartet, one of Sistema Venezuela's virtuosic touring ensembles. "The first violinist, Ollantay Velásquez, said to me, 'Your students are capable of more than you are asking them for.' It felt like an encouragement, not a criticism."

Richard Holloway spoke of this visit as the "first crisis" of Sistema Scotland. "They were a bit concerned that the intensity of our aspirations was not high enough," he said. "We wrestled with this: was musical excellence intrinsic to the social transformation or just simply an add-on feature? The Venezuelans were certain it was intrinsic."

Sistema Scotland made substantial changes in response to the Venezuelans' observations. They added prominent musicians to their board, including the violinist Nicola Benedetti, and hired an experienced music director, Francis Cummings. "With Francis's direction and a more cohesive curriculum evolving, our teachers felt confident in beginning to gently push the students a little harder," said Nicola

Killean. "And it turned out that Ollantay was right. The students rose to it. Actually, they loved hearing themselves play better. Then they wanted more."

Nicola and her colleagues got dramatic proof of their students' capacity for high aspiration during a catalyzing event in June 2012, when the Big Noise program in Raploch played in a concert with the Simón Bolívar Youth Orchestra of Venezuela, conducted by Gustavo Dudamel. Dudamel and his orchestra members rehearsed with the Big Noise orchestra for several days, with Scottish children paired off with the Venezuelan musicians as stand mates, to prepare for a joint performance of Beethoven's *Egmont* Overture. On the first day of rehearsal, a few of the most advanced Scottish kids compared the simplified parts they were using with the real-Beethoven versions their Venezuelan stand partners were playing. They asked their stand mates, "Do you think we could learn to play what you're playing—in three days?"

The Venezuelans' unsurprising response: "Of course you can!" So without mentioning it to their teachers, the kids found the full orchestral parts online, downloaded and printed them, and practiced the new parts until late that night, slipping them onto the rehearsal stands the next day. "It had never occurred to us," Francis Cummings told us, "that these kids would be capable of playing the real parts, at this stage in their development. They showed us they could."

Nicola told us that Big Noise students are capable of turning their aspirational energy in a very practical direction as well. The program regularly holds ceremonies at which students are invited to take their instruments home for the first time; this is a rite of passage, affirming that they have shown responsibility and are trusted to care for the instrument on their own. Nicola recalled three kids who, after the ceremony, left school but didn't head home. With their violins strapped to their backs, they walked directly to the Raploch village center, opened their cases on the sidewalk, and started busking for change.

Achieving high musical ambition can be especially hard for new programs with very young children. Often, such programs don't find their way to musical drive in the first few years, concentrating instead on developing a nurturing atmosphere and making all children feel valued and accepted. As they develop, they discover that a nurturing environment, while essential, isn't enough; musical hunger is crucial to their ultimate goals. It's at this transitional point that the mentorship of Venezuelan and other Latin American Sistema master teachers can be crucially helpful. We have seen the Libertadores Quartet bring their musical high spirits and pedagogical fervor to the young orchestras of developing Sistema programs not only in Raploch but also in Fukushima, Japan, and in Midtown Manhattan. They convey the clear assumption that it's possible to fuse excellence and inclusion into a single aspiration—a goal that's perhaps never completely realized, but that activates every aspect of Sistema teaching and learning.

In late 2015, Roberto Zambrano, the núcleo director in Acarigua, Venezuela, visited three U.S. programs (Kidznotes in North Carolina, OrchKids in Baltimore, and Soundscapes in Newport News, Virginia), spending a week at each. Rey Ramirez, program director of Soundscapes, told us: "In one week he completely changed our game. He lifted us to a new level of intensity and success with the students, more than we thought was possible. He got our teachers to try a new, Venezuelan paradigm in their teaching; and when they tried it, it felt right."

Many other Latin American master teachers engage in similar ambassadorial pursuits. Venezuelan conductor Manuel López-Gómez, who has also worked extensively in Colombia, sometimes conducts the children of Sistema Sweden. Ron Davis Álvarez, the twenty-six-year-old Venezuelan who has already directed a Venezuelan núcleo and founded one in Greenland, plays a similar role. At a June 2015 seminario in Gothenburg, Sweden, we watched him work with a youth orchestra composed of young people from both Sistema and non-Sistema programs. They were rehearsing Tchaikovsky's *Marche Slave*, and Ron lit into the work with attention to every dramatic detail. To the double bass players who begin the piece with an ominous repeated growl on the tonic note, he said, "You need to dip your heads when you begin to play, to help the audience understand the feeling of the music."

When the double bassists played the passage again, dipping their heads, their playing became edgier; simply being aware of what they were communicating to the audience had moved them to communicate more. "Fan-*tas*-tic," said Ron. He is a slight young man with a spur-of-the-moment mustache, and his rehearsal mode was characteristic of Venezuelan Sistema conductors; in constant motion, he often bounded from the podium into the orchestra to address specific sections, and he combined a focus on emotional connection with an implacable clapped beat. The kids, who were mostly Swedish, sometimes had trouble understanding his English. "This part is like— what do you call that pan you put on a stove, and you put a lid on it, and then it starts to boil?" A moment of puzzled silence, then: "Pressure cooker?" ventured a student. "Yes, yes, that's it!" said Ron. "The violins in this part, they have to be like a pressure cooker. More and more vibrato . . . a *lot* of vibrato, to tell the listeners, something crazy is going to happen, something is coming to 'splosion!"

During a break, we asked one of the double bass players, a Swedish boy named Jakob with shoulder-length blond hair, how it was to work with Ron. "It's really different," he said. "He pushes us so hard, and sometimes he laughs at us, but somehow it is always fun."

In Korea, the music director of the Bucheon Núcleo, Maestro Chae, told us that when their program was in its early stages, the Venezuelan maestro Rafael Elster paid them a visit. After their fledgling orchestra performed for him, Rafael told the teachers: "You are not pushing these children hard enough; they can do more. They can read music. They are smart. They should be playing Mahler a year from now!"

"I was shocked," said Chae. "Mahler was never on my list. The kids had only been in the orchestra for about a year or so. But we decided to believe him and give it a try. The first thing we tried was

Beethoven—and the kids could do it. So maybe we will try Mahler next time. We thank Rafael for giving such inspiration."

The Italian Sistema has benefited by hands-on learning from several Venezeulan master teachers. Jhonny Gómez and Naybeth García, the Venezuelan creators of the White Hands chorus concept, have visited Italy several times to help create White Hands choruses at a number of Italian núcleos.

Orquestra Geração, Portugal's highly developed Sistema initiative, may be the most musically ambitious program outside of Latin America. This is partly because the program is the oldest Sistema initiative in Europe, having been founded in Lisbon in 2007; it's also because Venezuelan teachers have been regularly involved with the program ever since, as mentors, advisors, and teachers. The program now has 820 students in 16 núcleos in the Lisbon area, and is expanding to other parts of the country. There are municipal Sistema orchestras in Lisbon, and regional orchestras are being developed. Founder-director António Wagner Diniz (usually just "Wagner") is a singer, conservatory director, and citizen artist with insistently high standards; he told us that often, the Orquestra Geração students who matriculate into local conservatories arrive with better musical skills than the more privileged kids have, and that the Orquestra Geraçao chorus can outsing the main conservatory chorus.

Observing a beginners' orchestra rehearsal, we saw teachers displaying a high level of attention to musical detail and nuance even as they taught the basics of getting the notes right. "Even the simplest pieces must be in time and be fully musical," said Wagner. He told us he is developing an intervention team of his best teachers who can be "deployed" to new sites or to núcleos that are musically underperforming.

All the Orquestra Geração leaders spoke with awe of visits from conductor Ulyses Ascanio, one of El Sistema Venezuela's leading maestros, whom they credit with advancing their sound beyond what they could have achieved on their own. Students and teachers find him a commanding, sometimes intimidating, presence and respect his ability to lift them to new levels.

The artistic director of Orquestra Geração, Juan Carlos Maggiorani, is also Venezuelan; a member of the internationally touring Matosinhos String Quartet, he grew up in Venezuela's El Sistema and moved with his family to Lisbon when he was in high school. In the sectional rehearsal we observed, his teaching moved from addressing technical problems to exploring emotional connections to the music in terms the teenaged players could instantly grasp. Even as he worked on techniques for adjusting timbre, he enlisted their imaginations and feelings: "Think of the heart pouring out of you into the life of that first note," he said. Throughout the rehearsal, he reminded them to keep their bodies moving as they played. The students stayed after the rehearsal, talking and playing—late on a Monday night—until they were physically ushered out of the building.

Rey Trombetta is an example of a Venezuelan who works in a different way to help Sistema programs elsewhere grow. Rey is not a peripatetic master teacher; a journalist by trade, he lives in England and is the communications and project manager for Sistema England. He is an articulate representative of El Sistema's philosophy and practices, an eloquent advocate of its central mission, and a tireless connector of Sistema-involved people everywhere.

The United States and Canada are also fortunate beneficiaries of Latin American Sistema mentorship. It's a primary axiom of El Sistema Venezuela that the Americas are, in many respects, one interconnected entity; Dudamel has said, "There is no 'North America' or 'Central America' or 'South America'—there is one America, and it is music that brings us together." That sense of unity is increasingly affirmed, as more and more Latin Americans assume leadership positions within the northern American Sistema movement. There are currently at least ten directors and more than thirty teachers in the U.S. and Canadian núcleos who come from Latin American backgrounds. The pioneer of this group is Guatemalan Alvaro Rodas,

BATUTA TO BEYOND

Juan Felipe Molano grew up in and near Medellín, Colombia; he studied clarinet and then conducting in that city's Batuta program, moving up to his first full conductorship in 1995. On a visit to New York, he bought a $10 ticket to observe a New York Philharmonic open rehearsal led by then music director Kurt Masur. He tried to speak to Masur after the concert, but a security guard blocked him; however, he found an unlocked door and wended his way through a warren of offices to get backstage, where he found Masur. Introducing himself, he asked, "Could I study with you, Maestro?" Masur agreed to let Juan Felipe audit a new course he was teaching. In the long run, Juan Felipe did more than audit; he found a mentor in one of the world's foremost conductors, who helped him begin his years of study at the Vienna Conservatory.

This story could well have ended with the precocious young Latin American conductor using sterling Old-World connections and credentials to achieve entree into the international conducting club. Instead, Juan Felipe went back to Colombia to become the Batuta national director of orchestras and the founding director of the Colombian Youth Philharmonic. In 2013, he came to California as director of the Sistema-inspired program Youth Orchestra of Salinas (YOSAL) and then moved to Los Angeles to become conductor of the L.A. Phil's Sistema-inspired program YOLA.

Clearly, Juan Felipe's great passion lies in bringing orchestral music to underserved children. His work in Colombia included consistent efforts to unite the energies of disparate organizations devoted to this goal. "Colombia is unusual," he told us, "in that it has many programs in addition to Batuta that are trying to bring social change to children through music. We make a great effort to maintain a collegial spirit between all these programs. Sometimes of course, the organizations fight with each other, because that's human nature. But the main thing is that we're always trying to connect around the needs of the kids."

The United States has hundreds of disconnected programs with sights set on those same goals. It's the good fortune of the U.S. movement that Juan Felipe has been selected as one of the faculty leaders guiding the creation of a U.S. Sistema Youth Orchestra.

founder of the Corona Youth Music Project in New York City. A successful symphonic percussionist before committing to the work of citizen artistry, Alvaro wrote his master's degree thesis in 2008 on the international growth of El Sistema,[27] and was the first Latin American Sistema Fellow. Other prominent examples of Latin Americans in leadership positions in the North American Sistema include Juan Felipe Molano of Colombia, the conductor of the flagship YOLA program of the Los Angeles Philharmonic; José Luis Hernández-Estrada of Mexico, founder-director of Sistema Tulsa, in Oklahoma; and Brazilian Diogo Pereira, founder-director of the Harmony Project Phoenix, in Arizona. The many Venezuelans in this list include Melina García and Samuel Marchán, founder-director and lead teacher of the Union City Music Project in New Jersey; Norma Núñez Loaiza, director of El Sistema Lehigh Valley; Antonio Delgado, music director of El Sistema New Brunswick; Jorge Soto, music director of the Sistema Side-by-Side Orchestra at Longy; teachers Margaret Gonzalez, Marielisa and Mariesther Álvarez, and many others. Rodrigo Guerrero, a longtime Sistema Venezuela administrator and translator for Maestro Abreu, is now the leader of an international El Sistema conferencing project of the Massachusetts Cultural Council.

Within Latin America, other countries continue to look to Venezuelan maestros for enduring inspiration. Marcos Rangel, the young horn player who conducts the advanced orchestra in Campos, told us that Roberto Zambrano has guided them for years, and that when Roberto works with them, there is an actual change in the sound of the program's orchestras. When we asked Marcos how the sound changes, he said, "I think the best way to describe the change is . . . the *pianissimos* are better!"

We had expected him to tell us that the *fortes* were better; Venezuelan Sistema orchestras love their fortes, and in fact Roberto Zambrano sometimes demands *fortes* of beginner orchestras, to instill a courage about playing boldly that is harder to internalize later. But Marcos's answer went straight to an aesthetic dimension. An orchestra can play *fortissimo* just by increasing its collective vigor, but it can play a great *pianissimo* only if its members are attending to the refinement of musical feeling. Roberto's attention to aesthetic detail is a reminder that when the Venezuelan master teachers advocate for excellence along with social inclusion, it is not only technical excellence they have in mind. It is also the capacity for revealing the nuanced beauty of musical details. Marcos's observation is proof that an ensemble born of radical inclusion can, in fact, achieve aesthetic distinction.

ALL TOGETHER NOW

In 2009, a music-loving Air Force colonel in the western Colombian city of Cali decided that the ninetieth anniversary of the Colombian Air Force should be celebrated with a huge musical event involving every single child in the area who could make music. Cali was a center of violence during the civil war; it is coming back to vitality and health, as are other Colombian cities, using the arts as a key investment for renewal. So when the colonel came asking for help, the local Batuta leaders mobilized all the music programs in the area that were working with children (including many non-Batuta programs) and brought them together in a massive *encuentro*, a huge gathering of orchestras and choirs. With the support of the Air Force, the best musicians in the region were hired to train and rehearse the children. The concert, with 800 young people performing for an audience of thousands, took place, appropriately, in an airplane hangar.

"They played Shostakovich and Borodin, and they sang the 'Hallelujah Chorus' from Handel's *Messiah*," says Juan Antonio Cuéllar. "While we had originally thought that beginners and advanced players would perform separately, all the younger musicians begged to play everything. So even the smallest children performed in all the pieces. For every single music program in the city, this concert raised the bar of excellence."

In telling this story, Cuéllar said several times, "We don't look for things . . . we find them." At first we weren't sure what this meant. Eventually, we understood it to mean a habit of high aspiration—a refusal to look for solutions to the needs of children without finding them. Juan Antonio was restating an adage that many use to describe Maestro Abreu's worldview: "No is not an option." The larger message seems to be the conviction that accomplishing Sistema goals means finding unexpected, unreasonable, close-to-impossible opportunities to succeed. An Air Force colonel offering an airplane hangar for a concert of 800 kids—what were the chances of that? And yet "no" was not an option.

The encuentro was so successful that the Air Force repeated it again the following year. Eventually, a regional orchestra emerged as a joint project of all the music programs. But the most important thing about the encuentro, perhaps, is the lasting memory, in 800 children's minds, of their teachers articulating a nearly impossible vision, and working with them diligently, patiently, and collectively, until the impossible became possible. In ways large and small, that is how Sistema programs work every day.

∞

There's no sauce in the world like hunger.
—MIGUEL DE CERVANTES

CHAPTER 10

Family and Community Involvement

In Venezuela, núcleo leaders see themselves not only as teachers and
orchestra conductors but also as community leaders. . . . they feel that
it's just as much of an honor to conduct a meeting of neighbors in the
community as to conduct an orchestra. . . .
Always, the life of the community is around the orchestra.
—JOSÉ ANTONIO ABREU

When a violin enters a home, the family rises to it.
It's the beginning of change.
—LUIS ALBERTO MORENO, PRESIDENT,
INTER-AMERICAN DEVELOPMENT BANK

The words "family" and "community" are close to sacred in
the dialogue of El Sistema. This is partly because the orchestra and chorus are seen as exemplars of healthy family and
harmonious community, but it's also because families and neighborhoods, as well as children and young people, are considered an essential part of the Sistema's transformative project. All over the world,
references to family and community involvement show up in the
goals, mission statements, and everyday conversations of Sistema-
inspired programs.

In previous chapters, we've discussed the abundant circumstantial evidence and growing body of research data affirming that strong

El Sistema programs achieve their mission of lifelong contribution to the lives of young people. It's harder to assess whether the mission of community change is widely fulfilled, as progress toward that goal is far more difficult to measure. The barrios of Caracas have not been transformed, in any way that we can reliably cite, by the many thousands of young people who have poured so much of their lives into neighborhood Sistema programs. Skeptics would argue that if there is no proven, large-scale positive impact in the country where the work has grown the longest and deepest, how can one propose that núcleos change communities?

A response to this question must include the fact that in the past few years, Venezuela has seen exacerbated levels of political turbulence and economic stress that make it difficult to perceive and document the possible positive impact of El Sistema on its most challenged communities. It is our sense that the community-building impact of El Sistema is fragmented and sometimes overwhelmed by the deafening demands of daily life in the distressed neighborhoods of many núcleos. Further, it's clear that on a macro level, Venezuela's social, political, and economic problems are so complex that no social program could make a measurable causal impact without involving many millions more people and more stable times. The Venezuelan Sistema is vast by many standards; still, with only some 2 million involved with it since it began, it hasn't had the capacity to foster change on a city- or country-wide scale. In addition, the young people who thrive and develop the most fully in Sistema work often move out of the barrios of their childhoods to build better lives in safer places. These factors make it difficult at this point to measure the impact of El Sistema on whole communities.

This doesn't mean the ripple effect of community benefit isn't happening; it does mean that amid dysfunction and chaos, the effect is harder to gauge. It seems likely that when the current crisis abates, the community impact of El Sistema will become more evident, as increasing numbers of Sistema graduates bring the social and emotional skills that now grow inside núcleo walls to bear upon civic reform and regeneration.

In the meantime, we have abundant observational evidence that in the Venezuelan Sistema, the active engagement of families and communities is a foundational principle and an essential practice. Families are drawn into the life of the núcleo in many ways—through bringing toddlers to musical play sessions and learning songs to sing with their children; through being part of frequent performances, some informal, and many in community venues; through learning to respond to their children's musical efforts with delight and encouragement. We have never visited a Venezuelan núcleo where there weren't some parents hanging out in the hallways or inner courtyards, listening to the music coming from all directions.

Finally, the presence of a núcleo means there is a space in a community that is dedicated to music. This carries tremendous symbolic weight, in a culture where music is deeply valued; it can make the whole community feel more valuable. Daniela Das Dores, the Venezuelan teacher and violinist who now works at In Harmony Lambeth, pointed out that in Venezuela, El Sistema "is not an after-school club. It's an orchestra." This simple statement is the accomplishment of decades. Instead of thinking of El Sistema as a "project" or "program," words that connote an encapsulated activity for young people, Daniela thinks of an artistic entity. It's not even "a youth orchestra." It's *an orchestra*. *Our* orchestra. This is what a núcleo can become, in the eyes of its community.

We visited the Núcleo Guarenas, about an hour from Caracas, with an international group of colleagues who were working hard to grasp the essence of El Sistema. Camilla Sarner, a visitor from Sistema Sweden, asked the young núcleo director, Andrés González (who is also the national director of El Sistema núcleos), "Can you tell us, in a few simple words, just exactly how El Sistema changes lives?"

"Yes, it really is simple," responded Andrés. "First we take kids out of the craziness of the streets. As much as we can, we grab them from the madness of the streets, the drugs and guns and violence. But even more important, what they experience here makes them feel *proud*. It makes them feel valued. Valuable. If a little kid knows how to play only one note, but she plays it well and for her parents and community—she is proud. Her family is proud too. Her friends and neighbors become proud. From there, things begin to change."

Andrés's words echo the more famous ones of Maestro Abreu: "Once a child discovers he is important to his family, he begins to seek new ways of improving himself. And hopes better for himself and his community." Families, friends, and neighbors provide the witnessing, resonating context that amplifies the many small successes of musical progress.

In the course of researching Sistema programs outside of Venezuela, we found many thoughtful and wholehearted examples of family and community involvement. Around the world, parents often sit chatting in corridors and common spaces while they wait to pick up their kids. Families fill performance spaces wherever Sistema orchestras perform, and walk home holding the hands of their excited players. Family members help out as volunteers. Family involvement in Sistema programs is frequent, in the global context; involvement by the wider community is naturally slower to evolve.

We also visited Sistema programs where family and community involvement was challenging at best, and sometimes impossible. The dynamics that keep families mired in cycles of need and social alienation are the very ones that can make them inaccessible or even hostile to the Sistema programs that are engaging their children.

Every program does its best to reach beyond the children and to connect somehow with their lives outside program walls. Every program comes up, sooner or later, against the limitations of those connections. It's a highly charged landscape, since it deals with issues of children and community identity and social norms and control. The stakes are high; the progress is slow. Community change, if it happens at all, happens over generations.

THE EPITOME OF COMMUNITY INVOLVEMENT: SCOTLAND'S BIG NOISE

In Raploch, Scotland, a depressed postindustrial district that lies literally in the shadow of the fifteenth-century Stirling Castle, nearly every elementary-age child in town is in the El Sistema program. One of the oldest Sistema-inspired programs in Europe, Big Noise in Raploch began in 2008 with funding from the Scottish Arts Council, supplemented by support from private trusts and individuals; in 2011, a rigorous three-year evaluation program proved so conclusively that Big Noise had a positive effect on its children that the city of Stirling, which includes Raploch, decided to take on the financial support of the program when its initial five-year funding plan ended.

This was an improbable stroke of good fortune for Raploch, which for decades has languished under that majestic castle—where kings and queens, including Mary, Queen of Scots, were once crowned—as a place mired in entrenched poverty and high unemployment. Sistema Scotland founder Richard Holloway has described it as "the archetypal alienated community . . . well before the deindustrialization of Scotland, it was associated with abandonment and on-the-edgeness."

Richard Holloway's career has included authoring numerous books on religious belief in the modern world, as well as long stints as the bishop of Edinburgh in the Scottish Episcopal Church and as a BBC radio and television presenter. He first heard about El Sistema in 2007, when he was the head of the Scottish Arts Council, and he immediately went to Venezuela to have a look. "What went to my heart," Holloway told us, "is that in Venezuela I saw children *playing*, in both senses of the word—playing with a joyous intensity that was transformative. I could see the immersive nature of the experience. I could see that for kids to be embedded in that was creating a reality stronger than the reality that would otherwise kill them."

Upon his return to Scotland, Holloway met with local officials in Raploch, which had recently received government funds for infrastructure rebuilding. "One of the standard political responses to a deprived neighborhood," he told us, "is to do something about the external infrastructure—the roads, the buildings, all of that—but nothing for the internal, spiritual infrastructure. If that was all they were going to do, they were about to make a colossal mistake. So I proposed this rather unusual experiment to them, of starting an El Sistema program. They were thinking roads and housing, not children with violins. But I told them that the Arts Council would fund it for five years. I proposed that if it started achieving its objectives, the city would then start paying for it. They said yes."

Because the overall goal was the regeneration of the town, community involvement was a top priority for the Raploch Sistema program from the outset. Nicola Killean, the gifted community arts educator Holloway hired to lead the project, assembled a staff of teaching artists whose first task was, quite literally, to go out and play. "Our teaching artists went all round the town," Nicola told us, "and they played everywhere—in the bingo parlor, in the post office, in the football clubs and the shopping centers. We really wanted to introduce ourselves to the community."

Holloway said, "They just flooded Raploch with music. People got curious: 'Who are they? What's goin' on in Raploch?'"

The program, officially dubbed Big Noise, began with very young children, ages five to eight, in two Raploch elementary schools that shared a campus. Once it was underway, Nicola and her staff invited all the parents to visit the classes and come to the concerts. They soon realized, however, that some families were never going to respond to such invitations. "So we decided to go to them," said Nicola. They created a "Take a Musician Home to Tea" ritual, an example many programs across the world are beginning to follow. Musicians make visits to kids' houses, meet relatives, and sometimes play and sing with the kids. "It's one of our teachers' favorite things," said Nicola, "and the children love it as well." This familiarity with the children's homes makes it possible for the program to keep close track of absentees. "If you stop showing up to the program," Nicola told us, "we will encourage you to come back in every way we can. We'll send 'Miss You' cards or 'Get Well' balloons, and we might come tapping at your door."

As Sistema Scotland, the charitable entity that supports Big Noise, expanded the program to more schools over the next several years—eventually including not only both elementary schools but also the local nursery school, a special needs school and baby/caregiver classes—parental involvement continued to be a central priority. Ali Gornall, a double bass player who was a teacher in Raploch and now directs the second Big Noise program, in Glasgow, said that one of the reasons Big Noise starts with children at a young age is that it's easier to engage parents that way. "Parents tend to be more closely involved when their kids are really young, so if we start at that age, we can build good relationships with families," she said.

As in Venezuela, the youngest children in Big Noise are often accompanied by a parent or caregiver, who learns the songs— "Everything is taught through songs, in the beginning," said Ali— and can then practice them with their children at home. When the children are older, the parents have the opportunity to learn instruments and play in a parent orchestra; this means they'll be practicing at home with the children (and learning from them, since the children often advance faster than the parents). There is a parent choir as well.

After seven years of nurturing this family-oriented learning culture, the program has engaged parents to the extent that almost all come to the concerts. "We perform all the time," said Nicola. "The children's orchestras are a great way to celebrate through performance. Parents always come. It is part of their lives now." Nicola has seen firsthand that family involvement in Big Noise can have a beneficial effect on family dynamics. "When parents develop that active interest in what the children are doing, it has a really positive influence on the family unit. They have a new language they're sharing together, and they are doing more together. Also, it raises parents' ambitions for their children. This helps to break the cycle of poverty. If we support the children and families to think bigger and wider, they all start to become a bit more ambitious and a bit more confident."

"Thinking bigger and wider"—that phrase defines the nature of Sistema Scotland. A crucial part of its vision is sustaining a close relationship with El Sistema in Venezuela. In 2012, Nicola Killean and Richard Holloway and their colleagues thought very big and wide: Let's invite the Simón Bolívar Orchestra of Venezuela, they proposed, to visit us. Let's have Dudamel and his musicians rehearse and work with our children. Let's have our children play with the Simón Bolívar Orchestra in a huge side-by-side concert!

Let's have the concert on the night of the summer solstice!

Let's have it in a gigantic field, for free, so that everyone who wants to come can come!

All of which they did. The concert entered the national calendar and became widely anticipated across the U.K. as a kickoff to the summer-long Cultural Olympiad celebrating the 2012 Summer Olympic Games in London.

The only thing they couldn't conjure was sunshine. During the concert, the field was pelted by torrential rain; the players were under the shelter of a band shell, but the audience members were drenched.

Weather notwithstanding, an enormous crowd turned out. Young couples pushing plastic-sheathed strollers, grandparents with rubbers over their shoes, small children dancing bare-limbed in the rain—it seemed that every person in Raploch had come out that evening to stand, along with a host of foreign visitors, in the sodden field in a downpour, listening to their siblings or cousins or children (or their neighbors' children, or their friends' children) play Beethoven with the virtuosi from Venezuela. The sound was huge and the sound system strong, and there were large video screens on either side of the stage, showing what the onstage cameras were catching. The cameras loved Gustavo, of course, but the shots that made the crowd catch its collective breath were close-ups of small redheaded or freckle-faced children sitting at stands with superstars from a far-off Latin American country—stars who, by virtue of the previous three days of joint rehearsals and learning sessions, were now role models, mentors, and friends. Each child was hearing and feeling his own sound as part of the grandest symphonic sound he'd ever heard. As Richard Holloway said: "They played till their wee hearts burst."

"That concert was really inspirational for our whole community," Nicola said. "It was just the idea that the Simón Bolívar Orchestra would think that we here in Raploch are important enough to come and work and play with us. And that the concert was in one of our hay fields, not a fancy concert hall in London. I think the community couldn't have imagined that was possible."

Maestro Abreu was there too, and in a rousing speech at the rehearsal hall beforehand, he invited Big Noise to come to Venezuela. Eighteen months later, in January 2014, 52 children from Raploch, Scotland, flew to Caracas, along with a host of teachers and volunteer parent chaperones, for a ten-day visit. The children, aged nine to fifteen, visited núcleos and rehearsed and performed a "bi-national Sistema showcase concert" with children of El Sistema Venezuela. The visit even included a rehearsal with Gustavo, who is the "official patron" of Sistema Scotland, and whom the kids now think of as a mate.

"That trip to Caracas was kind of an insane thing," Richard Holloway acknowledged cheerfully. "But it turned out to be a catalytic moment in the history of Raploch. Because it had an astonishing effect on the children. When I go and listen to them play now, I can hear how the trip galvanized them. The quality of their playing is so much higher. They really want to play and work hard."

Nicola noted that it was galvanizing for the parents and the community too. "The parents themselves were suddenly thinking big. Asking questions like, 'So what will we do about auditioning the children to get into the national orchestra and the national choirs?' 'How can we be involved in the Commonwealth Games when they come to Scotland?' I hear them and I think, wow. This is really thinking big."

Big Noise's "Big Trip" became news throughout the U.K.; a documentary film about the trip was broadcast on BBC1 a few months later. We were told by a number of Big Noise staff members that the program has helped everyone in Raploch, even those who don't have kids in the program, feel proud of their community. Holloway said, "Big Noise has given the community of Raploch a new and positive consciousness about itself."

Even the cabbie who drove us from the Stirling train station to Raploch knew about Big Noise. "It's an amazing music program we have here," he told us in his barely intelligible brogue, not knowing we had any connection with the program. "People know about Raploch now because of the children playing music. It used to be that they only knew about us for the unemployment and that. But this gives us something to be proud of. It lifts up our whole community, and gives us hope for our children."

We asked him how it has lifted the community. He said, "We have just had a new university campus built at Raploch. The government could have put it anywhere, but they put it here because of the orchestra, I'm sure of it. The kids have made us look good. They make us look like a place with a future."

BIG NOISE'S LANDMARK RESEARCH RESULTS

Big Noise is distinctive among Sistema programs around the world for its especially rigorous evaluation system, which began during its first year and was conducted by GEN, an independent evaluation team jointly commissioned by the Culture, Education, Youth Justice and Early Years departments of the Scottish government. The researchers studied not only the children themselves, but also the families and communities. Their aim was to determine whether Big Noise was attaining its goals of "transforming children's lives through music; empowering communities; and growing future inclusive orchestras."

A first report issued in 2011, after three years of research, revealed highly positive findings. Regarding the families, the report stated: "As a result of Big Noise, families report improved relation-ships at home, wider social networks and more shared activities between parents and children. It has also allowed the parents to see a more positive future for their children and has engendered a sense of pride in what they have and will go on to achieve in their lives."

Buoyed by the success of Big Noise in Raploch, the leaders of Sistema Scotland decided to expand, and there are now Big Noise programs in Glasgow and Aberdeen, with a fourth in the making. Nicola spoke of the challenges of expansion: "We are ambitious about growth, but we want to be really responsible about the children and communities we're already committed to. We will always make sure that the program in Raploch is developing and growing and thriving. But at the same time we really want other communities in Scotland to feel the benefits of this work."

Another independent research initiative is now underway, with an even more impressive pedigree than the first: it is being conducted by the Glasgow Centre for Population Health, a government welfare agency, in conjunction with Audit Scotland, Glasgow Caledonian University, and Education Scotland. Because this study is so rigorous, long-term, and large-scale, its initial findings in May 2015 are some of the most significant research findings about El Sistema to date.

As were the 2011 findings, these results are strongly affirmative. Researchers found a wide range of benefits to students in the short and medium terms, and predicted a long-term potential to enhance participants' lives, prospects, health, and well-being. The findings reflected significant improvements in school learning and atten-dance, in self-confidence, in socialization, and in family and com-munity functioning. All in all, the researchers reported "convincing evidence of positive change in children's lives," and concluded, "The program represents a good investment for society." Big Noise, they said, has "the potential to quickly generate social benefits greater than the cost of delivery."[28]

Generating social benefits greater than the cost of delivery: what that means, simply put, is that the study compared the costs of delivering the program to the costs the government would have had, without the program—costs like truancy services, medical services, police intervention, and juvenile detention. (This kind of calculation is known as Opportunity Cost.) As a case in point, when researchers applied this cost-benefit analysis to the Glasgow program, they predicted it would be slightly negative for the first six years, but after those six years, the program would begin to save the city money, eventually to the tune of millions of pounds. Within fifteen years, the researchers predicted, Big Noise in Glasgow would save the city a total of 29 million pounds. (This study's finding is consistent with a 2008 cost-benefit study of Venezuela's El Sistema, which calculated $1.68 of benefit for every $1.00 invested, or an Opportunity Cost benefit of $56 million in 2007, a time when the Sistema reached half as many students as it does today.[29])

Overseeing the Big Noise research is a panel of experts chaired by Angiolina Foster, Scotland's chief executive for Health Improvement. At the press conference announcing the findings, Ms. Foster said: "Established approaches are not meeting some of the challenges in our society. It is essential we learn from innovative programmes like Big Noise. These first findings are impressive and fascinating. It is clear that over the next few years we could see even more exciting outcomes."

COMMUNITY INVOLVEMENT ACROSS EUROPE AND ASIA

As an example of conscious, consistent family and community involvement, Sistema Scotland sets a high bar for Sistema programs around the world. But many programs are making progress toward meeting that bar. One program that particularly resembles Big Noise, and has consciously made the Scottish program its exemplar, is In Harmony Liverpool. Located in Liverpool's West Everton neighborhood, the program is housed in the Faith Primary School, and like Big Noise, it makes a priority of inclusive community; every child in the school is in the program. Taking inclusivity even further, all of the classroom teachers participate alongside their students in the ensemble music learning. As we walked through the halls, we heard music breaking out at frequent intervals and from all directions. It is as though music has become the language of the whole school.

Life expectancy in West Everton is shorter than in any other community in England—and that's just one headline indicator of a district in difficult social and economic circumstances. Community engagement is therefore a principal goal of In Harmony Liverpool, and tracking progress in that area has consistently been a key aspect of its evaluation process. In 2015, the program released a five-year evaluation report that documented a huge increase in the number of parents who felt more involved in the community as a direct consequence of In Harmony. The study yielded "strong and compelling evidence that self-determination and social capital are building within the West Everton community," wrote the researchers. "We have identified a cycle of change that is compelling."

This research is important for the overall Sistema movement, as is the Scottish evaluative report described above, in that it was independently conducted, rigorous, long-term (by Sistema standards), and resoundingly positive. Among its many findings were that the children's academic achievements were improving substantially, and that this had a direct bearing on feelings of increased self-worth and self-confidence. "There is strong evidence," wrote the researchers, "that it [the program] is contributing to enhanced family and peer relationships. We also believe that it is contributing to improved behaviour and mitigating risk."

In conclusion, the report states: "We have seen that In Harmony Liverpool can play an important role in public health provision, clinical health services, educational attainment, developing well-being at individual and community levels and in families. We believe the programme is generating important outcomes and life chances for children and families."

In Harmony Liverpool is run by the Royal Liverpool Philharmonic Orchestra. In 2014, the orchestra joined with a group of other local organizations to buy and renovate an abandoned church in the middle of West Everton and convert it into a community center called the Friary; In Harmony orchestras and choruses often rehearse and perform there, and other community events take place there as well. "The Friary is really the hub of the community," said Peter Garden, the orchestra's director of learning and engagement. "The parents love stopping in and hearing the children play." The orchestra musicians themselves often rehearse in the space, he told us, and get to know the In Harmony kids and parents.

Establishing an actual community center instead of operating within a school has also made a positive difference for In Harmony Lambeth, located in a poor neighborhood of London. The program moved several years ago from a school setting to the Wheatsheaf Community Center, an old-fashioned Gothic-style hall with a vaulted ceiling and balconies. Several teachers in the Lambeth program told us they saw a big improvement in overall behavior and attention when they moved to Wheatsheaf; it gave them a strong community presence, and it provided a nonschool atmosphere in which young people could create identities for themselves that were different from their school identities. A thirteen-year-old double bass player there told us that he wouldn't have been willing to go back to his old primary school in the afternoons to play music, but going to the Wheatsheaf Center "feels kinda all right."

Elsewhere in London, we visited the Nucleo Project, a small but vibrant Sistema-inspired program launched and run by Lucy Maguire, who is herself small and electrically vibrant. Her program, which began on the basement level of a West London flat, is highly family-centric, always teeming with parents as well as children. "I basically require the parents to stay for the program whenever they can," she says, "because they can be a real help with the kids. Also, they can learn what their kids are capable of."

Lucy dreamed as a child of being a conductor, and had some bouts of conservatory education, but a restless spirit took her to Venezuela in 2009, when she was nineteen. She didn't speak Spanish; she didn't know any Venezuelans. But she had her violin. "I went to visit the núcleo in Guarenas, and the next thing I knew, I was conducting these amazing young teenagers in Tchaikovsky's Fourth Symphony. I felt like I had found what I had always been looking for. I just decided to live there."

Several years later, she says, when she finally came home to London, "I went on eBay and ordered a bunch of secondhand violins and had them delivered to my parents' address. I forgot to tell my mum they were coming, so she was a bit surprised." Recruiting children with flyers at local primary schools, she started an El Sistema program in a vacant basement flat in her parents' apartment building.

When we visited on a weekday afternoon, parents and siblings took up fully half of the room. (The program has since moved to a larger space.) Lucy was leading the beginners' orchestra of tiny children with tiny stringed instruments. "Lucas, your bow hold is just beautiful!" she said to a six-year-old. "You must have practiced it a lot at home!"

Lucas, whose family had recently migrated to London from northern Africa, looked over his shoulder at his father, who was sitting among the other parents and watching intently. His father gave him a thumbs-up, and Lucas went back to contemplating his bow hold. Several more times during the session, he looked back; the thumbs-up was always there. At one point he ran back to his father, who hugged him and sent him back to his chair in the orchestra.

In cities across the country, England's Sistema-inspired programs strive for parent and community involvement. All encounter difficulties related to the ethnic heterogeneity of their student populations; they are meeting this challenge with varying degrees of success, and learning from one another in the process.

The same is true, on a wider scale, for the Sistema programs of other European countries. In many programs, tensions among different ethnicities, as well as dysfunctional family patterns within cultures of poverty, make it difficult to achieve substantial family and community involvement. In Lisbon, many of the students are from North African immigrant families. "Some of them are second- and third-generation, but they are still poor and live in closed communities," said Mariana Pinto, a young Portuguese violinist who taught in the núcleos of Portugal's Orquestra Geração for years, and has moved to Italy and now teaches at a núcleo in Florence. "Their cultures are sometimes different from our value systems; some still practice genital mutilation of girls and forced prostitution. It can be difficult for Sistema teachers to make connections with these families."

In Romania and in Bosnia, children in Sistema programs are often forbidden by their parents to sing in one another's languages. The Bosnian program's anthem "Love People" has the students singing, in English, "We are all the same, a brotherhood of man," in spite of the fact that some of their parents, traumatized by a history of genocide, won't speak to one another.

But some programs are making headway, even against such substantive odds. The "Vänstay" tradition of El Sistema Sweden has created a lively, welcoming multicultural civic space in which some parents and family members have begun to relax long-standing ethnic prejudices. In Srebrenica, Bosnia, the parents of those English-singing children allowed them to travel together to Austria in 2013 to join a Sistema Europe gathering, even though the parents themselves would not congregate together on the parking lot where they waved goodbye to the bus. The multiethnic young people in the Orquestra Geração of Portugal in Lisbon have achieved a comradeship that shines through in their exuberant performances.

Only a few of the Sistema-inspired programs in Africa and Asia involve students and families of immigrant populations. One interesting anomaly is the Crashendo! program in Melbourne, Australia, where over 80 percent of the children are from immigrant families. According to program manager Erica Rasmussen, the majority of these children are from the Karen ethnic group of southern Myanmar, many of whom have fled from Burmese persecution and live in refugee camps along the Thai border; Australia accepts a yearly quota

A MAORI WELCOME FOR ERIC

Sistema Whangarei (called Toi Akorangi in Maori) in northern New Zealand has exceptionally rich connections with its Maori community. At a performance by a violin ensemble of twelve beginners, I was greeted with a traditional pōwhiri, a community welcome ceremony that began with the karanga, a haunting song of welcome, as I walked into the school gymnasium hung with large banners of Maori sacred sites and artworks. After several adult welcomes and songs sung by the whole assembly, three students made speeches in Maori—all speaking and singing in the same driving, assured, extroverted style.

I was invited to "hongi" with the principal and the four lead students. This is a handshake followed by a pressing together of foreheads with noses touching, to share the "breath of peace." It is remarkably intimate. Participants closed their eyes, as if in prayer, in the two or three seconds of sharing head-to-head.

Then the new string orchestra performed; the pieces were rudimentary, but played with pride and flair. Afterward, the orchestra director, Samantha Winterton, invited me up to the stage. She explained to the children and the audience that I had never held a violin, much less played one, and she enrolled the children in teaching me. Before long, I was playing open strings in rhythms as the kids played harmonies. In effect, Samantha was honoring the art of teaching by putting it onstage along with the performance. She was modeling for her students the dual skills of teaching and performing, blending rather than separating them, and she was enabling the student performers to become instant teachers onstage before an audience of their families and friends. There was a lot of laughter at the halting efforts of the older white foreigner, providing an equalizing element in the room that could have been rife with cultural imbalances.

Fiona Douglas, the program director of Sistema Whangarei, told us that the Maori word *awhi* (pronounced "affie"), which means "to lend support," is a primary concept among her students and in Maori culture. It is the essence of Maori community, and the Sistema program is steeped in that community spirit. (This same concept surfaced again in Sistema-like programs in southern Africa, in the Bantu word *ubuntu*.) Fiona sees it as a cultural birthright, indeed a human birthright, which appears naturally when the social environment is receptive.

of Christian Karen immigrants for resettlement. "I'd say close to all these parents are quite happy their children are in the program," said Erica. "They come to every performance. Our performance space is always packed." Perhaps because the immigrants are themselves a fairly homogeneous community, and because they have escaped persecution based on both ethnicity and religion, the Crashendo! program is experienced by these parents as an uncomplicated benefit in their lives.

COMMUNITY INVOLVEMENT IN LATIN AMERICA

Culture is love. Art is sex. This is how cities propagate to stay alive.
—EDUARDO PAES, MAYOR OF RIO DE JANEIRO, BRAZIL

In Latin America, even though the tradition of community and family involvement is strong because of the relative proximity of Venezuela's example, some programs encounter parental resistance, but the cause is not usually ethnic discord or cultural convention. Here, it's more likely to be sheer poverty; once children turn twelve or thirteen, parents often want them helping out in the nonschool hours (school days are half-days in much of Latin America, with two shifts each day) by selling things in the streets, or even scavenging. In a few countries, most prominently Venezuela, programs can provide a small stipend for their most committed teenage students, especially when they move up to higher-level orchestras; this not only eases parental pressure to help support the families, but also is a tangible acknowledgment of the value of the students' dedication to music. This modest stipend sometimes comprises a significant share of a family's income.

In Colombia, at the Escuela de Música Desepaz in Cali, the program coordinator told us, "We try to solve the parental involvement problem by inviting them to come and hear the orchestras play, hoping to convince them that their kids are learning something

important for life here." We asked her if this works, and she smiled cautiously. "Sometimes it does," she said.

There is a similar intentionality in the way the Bairro da Paz núcleo in Salvador, Brazil, approaches the families of its students. "We do a lot of talking with the parents," said the young director, a trumpet player named Esdras Efraim. "We try to build it so it's a team: the kids, the parents, us. The same team."

We visited several núcleos elsewhere in Brazil where the ideal of community involvement means bringing social services into the núcleo. At Ação Social pela Música in Rio de Janeiro, health workers are part of the program staff. Said Julio Camargo, the program's pedagogy coordinator: "We don't lose sight of our primary goal, which is social transformation. We think this is best done through integrating support services into our program." Families' sense of urgency about money is assuaged in part by the food stamps the program distributes to kids who come regularly. Many programs here and elsewhere in Brazil take place in Pentecostal churches, which have become important community centers and hubs of connection.

Mariana Andrade, the staff social worker at Orquestranda a Vida in Campos, Brazil, has experience in psychological family therapy. She told us that the children in the program are sometimes pressured to leave it by parents who want them to be earning money. She has found that it's more effective to address this problem by counseling the children rather than trying to persuade the parents. "If the kids want to be in the program but the parents are resistant, I don't bring in the parents to talk to them myself. I talk with the kids to help them convince their parents: 'Find a way! You know how to do it!' Every kid knows his or her family better than I do. And they usually do find a way." She added that most of the kids understand that the program gives them choices in life that they would never have otherwise. "It's the first time in my twenty-five-year career that I have seen kids being offered a choice in this way," she said. "I find qualities here that I struggled to find in other social projects."

For the children who grow up to be musicians, says Campos program director Jony William, the financial problem sometimes continues on a larger scale. "We've lost many excellent young musicians, excellent teachers, because we couldn't pay them enough to satisfy the pressures of their families," he told us. "We do our best to pay them as well as we can, but the families exert great pressure on them to find more lucrative work."

COMMUNITY INVOLVEMENT IN THE UNITED STATES AND CANADA

An authoritative study on education improvement in the United States concluded: "A synthesis of research on parent involvement over the past decade found that, regardless of family income or background, students with involved parents are more likely to earn higher grades and test scores, enroll in higher-level programs, attend school regularly, have better social skills, show improved behavior, adapt well to school, and graduate and go on to post-secondary education."[30] Most program leaders and teachers in the U.S. and Canada have pursued the goal of parental involvement persistently and inventively, and as a result, robust evolving connections with family and community constitute one of the strengths of these programs. Many involve parents as volunteers, and often those volunteers carry out essential responsibilities like providing healthy snacks and chaperoning trips. At the Union City Music Project in New Jersey, the smiling ladies at the attendance table are often parent volunteers, checking off names, noticing who's absent, keeping track of who's sick and who's away. Some programs have regular potluck dinners starring the parents as cooks.

The leaders of B Sharp Youth Music in Fort Worth, Texas, felt during the program's early stages that there was some kind of invisible door blocking parental and community engagement. In 2014, program coordinator Dorsey Griffin recruited men from the community to join Men 'N Position—men willing to put themselves in the position of guiding the boys in the program, serving as role models and mentors for the two-thirds of the program's boys who are without fathers. Following the men's lead, the mothers and other female caretakers formed their own group, #sharpmoms, whose members work together to help the girls in the program be more successful in school, in music, and at home.

At Sistema Toronto, committees of parent volunteers are entrusted with running one major fundraising event each year, and parent volunteering for concert support is presented as a program requirement. This has resulted in parents making friends across site communities; one parent, for example, shoots photos for his own

COMMUNITY MUSICWORKS

Community MusicWorks in Providence, Rhode Island, was founded in 1997, a decade before the U.S. Sistema movement arose, but it holds a number of principles in common with El Sistema. CMW has kept its enrollment small (currently 110 students) in order to provide in-depth contact and guidance for each student. Founded by the Providence String Quartet, it has emphasized lessons and small ensembles, introducing an orchestra only in the past few years, but its work has had research-affirmed life-changing impact on students and families.

CMW has become a national learning center, providing conferences, fellowships, and consulting, and always leading by example. On a warm summer afternoon, community members can be found sitting in folding chairs outside the program's small street-side building, listening to rehearsals through speakers set up on the sidewalk. CMW's leaders are in constant contact with community leaders and families, regularly hosting public events and parties in the neighborhood; faculty members are strongly encouraged to live in the neighborhood. CMW is a part of the community, not just a program that happens there; everyone knows them and is proud of their students and accomplishments. Founder Sebastian Ruth is a MacArthur "genius grant" awardee and a recipient of many awards, for demonstrating what long-term investment can do for the children and families of inner cities in the United States.

child's site, and crosses Toronto to photograph another program site. To Sistema Toronto director David Visentin, "This is the beginning of real social development and cross-community linkage."

Almost all programs make sure to arrange plenty of performances for parents. Some devise as many ways as possible to have students perform in public spaces in the community. Katie Wyatt, the founder-director of Kidznotes in Durham, North Carolina, has said that one of her ultimate goals is for her kids to perform in every single public space in the city.

A number of Sistema programs have created ways to bring parents and community members further inside the program by inviting them into parent choruses and parent recorder ensembles. These are often occasions for the sudden flash of understanding that comes only through actually diving into music-making: "What my kid is doing is HARD!" El Sistema Somerville, in Massachusetts, runs a community orchestra that accepts all interested comers and rehearses twice a week.

PROGRAMS THAT LIVE WITHIN COMMUNITY: GUADALAJARA AND BULACAN

"Always, the life of the community is around the orchestra." This vision of Maestro Abreu's is a beautiful ideal, and every El Sistema-inspired program strives toward some version of it—often, as we have seen, against complicated odds. In Guadalajara, Mexico, at the Lomas del Paraiso program, the life of the community has to be around the orchestra—because the orchestra is smack in the middle of it. The combined orchestra always rehearses outside, since there is no room inside the cramped núcleo building for all the kids to play together. As a result, the plaza and streets around the outdoor rehearsal space have become places where parents visit with friends and listen to the orchestra while their toddlers run around the sunny plaza. The music fills the neighborhood. A local television crew came to videotape the orchestra a week before our arrival, and they didn't need to ask where it was; they just followed the sound through the cramped barrio streets.

Because the parents and families are right there, watching and listening, they are, in a sense, in the program along with their kids. They witness the teaching and learning in daily detail. "It's amazing for the kids," we were told by Carla, whose daughter Estrella is in love with percussion. "They learn to work in teams. They are given real responsibilities to take care of themselves and each other." Her friend Maria, mother of Lizbet, who plays the flute, added, "They learn the hard discipline of practicing, and they learn it willingly because they are doing it together."

The mother of a particularly shy flutist told us that even though the program had not been in session the day before, because of a national holiday, her daughter had insisted on coming anyway. "She unpacked her flute and stood in the plaza and played, for everybody passing by," said the mother. "Everybody was so happy to hear her. She felt proud—like she had something to give them for their holiday. She had music to give them."

A few months later and half a world away, in the Bulacan district of Manila, 150 kids in the Ang Misyon Sistema program crowded under a tin-roofed shed to perform for us. Hanging behind them was a small chalkboard with musical staves; the shed becomes their classroom when they turn their plastic chairs around. The bandleader, Federico Frayna, teaches every instrument to every one of the 150 children, so he is glad that he can begin to rely on the advanced students of the Orchestra of the Filipino Youth who come to help out with teaching.

We sat on folding chairs in a dusty red dirt plaza in front of the shed, surrounded by family members and neighbors. Around the plaza, a few shack-shops and an ice-cream cart delineated the community agora, which is surrounded by pig farms. As in Lomas in Mexico, the orchestra is the heartbeat of the community.

At high noon, in three-digit temperatures, the kids played a lively concert, ending with the full orchestra tearing through the last movement of Dvořák's Fifth Symphony. During the performance, a dozen mothers were busy in the plaza preparing a special lunchtime ceremony called a boodle fight. Long narrow tables were laid with giant banana leaves. A column of cooked rice as thick as a fire hose was placed down the center, and the mothers ladled *adobo*, the soy-and-vinegar-flavored meat and vegetable stew that is a signature dish of the Philippines, on top of the rice.

After their performance, the players lined up on both sides of the tables, jostling for places; they restrained themselves for a brief blessing and then, at the signal, dove in, scooping food into their mouths with their fingers. It wasn't a fight at all; it was a sublimely silly how-fast-can-you-eat contest. Afterward, they immortalized the moment using a selfie stick so long that the photo could include the entire orchestra, plus guests, plus a few stray dogs.

Can we—can anyone—prove conclusively that the children's orchestras of Guadalajara and Bulacan have helped to knit their communities tighter, or improved their circumstances? Probably not; at least, not yet. For now, however, we can report that in both programs we spoke with parents who could see new possibilities for their children that they could never have seen before. In both places, we saw communities burdened with punishing poverty find a haven of friendship and cooperative endeavor in the space where the orchestra plays.

PART III
Overview of a Movement

For all its brilliant attributes, El Sistema's greatest genius may be its flexibility, its adaptability to so many different cultures.
—ANGELIKA LOŠEK, MANAGING DIRECTOR, SUPERAR

Sistema Europe Youth Orchestra (2015) performing at
La Scala Opera House in Milan, Italy.

PHOTOGRAPH: © MARCO CASELLI NIRMAL

CHAPTER 11

Different Cultures,
Different Needs

No pessimist ever discovered the secret of the stars, or sailed to an
uncharted land, or opened a new doorway for the human spirit.
—HELEN KELLER

If we heal our children, our children will help to heal us.
—KENICHI MURATA, PRINCIPAL INSTRUCTOR OF
THE BOARD OF EDUCATION IN SOMA, JAPAN

In Venezuela, El Sistema exists first and foremost to combat the
effects of poverty in the lives of children and young people. As
we have seen, the goal of poverty alleviation is also paramount
for many El Sistema-inspired programs across the world. We've also
discussed another kind of primary goal in European Sistema-inspired
programs, that of defusing the damage wrought by ethnic segregation
and prejudice in the lives of children and young people. When we
began our research, we envisioned an exploration of how Sistema
programs address these two worldwide goals. Along the way, we
found places where El Sistema has been adopted to address other
goals as well—goals equally as daunting, and equally resistant to
other remedies.

"READY FOR JOY": EL SISTEMA AND NATURAL DISASTER

Soma, a small seacoast city in the Fukushima Prefecture, lost almost 500 people in the earthquake and tsunami disaster of 2011. The water surge rose as high as 30 feet in many places and destroyed large areas of the city. When we first visited Soma in July 2012, we saw bridges that had been twisted in knots or broken into random pieces, apartment buildings ruptured as though crushed by a giant hand, and whole neighborhoods reduced to uninhabitable marshes littered with foundation stones and rubble.

We were told that just before the tsunami hit, parents raced to the schools to get their children. Some of the schools are built on higher ground than the residential neighborhoods, and schoolteachers pleaded with the parents to leave their children in school. But many parents, operating on the primal feeling that home is the safest place, took children home. Hundreds of families were lost when the tsunami swept them out to sea.

The rice paddies were ruined by salt water; rice had been one of Soma's two main sources of income. The other source was the fishing industry, and that was destroyed too, because Soma is also only twenty-eight miles from the Fukushima Daiichi Nuclear Power Plant, where the tsunami caused a major nuclear accident. No one in the country would buy seafood from the waters of Fukushima, and the fishing fleet lay broken and scattered in the harbor.

Many children in Soma lost a family member or friend in the disaster. Many more lost their homes and were living for extended periods in temporary housing quarters. Outside of every city school a monitoring station still stands, setting off an alarm if radiation levels rise too high. For a long time, the alarms rang often in the morning, and the children of Soma didn't go to school.

"The children you see here are neatly dressed and well behaved," we were told by Koichiro Yamada, the city superintendent of schools. "They are quiet; they do their schoolwork. You may think, 'Oh, these children are fine.'" Mr. Yamada, an austere elderly gentleman, shook his head. "The children are not fine. They are traumatized. They are deeply hurting inside. That is why we have brought El Sistema here."

Soma has deep traditions. An annual summer festival that includes a parade of samurai on horseback, clad in ancient armor and bearing flags of clan lineage, follows rituals that have been reenacted in exactly the same way nearly every summer for a thousand years. The city's music education tradition isn't as long as its samurai history; but for decades, school music ensembles from Fukushima have competed successfully against youth orchestras from other areas of Japan. In general, Japan is known for having one of the world's most extensive public music education systems, and Soma's music education has attained national prominence in a field of many wealthier and larger districts. We asked Mr. Yamada and other school officials why they had chosen El Sistema to address the suffering of Soma's children, given that its children have such extensive access to music education.

The answer was simple and consistent. "El Sistema is a pedagogy of joy," they said. "Joy is what our children need." We understood what they meant when we observed several school music programs in Soma. Excellence was obviously being achieved, but the students were subdued and seemed reluctant to risk being singled out for criticism by the teacher; there were no smiles, and there was little eye contact other than with the conductor.

How did word of El Sistema reach the local school board of a small seaside city in Japan? As with so many stories about the international spread of El Sistema, the answer involves a few improbable degrees of separation. Several months after the tsunami struck, Yutaka Kikugawa, a Japanese UNICEF national committee official helping to lead Soma's recovery effort, had a chance to work with the Berlin Philharmonic (one of the UNICEF goodwill ambassadors for tsunami victims) and happened to meet up with one of the orchestra's French horn players, Fergus McWilliam. Fergus is a Scot and a board member of Sistema Scotland; he has worked with Venezuela's El

Sistema for over a decade. As they talked together about what could be done to help Fukushima, Fergus remarked to Yutaka, "Perhaps you need El Sistema."

Yutaka is not a professional musician, although he played piano and jazz saxophone growing up and was the conductor of his high school wind orchestra. He has pursued a distinguished career of service in international humanitarian efforts, spending years in South Africa, Lesotho, and Eritrea before returning to Japan as a UNICEF official. He was struck by Fergus's tales of El Sistema in Venezuela and in Scotland, and spoke with members of Soma's Board of Education about the idea. They all agreed that the Sistema's joyful spirit and interdependent practices could help to heal their children's invisible wounds.

We heard Kenichi Murata, principal instructor of the Soma City Board of Education, elaborate on this choice when he spoke at a symposium about bringing El Sistema to Japan. "Children are the treasure of Soma," he said. "It is they who will revitalize and invigorate the adults. Music can heal people; everyone understands that. El Sistema is what we need, because when children are engaged, parents and grandparents and community will come together."

At a ceremonial dinner on our first night in Soma, school board officials expressed their interest in the Sistema vision and their excitement about bringing it to Soma, even though it had taken professional courage to propose an unorthodox program that challenged their successful musical traditions. One of the officials had been inspired by seeing the documentary *Tocar y Luchar*. Others were simply won over by Yutaka's clarity and eloquence.

They all said that when they were teenagers during the 1970s, a time of hope and inspiration in Japan, they had experienced music as life-changing. Three of them had been in rock bands. "I loved it," said the most senior official. "It brought me the greatest feeling of freedom I ever had. That's the kind of joy I want to bring to the children of Soma." We asked him what kind of music he had played with that band of his youth. What groups had influenced him? The sake had been flowing freely, and he confessed. "Deep Purple," he said.

A school official who learned the power of music through Deep Purple, plus a Scottish horn player in the Berlin Philharmonic, plus a farsighted and tireless UNICEF official: thanks to the somewhat random intersection of these forces, El Sistema Japan was born in Soma. In some ways, it was not such an unlikely coincidence. There are strong affinities between El Sistema and the Japanese Suzuki tradition, which was inaugurated after the Second World War with the goal of restoring joy and beauty to the lives of children who were victims of the war. Shinichi Suzuki's concept of music education resonates strongly with Sistema philosophy. "Teaching music is not my main purpose," he once wrote. "I want to make good citizens." Maestro Abreu's close colleague Frank Di Polo was in Japan as early as 1979, recruiting a master Suzuki teacher to come to Venezuela and work with the youth orchestra. Nearly four decades later, many of the early childhood pedagogies of Venezuela's El Sistema are closely related to Suzuki teaching techniques.

Sistema teachers everywhere, in fact, are finding that some elements of Suzuki pedagogy work naturally and usefully within Sistema learning environments. Suzuki's emphasis on learning simple, engaging songs by ear works well with children in a group setting as well as individually, and can complement the process of learning to read notes. Even deep in a Nairobi ghetto, American Karis Crawford uses Suzuki methodology to teach the beginning violinists in her Sistema program.

Our first visit to Japan, in July 2012, was with a small delegation that included two experienced El Sistema teachers from the United States, Lorrie Heagy and Dan Berkowitz; the delegation was invited by the city's school officials to help launch Sistema Soma. Local music teachers who attended Lorrie and Dan's demonstration sessions were curious but wary about the unorthodoxy of Sistema methods. "They understand that El Sistema is about nurturing the spirit," Yutaka told us. He relayed the eloquent, if not linguistically perfect, comment of one teacher: "I begin to believe that it is possible to nurture humanity if we can access the hungry spirit among joy." But he added that the teachers were skeptical about how it actually works. "And since there is no manual or guide," he said, "they wonder how they will know if they're doing it right."

When we returned to Soma fifteen months later, we found that several Soma music teachers had overcome skepticism and become lead teachers in the program. They were doing many things right, and the program had grown to include 100 children ages four to seventeen. According to Yutaka, they hadn't intended to expand quite so fast. "But the little brothers and sisters all wanted to be a part of it, and when we let some of them join, the parents of the others insisted." The teachers told us that many of the students who lost family members or homes in the tsunami have started calling the program "my family."

During the months since our first visit, Mr. Yamada had passed away; still, the Soma school board had been unwavering in its dedication to the program, and had brought five master teachers from Venezuela to work with the teachers and students. There had also been a visit by Fergus McWilliam, the Berlin Philharmonic French horn player who had first imagined El Sistema in Fukushima; he brought his wind quintet to Soma to play *Pictures at an Exhibition* with the Soma Sistema orchestra. And there was strong support from the Venezuelan embassy in Japan (Cultural Affairs Attaché Maurice Reyna, an ebullient extrovert in a culture of restraint, teaches Japanese university students to play Venezuelan folk music).

The program has a cadre of college-student volunteers who take the three-hour train-and-bus trip from Tokyo to Soma, and back again, every Saturday. They discovered the program via the website or Facebook; many are not music majors, but they all want to experience and contribute to the social aspects of the program. Those aspects were strikingly on display when we heard and saw the Soma Sistema orchestra play Vivaldi and Mozart (very well, for beginners; this was Japan, after all). Most noticeable was the mingling of younger and older, beginners and more skilled players, often paired at the same music stand. There were middle-aged and elderly players sitting among the children; they were not music teachers but older beginners, mostly retired schoolteachers, who wanted to be part of this different kind of orchestra. Small children freely offered help to grandmotherly ladies; older children helped little ones stay on track.

The program has found a strong music director in Yohei Asaoka, a Juilliard-trained conductor who is devoted to the work and ideals of El Sistema. Asaoka looks a bit like a young Seiji Ozawa, with long hair and a flowing white shirt; he dances as he conducts, and sometimes the children start to move with him. "Whole body movement," he told us, "that's very important." During his time at Juilliard, he included Dalcroze and Alexander technique in his studies. He says he uses both techniques in working with the Sistema students. "They need to be relaxed when they play—ready for joy."

El Sistema as a conduit for joy: we never heard this articulated so consistently as we did in Japan. Japanese children do not experience the deep destitution of other cultures where Sistema flourishes. They are usually well housed, well fed, and decently clothed, and they know they are loved. But for the children whose lives were devastated by the tsunami, real joy is largely inaccessible.

Yohei Asaoka and the teachers believe that peer-to-peer teaching, which helps to build strong empathic connections, will help them rediscover joy. "Peer learning is our main goal," Maestro Asaoka told us. "Pedagogically, it's the key thing." Yutaka, the program's founder, stressed that helping children build strong relationships gives them a skill that will help them succeed in life and also bring them happiness. "Helping their friends to learn, and learning from their friends," he said, "these are life skills that will help them overcome their grief and dislocation."

Peer learning is so central to the creators of El Sistema Soma that it has top priority in their formal evaluation system; the evaluators have developed tools that measure how frequently and how successfully it goes on within the program. "We are building peer learning into the program as a pedagogy and as a measurable goal," said Yutaka. "We are working hard to create an environment that enables the habit of learning from one another." The first-year evaluation found that 69 percent of children reported they had collaborated with their peers on teaching and learning. When the question was phrased differently—"Have you been taught by one of your friends?"—a full 94 percent said yes. Younger children often reported being able to teach older children. "The peer teaching and learning regardless of age is a unique feature of this project," the independent research report concluded.

The habit of learning from one another can be complicated to acquire in a Japanese cultural setting, where instructional hierarchies are firm. Just as the idea of prioritizing emotional expressiveness can collide with the tenets of established Japanese music education, the idea of peer learning can be overruled by the tradition of *sempai/cohei* (dominant elder/submissive younger) hierarchy. According to Andrew McDermott, a Sistema observer who supports the Valley Vibes Sistema program in Sonoma, California, and is familiar with Japanese culture, this tradition "kicks off in junior high school via the after-school club system." The phenomenon of older students demanding submission from younger students, and sometimes bullying them, appears across the world; in Japan, it is sometimes reinforced by a cultural tradition of ordering social and professional relationships through such hierarchies. "There is team spirit," wrote McDermott of the afterschool clubs, "but there can also be a mean streak; these clubs have their own dynamics that have lasted for decades and are in many cases the antithesis of what El Sistema stands for."

Thus Yutaka and his colleagues are challenging some deep-rooted traditions in seeking to instill habits of mutually respectful peer teaching and learning. The program in Soma is funded partly by the central government as a psychosocial program; the teachers are listed on the payroll as "counselors"—which is fine, said Yutaka, "because that's exactly what they are."

Yutaka and his colleagues have led the development of El

Sistema Japan with steady attention to the synergy between social and musical goals. They are clearly excited about their progress. But perhaps not even Yutaka could have imagined, on the occasion of his first talk with Fergus McWilliam, that in March 2016, the children of El Sistema Japan would be invited to Berlin to play Beethoven's Fifth Symphony side by side with members of the Berlin Philharmonic, as part of the five-year commemoration of the tsunami.

"THE MUSIC KIDS ARE SAFE": EL SISTEMA, CIVIL WAR, AND GANG WAR

The week before we arrived in Medellín, Colombia, an eighteen-year-old boy who had been involved for years in the music program La Red was approached by a gang and ordered to join. He wasn't carrying his instrument and wasn't actively engaged in the music program anymore, but he still thought of himself as part of it. He felt protected by this identity; he was confident that there was a long-standing custom among local gang members to leave the music program alone. So he told them, "No, I'm a musician; I don't get involved in that stuff." They killed him. The killing was not for identifying as a musician, we were told, but for disrespecting their authority.

For the teachers and leaders of La Red, this tragedy was the realization of a perennial fear. "The gangs are a constant part of our lives," said Juanita Eslava, La Red program's psychologist and curriculum developer. "Their territories are where our program operates. Usually, we know how to deal with it, and our kids know where to go and where not to go. But when two gangs are fighting over turf, sometimes it's permissible to walk here or there, and sometimes it's not. Sometimes the rules about who owns what turf changes overnight. There are days when it's too dangerous for the children to come to the music school."

La Red leaders have trusted informants in the neighborhood who keep them aware of what they need to do to keep the kids safe;

this helps, but they know it's not foolproof. Within a week of the murder, the program had revised its curriculum to include more in-depth instruction for kids on how to deal with gang encounters.

The dangers notwithstanding, Medellín teems with Sistema-esque activity; the city is unique in our experience for the depth and breadth of its youth music programs and for the highly collaborative way these programs, funded and organized in different ways, work together. La Red, a city-funded program, serves 4,500 children in 27 núcleos across the city, bringing the more advanced students together in a variety of ensembles for long weekends of rehearsal. The program provides free busing for all students. "That is a huge expense," said Ana Cecilia Restrepo, the director of La Red, "but we have to do it. It helps to keep the kids safe from gangs."

We stood with Ana Cecilia on the rooftop of the Casa de la Música, the large modern building where the older students come to play and sing on weekends in ensembles including orchestras, wind bands, folk bands, and choruses. La Red has free use of the building, which is owned by a municipal power company; from the roof, it's possible to see that the Casa de la Música is part of a huge cultural complex that includes a "Plaza of Wishes," a huge park, a planetar-ium, an amusement park, and a botanical garden. Recently installed cable cars run from the downtown to new "library parks" the gov-ernment has created in the barrios atop the steep hillsides, to connect those barrios more directly with the rejuvenated downtown. Medellín spends over 30 percent of its city budget on arts and culture. (We asked Ana Cecilia to repeat that statement, to be sure we had heard it cor-rectly.) "The government recognizes that one of the essential ways to bring a war-devastated city back to life is vigorous investment in arts and culture in every corner of the city," she said. We asked her why the city, in an effort to overcome its legacy of drug war and gang violence, has decided to prioritize arts and music. "Music is still a sacred space in this culture," she replied.

La Red has developed a meticulous sequential curriculum that integrates musical, social, creative, and cognitive developmental goals in a multiyear sequence, a pedagogical pathway that carefully guides children from hard poverty and gang neighborhood backgrounds through school and toward new lives. Ana Cecilia told us that the students who become musically advanced often attend the University of Medellín, which is affiliated with La Red; there are 400 La Red students currently in the university. Ana Cecilia, who is not much older than these university students, speaks perfect American English; she grew up in the United States and was a dance major at the University of Maryland. But Medellín is her birthplace, and she is devoted to its project of rejuvenation through the arts. "We take the music everywhere in the city—the parks, the libraries, the city offices," she said. "We give three hundred concerts a month."

Visiting a La Red núcleo in Medellín, we met Andrés Felipe Villegas, a soft-spoken trombonist who grew up in the countryside but came to the city to join in the gang-combatting work of La Red. "I had heard about what happens here, and I wanted to be part of it. I took the bus from my small town, seven hours away, to Medellín. I started to teach here, and now I am the director." Andrés is twenty-five. Some of his students are older than that. He knows that the program is the only reason these young people are not gang members, and he sees it as the only effective kind of resistance to gang culture and values. "The objective here is not to make musicians, but through music, to show the importance of every human being. To really bring a message about human unity."

La Red is a remarkable example of committed, large-scale municipal funding for a Sistema program. Even more remarkable is that Colombia in general has a far-reaching network of government support at the federal, state, and local levels for music programs with social goals. For the most part, these funding streams are mutually supportive and reinforce a general policy agreement that music, and culture in general, are pivotal in the drive to revitalize and restore a society broken by drug and gang wars. Juan Antonio Cuéllar explained that in Colombia, "the government is involved at every level in supporting music programs for social purposes. It happens at the federal level, in several ministries, and it happens at the levels of state and city governments as well. It's a huge priority."

Batuta, the federally funded Sistema program, serves almost 40,000 children across the country; it is by far the nation's largest Sistema program (and one of the three largest in the world, along with those of Venezuela and Mexico). Because Colombia has so many Sistema-like programs, Batuta plays a dual role: creating collaboration between other Sistema-like programs, to help advance them all, and providing music programs in the areas that fall between the cracks, often serving the neediest kids in the most dangerous barrios.

As with La Red, this means, first and foremost, dealing with gangs. María Claudia Parias Durán, the director of Batuta, told us, "Everywhere, our programs deal with the 'invisible borders' that the gangs constantly draw and redraw within the barrios. Overnight, it can become lethally dangerous for kids to come to the program." When gang disputes break out in a particular area, Batuta cancels the program in that area for the day. If the fighting subsides, it is up and running again the next day.

María Claudia stressed that since Batuta was founded in the early 1990s, its charter commitment has always been to serve the victims of the civil war that ravaged the country during that decade. The program originally began in tent encampments for refugees, providing musical group play to keep kids occupied amid the grim boredom of refugee life. Much of the federal government funding for Batuta comes from the Department of Conflict Resolution, and nearly half of its students have been direct victims of the civil war. Increasingly, Batuta's work involves gang prevention across the country. "The government knows that Batuta is a vitally important social project for the country," said María Claudia. "The government believes in art for social change. Now that we are facing a social situation, Batuta needs to reach both the victims and the victimizers."

Colombia's gang-related violence has significantly diminished in recent years, but in spite of ceasefires and truces, it is far from over; gang lords still control the territory in many barrios. Given the ongoing nature of the conflicts, it's impressive that the country's public policy is capable of acknowledging that the perpetrators are themselves in need of social support.

In the southwestern city of Cali, we visited three Sistema-inspired programs that highlighted the starkness of the country's class divide even in this city known for leisure-time pursuits like salsa and sports. The Notas de Paz (Notes for Peace) program is in a ghetto located directly across the street from a new high-rise luxury apartment development, the priciest in the city. Its directors are a married couple, a professional violinist and conductor, who told us that creating this program has been their lifelong dream. "These kids are the poorest of the poor," said codirector Lilly Scarpetta de Pumarejo. "But they are here practicing six days a week. They would come the seventh day if we were open." In the beginning, she and her husband Felipe Martínez were worried that gangs would vandalize the building and steal the instruments. "But the gangs saw the little kids coming here, and . . . nothing ever happened."

At the Desepaz Núcleo in Cali (an acronym for "Development, Security, and Peace"), we again encountered superb musicianship in a highly developed sequential curriculum; here, too, we found a mixture of confidence and anxiety in relation to the surrounding gang dangers. Beatriz Barros, the director, said, "The uniform of the music program protects these kids. It's like a magic cloak!" But we were also told that the chorus teacher, who lives in the neighborhood, stays vigilant about what is going on with the gangs.

Our final stop was a Batuta program in Cali housed in a special school called the Arts and Techno School, a big building with an industrial look but filled with music-making. On the top floor of the building was "the clubhouse," an informal lounge managed by an enterprising student, with desktop computers where kids were learning to do graphic design and tables full of Legos for robotics experiments. In a small recording studio, three teenaged boys were creating a hip-hop piece using samples from classic rock songs. We asked them what their lyrics meant. "This song is about war," one of them said. "Gang war. Civil war." Another boy added, "We write music of conscience. Messages of peace during war. Hip-hop is good for this."

Only after we left the Arts and Techno building did our hosts tell us why fewer students than usual had shown up to play that day. A gang war in the area had been scheduled for that afternoon. In the morning, program leaders and community liaisons had negotiated a ceasefire between 2:00 and 4:00 P.M., the planned hours of our visit, so that students could come to the building and play for us and safely return home before shooting began at 4:00. However, our earlier visits to the other núcleos had run overtime, so it was well after 3:30 when we arrived. The students in that area had been called or texted at the last minute and told not to come.

One surprising aspect of the gang issue in Colombia is that in communities where music programs are strong, gangs sometimes try to protect the children of these programs from the violence. "The teachers in our programs are closely attuned to the communities, and they communicate regularly with the gangs," Juanita told us. "Sometimes gang members will call our teachers and say, 'It's not safe for your kids today in such-and-such a neighborhood; keep those kids home.'" Marysabel Tolosa, an administrator with the Ministry of Culture, told us that in rural areas there are many folk bands and ensembles that move from town to town to rehearse or perform together. (For many young people, she told us, these ensembles are the only things to do after school that don't involve drugs and violence.) "There are a number of places," she said, "where gangs halt their conflicts when a band moves from one town to another."

Among the many countries we visited, Colombia was the only one where gang war had escalated to the level of civil war, a result of the decades-long triangulated conflict between the drug cartels, the government, and the paramilitary opposition. It was also the country in which addressing this problem was most highly prioritized by a national government, and in which Sistema-inspired programs were most widely seen and used as a solution to the problem. But gang war was a central issue in many of the countries we visited.

In Rio de Janeiro, Brazil, gangs financed by drug trafficking essentially ruled the city's vast favelas for decades, until in 2008 the federal government began a massive "pacification" program involving the permanent installation of police and military forces to drive out gangs. Fiorella Solares, who has carried on the mission of Ação Social pela Música in Brazil since her husband died two decades ago, recounted the way the program began in Rio's Dona Marta favela. "For thirty years, cocaine trafficking completely dominated this place," she said. "It was the only business; it was the entire economy. Ação Social obtained a sponsor for the Dona Marta project in 2008, and we tried to start the project in 2009, after the pacification began. But we struggled, because many gang members were still there. They waged a kind of war of terror on us; they intimidated residents who wanted to send their kids to the program. The teachers I hired were afraid to come there to teach. I was afraid we would have to return the money to our sponsor." Fiorella said that feeding the children nutritious cooked meals has always been an important part of her program, because they so often come hungry and ill nourished. "The gangs made even this impossible for us. They stopped the flow of gas into our building, which made it impossible for us to cook."

By 2010, the pacification effort was beginning to be more substantial and effective. "Finally, more children of Dona Marta began to come to the program," said Fiorella. "We have hundreds of children now. Now the teachers are no longer afraid of coming into the favela to teach." Ação Social pela Música now has programs in three other favelas in Rio, which have also benefited from pacification, although they are still far from gang-free. We visited the program in Complexo de Alameo, a cluster of favelas on a hilltop. "Before the pacification in 2010, the gang flag flew on this hillside instead of the Brazilian flag," said our guide, Julio Camargo, the pedagogy coordinator for Ação Social. "Then the army came to kick out the gangs and confiscate their guns. But there are still lots of shootouts between gangs and cops, and between gangs and gangs. Some people think that the cops actually sell the guns back to the gangs, for a big profit."

When we arrived at the program, which is housed in a Pentecostal church, there were policemen at the entrance. A cop had been shot and killed there the night before, and the police were telling the children that it was not safe to be there, and they should go home. Some went home, but some stayed. The núcleo was clearly open for business, so we stayed too. The courtyard was decorated with strings of small flags, looking incongruously festive in light of the report we had just heard, and there were kids playing everywhere as we walked through a little warren of practice rooms and up the stairs to an airy sanctuary. A string orchestra of about forty children was playing a schmaltzy arrangement of "Love Me Tender." Then they segued to a samba, with some complex counterrhythms and lots of pizzicato, and then a classical medley. They seemed equally at home in all the different genres—and at ease in that room overlooking the site of a police shooting.

When the orchestra took a break, the conductor, Edvan Moraes, introduced us to two boys, Nathaniel and Gabriel, and brought them out to a little balcony to play a violin duet for us. The view from the balcony included the highest hilltop favela, which we had been told was the most dangerous. "That's where we live," Nathaniel told us, pointing. The boys, probably twelve or thirteen years old, played a Baroque duet for us, and they played well and in tune, although twice Nathaniel forgot an entrance, Gabriel stopped playing and set him straight, and they went at it again.

The church bells suddenly began to ring, their melodies veering in and out of tune, in and out of rhythm, with the boys' music. We thought the bells would confuse them, but they seemed to relax and play better, leaning into the clangor. We asked them, was it easier or harder to play together when the bells began? "Harder," said Nathaniel. "Easier," said Gabriel at the same time, and they both began to laugh.

"THE TALKATIVE PROGRAM": EL SISTEMA AND SOCIAL ISOLATION

The Korean Sistema program is called Orchestra of Dreams. Funded by KACES (Korea Arts and Culture Education Service, a federal agency), it began as a pilot program in 2010, signed a friendship agreement with El Sistema Venezuela in 2012, and by the end of 2015 had rolled out thirty-eight programs across the country. The program is targeted to lower-income children, orphans, and children of single-parent homes; its stated goal is a distinctive expression of Sistema goals around the world: "The Orchestra of Dreams helps children and adolescents grow as cheerful and healthy citizens with self-esteem and communal character through the orchestra activity focused on peer teaching and cooperation."

By most measures of wealth distribution and economic mobility, South Korea is already among the world's most progressive nations. Yet even with such relative success, the government is concerned that economic mobility seems blocked for the next generation of low-income young people; hence the decision of KACES to invest in El Sistema. We were told that in the government's view, children from poorer families in South Korea do not ascend professionally because they haven't developed the necessary social skills. There are several suggested reasons for this: a lack of after-school programs where children socialize together; many single-child homes; extreme homework pressure, imposing hours of solitary work during after-school time; and electronic media, especially video games, absorbing most spare time. Lacking face-to-face social experience, children become taciturn. Around puberty, the silence often turns to anger. Some joke that nobody worries about an invasion from North Korea, because South Korea could just send out the twelve-year-olds to scare them away.

The government is investing in youth orchestras as a way to develop the social skills that will reduce the difficulties of adolescence and lead to greater professional opportunities. The evaluation protocols for Orchestra of Dreams programs focus on social development, and the feel of these programs is more personal and playful than that of Korean music programs for more advantaged children. We saw students stepping up to the podium to conduct warm-ups, trying to keep the D scales interesting, and teachers having students switch chairs in sectionals and rehearsals, sometimes switching up the entire orchestra placement so that the brass or winds were closer to the conductor. Conductors often spend rehearsal time brainstorming with students about a piece before they start rehearsing it—looking through it, asking questions, and trying out bits. They find that this gives students a stronger, more engaged relationship to the piece.

Families began to call the Orchestra of Dreams "the talkative program," because after a few months, children who had always sat silently at the family dinner table became chatty about the orchestra. Over time, there were deeper changes. During the first year, a high percentage of students, especially the fearsome twelve-year-olds, complained about having to attend orchestra during school holiday breaks, but those complaints disappeared in the second and third years, and some children even came voluntarily for extended hours. A 2014 evaluation of the program's effectiveness showed that children in the Orchestra of Dreams demonstrated growth in the areas of self-esteem, social abilities, and family relationships as well as in musical abilities.

Many parents tell their children, "You can join this orchestra as long as your grades don't go down." Because students spend so many hours a week in orchestra, they need to become more efficient with their school studies—and they do. Parents are confused but pleased to find that their children spend fewer hours per week doing homework, and yet their grades stay the same or go up. (This pattern appears in many countries.)

KACES mandates a series of benchmarks that each program site must meet in order to sustain government support. One of the benchmarks is community inclusion; the student orchestra must connect with the community in some way, to expand the social component of the program. We visited a program in Wanju where the community inclusion requirement had been fulfilled by creating a citizen chorus to perform with the student orchestra at the yearly Dynamic Festival of Wanju. The student orchestra numbered about a hundred—and there were a thousand people in the citizen chorus.

The social development aspect of the program escalates during the summer, through weeklong camps that bring children from different sites together by the hundreds to rehearse and perform. The 2014 program evaluation found that the camp experience produced significant change in personal growth, social abilities, and "communal character." The report also found that after the camp experience, there was a "significant increase in frequency of conversation with family, so the relationship with family improved." In other words, children returned from camp chattier than ever.

TEACHING ARTISTS IN KOREA

By definition, teaching artists dedicate themselves to activating many kinds of highly engaged learning, by connecting what they know as artists to what they have learned as educators. Although the U.S. field of teaching artistry has grown steadily in size and efficacy, it remains underfunded and under the radar, even while being widely utilized in many settings. Teaching artistry thrives around the world too, under various names, but usually without commensurate recognition or support.

The South Korean government, in contrast, has made a significant commitment to teaching artistry in general, and, in particular, to teaching artists in its El Sistema program. The South Korean federal agency KACES (Korea Arts and Culture Education Service) was authorized to hire 5,000 teaching artists in the last few years, as a part of its 1,260 percent increase in arts and cultural education funding, and to train and certify these teaching artists. The stated purpose was to reduce Korean society's stress-related high suicide rate and to increase "stabilization, harmony and social adjustment."

Yes, that basically means hiring thousands of teaching artists to increase national happiness. This would be the statistical equivalent of the U.S. government hiring 48,000 teaching artists to make the U.S. population happier. Even at the lowest point of the Great Depression, only half that number of artists was hired by the WPA.

"STARTING BELOW SCRATCH": EL SISTEMA AND POLITICAL OCCUPATION

Ahmad Al'Azzeh is the program director of the Sounds of Palestine, a Sistema-like program in the Aida and Al-Azzeh refugee camps in Bethlehem, Palestine. "We didn't start our program from scratch," Ahmad told us. "Scratch means starting with nothing. We started ninety degrees below scratch, because we had so many nos against us before we began. Authorities were against us. Parents were against us. Schools were against us. Religion teachers and nonreligion teachers both were against us. For the first year and a half, we fought all this resistance every day."

The struggle to create Sounds of Palestine can only be understood in the context of the subjugation and occupation that gave rise to the refugee camps. Palestinians telling this story invariably arrive at the sentence "The wall changed everything." In 2002, the Israelis began erecting a 430-mile security wall between Israeli and Palestinian lands, along the "green line" of the disputed 1949 armistice. The security wall stands 10 to 40 feet high along the border of the Aida Refugee Camp. It slashes through the neighborhood, truncating streets, cutting people off from their work, severing families from inherited olive orchards. Its guard towers overlook the camp. Over the course of the building of the wall, which was completed in 2007, 186 protesters were arrested.

The entrance to the Aida camp, a compound of low tan stone and concrete buildings, is marked by a gateway with what's called the world's largest key on top of it—the "key of return." The frequent protests near the key, with the wall and its guard towers looming overhead, usually begin as nonviolent demonstrations but frequently tip into violence with the toss of a rock. Tear gas, rubber bullets, and arrests predictably ensue. After the shouting has subsided and the air begins to clear, small boys gather bullet shells and empty gas canisters and even live ammunition, to use as play toys. In the elementary school where the students play their instruments, the smell of the new, more devastating tear gas now used by the Israeli military is permanently embedded in the window frames.

The school's outer gate is pocked with bullet marks. Stenciled into the wall are the names and faces of young men currently held in Israeli prisons—a fate most boys anticipate as a matter of course. People tell stories of Israeli killings and atrocities. They tell of watching a female Israeli soldier be upbraided for talking to the residents. "You must not see them as human," she was told. On the day we arrived, we saw a reckless driver scaring pedestrians and made an innocuous joke about crazy local drivers; the unsmiling answer was that the car had a yellow license plate, meaning it was an Israeli car. Israelis can drive as dangerously as they like here, because they can't be given driving tickets in Palestine.

In an occupied land, children regularly suffer many kinds of trauma, large and small—daily scarcities and humiliations; families in disarray and depression; poor schools and unhealthy living conditions. There is little hope, which over time wears down to no hope. The Aida camp has 5,000 people densely packed into two-thirds of a square kilometer, and in the adjacent Al-Azzeh camp, which Sounds of Palestine also serves, there are 2,500 people living in a fifth of a square kilometer. Of the combined population of 7,500 people in these camps, over half are children under age eighteen. Most of the children show evidence of emotional trauma; domestic violence is common, in addition to regular neighborhood violence by the Israeli military and the daily humiliations of subjugation.

The Sounds of Palestine program seeks to provide children the same learning benefits that many Sistema programs around the world aspire to: enhanced concentration, cooperative skills, a sense of mastery, fuller lives. But with these children, psychological trauma is at the forefront, and the program's highest priority is helping the children develop resilience and self-esteem. There are social workers on staff and available during the teaching day to deal with kids in crisis. The week before our arrival, a child who was pulled aside for disruptive behavior said, "My cousin was arrested last night, and they took him away, and I don't know if I will ever see him again." The social worker sat with him and talked quietly until he wanted to return to friends and music. Such interventions are an almost daily occurrence.

When the program began, in 2012, parents were slow to understand what it was about. This is the only place we visited where the word "orchestra" evoked no image in people's minds. They didn't consider it either elitist or attractive; they had never thought of it at all. In the early pages of this book we remarked that a youth orchestra was an implausible idea to offer as an effective solution to intractable social problems. In Palestine, it was beyond implausible; it was literally inconceivable.

But after Sounds of Palestine's first year of working with kindergarten children, mothers were saying to Ahmad and to Fabienne van Eck, the program's artistic director, "We don't know what you are doing with the kids, but whatever it is, keep doing it." What they were doing was basic musical engagement; the students were learning to focus, to play notes together, to cooperate, and to sing songs and master them, in a safe, welcoming atmosphere. What mothers were seeing at home was social engagement; their kids were no longer sitting passively in corners.

We were told about Shamekh, who said, "I love to come to play music, it is the only place in my life that is easy." And about Daysam, a boy who had become so depressed that he spent all his time at home wearing the face-hiding gear protesters wear to disguise their identity. Within weeks of starting to learn his instrument, he stopped wearing the mask.

Artistic Director Fabienne van Eck is a citizen artist dynamo— articulate, vibrant, fiercely dedicated. A conservatory-educated Dutch cellist who married an Israeli double bass player, she has always been both a teacher and a peace activist; she also works for Musicians Without Borders. She has worked hard with her teaching staff to move them from the milder affect of conventional music teaching to the drive, positivity, and personal relatedness of Sistema teaching. She encourages them to see and respond to the needs of each child, and to take responsibility for embodying the habits of mind and heart that can teach by slow example. She also serves as a music teacher for her teachers, since few have had opportunities to develop as musicians.

Both Ahmad and Fabienne assert that they teach resilience above all else. Given the unpredictable violence and turmoil that attend these children's lives, this is the clear first priority. During the latest outbreak of violent rioting, in 2013, they didn't want to shut down the program; they felt that wartime was exactly when children needed stability and connectedness the most. They relocated lessons to what they thought would be a safer neighborhood. But one day, shots rang out around the school. Ahmad and a colleague raced through narrow streets with two children at a time, one tucked under each arm, to get them to cars a few blocks away and drive them to safety.

Danger escalated again during the 2014 war in Gaza. The program leaders decided to hold their summer music camp anyway, and children came, but they were nervous. Some sat inert, refusing to play music out of fear that something terrible would happen if they made noise. Ahmad and Fabienne persisted, and within two weeks all the children were playing again. After the final camp concert, many parents came to thank the team, saying that at the beginning of the summer, fear of war had been so great that they hadn't been able to reach their kids anymore; some had become aggressive, and some had stopped talking altogether. Ahmad said that parents told him, "After the summer camp, they are our kids again, and they behave as they did before the war began."

We attended a student concert at the Aida Community Center, a building that is too dangerous for regular use because it is right by the Israeli wall at the entrance to the camp. There had been a political protest scheduled for that day, but the protest leaders were willing to postpone the action in deference to the concert. It is a chilly building even when the sun is warming the neighborhood, because the wall casts a permanent shadow over that part of town.

The concert involved about 70 children, six to eight years old;

their playing and singing was at a fairly elementary level, with a few beginning to show musical promise and a few showing developmental challenges. But Fabienne was thrilled afterward. For one thing, she said, her staff was working together better than ever before, anticipating needs and jumping in to organize things rather than waiting for instruction from her. For another, a few fathers had shown up—a surprise, since the fathers are almost completely uninvolved; some don't even know their children are learning an instrument. Finally, she was proud that her students rose to the occasion, playing better than they ever had, and mostly maintaining concentration despite distractions that included nonstop loud talking in the audience. To the children, the performance meant that they were seen and recognized by their community as accomplishing something different and difficult. After the concert, a few fathers offered acknowledgment in the form of a gentle touch.

Funding for Sounds of Palestine comes through a Christian charity in Switzerland that collects donations from churches and has proven to be a generous partner. Ahmad and Fabienne envision the program having its own building in a few years. "Land is expensive," they told us, "and we have no idea where the money for this will come from. But we have never known how any of this would happen. And somehow it has happened."

The program's relationship with local authorities has had its ups and downs, but seems stable now. Ahmad, who is Palestinian, has considerable skills as a trusted community organizer, an advocate for children, and a tireless explainer of what an orchestra can do for children. "We are beginning to find believers," he told us. He knows that, in time, the youth orchestra will be able to advocate for itself with its musical accomplishments and successful students. Perhaps Ahmad's most powerful advocacy argument to doubters is that three of his five children are in the program (the other two are still too young) and are becoming strong, proud young Palestinians and better school students as a result.

For the children of Sounds of Palestine, the political tension between Palestinians and Israelis is a hard fact of daily life. While all of the children are Muslim, half of the faculty members are Christian; the camp is a short walk away from Bethlehem's Manger Square, the literal birthplace of Christianity. Somehow—ironically, perhaps auspiciously—there is no religious tension in the Aida Refugee Camp. And now there is music, which for some parents and children feels like the beginning of hope.

RESCUING THE MUSIC: EL SISTEMA AND CULTURAL RENEWAL

A generation ago in Afghanistan, one could be killed (and many were) for being a musician, for playing music at a wedding, or even for playing a CD in a car. The Mujahideen, and subsequently the Taliban, banned all music as a distraction from focus on religious matters and as an invitation to proscribed behaviors; this edict derives from a particular interpretation of a few verses amid the 600,000 words in the 1,300-year-old Koran. It was common to see a soldier toss a hand grenade into a piano, to turn it into firewood; tablas were used as flowerpots; trumpet bells were severed and sealed and used to pass gravy at dinner tables. There are reports that as recently as 2012, the Taliban slaughtered 15 people in a remote village for playing music at a wedding.

Ahmad Sarmast was studying music in Moscow when the Mujahideen drove the Russian occupiers out of Afghanistan, and he was unable to return to his native Kabul for two reasons: because having spent time in Russia, he was automatically deemed a KGB spy, and because he was a musician. Both were grounds for execution. In 1994, he fled to Australia, where he made a life for his family; he earned a Ph.D. in musicology, focusing on Afghan music, and waited for an opportunity to bring music back to his homeland.

Around 2006, he began to see signs of possible openings. He made connections and lobbied government officials for his vision of

A LIFE REDIRECTED BY 9/11

The U.S. teacher William Harvey was ANIM's lead violin teacher, orchestra arranger, and conductor from 2010 to 2014. William's first experience of how much music can matter occurred a few days after September 11, 2001, when he was in his first weeks at Juilliard. On September 16, he and two friends went downtown to the 69th Regiment Armory to play for families who were waiting for news of their missing loved ones. Later that evening, when his friends left, the sergeant major of "the fighting 69th" asked William if he would stay on and play for the soldiers who were resting on the second floor between shifts of digging through the rubble of the World Trade Center.

He stayed, played everything he knew by heart, and then played it all again. After many hours, his hands were numb, the nuances of violin performance that mattered so much in his uptown Juilliard life were gone, and the exhausted soldiers told him it was the most beautiful music they had ever heard. He finished with "The Star-Spangled Banner" as the soldiers stood at attention. One of the colonels gave him the honorary coin of the regiment.

transforming a nearly defunct secondary school for the arts into a national institute for music. With an agreement in place, Sarmast moved back to Afghanistan and began to create the Afghanistan National Institute of Music (ANIM) in a place devoid of music. Funding was the first priority, and it did not come easily. But waiting in an airport during a flight delay one evening, he began to talk to a man waiting next to him; the fellow seemed interested and asked a number of questions. He turned out to be a leading officer at the World Bank, and he invited Sarmast to submit a proposal. In short order, ANIM was funded.

Sarmast spent the next two years renovating the building, to provide study and practice spaces, and looking for instruments. Faculty recruitment was another high priority, since there were so few Afghan musicians, so Sarmast recruited a number of faculty members

The next afternoon, he wrote an email about his experience to his family and friends. This letter moved many people and was widely shared in newspapers and on television; he got hundreds of grateful emails echoing his belief in the power of music to heal. He decided to form an organization called Music for the People, to bring teams of U.S. conservatory students into countries across the world that are not friendly to the United States. This organization, now called Cultures in Harmony, is still flourishing, with teams in thirteen countries making friends through musical residences in communities.

In 2010, William began working in Afghanistan with Ahmad Sarmast at ANIM, guiding the violin instruction and in additional roles required by the new school. He says the direction of his life changed that night at the armory. The musical debates that happen within Juilliard and every other corner of the classical music world—i.e., "Which virtuoso plays Beethoven sonatas best?"—paled in interest for him after that turning point. What had happened in the armory was more important: even with his many technical mistakes, the music had mattered to people. What happens in a walled school in Kabul matters deeply to the children inside, and helps to make a musical mark on the future of a country in crisis.

from other countries, including William Harvey, a Juilliard-trained violinist. What Afghanistan doesn't have is a music industry, and Sarmast understands the need to re-build that industry. His goal for ANIM is to revive the musical life and spirit that was quenched for so long in his country.

During ANIM's first six years, Sarmast developed it into the most important arts learning institution, and perhaps the most important cultural organization, in Afghanistan. ANIM now has 220 students, 60 of them girls, and runs a full-day, degree-granting program that includes academics and a hot meal. Within its highly guarded and armored compound, there is not only the restored secondary school of fine arts but also a new building of practice rooms, an instrument repair workshop, and a girls' dormitory, which will enable girls from outside of Kabul to study there. There is also a new performance hall, the first of its kind in Kabul, which will provide an income source for ANIM, since it can be rented out for concerts and convenings—part of Sarmast's "earned income" sustainability strategy. Sarmast is in conversation with President Ghani to change the designation of musicians under Afghan law; they are currently categorized as clerks, and Sarmast wants to raise their pay in recognition of the special skills and special conditions required for their work. ANIM charges a fee for all its performances, even the ones for the president, to build awareness of the value of live music. The income gets split fifty-fifty, half going to ANIM and the other half to the performers.

ANIM is not explicitly modeled on El Sistema, but there are cordial connections with the Venezuelan Sistema (moving toward official connections), and the lively, friendly environment of the program has the feel of Sistema núcleos everywhere. There are a senior and a junior traditional instrument ensemble, a wind orchestra, a percussion ensemble, a 20-player string ensemble, and a chorus. There is a 35-member women's ensemble, with a female conductor, and there is also an international touring youth orchestra that mixes orchestral instruments with Afghan instruments. Students are invited to explore their own interests and form their own ensembles. There is—yes, even in Afghanistan—a rock band.

Sarmast is courageously proactive in advancing female equality. The fact that girls study next to boys is a significant cultural statement in itself—and a point of tension with local fundamentalists and some prospective parents. Outside their guarded gate, women are completely covered in burqas; inside the gate, young women wear their headscarves casually and talk and play music with young men.

ANIM offers a number of students monthly $30 stipends, to discourage their families from making them leave the program and go to work hawking wares in city traffic to earn a dollar a day. Poverty is deep and widespread in Kabul and in Afghanistan as a whole, and a small stipend is an act of consequence, an affirmation of the students' work. We witnessed an all-female ensemble get paid after a performance, and it was clearly a significant moment for all the young women. While most had worked before, selling items on the street in traffic, few had experienced payment as a prestigious recognition of their accomplishments. The handing out of money in white envelopes, one by one, was like a graduation ceremony; several of the girls clutched the envelopes to their hearts.

Already, ANIM graduates are among the best musicians in the country, and Sarmast wants to make sure they can support themselves. He hires some of them as teachers and arranges internships elsewhere for others. With the seven 2015 graduates and the eight 2016 graduates, he plans to form an ensemble that will become the spine of a future National Orchestra of Afghanistan. He also plans to open ANIM centers in three additional cities in the next two years, and eventually across the country, but at this point most areas are still too dangerous for teachers, for female students, and for music.

The balance of tradition and change at ANIM is always delicate. Students are required by the state to take religious studies, and Sarmast tries to select imams as instructors who will be sensitive to the school's musical mission. But when we were there, students had been taking pictures of their favorite composers—Bach, Mozart, Chopin—down from the walls of their practice rooms, because their religious studies teachers had told them that the way they loved these great masters was too much like idolatry.

Relations with the students' families are perhaps the most delicate issue of all. Many parents remained mistrustful and unsupportive of the program for months, and some parents have never come around. One student who had become an especially advanced violinist was offered a teaching job at ANIM, but confessed that he had never told his family where he had been going every day for the past five years. Sarmast and William Harvey insisted that he tell his family, since this was an important life marker for him. The student did so, and his father disowned him on the spot, telling him to leave the house and never return. As of this writing, the student resides in Solothurn, Switzerland, receiving free housing and German lessons from the Swiss government.

However, as ANIM builds presence and credibility, many parents are beginning to trust. The monthly family events are well attended. The music is good, and getting better. The student orchestra has managed international tours, one to the United States, with performances at the Kennedy Center and Carnegie Hall. "We like your hometown," they told us when they came to New York.

ANIM is entirely dependent on Ahmad Sarmast at this point; he is an omnipresent leader who loves the students and pushes them hard about their musical improvement. In 2014, the whole program

LEADING A REBIRTH IN AFGHANISTAN

Ahmad Sarmast was born during a peaceful time in Kabul. His father, Salim Sarmast, was a composer and songwriter, and the founder of the first professional orchestra in Afghanistan. Ahmad studied trumpet in his youth, played with a jazz ensemble, and discovered his love of musicology as a conservatory student in Moscow during the Russian occupation.

Sarmast told us that the idea of establishing a school of music for disadvantaged kids of this country comes from his father. "He was the source of inspiration for me," he said. "He grew up in an orphanage and became the superstar of Afghan music." He added that some of the pieces the ANIM orchestra has played on tour were originally arranged, performed, and recorded by the orchestra his father had founded.

A vigorous man in his early fifties, Sarmast has a visionary energy; like Maestro Abreu, he is a skillful politician, a devoted educator, an imaginative administrator, and a lifelong artist. And he believes in music's contribution to a just and civil society. "Music is not just a type of entertainment," he said. "Music is a powerful source that can enormously contribute to various aspects of life in this country. No civil society can be established without investing in art, culture, and education. It's impossible to get stability in Afghanistan, and peace in Afghanistan, and economic development, unless we invest in art, culture, and education."

went into shock when a terrorist struck at a theater performance in which ANIM students were performing. The play itself was about terrorist bombings. "About twenty minutes into the play," Sarmast said, "just as the actors were portraying what happens right after a suicide bomber strikes—a suicide bomber struck the theater. We were suddenly living what the actors had been acting."

No ANIM students were harmed in the explosion, but Sarmast was seriously injured by shrapnel to his head. He describes coming back to consciousness on the floor of the theater, wondering if he was dead or alive. As soon as he was rushed to emergency medical care, a crowd began to gather at the hospital. It grew to include hundreds of students, families, and supporters, all standing in the street below his hospital window. The president of Afghanistan paid him a visit.

A year later, he is still under medical treatment for damage to his sight and hearing. He has had to increase security measures at the program in response to a wave of threats directed at both him and the program, in the wake of the bombing. When we asked him how this incident had affected him, he replied, "I will regain my strength, and it has redoubled my commitment."

His closing comments in our most recent conversation were about his excitement that he has found the right person to replace him when he is gone. "I have found the future leader of ANIM, who is a young, strong, hardworking, talented eleventh-grade student," he said. "I have complete confidence in her." True to his crusading spirit, Ahmad Sarmast has decided that the next leader of ANIM will be a woman.

CHAPTER 12

Following the Money

The arts are the best insurance policy a city can take on itself.
—WOODY DUMAS, FORMER MAYOR OF BATON ROUGE, LOUISIANA

Arts education is arguably a national security issue, when we consider
its relationship to creativity and innovation, academic and social
engagement by at-risk populations, and even economic productivity.
—SUNIL IYENGAR, DIRECTOR OF RESEARCH, NATIONAL
ENDOWMENT FOR THE ARTS (USA)

In 2009, when concert pianist Ricardo Castro decided to start a Sistema-inspired program in his home city of Salvador, in the Brazilian state of Bahia, he went to see a state government official to ask for funding. The official's first response was that most kids in the favelas wouldn't have the talent to learn to play an instrument. Ricardo told him that in fact anyone could learn to play an instrument if given the chance.

"He said, 'You have five minutes to prove that to me,'" Ricardo recalled. "And somehow I did." Ricardo is revered in Bahia for being the local kid who became an internationally acclaimed classical musician. Once he had secured state support, however, he realized how daunting a task he had signed up for. "It was scary in the beginning," he told us. "Nobody here believed it would work—only the government did, because they knew so little about music that they didn't know it was impossible. They just thought, 'Ricardo is famous, he must know what he's doing.' Had they known how hard it is to make good music, they never would have supported me. I mean, kids from favelas, playing Beethoven in the big downtown theaters? It was the first time those kids could even enter these theaters."

The way Ricardo went about meeting the challenge was unusual among new Sistema programs across the world: he decided that he would not start from scratch with beginners from favelas, but would seek out talented local music students and begin by creating an advanced youth orchestra. He was doubtful at first that he could find such kids in Salvador, but Maestro Abreu, with whom he had had a long friendship, assured him they would appear and rise to this opportunity. Within a year, he had put together a youth orchestra that sounded good enough to impress sponsors and enlist their support for launching a fuller program—very much like the way Maestro Abreu himself began El Sistema forty years ago with a hastily cobbled-together orchestra of teenaged and young adult music students. "Actually, Maestro Abreu advised me to do it this way," Ricardo said. "I have enormous respect for the Maestro, and so I do whatever he tells me to do. If he had told me to jump off a ten-story building . . . well, it's a good thing he never did."

Ricardo's initial orchestra rehearsed together for several months and then played a debut concert under the baton of Venezuelan conductor Manuel López-Gómez. "That first concert was surprisingly emotional," said Ricardo. "The kids were crying; they couldn't believe they could sound like that." The concert served its intended purpose: Bahia government officials announced their commitment to the program, and NEOJIBA (Núcleos Estaduais de Orquestras Juvenis e Infantis da Bahia) was born. In short order, there were núcleos serving hundreds of younger children in poor neighborhoods in the city of Salvador and the surrounding countryside, and the youth orchestra musicians were serving as assistant teachers in the núcleos. Institutional Director Beth Ponte explained to us that 80 percent of the funding for these sites comes from the state of Bahia and is managed by an NGO.

We visited several NEOJIBA núcleos in Salvador. Touring the SESI núcleo with us, in the poor neighborhood of Itapagipe, were several state officials who spoke enthusiastically about the program's mission. "Music learning corrects the feeling of selfish individualism in modern society," one official said. "This ensemble work transforms the human being. It is stronger than sports learning, because it transforms both the young musicians and their audiences."

The SESI núcleo is funded by a "social tax" the state requires every industry to support educational and social projects that contribute to public welfare. Another official asked us about governmental support for El Sistema in the United States. "The United States has so many good musicians, and the government has so much money," she said. "They could serve as a model for a social tax!" We told her that in fact, Bahia could provide an inspirational model for the U.S. and for other industrialized countries where this commonsense idea is still largely absent.

"HOW ARE EL SISTEMA PROGRAMS FUNDED?"

This is one of the most common questions we are asked, whenever and wherever we speak about El Sistema. Since programs are free for all students (in the few instances where there is a fee, it is nominal) and expenses—including facilities, instruments, and high-quality teachers—are considerable, people who want to launch and develop them are confronted with a challenge to which there are no formulaic answers.

But the question about funding is more than a practical, how-to matter. It's also a question about cultural values. The way a society funds its Sistema programs illuminates much about what its members consider most important. How does the society deal with problems of equity and social justice? Are these issues seen as urgent, calling for public intervention; or are they implicitly accepted as the inevitable underside of a market economy, to be addressed in entrepreneurial ways if the private sector cares to do so? Further, are the arts, and arts education, perceived as effective, vital tools of social welfare or as enrichments to be indulged in after the important things are taken care of?

Latin American countries stand decisively at the forefront of progressive, arts-oriented answers to these questions. In Colombia, Mexico, and other Latin American countries where the example of Venezuela is close at hand, the ideal of arts learning for social welfare has been ripening for decades. Sistema programs in these countries are substantially supported by public funding; governments have decided that improving the social and emotional lives of at-risk children through musical engagement is *not* such an implausible idea but, in fact, a potent way to address entrenched social problems. This government commitment occurs sometimes at the federal level, sometimes regionally or locally, and sometimes at all three levels. (Brazil's Bahia is an example of substantial support at the state level in a country where there is little or no support at the federal level.)

There are some examples of large-scale government support in countries outside of Latin America (for example England, Scotland, Portugal, South Korea, Sweden, and New Brunswick in Canada), but they are relatively few. More commonly, Sistema-inspired programs in the United States and Canada, Europe, and Asia rely on private foundations, nonprofit arts institutions, wealthy individual donors, schools, or some combination of all these. There are already some noteworthy examples of wholehearted long-term support by private foundations and philanthropic donors. The Hilti Foundation in Europe, a large private foundation with a broadly progressive social mission, is a unique player on the worldwide Sistema scene; it is the principal supporter of the European multinational organization Superar. A significant number of programs are launched and supported by symphony orchestras, in the United States and Canada and elsewhere around the world. A few programs are supported by corporate money. And support for El Sistema from academic institutions is beginning to emerge.

Along the continuum of government/private support, Venezuela with its abundant government support is at one extreme, and at the other sits the United States, with virtually no government support, beyond an occasional instance at the local level, for its hundred-plus programs. In between the two extremes, countries and cultures go about answering the question in a myriad of ways. Each country, and sometimes each program within a country, has its own particular mix, and the balance can shift in response to opportunity and change. To exemplify the wide range of possible funding paradigms for El Sistema-inspired programs, here are three different and imaginative ways that Sistema support is being created across the world.

CORPORATE/GOVERNMENT PARTNERSHIP

We have seen that the El Sistema tradition in Mexico is long and deep. For decades, federal agencies have funded nationwide Sistema initiatives as a strong force for youth development and social welfare, supporting the development of 130 music centers across the country. In the past decade, a new project called Esperanza Azteca has added another dimension to the Mexican Sistema scene: a partnership between corporate philanthropy and government. Esperanza Azteca is an initiative of the Fundación Azteca, which was created in 1997 by Mexican billionaire Ricardo Salinas (Grupo Salinas owns a TV network, a telephone company, a chain of retail furniture stores, and many other businesses) to fund a wide variety of social and antipoverty causes.

The director of Fundación Azteca is Esteban Moctezuma, who has served in the Mexican government as minister of the interior and minister of social development. He works closely with Ricardo Salinas to develop projects that address Mexico's social challenges. "The foundation has many, many great projects," Esteban told us. "We have Vive Sin Drogas, a campaign to influence kids not to use drugs, and Limpiemos Nuestro México, which gives prizes to teams of volunteers who clean up trash and litter. We have a program to teach robotics to talented kids, a program to train midwives, and an initiative to maintain a tropical rainforest."

The foundation's Esperanza Azteca initiative adds a musical dimension to its activities: Esperanza Azteca launches Sistema-inspired programs across the country and partners with the government to support them financially. Esteban explained that this initiative began when he and Salinas were visiting the city of Puebla and were approached out of the blue by the mothers of children who were taking free violin lessons from Julio Saldaña, a charity-minded violinist. "They wanted us to start an El Sistema program in Puebla. So we met with these moms to find out about El Sistema. They brought the movie *Tocar y Luchar*, and we all watched it together. It was incredibly moving. Ricardo Salinas was crying. Afterward, the moms said, 'Could we have an orchestra like that?' Salinas said, 'Of course we can!' "

With Fundación Azteca's support, and under Julio Saldaña's direction, Esperanza Azteca was launched with 350 children in a restored factory in Puebla. "I went there to visit every other month," said Esteban. "Every time I heard the children's orchestra, they were playing better. So I said to Ricardo Salinas, what's happening is so incredible that we have to replicate this model." Within five years from its inception, the program multiplied exponentially; there is now at least one Esperanza program in every one of Mexico's thirty-one states.

Esteban stressed that what makes Esperanza Azteca important is its unique alliance between government social development initiatives and business philanthropy. "Our funding design gives us great stability," Esteban told us, "because we involve a combination of corporate foundation money, federal government money, state government money, municipal money, and private donor support, usually from local patrons. Our stool has five legs, so it's solid and sustainable even if something goes amiss with one leg."

The federal government money Esteban refers to is not money from the federal cultural agency; Fundación Azteca's government connections are so strong that it can go directly to the national Congress to ask for funding. Despite the potential friction with SNFM, however, the people we met from both SNFM and Esperanza Azteca were consistently respectful and generous when they spoke about one another's programs. "There are enough needy children in Mexico," said Armando Torres-Chibrás, "that we should celebrate all programs that can reach them with music and hope!"

Esperanza Azteca's flagship site in Puebla looks more like the campus of a private school than like the núcleos we were used to seeing. Originally the first textile factory in the Americas, the plant has been transformed into an estate-like landscape of buildings painted a rich red, arranged around verdant courtyards and connected by cobblestone pathways. On the gleaming dark wood doors are brass plates announcing what happens inside each room—e.g., "Orchestra A violins," "Orchestra B woodwinds."

When we asked Julio Saldaña how Esperanza Azteca managed to grow so fast, he answered like a businessperson. "We have a system," he said. "It's preestablished, like a franchise—like McDonald's. We always start with a certain number of children, a certain repertoire and methodology. We have found out what works, and we replicate it." This was the first time we had ever heard McDonald's cited as a possible model for El Sistema growth. In fact, an absence of franchise thinking—even an aversion to it—is one of the most consistent features of El Sistema as it spreads around the world. Its appearance here seemed to be a reflection of a corporate culture that relies on quantifiable core practices.

However, when we asked Julio what is the most important aspect of his work, he answered like a citizen artist. "It's about working together in a community," he answered. It's not just playing; it's a philosophy of life. I look for teachers who will tell children, 'It's fine if you don't become a musician. I want you to learn service, to find solidarity, to become finer human beings."

Esperanza Azteca is in the process of finding its dynamic balance between two strong value systems—corporate franchise and organically created núcleo. Both Esteban and Julio are confident that the Esperanza Azteca program meets a vast, nationwide felt need for addressing youth development through music and the arts. Soon after the program's inception, they told us, more than twenty of Mexico's thirty-one state governors attended a concert of its children's orchestra.

"Governors don't usually come together in those numbers," said Julio. "Maybe for national security issues they have—but for something about children? And music? It was kind of unbelievable. We had 350 children onstage, and they played and sang the "Hallelujah Chorus." Every governor said, 'I want this in my state.'"

Esteban added: "I think that the government leaders in all the states really believe in El Sistema. When children are involved in music, they are off the streets and safe, and have the chance to become better human beings. Our political leaders know the power of orchestras, and the urgent need of giving children and youth something constructive and valuable to do."

Another notable example of corporate/government partnership is Sistema New Brunswick, the only one of Canada's twenty Sistema-inspired programs that receives substantial government funding. Its six sites, serving 800 impoverished children, including First Nations children (a term adopted by some of Canada's aboriginal people), receive over 50 percent of their funding from the provincial government. Ken MacLeod, who founded and leads Sistema New Brunswick (SNB), is a former local legislator, fundraiser, and philanthropist. He told us that before he launched the program, he spent six months approaching every influential government and business leader he knew to ask for support. "By the time we began," he told us, "I had solicited 50 percent of our funding from the government of the province of New Brunswick, and 50 percent from the private sector. I knew that having substantial public funding was going to be essential for us to flourish."

It helped that the New Brunswick Youth Orchestra, a much-respected institution, was going to be the program's sponsoring organization, and that Ken was its president and CEO. But he believes that the power of the idea itself was what sold it. "It's so compelling," he said, "that people invariably end conversations by saying, 'Let me know how I can help.' They want to be a part of it."

Now, over four years later, the programs' ensembles perform frequently; when Ken approaches potential supporters, there is plenty to show. "The children's ensembles are the best PR tool we have," he said. "People can't leave the performances without being moved and touched, and having a sense of joy and hope." Sistema New Brunswick is expanding into a "cultural ecosystem" for the province, he added. "Its effects are being seen and heard all over the province. Each community has an orchestra. There is a provincial youth orchestra and professional orchestra. Many superb teaching artists have moved here to make this work their career, and they add immensely to our entire cultural and even economic life." The faculty has created a professional orchestra called Tutta Musica, which, among other gigs, partners with the Capitol Theatre to perform in musical theater productions.

Ken is confident that the province's financial support will continue to be strong. "I am convinced," he told us, "that we could not build a large, robust, and sustainable organization without that support. Don't get me wrong; small programs that are privately financed can be great. But if you want large, robust, and sustainable, you have to have public funding."

GOVERNMENT-CIVIC PARTNERSHIP: ENGLAND AND SCOTLAND

In August 2007, London was the scene of a "Venezuelan Invasion" that, although not quite the mass culture phenomenon the pop music "British Invasion" of the U.S. was in the 1960s, was greeted by the same kind of hyperventilating media excitement. The day after Gustavo Dudamel and the Simón Bolívar Youth Orchestra of Venezuela took London's classical music establishment by storm with their performance at the BBC Proms, critic Andrew Clements wrote in *The Guardian:* "Whatever you have read about the Simón Bolívar Youth Orchestra . . . can't convey the brilliance and disarming exuberance of their playing. There are some great youth orchestras around today, but none of them are as exciting to behold as this."

"Their electricity almost burned down the Royal Albert Hall,"

wrote Geoff Brown in *Classical Music* magazine. "Was this the greatest Prom of all time?" critic Paul Gent exclaimed in the *London Tele-
graph*. "It was a night that anyone who was there will never forget."

Julian Lloyd Webber, the U.K.'s most famous cellist, was there.
He told us that, like everyone else, he was thrilled by the orchestra's
performance, but that for him, the most significant thing about it was
the program it had sprung from. Lloyd Webber had long been a
high-wattage advocate for public music education. For years, along
with a number of fellow musical luminaries, including Irish flutist
James Galway, Scottish percussionist Evelyn Glennie, and
American-born composer Michael Kamen, he had lobbied the government for more support of music education at a national level. In
2007, the government had responded by dedicating an extra 332 million pounds for music education.

Thanks to the excitement about El Sistema generated by the
Venezuelans' BBC Proms concert, 1 percent of that 332 million
pounds was dedicated to a three-year experimental project to see
whether El Sistema could work in England. The project was named
In Harmony and chaired by Lloyd Webber, who made a visit to Caracas his first order of business. "I was totally blown away by everything
I saw," he told us, "and I knew this is what we needed in England."

Under Lloyd Webber's stewardship, In Harmony launched sites
in three cities in 2009. Over the next few years, the experimental
project proved so successful—a government-commissioned review
declared that "there is no doubt these programs deliver life-changing
experiences"[31]—that it was expanded, and as of 2015, In Harmony
programs serve nearly 3,000 children in cities across England, including Liverpool, Newcastle/Gateshead, Telford and Stoke-on-Trent,
and London. (There are also Sistema-inspired programs in Norwich
and Nottingham.) The funds for In Harmony programs come primarily through the Department for Education and Arts Council
England. "Now, wherever I go in this country," said Lloyd Webber,
"people say to me, 'We really need an In Harmony program here.'"

A substantial funding commitment at the national level for

Sistema-inspired programs is rare among European nations. While in England this commitment is strong, the funding is still insufficient to cover all the expenses of the programs, and there's a constant quest for other sources of support. The umbrella charity Sistema England, founded by Lloyd Webber and two close colleagues, Nina Kaye and Richard Hallam, helps to support the In Harmony sites and two other Sistema-inspired programs, Sistema in Norwich and The Nucleo Project in London. (Nina Kaye is renowned for her ability to rush large quantities of donated instruments to programs in need of them.) In Liverpool, the Royal Liverpool Philharmonic Orchestra partners with and supports the In Harmony project. In the other cities, networks of partnerships with local musical and social organizations help the programs to thrive and expand.

THE "DEAN" OF SISTEMA ENGLAND

Richard Hallam is the quintessential citizen artist as diplomat. He has had a long and distinguished career in English music education and is currently the chair of the Music Education Council in the U.K.; along with his wife Susan Hallam, a professor who studies music learning and the effects of music education on children's development, he has been a lifelong advocate for the central importance of music in children's lives. Having come from a working-class background and begun his musical life as a cornet player in a local Leicestershire brass band, he knows firsthand the transformative potential of music learning. One could say he has been the unofficial dean of music education in England.

With the advent of the El Sistema movement in England and beyond, Richard has become its unofficial dean as well, straddling the worlds of traditional music education and the more unconventional Sistema. He is a leading administrator within Sistema England and Sistema Europe, and his gentle, diplomatic approach has been key in building strength and consensus within both spheres. Working often behind the scenes and always in the interests of greater collegiality and stronger collaboration, Richard reminds us that the ideal of music education as civic service has been around for a long time.

For England's neighbor to the north, government funding has also been critical to the development of El Sistema. As in England, the Scottish national government has declared a solid commitment to provide music instruction to every child in the public education system. Sistema Scotland began in 2008 with startup funding from the national arts council for its first Big Noise program in Raploch, a district of Stirling; as we've noted in Chapter 10, funds for that program now come from the Stirling city government and several private sources. "There is a lot of talk these days about the importance of early intervention and preventative spending," said Nicola Killean. "I think the city of Stirling understood that in Big Noise they were seeing it in action."

To launch Sistema Scotland's second Big Noise site, in the Govanhill area of Glasgow, a partnership was formed with the Govanhill Housing Association, a forty-year-old community organization that takes responsibility for housing and quality-of-life issues for the 15,000 people in this lower-income district. Housing authorities do not usually support ensemble music programs, so this was a bold move for GHA leadership, and they went further; they moved out of their own offices in a former church and moved the Big Noise program in, helping with renovation.

Across Europe, there are a few other examples of Sistema programs that have significant government funding. Portugal is an important one; 85 percent of the funding for the nationwide Orquestra Geração program comes from the government. Antonio Wagner Diniz, the conductor/opera singer/conservatory leader who founded and directs Portugal's program, spoke bluntly about the importance of government support. "The government *should* pay for the program," he told us. "After all, they helped to create the problems we are working to alleviate."

But for the majority of European programs—and they are legion, sprouting in twenty-six countries so far—there is little government support as yet. Roberto Grossi, the head of El Sistema Italia, is a leading crusader in the effort to change this situation. "The Italian

Sistema needs to have a collaboration with the state," he told us, "because our goal is a public goal. We are a public service! Public-private collaborations are essential."

Roberto launched Sistema Italia with Claudio Abbado in 2010, after Abbado took him to visit Venezuela. "It was a very emotional experience for both of us," he told us. "I think meeting Abreu caused Maestro Abbado to change his view of music forever." When they returned from Venezuela, they lobbied the Italian Senate to support an Italian Sistema program, but support was not forthcoming at that point. "So we rolled up our sleeves and created a civil association," he said. "Maestro Abreu is our honorary president."

In December 2013, the national orchestra and the White Hands Choir of Sistema Italia performed for the Italian Senate under the direction of celebrity conductor Nicola Piovani. Roberto Grossi hoped, and still hopes, that federal government officials will be moved to commit funding to the program. In 2014, he arrived at an accord with the Ministry of Education. "But it's not enough. We need partnerships with municipalities and regions as well. After all, this is the country of music! We have perhaps the world's most important cultural heritage—we must invest in keeping culture alive and available to every child."

THE CORPORATE MODEL: THE PHILIPPINES

In 2012, Jovianney Emmanuel Cruz was asked to play a private concert to celebrate the arrival of a new Steinway concert grand in the spectacular forty-third-floor penthouse home of Federico (Piki) Lopez, a wealthy industrialist in Manila. Piki runs the Lopez Group's power generation division (much of it focused on renewable sources) of the First Generation Holdings Corporation. The Lopez family is one of the most powerful and cohesive families in the Philippines, with a two-hundred-year tradition of commitment to country, philanthropy, and corporate social responsibility that has helped Filipinos

AN ARISTOCRAT OF EL SISTEMA

Maria Majno is not a musician, but she grew up steeped in the traditions of Western classical art music and the culture of the European artistic intelligentsia. Her family home in Milan had a private theater where her uncle Guido launched an orchestra; as a child, she studied the violin and pursued a French classical education, and within "the Majno family musical texture," as she puts it, she met a host of classical music luminaries. She married an American pianist, David Golub, and pursued graduate studies in musicological philosophy and the history of ideas. Her professional life has ranged widely, including both a sustained inquiry into pediatric neuroscience and a long stint as artistic director of the Società del Quartetto di Milano, the oldest chamber music society in Italy.

Given this background, Maria was an unlikely candidate to become an international El Sistema leader. But on Christmas morning in 2008, she received a phone call from Claudio Abbado, who was a family friend. He needed her, he said, to help him start El Sistema in Italy. "After having received so much from music and musicians," she told us, "I felt it was high time for me to start giving back." Her genius is in building organizations and recruiting teams of talented people; she is the founder-director of Sistema Lombardia, a major coordinator of Sistema Italia, and vice president and treasurer of Sistema Europe.

She has also led the way for others from her high-art world to support El Sistema in Italy. It was Maria who made the vital connections that brought the Sistema Europe Youth Orchestra together with La Scala Opera House when the great orchestras of El Sistema Venezuela were in residence there in 2015. And it was Maria who reached out to Signora Giuseppina (Pina) Antognini when that Milanese lady lost her husband Francesco Pasquinelli, a prominent businessman and collector of modern art. Maria telephoned Pina—just as Abbado had telephoned Maria—and said that Sistema Lombardia needed her support.

"I have never made a big decision without my husband," Pina told us, recalling that conversation, "and so I asked Francesco"—she pointed upward—" 'What about this El Sistema? Maria Majno wants us to support it. Should we?' And I got a very clear message back. He said yes."

through harrowing wartimes and endemic economic difficulties. In a country of financial extremes, with a small middle class, the Lopez corporate ethos has been an abiding belief that private wealth must intervene to help where government cannot or does not.

Jovianney's dazzling performance at the penthouse party sparked a friendship between him and Piki Lopez—and a conversation about reviving the musical culture of the Philippines. The ABS-CBN Foundation, a large broadcast network run by Piki's brother, had just established its own professional orchestra in order to widen concert opportunities in the country. Jovianney suggested that a concert hall should be included in a huge new real estate development the Lopez Group was involved in, and Piki loved the idea. "So of course," Jovianney told us, "the next logical idea was 'Let's bring El Sistema to the Philippines!'"

That may not have been everyone's next logical idea, but they were all for exploring ideas about how the combination of a new professional orchestra, a new concert hall, and an El Sistema program might benefit the wider population of Manila in multiple ways. In just a few months, the groundwork was laid for the Ang Misyon (The Mission) Sistema project, with initial funding commitments from the First Generation Holdings Corp. and the ABS-CBN Foundation.

As Ricardo Castro in Brazil had done, and as Maestro Abreu had done decades before, they decided to start by creating a youth orchestra of teenagers who could already play well and would give the project an immediate positive high profile. Jovianney sent out a call to music teachers across Metro Manila, recruiting promising young musicians, and auditions were held for the Orchestra of the Filipino Youth (OFY). According to Jovianney, some of these young people came playing fairly fluently. "But their technique tended to be terrible," he added, "because most of them had only had You-Tube to teach them. So we had to begin right away rebuilding their technical foundations."

Very quickly thereafter, Ang Misyon initiated ten satellite programs (more are planned) in slum areas—programs similar to Venezuelan núcleos, where children of all ages and skill levels receive intensive ensemble music learning experiences. A conscious effort was made to choose neighborhoods where the musicians of the OFY lived, so that they could become mentors, leaders, and teachers in their community programs, sharing what they were learning in their OFY rehearsals and concerts.

The support of the First Generation Holdings Corp. for Ang Misyon goes deep: the program was invited to establish its base of operations in the company's downtown headquarters building in a street-level retail space that was once rented by a bank and had been converted to a fitness center for the wives of the company leadership. The wives agreed to give the space to Ang Misyon, and now it is the program's headquarters and main rehearsal space. Administrative offices are in the original bank vault; the gigantic door of the vault stands ajar so that Jovianney, Tinky, and their colleagues can listen as the junior and senior youth orchestras of Ang Misyon take turns rehearsing. In the lobby of the building, on a raised dais, student ensembles sometimes give short impromptu performances for any businesspeople who happen to be waiting for an elevator.

When we talked with Piki Lopez about Ang Misyon, he spoke of El Sistema's resonance with Filipino culture. "We have such musicality here, and also such brutal poverty," he said. "El Sistema can give meaning and purpose to these children's lives. And not only their lives but the lives of their parents too, when they see how their children have changed and have more discipline, more purpose, more joy."

Ang Misyon is a prime example of a Sistema program funded almost entirely by corporate money—a dramatic case in point of a corporate entity meeting the obligation of corporate social responsibility. CSR, as this concept is often called, has been gaining traction for some years, in the Philippines and around the world. Its appearance in this instance is a fortunate coincidence, the result of a chance meeting between a philanthropically minded businessman and a concert artist yearning for social activism. Jovianney calls it "the 20/20 plan;" he had been dreaming of it for twenty years, and it took a twenty-minute conversation with the right person at the right time to make it happen.

A number of Sistema-inspired programs have gotten startup grants from corporate foundations, as did the Atlanta Music Project from the Atlanta Coca-Cola headquarters. But for such startup funding to turn into long-term support, the relationship must be seen as mutually beneficial—meaning that the corporation has to see what it will get for its social investment. Sometimes, corporate leaders see that clearly. When the Kenyan cellular network company Safaricom created an employee choir some years ago, bringing together workers at all levels, from delivery truck drivers and secretaries to managers, the company discovered that multiple benefits accrued: higher morale, enhanced employee retention, and uplifting entertainment at corporate events and public occasions. Safaricom's "Niko na Safaricom" ad campaign, the largest brand-identity TV advertising campaign in Kenyan history, featured the Safaricom Choir singing in a number of scenic locations around the country. The patriotic identity of the choir and the spectacular scenery made it the most popular advertisement of the era and made the chorus nationally famous. That chorus is not going to lose company funding anytime soon.

Deepening its commitment to the ideal of corporate social responsibility, Safaricom has recently created the Safaricom Youth Orchestra, comprised of a socioeconomic mix of young musicians in Nairobi (including some graduates of the Ghetto Classics program we described in Chapter 8). The company opens its corporate headquarters for the orchestra's regular Saturday rehearsals, and the orchestra kids take over the building: the reeds rehearse in a conference room with panoramic views of the city; the flutes are in the Mugumo Conference Room; perhaps most incongruously, saxophones are in the Crisis Management Room. Percussion rehearsal happens in an elevator lobby decorated with Safaricom motivational slogans like "We create game changers to achieve the impossible." After three hours of these sectional rehearsals, the full orchestra convenes for several more hours. Safaricom President Bob Collymore, said to be the highest-paid person in Kenya, takes an active personal interest in the orchestra and is sometimes seen observing rehearsals, asking how he can help.

THE SHEER GRIT MODEL

Finally, some programs get by on next-to-no funding, surviving through a heady but precarious mix of passion, volunteerism, and ingenuity. One example is Sistemang Pilipino, a small program in the Philippines city of Cebu that is not connected with Ang Misyon. Its founder-director, violinist Lianne Sala, has deep roots in the musical community of Cebu, where her family ran an orchestra development program in the 1990s; in 2012, a group of musician friends raised funds for her to take a four-month international tour of Sistema programs, to learn about starting and running a program. She has relied on her strong local connections in building her small initiative, which currently serves about 70 children, over half of them orphans. The teachers are music students at a local college who volunteer their services, and partnerships with local service organizations help sustain the program. But money is always short, and while Lianne and her colleagues would love to expand, that goal remains elusive.

The "sheer grit" model, usually led by a doggedly resolute citizen artist, shows up across the world. Adeyemi Oladiran's Music Enlightenment Project in Johannesburg/Braamfontein, South Africa; Karis Crawford's Sistema Kenya, starting with 23 students in one of the most dangerous slums of Nairobi; Brazil Strings, launched in a Rio de Janeiro favela by Canadian Vanessa Rodrigues, who left a successful musical career in her home country; Pablo Yang's Bamboo School in rural Vietnam; Aryiole Frost's Shift: Englewood program on Chicago's dangerous South Side; David France's Revolution of Hope for high-schoolers in the Roxbury district of Boston—these programs and many others like them survive on perennially low budgets. Their leaders risk burnout from the enormity of the workload

and stress; indeed, some do burn out. They know they need to cultivate long-term funding, but are stretched so tight with daily program-
matic responsibilities that they don't have the time this task requires.

Still, few programs close. In general, the wave of international
Sistema expansion that has been happening since 2007 has seen
little attrition, even during a worldwide recession. Economists estimate that 80 to 90 percent of new businesses fail; we estimate that
fewer than 5 percent of new Sistema programs close in their early
years. The percentage of programs that close may increase as programs approach the transition from eager startup funding (sometimes called honeymoon funding), which eventually goes away, to
more sustainable support. Attrition could become more acute for
the nearly 130 independent programs in the United States than for

FOUNDING AN AFRICAN SISTEMA PROGRAM

In 2006, Adeyemi Oladiran moved from his home in Nigeria, where he
had studied music education, to pursue advanced studies in classical
music at the University of the Witswatersrand in South Africa. Financial
difficulties interrupted his studies (he subsequently completed his music
degree from the University of South Africa), and as he searched for financial support, he began to work with an NGO, teaching young children in
Soweto to play the recorder.

In 2009, he and some friends had the idea of starting Music Enlightenment Project in their Braamfontein neighborhood, with its mixed population of Africans from many other countries and, recently, some white
residents as well. Adeyemi got things moving fast, starting a recorder
ensemble in partnership with a local progressive primary school. When
he heard about Venezuela's El Sistema from a friend in 2011, he was
inspired, and proposed to his school partners that they could have a
children's orchestra within two years. Together, they made it happen.
Children in the program start by learning recorder and basic musicianship and progress to playing orchestral instruments.

We were there the day Ade received the keys for the large new programs in other countries that already have a larger share of public funding.

LONG-TERM SUSTAINABILITY

The mixture of funding sources we've been describing is a lively but unstable status quo. In the United States and Canada, most programs are still small and seek funding support independently and annually; this is true as well of many European and Asian programs. Indeed, the global Sistema movement has, as yet, few exemplars of sustainable, long-term funding. We are convinced that in general, and in most countries, sustainable long-term funding must be anchored in public

space that will be Music Enlightenment Project's first home, a derelict commercial warehouse donated by a landlord who was taking advantage of a government Community Social Investment policy. A volunteer architect designed the renovation, and Ade and his faculty have joined in the enormous work of renovation. With their scarce funds, it may take years to complete. But as he walked us through the trash-strewn, malodorous concrete shell, Ade pointed out in precise detail how the spaces will be used; he has envisioned the use of every square foot.

Ade said the space will enable MEP to "rebrand and remodel ourselves" for the children and "begin to come alive" for the whole neighborhood. There is the matter of raising money, which he admitted he is just learning about, but he has no doubts he will succeed, "because the example of El Sistema and Abreu's orchestra shows us what is possible." As of this writing, the kids are already using the new space for rehearsal, even as reconstruction goes on all around them, and Ade has begun to request donations for building supplies from friends around the world. Ade wrote, "Sometimes the students just want to stay in there all day on weekends after practice, as it seems to be the only opportunity to be together outside of school. You should see how relaxed they get in our space."

THE HARD CHALLENGE OF HARD DATA

We assume you are curious to see hard data about key issues, and we have made sure to share the hard data we know about thus far. But it's simply too soon in the lives of most Sistema-inspired programs to have a substantial show of numbers. There is abundant qualitative and anecdotal information, and program-specific evaluations have already provided a good deal of information, but the findings are not yet widespread enough or coordinated enough to lead to an unassailable case. Reliable quantitative research data is in development in many places, but will take some years to emerge as substantive, simply because the effects of El Sistema programs happen over years, sometimes many years.

In addition, conducting good research and evaluation takes money. In a world where funders often require data about program effectiveness—but where doing research that proves effectiveness requires funds—many young programs are caught in the Catch-22 dilemma of not being able to afford the quality evaluation projects that would make their programs more sustainably fundable.

There are other data challenges. It's difficult to come up with consistent numbers for what a Sistema-inspired program costs; many young programs are experimenting, so costs can vary drastically year to year.

funding. We are also convinced that in most cases, relying solely on public funding will not be enough. Almost by definition, government funding is bare-bones funding, at least in the areas of social welfare and the arts. It works best when it is based on long-term commitment and supplemented by funding from other sources. In our opinion, the best long-term sustainability scenario for Sistema-inspired programs is the public/private, public/civic, or public/corporate partnership. With government commitment plus civic engagement, Sistema programs have a shot at realizing their multiple goals of intensity, excellence, youth development, and social change. This means that the value of El Sistema must be recognized so strongly that governments, civic organizations, businesses, and donors choose to invest in the

Donated space one year can turn into large location costs the next year if a program moves from a school to its own center. Cost per child can almost double when a small program takes on new faculty for growth, or halve when it takes on more students without increasing faculty.

It's also true that in a young field comprised of widely varying programs, early data is sometimes just not very meaningful. For example, in the United States, statistics about averages don't shed much light, because annual program budgets range from $1,058 to $2,715,079; costs per student range from $12 to $7,118 per child per year; program hours fall between 3 and 40 hours per week; and program size runs from 8 to nearly 2,000 students.

The data situation is no simpler when it comes to global comparisons. The numbers have little meaning when we are comparing high-cost Western European countries and low-cost settings like Vietnam, Kenya, and the Philippines. Common impact measurements are not yet developed. The field isn't mature enough for us to make valid estimates of norms or averages or reliable statistical outcomes in any category.

Five or ten years from now, revised versions of this book will be substantively bolstered with data. We are confident that most of it will support our current observations of this field in formation, and we're interested to find out which parts of the data will challenge us to expand our understanding.

long-term viability of the programs. Sistema programs must continue to prove they deliver the results they describe.

Proving value to public funding agencies is probably the single biggest challenge facing the young global Sistema field. The proof doesn't have to be so compelling that it converts diehard skeptics, who will probably not believe it anyway (consider the attitude of diehard skeptics toward the reality of climate change, as sea levels rise). But it will have to be solid enough to convince the officials and legislators who can tip the policy balance. The subjective impact of visiting Sistema programs, seeing children perform, and hearing personal testimonials is, of course, an essential tool in attracting support. But a strong objective case of public benefit and government savings is essential as well.

This imperative is complicated by the difficulty of evaluating youth development work in statistically reliable and convenient ways, in a funding climate where metrics and quantifiable data are increasingly considered the ultimate criteria of program worthiness. Further, youth development goals are not quickly achieved; it can take years before the impact of a Sistema program upon young people's lives is clearly visible. Sistema leaders often feel they are selling long-term benefits in a hyperactive short-term funding world that demands guarantees of impact by metrics.

Challenges notwithstanding, there are already some examples of independent research that strongly affirm programs' claims. We have seen that Sistema Scotland's startup success has been amplified by its extensive evaluative research, and that studies of In Harmony Liverpool show compelling evidence of the program's positive impact. Researchers studying the Pizzicato Effect program in Australia found statistically significant improvements in children's academics, self-esteem, and social and emotional well-being as a direct result of the program.[32] In the United States, programs that have been running for four or more years have begun to show statistically verifiable results. Many U.S. programs have found clear affirmation of positive academic benefits, among them Kidznotes in North Carolina, Play On, Philly! and the Community Opus Project near San Diego. At YOLA (Youth Orchestra of Los Angeles) there are early data showing that the program is associated with higher graduation rates and college matriculation percentages. As of this writing, all thirty-one YOLA students who have graduated from high school while in the program have gone to college; these are students living in communities with relatively low college-attendance rates.[33]

YOLA is also part of several long-term academic research projects. One of these involves collaboration with the Brain and Creativity Institute at the University of Southern California on a research initiative investigating the cognitive effects of El Sistema-inspired musical training on childhood development. Results obtained by the third year suggest that participation in the program has positive effects on

child development.[34] Another YOLA collaboration, a study with Stanford University researchers, is investigating which elements in a Sistema learning environment seem to make the most difference in providing social and emotional benefits to children.[35]

In addition, the first U.S. national research study of El Sistema-inspired programs, led by the consulting company Wolf-Brown and the Longy School, will report its findings in 2016 regarding the conditions under which programs have positive effects, the assets they build in children and families, and key outcomes such as achievement and prosocial behaviors. Preliminary results from this methodologically strong research confirm the anecdotal reports from around the world: students enrolled in Sistema-inspired programs scored significantly higher on standardized tests of English language arts and math, and earned higher grades in these same subjects, than their non-Sistema peers attending the same school.[36]

Even before hard data is widely available, many program leaders are beginning to use the Opportunity Cost argument, discussed in Chapter 10, to make a case for the benefits of Sistema programs. Just consider, they say, that the average cost of a single young person's involvement with the criminal justice system in some U.S. cities is $200,000 per year. If a Sistema program, which averages less than $2,000 per child per year, can be shown to help keep kids out of legal trouble, then clearly there is a potential here for massive long-term savings. Even an allocation of several million dollars to a Sistema program is a public funding bargain.

SIGNS OF PROGRESS

In 2014, the Massachusetts Cultural Council allocated a million dollars over three years to support Sistema-inspired programs—to date, the only state government funding for Sistema initiatives in the United States. The council received applications from thirty-one programs in its second year, an indication of the tremendous hunger for this

kind of funding. Also included in the council's initiative are funds for a music instrument library that will lend instruments to Sistema students across the state, and funds for a research project to document the development of "executive function" in students (the suite of self-management capacities discussed in Chapter 8). In New Jersey, the first instance of private support for growing a statewide El Sistema network has come from the Dodge Foundation, which has funded the El Sistema New Jersey Alliance's efforts to build connections between programs in different areas of the state. The three largest Sistema programs in the Canadian province of Ontario (in Toronto, Ottawa, and London) have created a provincial organization that advances the prospects of all ten programs in the province.

A particularly imaginative funding idea comes from Creative Scotland's CashBack for Creativity program, which has used millions of pounds recovered from crimes (i.e., taxation of profits generated by crime, confiscation of property purchased with the proceeds of illegal activity) and reinvests them in building healthier communities, especially creative opportunities for young people in struggling neighborhoods.

There's another promising option for the future in the form of "social impact bonds," or SIBs, which are also known as "social innovation financing" and "pay for success." This approach enables cash-strapped, risk-averse local governments to address expensive, difficult social problems in long-term ways without financial risk. A government targets a particular social problem—prisoner recidivism or homelessness, for example—and partners with an intermediary bond-issuing organization that raises bond money from private investors (individuals, banks, foundations). The bond allows for the hiring of social service providers with established track records of success to address the challenge. If the intended goal is achieved, the government repays the bond investors, with interest. If the intervention does not meet the goal, investors are not repaid, and there has been no cost to government. Even though the first few SIB projects didn't pay off as quickly as intended (and the first U.S. SIB, addressing Riker's Island

recidivism, may not reach payback at all), the use of SIBs is spreading. By 2015, there were 16 social impact bonds in the U.K., 4 in the U.S., 2 in Australia, 5 in various other countries, and over 100 proposals in the works worldwide.

Why not a gang membership reduction SIB, with a Sistema program as the lead provider? Why not a school dropout-rate reduction SIB? As Sistema programs grow into maturity and can demonstrate through independent evaluation that they achieve their social goals, they will be ideal partners to deliver government cost savings. SIBs could provide a sustainable win-win-win way for Sistema programs to thrive—for governments to save money while improving communities, for investors to gain financially, and for the children whose lives begin to change. When the self-interest of the wealthy can be turned into life change for children of need, there is every reason to seize the chance.

"HOW DO YOU BRING IT TO SCALE?"

This is a common question from politicians and business leaders who are enthusiastic about the local Sistema program but want to know, before they provide support, how it can expand to reach all the needy kids in an area. It's a question that is sometimes daunting to program leaders; funding such slow, time-intensive work over years is difficult even with a limited number of kids, so multiplying the number of students by a factor of ten or fifty or a hundred can seem inconceivable. Furthermore, Sistema leaders are reluctant to accommodate the impulse to reach more kids if it means scaling back the intensity of the programs and thus diluting their effectiveness.

There is one U.S. program that accomplishes both the sustainability and "scale" questions in a unique way. The school district of Chula Vista, California, has 50 percent free-lunch-qualified students and 50 percent English language learners (measures that indicate significant poverty and significant recent-immigrant population, respectively) among its 29,000 students. Throughout the 2000s, the district's budget for arts education was exactly zero. Chula Vista is in the San Diego area, and when the San Diego Youth Symphony (SDYS) was looking for a community partner to launch an El Sistema-inspired initiative, it found an ally in Margarita Holguin, executive director of the Chula Vista Community Collaborative. In 2010, Holguin and SDYS CEO Dalouge Smith led the launch of the Community Opus Project in Chula Vista, with 65 students at two elementary schools.

From the beginning, Opus was unusual among Sistema-inspired projects because it aimed to restore in-school music by leading with after-school music. Within eighteen months, Opus had expanded to a total of six schools in the after-school program, and plans for in-school music at all six sites were underway. The SDYS provided the Opus after-school orchestra program, and the school provided Sistema-inflected in-school music classes with the same teachers.

By 2014, eighteen schools had piloted in-school music programs, and six of them had hired full-time music teachers. The after-school Community Opus Project had grown to over 200 young musicians. When a district-wide evaluation of the results of the music program cited many positive benefits for students, the school district was delighted. The superintendent and the school board became believers in the power of arts education. As the numbers of students grew, the quality of the music rose. All the kids were musically engaged, and those moving into the Opus orchestra were excited and ambitious.

In 2015, a new opportunity suddenly appeared when Governor Jerry Brown lifted funding controls on California districts with disadvantaged students, letting them make their own decisions about how to spend their money, and providing them with more to spend. Of the many districts around the state affected by this decision, only Chula Vista voted to apply 15 million of its new dollars, 5 million a year for three years in a row, to bring arts education to every one of their schools.

As we go to press, the district has hired a total of sixty-two new teachers across all arts disciplines, to reach every child. The after-school Opus Project is now open to students from all elementary and middle schools in the community, and over fifty Opus students have moved into the San Diego Youth Symphony and other youth ensembles, joining the more affluent students who got there by the standard pay-to-play pathways.

It's a dramatic success story: because of the positive results of the Sistema-inspired Community Opus Project, a school district's arts budget of zero turned into a budget of over $5 million a year. The model is now being adopted in other San Diego area school districts. Dalouge Smith stressed the potential for public funding of El Sistema programs. "We knew from the outset," he said, "that we could never reach the hundreds of thousands of children in San Diego County who have little or no access to music education with private resources alone. By structuring the goal of public education funding into the earliest strategic framework of the Community Opus Project, we made it possible to move toward our vision of making music education accessible and affordable for all children."

A LONG-TERM VISION: CSR AND ASR

Jovianney Cruz of Ang Misyon in the Philippines sometimes tells fellow musicians and Ang Misyon students that as the concept of corporate social responsibility (CSR) begins to spread within the international corporate world, it's imperative for artists to include artistic social responsibility (ASR) in their definition of what it means to be an artist. The citizen artists we have profiled in this book, and many more like them throughout the world, have a powerful feeling of social responsibility. Their sense of obligation seems to be the opposite of a burden: it feels intuitive, urgent, and joyful.

Is it possible that as their numbers grow, alliances between ASR and CSR will begin to multiply? Might a new generation of citizen artists, without some of the anticorporate prejudices of previous generations, find new ways to join forces with business and industry, in the interests of advancing agendas of social change? Could the successes of Sistema-inspired programs and similar endeavors convince business leaders that artists, and the arts, have a crucial role to play in the process of social regeneration? As evaluative research on the effectiveness of these programs begins to produce positive results, might the corporate sphere become more receptive to the idea that one of the best ways they can "give back" is to give the poorest and most at-risk children in their communities an intensive, long-term experience of artistic immersion?

If so, the energy of ASR combined with the energy of CSR could become a vast and combustible force for social change. Children's orchestras, choruses, and bands—and perhaps dance, theater, and visual arts programs as well—would proliferate in places they have never been before. Government and civic leaders might identify ASR/CSR as a way to help them accomplish what they have been unable to do alone.

Blue-sky thinking? Perhaps. But . . .

As our hypothetical social change agent said on the very first page of this book: It's already underway. And it's working. The examples in the global Sistema that we have cited—the alliance between the Lopez Group and Ang Misyon in the Philippines, born of the collaborative friendship between a concert pianist and a business leader with a social conscience; the partnership between the Safaricom company and the youth orchestra movement across Nairobi, Kenya; the partnership in Mexico between corporate magnate Ricardo Salinas's Fundación Azteca, former government minister Esteban Moctezuma, and citizen artist Julio Saldaña, which supports Esperanza Azteca in Mexico—these represent such connections in practice. We believe that they offer one of today's most hopeful models for social change, and that corporate social responsibility and artistic social responsibility, working together respectfully and cleverly, and ideally with the supportive participation of government, can lead social change perhaps more than any other single force. El Sistema is in the vanguard of this phenomenon.

CHAPTER 13

Connecting the Dots

Inapparent connections are stronger than the apparent ones.
—HERACLITUS

In August 2015, Milan, Italy, became a little bit Venezuelan—similar to the way Salzburg, Austria, took on a Latin feel in 2013, when hundreds of kids from Venezuela came to play music there. For four weeks, the world-famous opera house La Scala—even more of a high-art icon, if that's possible, than the Salzburg Festival—opened its doors to the children and young people of El Sistema, hosting six full instrumental and choral ensembles from Venezuela. This "Progetto Sistema" was the brainchild of Alexander Pereira, the impresario who had shaped the Sistema's Salzburg residency; he had subsequently become the director of La Scala and had brought with him his zeal about El Sistema.

In Milan, the Sistema-esque vision for the residency went even further than it had in Salzburg. La Scala's doors were open not only to the young performers, but to an entirely new audience; the poor and underserved children of Milan were invited in to listen for free. "There are thousands of children in our city whose families cannot go away for an August vacation, and cannot afford tickets to concerts," said Pereira at a press conference. "We want to gather those children and give them the possibility of hearing music and seeing theater—to open the doors and give tickets to young people who would normally not have had the chance to enter this theater or to encounter classical music."

At the same time, 180 Sistema students and teachers from

twenty-six countries across Europe (and beyond) converged on Milan for the Sistema Europe Youth Orchestra (SEYO) summer camp. Over nine intense days, they dove into long, rigorous rehearsals under the batons of Sistema Lombardy conductor Alessandro Cadario, Sistema Portugal conductor Juan Carlos Maggiorani, and Sistema Europe Youth Orchestra conductors Bruno Campo and Etienne Abelin.

Along with the serious play of rehearsal, they joined in more lighthearted kinds of play: workshops in improvisation, movement and dance, and the storytelling dimensions of classical music; empathy games and sound-visualization sessions; flash mobs at a castle and an EXPO 2015 site; a session on Baroque performance. Some of the young musicians remembered one another from the SEYO summer camp the year before, in Istanbul, and the few who were alumni of the first SEYO gathering in Salzburg in 2013 became instant mentors and assistant teachers to the newer players.

Maestro Abreu has said that the orchestra is the only form of association whose sole purpose is agreement. The young musicians of SEYO worked together that week to arrive at expressive agreements inside eleven musical masterworks, including Shostakovich's *Festive Overture*, Tchaikovsky's *Marche Slave*, a movement from Beethoven's Fifth Symphony, *Danzon No. 2* by Márquez, and Bernstein's "Mambo"—agreements that were far more nuanced, complex, and large-scale than any they had experienced in their home núcleos. Together, they created a sonic grandeur they had never imagined themselves capable of. They ended their week with a final concert in the historic Teatro degli Arcimboldi, a special rehearsal with Dudamel, and a side-by-side performance with the Youth Orchestra of Caracas at La Scala, with Venezuelan conductors Dietrich Paredes and Jesús Uzcátegui.

International youth orchestras have long been a way for young musicians to join forces, work and perform together, and create bonds across cultures. But an international Sistema ensemble is something new: children and young people of traditionally excluded communities, who are there not by virtue of family tradition, private lessons, or conservatory training, but because they have developed musical strength and social cohesion through ensemble learning. These young people, many of whom have never left their hometowns, come together already practiced in the inclusive, empathic habits of heart and mind that are nurtured in Sistema learning environments.

It's new, and it's happening more and more. It happened in January 2014, when the children of Sistema Scotland went to Venezuela to play music with the children of Caracas. It happened in 2015, when 50 young people from Sistema England and Italy traveled to Canada to play with 140 young Sistema musicians, and in the other direction four months later, when a delegation of students from Toronto and Ottawa went to Sweden to play with students from eight European countries. In March 2015, when the Los Angeles Philharmonic Orchestra went on tour in Japan, they brought along the young musicians of YOLA to play in Tokyo's Suntory Hall with a Sistema orchestra from Fukushima. It will happen in the summer of 2017, at the summer camp and first performances of the national Sistema orchestra of the United States.

"THE GLOBAL EL SISTEMA MOVEMENT"

We find ourselves using that phrase often, to describe the shared urgency, common goals, and similar vocabulary and practices we have encountered in our travels for this book. The increased frequency of international Sistema ensemble gatherings is an indication that El Sistema is a global phenomenon. But is it a movement?

We'd propose that a genuine social movement has three fundamental characteristics:

- It addresses and seeks to change a social, political, or economic reality.
- It includes coordinated and sustained actions.

- It is comprised of an organized group of individuals who work together toward a common purpose.

It seems clear that the global Sistema qualifies on the first two points: across the world, leaders and programs seek to change social and economic realities—that's the whole point!—and the programs are aligned and built around sustained action. As for the third criterion: inarguably the wide array of programs coalesces around a common purpose, but is there sufficient organization and collaboration to call it a movement?

El Sistema leaders in Venezuela would seem to be the obvious ones to take on the role of international organizing, but Maestro Abreu and Fundamusical have made a clear decision not to do so. Eduardo Méndez, executive director of Fundamusical, describes their approach: "The beauty of this phenomenon is to see how each Sistema-inspired project in the different countries adapts the Venezuelan idea to the needs, culture and reality of its community. We like being able to help through technical support and training, but we think it's important to provide the space that allows their own development to take place freely. The growth of local leadership and identity is pivotal to the sustainability of the project in time and to the process of pursuing social change through musical excellence."

This approach accounts for the fact that Sistema-inspired programs around the world can differ widely and strikingly in many ways, but to a remarkable degree, they operate according to the same principles and are guided by the same goals and vision. The unity of vision combined with flexibility of implementation is one of El Sistema's greatest strengths. Alix Didier Sarrouy, a sociologist working with the Sorbonne and the Minho University of Portugal, has undertaken a study of this subtle accomplishment of Sistema programs; he is doing in-depth field research on Sistema-inspired programs in Venezuela, Brazil (NEOJIBA), and Portugal (Orquestra Geração), to explore the ways El Sistema principles are practiced and shared within different cultural, social and political contexts.

The very use of the name El Sistema seems to depend on a global honor system. The term is understood to be used only by programs that adhere to the basic set of values and social goals that characterize El Sistema in Venezuela. (See Appendix III.) There is some risk involved in this approach, because non-Sistema-like programs could legally use the name to burnish their image, but generally, the honor system works. There are cases of not-very-Sistema-like programs claiming the name and association, but these have been few, and the damage has been negligible.

Maestro Abreu continues to shun anything that looks or feels like franchising. His position is remarkably trusting; it is hard to imagine other organizations with similarly international scope being so hands-off and noncontrolling about their name and practices. In essence, he has been a superb mentor. Mentorship is a central pillar of El Sistema pedagogy; everyone, young and older, at a mature núcleo develops the habits of mind and heart to be good at it. These same habits of mind and heart seem to characterize international relationships, as if the global Sistema were one large orchestra of peers and mentors.

Organizing the global movement, therefore, is left to the mentees. Programs reach out to one another and create collaborative networks in a myriad of informal ways. In the United States and Canada, there's a great deal of regional coordination through seminarios, conferences, and projects.

The Los Angeles Philharmonic provides a substantial level of support for national network-building through its Take a Stand partnership with Bard College and the Longy School of Music at Bard College. "We feel a strong responsibility to support the growth of the national field, and we are looking to deepen that support," said Deborah Borda, the president of the L.A. Phil, who led the process of forming the first U.S. Sistema program, Youth Orchestra of Los Angeles (YOLA), in 2007. Take a Stand has hosted several major national conferences that serve as gatherings of the clan, and has created the only national teacher-training degree program in the

United States, Longy's Master of Arts in Teaching, housed in YOLA at HOLA. In 2016, Take a Stand is sponsoring two regional orchestras to lay the groundwork for a national El Sistema orchestra that will convene in 2017, with Dudamel conducting. Another initiative involving nationwide connectivity is the national research project led by the Longy School and WolfBrown.

As for formal national organizations in the United States and Canada—they are taking shape, although slowly and haltingly, in both countries. In the U.S., a dues-paying nonprofit organization called El Sistema USA (ESUSA) has established a website with useful information, has hosted several gatherings, and is planning to expand its services to the field. In Canada, a promising initiative to establish Sistema Canada was carefully and collaboratively conceived and designed, but the plan awaits funding before it can be realized.

In Europe and Latin America, many (though not all) countries have national Sistema organizations. The programs of six central and eastern European countries are formally united through Superar, headquartered in Vienna. The social and musical strength of this collective entity is growing; in 2015, the Superar orchestra performed for the heads of EU countries gathered in Vienna for the Western Balkans Civil Society Forum. Superar leaders Angelika Lošek and Irena Klissenbauer wrote to us: "Our kids from Austria, Bosnia, and elsewhere opened this forum with their music, showing the politicians what power really means."

By far the largest international network of Sistema programs is Sistema Europe, the entity that has created the Sistema Europe Youth Orchestra (an ensemble reconstituted with new students every summer). This group consists of representatives from all of the European countries with Sistema programs, including the Superar countries. As we go to press, 21 countries are represented; the largest program member is Sistema Italy, with about 9,000 students in over 60 núcleos, and the smallest is Sistema Lichtenstein, with 37 children eighteen months to three years old. Sistema Europe definitely meets our third criterion for a social movement—"an organized group of individuals who work together toward a common purpose." Since its inception in 2012, Sistema Europe has brought together children, teachers, and leaders from across the continent (and sometimes from Canada) to sing and play together and inspire each other. It has also established strong links between Latin America and Europe, won several substantial European Union grants that have strengthened the alliance, and provided a united voice in the political landscape.

Equally remarkable is the democratic and flexible process through which it accomplishes such things. The Sistema-inspired programs that have sprung up across Europe exhibit a lively diversity that reflects the many cultures sharing the small land space of the continent. Marshall Marcus has written of Sistema Europe: "We are (in no particular order) friendly, visionary, chaotic, complex, innovative, unresolved and deeply aspirational." We can add that they are also scrupulously collegial. The same generous spirit that characterizes Sistema learning environments pervades the meetings of Sistema Europe; we have watched with admiration as members from various countries plan and develop shared projects, working as equals, regardless of the size and budgets of their programs. Sistema Europe is an example of a network that is both egalitarian and flexible, a vivid proof that direct democracy need not be procedurally cumbersome.

In June 2015, the Gothenburg Symphony sponsored an international gathering that pushed the ideal of "inclusion" to mean including non-Sistema children and teachers. Kids from El Sistema Sweden were side by side not only with Sistema kids from eight other countries, but also with the young middle-class musicians of Sweden's many community "culture schools." In addition, side by side with the young people's encounter, teachers from Sistema programs engaged in constructive debates with culture school teachers. The tensions between these two groups can turn negative when they simmer without communication, but in this context of mutual curiosity and inquiry, some substantial peer learning was achieved. This new kind

THE VERY MODEL OF A MODERN CITIZEN ARTIST ADMINISTRATIVE LEADER

The contribution of Marshall Marcus to the growth of the worldwide Sistema movement cannot be overstated. Marshall studied philosophy and psychology at Oxford before becoming a violinist and performing with ensembles across the world. He was one of the founders, and also chairman and CEO, of the Orchestra of the Age of Enlightenment, and went on to serve as Head of Classical Music at Southbank Centre and then as CEO of the European Union Youth Orchestra. Through a fortunate coincidence early in his prolific career, in 1979, he became the concertmaster of the Orquesta Filarmónica de Caracas, where he met José Antonio Abreu and began teaching for El Sistema—which he has been doing, on and off, ever since. In February 2011, Maestro Abreu asked him to form a Baroque orchestra within El Sistema; the result was the Orquesta Barroca Juvenil Simón Bolívar.

Amid the pressing demands of his day jobs, Marshall launched Sistema Europe, which now includes some 32 programs in 21 countries. Even though he himself is a product of traditional music training, his understanding of Sistema principles has informed his intuition for the qualities of interdependence needed in a Sistema network: consensus, inclusion, experimentation, and efficiency. Marshall has managed to keep the group hewing to those qualities even as it became a legal entity, quadrupled in membership, and secured significant grant monies.

Marshall is a citizen artist who combines a deep knowledge of music with creative skills in organizational development and administration. He has launched the beginnings of a Sistema Africa network, which is slowly beginning to grow, and also the Sistema Evaluation and Research Archive, an initiative valuable both to the Sistema field and to the larger education community.

of seminario, fostering exchange between Sistema-oriented programs and more established music learning organizations, and widening the circles of teaching and learning, may become pivotal in the long-term Sistema story.

Another important connecting agent is Sistema Global, an Internet communications hub that includes a website, discussion opportunities, a resource library, and a research arm that sponsored the first major research project in the field, the *Literature Review of El Sistema and El Sistema-inspired Programs Worldwide: Research, Evaluation and Critical Debates*. Sistema Global was founded by Glenn Thomas, a mostly retired San Diego businessman who fell in love with El Sistema and understood its worldwide potential. On his own entrepreneurial initiative, Glenn saw a niche for global communication and connectivity, and jumped to fill it; he is one of the first individuals to invest deeply in supporting the global Sistema. The "REP + Resource" section of Sistema Global has already proven invaluable to the worldwide movement, offering a wealth of free teaching resources, downloadable arrangements, and public-domain repertoire. Created by Louise Lanzillotti (founder-director of Kalikolehua, the Hawaiian El Sistema program) and a team of U.S. volunteers, it has grown into a generous library, helping Sistema programs around the world save time and money.

One of the striking dynamics of Sistema Global is one that Glenn may never have anticipated. On the LinkedIn discussion forum that is the most prominent face of Sistema Global, not a month goes by without someone in a remote country posting a new thread: "Hi, I live in Mongolia (or the Seychelles Islands, or Bangladesh), and I am trying to start an El Sistema-inspired program. Can someone please tell me how to do this?"

Always, people respond. Sometimes it's simply "Great to hear about you—you are doing the right things, just keep going!" At other times, resources are cited or substantive advice is offered. A thread in a discussion forum is clearly a haphazard way to launch a social program, but these virtual conversations are an indication of the strength and urgency of the Sistema-inspired impulse across the world.

Such messages in a virtual bottle, appearing out of the blue, are reminders of the unpredictability of the growth of El Sistema. The

HUNGRY FOR INFORMATION

To accelerate the growth of international connections, we began publishing a quarterly electronic newsletter, *The World Ensemble*, modeled on the monthly newsletter *The Ensemble*, which we have been publishing since 2012 to help connect Sistema programs and people in the United States and Canada. The global edition has built information exchange networks where none existed before, and helps programs across the world learn about one another and share innovations and successes. There seems to be a palpable hunger for connection and dialogue across the world of Sistema-inspired programs; during our research travels, we spent almost as much time answering our hosts' questions about how other countries address Sistema challenges as our hosts spent telling us about their distinctive solutions. In a grassroots phenomenon like this one, often the only way to learn how to create a program is to study others who are already doing it.

serendipity of an inspired individual, an atypical funder, a chance encounter with an attention-grabbing YouTube video or book, a Google search that pops Sistema Global to the top—these are more likely to be the first sentence of a Sistema program's founding story than is a feasibility study of a new project by an established music education institution.

Informal, often serendipitous networking among Sistema programs has been happening for decades in Latin America, where Sistema teachers and leaders of many countries visit one another (and especially Venezuela) to learn new teaching techniques, hear new orchestras, and build solidarity through connection. In more recent years, the informal networking has begun to reach around the world. A particularly vivid example is the "paper orchestra," developed several decades ago by Josbel Pulce, director of the Caracas núcleo La Rinconada, as a solution to the scarcity of small-sized instruments for young children.

HIGHLIGHTING SOME ADDITIONAL PINS ON THE MAP

Unfortunately, we aren't able to include in this book all of the noteworthy programs and people involved in Sistema-inspired work around the world. Here are brief introductions to some distinctive programs we haven't been able to describe in detail elsewhere.

Armenia

Based in Yerevan, Sistema Armenia started in 2013 with students who already played instruments, and then expanded to bring in younger players who are mentored by the more experienced musicians. The program, now with 120 students, has a primary goal to build a "more fair, prosperous and beautiful Armenia," according to Executive Director/Founder Anna Mikaelian Meschian. Anna said she and her colleagues have discovered that in a former Soviet state with strong but traditional music instruction, this goal requires a more holistic approach than a sole focus on music, so the program includes critical thinking, sports, and hands-on social impact projects, in addition to music.

China

El Sistema came to China in late 2012 with the pilot of Music for the Growing Mind, for 60 six-to-nine-year-olds; it has grown to include a hundred students in Hong Kong's poorest district, with the highest suicide rate. The program has forged a strong partnership with the Chicken Soup Foundation, an NGO, and has hired the violinist Melissa Niño, who grew up in Venezuela's El Sistema, to manage the program. Students regularly perform in end-of-life facilities, bringing lively energy and finding grateful audiences in return. Ambitious growth plans for the program project over a thousand students involved within a couple of years, and wider expansion in Hong Kong and into cities of mainland China in a few more years.

Croatia

SO DO is the musically memorable name of this program; the acronym stands for Sustav Orkestara Djece i Omladine, or System of Orchestras for Children and Youth, but it is also instantly singable, since those syllables, in solfège practice, refer to the fifth and first notes of any scale.

Carmen Hiti, the founder-director, has led the program's expansion in less than two years to three sites (in Zagreb, Lekenik, and Pula) serving 170 children. "The most pressing social need in our country is moral poverty," Carmen told us. "For the last 20 years, politicians have set very bad examples of behavior—corruption, nepotism, and theft in 'privatization' and in every other aspect of daily life. Young people are adopting unacceptable social and moral standards." SO DO attempts to reverse this trend by setting positive examples of social interaction, including compassion, helpfulness, and ethical behavior.

Greenland

Eighty students (45 from an orphanage, 35 from the town) play in the string-and-wind Uummannaq Orchestra in a remote area of Greenland. Founded in 2011 by Venezuelan El Sistema leader Ron Davis Álvarez and orphanage director Ann Andreasen, the program is funded by the government and many other sponsors (including the Uummannaq Polar Institute) and led by a faculty of three, including Music Director Jonna Faore. Kids sometimes travel on dogsleds to perform concerts in remote fishing communities, in schools and community centers and on ships. Often they play on the pack ice, using an ice wall for acoustical resonance. Their repertoire is a mix of orchestral music and the traditional music of Inuit culture. Venezuelan musician and teacher Sofía Hernández now lives there, helping the program build links to other towns to create a Sistema musical movement across Greenland.

India

Music4All works with 400 extremely poor children in New Delhi. It is run by volunteers and led by esteemed classical musicians Shubhendra Rao and Saskia Rao de Haas; studies center around Indian classical music, but in a way that is aligned with Sistema goals of youth development. The program uses multisensory approaches integrating age-old Indian music traditions with western teaching techniques, and moves from vocal work for beginners to a full range of Indian classical instruments. Sageet4All, an in-school Indian classical music curriculum also in New Delhi, serves 500 needy children.

The Child's Play (India) Foundation has four sites in the state of Goa. Founder/director Luis Diaz is an obstetrician who was so inspired by the

Venezuelan example that he left his practice in the U.K. and relocated back to his native India to start this program. Currently, 120 children are learning to play violin, viola, cello, recorder, and transverse flute, and to sing in a choir.

Iran

The Iranian Youth Orchestra (IYO) was founded in 2014 by a group of musicians who were disheartened by the demise of the Tehran Symphony Orchestra and decided to revive classical music in Iran by working with young people. They were inspired by visiting the Sistema Europe Summer Camps in Istanbul (2014) and Milan (2015). The inclusion of four young Iranian musicians in the Milan summer camp sparked the interest of more young people, and the orchestra (with many female members) currently numbers over 45. The mission of the IYO is to revive public interest in orchestral music and music-making for young people.

Mozambique

The Xiquitsi Project in Maputo now has 150 students playing strings, clarinets, and singing in choir in a country that has no resident or touring orchestras. Founder Eldevina (Kiki) Materula, an oboist, worked with NEOJIBA in Brazil and was inspired to bring the Sistema vision back to her home city. Its impressive success over three years has persuaded the Education Ministry to use it as a model for other school projects, and to introduce musical instruments into school learning.

Taiwan

Sistema Taiwan teaches 230 students in 10 rural orphanages and one community center; the program focuses primarily on "developing positive emotions" in troubled students who come from dysfunctional families. Particular challenges include students' lack of schooling and turnover when children are released from the orphanages.

And . . .

As we go to press, we have heard recent updates about programs that have begun or are in formation in Bulgaria, Germany, Iraq, Indonesia, Malaysia, Mongolia, Pakistan, Poland, Samoa, and, quite possibly, your home city.

Josbel's four-year-old students create and decorate papier-mâché violins, and use them to learn the basics of how to hold and care for an instrument, and to practice the feeling of personal ownership. "Your instrument is a part of you," Josbel tells them. Families help create the instruments, and the children often begin to love and feel identified with their colorful, sometimes sparkly creations. Josbel's students culminate their three months in the paper orchestra with a concert in which they sing songs about their instruments as they "play," and then are given their first actual instruments.

Josbel grew up playing in the La Rinconada núcleo; she went on to study early childhood education and then returned to the núcleo, first as teacher and then as director. Of the paper orchestra, she says, "Sometimes there are limits to our supplies, but there are no limits to our creativity as teachers."

Many international visitors to Venezuelan Sistema programs have been enchanted by the paper orchestra and brought it back to their own programs. Some also share the idea with other programs around the world. We've watched teaching artist Lorrie Heagy, founder-director of the program Juneau Alaska Music Matters, show teachers in Soma, Japan, how to implement the paper orchestra. We've also seen teachers from New Brunswick, Canada, share the technique with dozens of teachers in the Orchestra of Dreams Sistema program in Seoul, Korea. The paper orchestra is now the gateway into Sistema playing for thousands of children in many countries. An idea born of necessity in a Venezuelan barrio is now enjoyed by children and families around the world.

Is El Sistema a movement? That third criterion we cited—*being comprised of an organized group of individuals who work together with a common purpose*—would not have described the international activity of El Sistema even a few years ago. Every leader in the worldwide Sistema has long felt that she or he is part of a global endeavor, but the neurons of the larger entity are just now forming their connections. We feel that the global field is at a kind of tipping point, coming together a little more every day. In Milan in August 2015, that impression felt incontrovertible.

Had Claudio Abbado, the founder of the Italian Sistema, lived to see the Sistema celebration in Milan, he would have been thrilled. "El Sistema," he once said, "is something great, something fantastic. It is musically, culturally, socially and humanly unique. Already it does not belong to Venezuela alone. All countries, even those with major musical capitals, are getting to know it and want to imitate it, because there is no program . . . with such noble purposes, anywhere else in the world."

Musicians everywhere share Abbado's sentiments. Israeli violinist Pinchas Zukerman said, "El Sistema has now evolved to a global level of absolutely the best there is. And it will continue to evolve in the depth of its understanding. . . . It will be part of an extraordinary evolution, I think, for the world."

U.S. composer John Corigliano said, "As a musical citizen, it is a pleasure but also a privilege for me to add my voice to the chorus of musicians who admire Maestro Abreu's contribution to our musical and civic life, which is unprecedented. The first time it was suggested, it was hard to imagine something like El Sistema in the world. Now, it is hard to imagine a world without El Sistema."

And conductor Mariss Jansons: "José Antonio Abreu has shown the world a wonderful way to give millions of children the prospect of escaping poverty, sharing the magical experience of music and giving them social and emotional stability."

El Sistema is a significant and genuine worldwide movement.

By the time you read that sentence, it will be true.

CHAPTER 14

What We Can Learn from El Sistema

In a time of drastic change, it is the learners who inherit
the future. The learned usually find themselves equipped
to live in a world that no longer exists.
—ERIC HOFFER, PHILOSOPHER

Almost always those who achieve fundamental inventions
of a new paradigm have been either very young or very new
to the field whose paradigm they change.
—T. S. KUHN, PHYSICIST, PHILOSOPHER

We write this book out of a strong conviction that music educators and social policy makers have a good deal to learn from El Sistema. But we are more and more convinced that the learning environment developed by El Sistema also has relevance and value for many other spheres of the arts and education. In this chapter we offer some thoughts about how El Sistema's principles and practices might prove useful and enriching for widening concentric circles of cultural and civic life. Our discussion will focus primarily on cultural practices in the United States, about which we know the most, but our sense is that the lessons are widely applicable in other parts of the world.

WHAT THE K–12 MUSIC EDUCATION SYSTEM CAN LEARN FROM EL SISTEMA

In-school music teachers sometimes think of El Sistema as a competitive threat. When a new Sistema-inspired program begins in their district or school, they often fear that the district will cut in-school music programs by using the excuse that music-learning opportunities are adequately provided by the after-school Sistema program.

These fears are understandable, but in our experience unfounded. We have never heard of an in-school music teacher being fired or a music program cut back because of the launching of a Sistema program. In fact, we often hear the opposite: that the enthusiasm stimulated by Sistema programs can help school music programs grow, and sometimes actually leads to the hiring of more in-school music teachers. (For a dramatic example of this, see our Chapter 12 story of the San Diego Youth Symphony's Community Opus Project.) In Paterson, New Jersey, the excitement about a clearly beneficial Sistema-inspired program prompted the financially strapped school system to hire more in-school music faculty. Sistema teachers in relatively long-running programs, like the Harmony Program in New York City and the OrchKids program in Baltimore, have told us that kids who are in after-school Sistema programs bring commitment and expertise to their in-school music classes and ensembles.

To describe the healthy relationship we envision between Sistema programs and the rest of the music education ecosystem, we suggest the metaphor of a generous laboratory.

Sistema teachers have more teaching time, more pedagogical autonomy, more direct access to students' families, and more collegial reflection time than do most other music educators; these advantages make the Sistema classroom a potent laboratory for experimenting with the musical and social dimensions of various pedagogies, curricula, and repertoire. It can sometimes be difficult to apply the findings of such experiments to the conventional music classroom setting,

KINDRED COUSINS

There are many remarkable initiatives around the world that are similar to El Sistema, simpatico in spirit and values, but unaffiliated with the Sistema movement—so many that we cannot begin to do justice to them all here. We can only cite a few prominent examples, in the hope that readers will be newly alert to hearing and learning about other such initiatives. The family of this wider movement goes by many names but shares some central assumptions and goals.

The DaCapo program in London offers a weekend music education program that guides students through years of musical development, including choruses, instrumental lessons, and an orchestra. The families of DaCapo students have become a kind of community, enjoying a common space that includes music lessons for parents and impromptu performances by students. DaCapo leaders know and respect the El Sistema programs in London and are driven by similar aspirations.

In the United States, some examples of Sistema-like but not Sistema-connected programs include the Young People's Chorus of New York City; the Chicago Children's Choir; Community Music Works in Providence, Rhode Island; the Settlement Music School in Philadelphia; Jazz House Kids in Montclair, New Jersey; and a number of Carnegie Hall programs that work quietly and steadily under the radar in correctional centers, health clinics, homeless shelters, and elsewhere to bring transformative music education opportunities to underserved communities. There are many other such programs across the country.

And across the world, there are an increasing number of programs that build community and seek social transformation through music. One of the oldest and most famous of these initiatives is the West-Eastern Divan Orchestra, founded in 1999 by the great pianist, conductor, and composer Daniel Barenboim and the literary scholar and social activ-

where teachers work with huge groups of children for only 30 or 40 minutes a week, bound by bureaucratic constraints even around these minutes. Still, we feel certain that some of the findings of the "generous lab" of Sistema can be useful for in-school teachers.

ist Edward Said. The orchestra brings together young Palestinian and Israeli musicians (now with members from other Middle Eastern countries and Spain) to play together—an "experiment in coexistence" which has evolved into a great orchestra. "We aspire to total freedom and equality between Palestinians and Israelis," Barenboim has said, "and it is on this basis that we come together to play music."

In the township of Soweto, South Africa, the MIAGI (Music Is a Great Investment) program is aligned with Sistema values and goals; it uses classes, lessons, and ensembles to guide students away from trouble and into patterns of success. Its home base is just a short walk from Nelson Mandela's childhood home and from the epicenter of the June 16th Youth Uprising credited with turning the tide of the nation's apartheid history. The South African program BuskAid also works "to give impoverished children in the townships of South Africa the opportunity to learn classical stringed instruments to the highest possible standards." In Kinshasa, Democratic Republic of Congo, the Symphonique Kinbanganiste, a youth and adult orchestra and choir founded and conducted by former airline pilot Armand Diangienda, has persisted through difficulties for over 20 years. In Paraguay, the Landfill Harmonic Orchestra is comprised of children and adults who have made their instruments out of objects found in a landfill dump. They were featured in a widely circulated 2013 documentary and now tour in other countries.

The international European charity Music Fund, founded by Belgian musician and scholar Lukas Pairon, brings free orchestral instruments and lessons in instrument repair to young musicians in poor and conflict-ridden areas in developing countries. MusAid, a charity based in the United States and Canada, partners with schools in Afghanistan, Haiti, Burma, El Salvador, and other countries to provide instruments and instruction by volunteer music teachers. Musicians Without Borders works in six war-torn countries.

One of the most useful findings may involve expectations about what children can accomplish. Sistema experience challenges several nuggets of received wisdom in public school music contexts—for example, that small children can't manage wind or brass instruments;

that recorder must be introduced before orchestral wind instruments; or that very young children can't sing complicated harmonies. We have seen children as young as seven and eight successfully playing small-scaled wind and brass instruments in Sistema orchestras. Similarly, we've heard Sistema choruses of young children singing in three- and four-part harmony. Public school music teachers are always interested in our reports of these observations. "How do they get kids to do that?" they ask. Often, they are stimulated to think more expansively about what their students may be capable of.

Another valuable finding from the Sistema "lab" is about performance. In-school music teachers usually gear their teaching around two or at most three concerts a year. Sistema teachers often gear their teaching around two concerts a month; some add pop-up concerts and flash mobs to the mix. The performances may not be as polished as those in school settings, but the motivational through-line stays higher, and that motivational habit of heart and mind is gold for a music teacher.

Beyond these specific pedagogical lessons for music teachers, El Sistema offers a learning model that could be of interest to all educators. This book is not the place to undertake a detailed investigation of how El Sistema sheds relevant light on school reform movements around the world; however, the habits of mind and heart we explored in Part II are key features of many education reform models. We strongly encourage those involved in or interested in project-based learning, collaborative-cooperative learning, experience-based learning, and other progressive models to consider El Sistema a strong colleague and partner by virtue of the depth and breadth of its ensemble practice and its emphasis on learning by doing.

WHAT THE CONSERVATORY SYSTEM CAN LEARN FROM EL SISTEMA

The often cut-throat environment of competition in
conservatory training can easily kill the "story" in the music.
Sistema training, rooted within place and community,
invites musicians to co-create their own story.

— VIJAY GUPTA, VIOLINIST
IN THE LOS ANGELES PHILHARMONIC
AND ARTISTIC DIRECTOR OF STREET SYMPHONY

In the United States, Canada, and Europe, pathways for training
musical professionals are based on the bedrock assumption that individual ambition in a competitive atmosphere, nurtured and shaped
in private lessons, is the way to create truly great musicians. Conservatories have been organized around this principle for centuries.
Many professionals in the music establishment are skeptical, to say
the least, about whether an ensemble mindset can produce musical
excellence. We've heard such professionals speak critically and sometimes dismissively about the Simón Bolívar Symphony Orchestra of
Venezuela and other top youth orchestras of the Venezuelan Sistema.
Always, it's about how the ensemble-learning environment compro-
mises technical perfection. The critique springs from a belief system
that prioritizes what we've referred to, borrowing the words from
Marshall Marcus, as "the virtuosity of technique."

Venezuelan teachers and students prize technical virtuosity as
well, and have always been eager to learn what the conservatory tradition has to teach them about the virtuosity of technique. But the
Western classical music establishment has yet to recognize how much
it has to learn from El Sistema about the virtuosity of communication,
and about how prioritizing passionate connection can help to expand
and engage audiences.

Imagine if the classical music establishment were willing to
learn from El Sistema about how to develop the spirit of collaboration

instead of competitiveness. Imagine if all music students, from interested beginners to advanced conservatory students, had their regimen of private lessons and isolated practice sessions leavened by regular ensemble learning that they experienced as fun, in which peer helpfulness, the spirit of mutual collaboration, and the goal of group excellence trumped the competitiveness of solo striving. Our strong guess is that technical virtuosity would remain robust, and there would be a surge in virtuosity of communication. If indeed it's true that "passion provokes precision," there might even be an acceleration of technical development.

A Sistema England initiative in November 2015 provided an imaginative example of what conservatories can learn, in a "Create Your Own Orchestra in a Week" project that brought together thirty-five music students with evident leadership potential from four Sistema-inspired programs across England. The students spent a week putting together their own orchestra; they were guided by teachers and mentors but made many of the important musical decisions and choices themselves. "This is your orchestra," Fiona Cunningham, CEO of Sistema England, told them at the end of the week. "It is up to you to lead on how it sounds, what it looks like, and whether it continues to exist." The students decided they wanted the orchestra to continue, and that on their own, they will be responsible for moving toward more complex and varied repertoire, more days and hours making music, and more performances. Two months later, the orchestra they created did a residency at the Southbank Centre in London.

WHAT THE PROFESSIONAL ORCHESTRA WORLD CAN LEARN FROM EL SISTEMA

The time we invited the Simón Bolívar Orchestra to the BBC Proms in
2007 was the most exciting experience of my musical life.
—NICHOLAS KENYON, MANAGING DIRECTOR
OF THE BARBICAN CENTRE, LONDON

Classical music may be the only professional field in which there are
more expert practitioners than ever before, and higher-quality training
for those practitioners than ever before—and yet the question "Is it
dying?" haunts the public conversation about the field. *The New Yorker*
music critic Alex Ross put it bluntly: "The modern orchestra concert
is not entirely unrelated to the spectacle of a Civil War re-enactment."
It's a bewildering cultural paradox: the pipeline of conservatory education turns out more and more qualified aspirants for fewer and
fewer orchestral jobs, in a field some say is headed for hospice.

Others say the orchestral field is in fact changing—maybe not
quickly, but heading in the right direction. Whether the doomsayers
or the optimists are right, orchestra leaders and musicians around the
world recognize the need to reimagine the identity of the traditional
symphony orchestra concert—a ritual that is considered irrelevant
and uninteresting, not to mention inconvenient and expensive, by a
growing number of people.

In the United States, orchestras began the process of self-
questioning in the 1980s, when school districts across the country
decided to cut their budgets by downsizing music and other arts programs in public schools. Many orchestras formed arts education
departments or projects to fill the vacuum. In general, these initiatives
have not had the impact that was hoped for; research shows that
orchestra education and community programs have not translated
into new subscribers for orchestra concerts, nor have most programs
had much lasting educational effect. Orchestras continue to experiment with community partnerships to find new connections with

audiences, but even their successful projects often remain peripheral to their main work of traditional concert performance.

When the Simón Bolívar Youth Orchestra burst upon the international orchestra scene in the first decade of the twenty-first century, its appearance had the force of revelation for many classical music lovers. Lines of fans stretched around city blocks, waiting for hours to buy tickets not for the latest pop sensation but for an orchestra of young Venezuelans. Lo and behold, classical music was alive!—and not only for traditional concert-goers, but also for people who had never heard an orchestra before.

The revelation has deepened as the international orchestral community has learned more about El Sistema—about its multiple touring orchestras and charismatic conductors, its flourishing counterparts in other Latin American countries, and the social impact of its nationwide network of children's ensembles in disenfranchised neighborhoods. The somewhat insular Western classical music establishment is beginning to understand that it is Latin Americans who are revitalizing the world of classical music, and that it is from Latin America that we can and must learn.

What can orchestras learn? Perhaps the most fundamental lesson is simply about emotional vitality. In 2012, when Carnegie Hall administrators were planning a Festival of Latin American Voices, they asked Argentinian composer Osvaldo Golijov to articulate a theme that would embody what Latin America has to teach the rest of the world through the arts. His answer: "To live for joy."

"Joy" is not the first word that comes to mind when watching the musicians of most professional orchestras perform in concert. "Virtuosic," yes. "Focused," absolutely. But there is little attempt to communicate the feelings of urgency and excitement that surely constituted the musicians' initial experience of the music. Orchestra players have unlearned the virtuosity of communication that should be at the center of live performance and that Sistema orchestras know so well.

Of all the world's non-Latin American professional orchestras, the Los Angeles Philharmonic has had perhaps the most intense experience of learning from El Sistema; not only have they played under Dudamel since 2009, but they've also played side-by-side with the Simón Bolívar Orchestra many times, in both Los Angeles and Caracas. Clearly, they have caught the fever. *Los Angeles Times* critic Mark Swed, reviewing a 2015 concert in which the L.A. Phil played Stravinsky's *Rite of Spring*, called the performance "riotous." "This concert," he wrote, "was a too-rare demonstration of the way an orchestra can still be an excellent and relevantly dangerous vehicle for agitation. . . . The 'Rite' left everyone reeling. The orchestra could barely be contained." What a sea change there would be in the orchestra world—and in our collective cultural life—if orchestra concerts more regularly left us reeling.

In addition, orchestras can learn that the dynamism we see in Latin American Sistema orchestras is connected to a strong community orientation that is the taproot of their vitality. Again, the L.A. Philharmonic is a noteworthy example of an orchestra that has taken this lesson to heart. "The most important thing an orchestra can do is really listen to its community," said Philharmonic president Deborah Borda. "Before we started YOLA, we spent months talking with people in our community about how best to partner with them, because every orchestra has to have specific meaning and value for its own community."

Borda told us that now, a decade after the L.A. Phil launched Youth Orchestra Los Angeles, YOLA has become as much a part of the orchestra's community identity as their subscription concert series at Walt Disney Concert Hall. "Orchestras sometimes have a strong urge to exist in a bubble, where their only commitment is to their artistic imperatives," she said. "YOLA is a driving force to connect us beyond that bubble to other community priorities." The orchestra often plays side-by-side concerts with YOLA students; sometimes when it goes on tour, a contingent of YOLA musicians is taken along and included in tour activities and performances. "We are committed to supporting YOLA for the long term," said Borda.

"It's like adopting a child: You don't do it just for four or five years. You have to really commit."

L.A. Phil musicians have embraced the commitment to YOLA; fully half of the musicians actively work with the YOLA program, and for all of them, YOLA is a matter of pride. "They have come to see how it involves balancing the social and musical imperatives," Borda said. "And they are on board with that. Partly, this is because our musicians tend to be highly flexible and open-minded. And partly, of course, it grows out of their love for Gustavo."

Dudamel's decision in 2015 to renew his contract with the L.A. Philharmonic for another six years, instead of making himself available to potential offers from other prominent orchestras across the world, was celebrated by Sistema advocates as a sign of his commitment to YOLA and to the mission of El Sistema. Indeed, there is abundant evidence of that continuing commitment. In addition to his work with YOLA, Dudamel remains the music director of the Simón Bolívar Orchestra of Venezuela, and when he is on tour in other countries, he sometimes meets and works with local Sistema orchestras. "I will keep working for this," he has said, "because it is something very important not only for my country but for the world."

Another striking example of community commitment is the Royal Liverpool Philharmonic Orchestra, where musicians now think of themselves as community builders valuable even to the poorest people in their city. A large majority of the orchestra's musicians are engaged in regular community-related endeavors, and the result has been to empower them as community music leaders, changing the nature of their professional identity. "It has brought the Liverpool Philharmonic into the community, in a deeper way than we've ever been before," said Peter Garden. "It's been a huge catalyst for how we work—for our company values."

Many Liverpool musicians choose to devote their community engagement time to the In Harmony Sistema program that the orchestra supports in the West Everton neighborhood; they work with the children individually and in sectionals. Others work in the early-childhood learning and mental health programs the orchestra also supports. Peter told us that when orchestra musicians come to rehearsal, their preliminary chatting is usually about their experiences in the community learning projects. "It's the most exciting and unusual thing in their professional lives," he said. "They are completely lit up about it." It's possible that such informal conversations at the music stands of symphony orchestras with bold community partnering initiatives may be more important to the future of orchestras than whatever goes on in the meetings of their marketing strategists.

A different paradigm for orchestra-community relations might also help to address a growing concern of orchestra managers: an increasing number of young professionals in classical music are losing interest in orchestras. They are piecing together careers in an improvisatory, entrepreneurial way, and many prefer this way because, even with its uncertainties, it provides creative control and the opportunity to pursue a variety of interests. In a recent survey of the alumni of the Sphinx Organization, which supports the advancement of young black and Latino classical musicians, only 11 percent envisioned or wanted a career in orchestras, in spite of the attraction of tenured employment and benefits. Among the eighty-three graduates of Carnegie Hall's two-year Ensemble ACJW Fellowship, a prestigious training program for teaching artists, fewer than 10 percent have taken full-time orchestral jobs; the rest have pursued a freelancing mix that includes small ensembles with a lot of creative control, edgier chamber orchestras, and part-time orchestral gigs.

The Liverpool example is proof that a stronger community orientation could help to reverse this trend. Peter Garden told us that top young musicians in Great Britain often seek out auditions with the Liverpool Philharmonic because its social engagement dimension appeals to them. If more orchestras cultivated this dimension, it's possible that emerging young musicians would be more lit up about joining their ranks.

Further, the example of El Sistema challenges the prevailing orthodoxy about developing new audiences. For decades, orchestras

AN ORCHESTRA CHANGING WITH ITS COMMUNITY

When Michael Eakin, chief executive of the Royal Liverpool Philharmonic Orchestra (RPLO), is asked to define his organization in a single sentence, he mentions two things: the orchestra, with its vibrant young chief conductor Vasily Petrenko, and In Harmony Liverpool, its El Sistema program. The RLPO has integrated its work with and for local communities into the basic fabric of its identity. The organization has three divisions, each with a director—orchestra performances, hall management, and learning activities. Peter Garden, director of learning, is paid and empowered equally with the other two; this equivalent prioritization of concert performance and community engagement is unprecedented in the orchestral world.

RLPO Learning has three major community initiatives. One is in-depth work with impoverished young children (infants to age five) that focuses on child-directed musical creation, so that peer learning and child-centric music learning is in place long before children begin playing instruments. The second initiative involves in-depth work with mental health programs. The third is the Sistema-inspired In Harmony program in the neighborhood of West Everton, one of England's poorest communities. As of 2015, the program involved 750 children, and the program was expanding to include a nursery school and another primary school.

have thought about attracting new audiences primarily in three ways: through cleverer marketing, through educating people as listeners, and through supporting talent development through conventional youth orchestras. But El Sistema is not about any of these things. El Sistema is about creating communities of players not by seeking out the talented but by seeking out the underserved. It's also about creating communities of listeners where they have never existed before—listeners to whom the music matters because it is so communicatively played.

The sponsorship of a community Sistema program doesn't necessarily mean that many of the orchestra's musicians are substantively involved in the program. Frequently, such involvement increases gradually over time, as musicians discover that working with the kids can be fun and invigorating. Regardless of the level of musician participation, however, the overall opportunity for orchestra leaders is to listen, experiment, and discover the ways they might make a difference to communities they've never reached before.

A number of orchestras across the world are now sponsoring or supporting Sistema programs. In the United States, in addition to the Los Angeles Philharmonic, the most prominent of these is the Baltimore Symphony Orchestra, whose conductor, Marin Alsop, is a strong believer in El Sistema. Other U.S. orchestras that have made serious commitments include the New Jersey Symphony Orchestra, the Allentown Symphony, the Orchestra of St. Luke's, the Waterbury Symphony, the Kalamazoo Symphony, the Santa Rosa Symphony, the Stockton Symphony, the Jacksonville Symphony, and Illinois's Fox Valley Orchestra—as well as several youth orchestras and one professional chorus, the Pacific Chorale.

Internationally, in addition to the Royal Liverpool Philharmonic Orchestra, a prominent example of a Sistema-oriented orchestra is the Gothenburg Symphony Orchestra in Sweden. The Gothenburg orchestra is a founding member of El Sistema Sweden; it partners with the ten local núcleos on many projects, and its CEO has a permanent chair on the board that oversees the national growth of El Sistema Sweden (now thirty núcleos in twenty cities). Some symphony musicians have gotten to know the students of Sistema Gothenburg, who frequently perform with them in side-by-side concerts. Petra Kloo Vik, the orchestra's main Sistema connector, said, "Through El Sistema, the orchestra gets the decisive opportunity to become relevant in a changing society. Thanks to our fantastic cooperation with the community music schools, our orchestra can be the force of change that every arts institution should be."

A recent addition to the community of major orchestras supporting Sistema programs is the Bogotá Philharmonic Orchestra, Colombia's premiere symphonic ensemble. In 2013, under the new leadership of music director David García, the orchestra launched an ambitious new El Sistema initiative that aims to provide daily ensemble music education for 20,000 children. The project has strong ties to Venezuela and will expand the spread of the Sistema ideal in Colombia beyond the already considerable reach of Batuta, the world's second-largest Sistema program.

It's important to note that some orchestras and other large music institutions are finding alternative ways, apart from Sistema initiatives, to make substantial community connections. Carnegie Hall, for example, is committed to a number of groundbreaking community programs that reach far beyond its traditional audiences and famous location; these include the Lullaby Project (now a national program), which involves professional musicians working with pregnant single mothers to help them compose lullabies for their unborn children, and the Musical Connections Project at Sing Sing Maximum Security Correctional Facility, where inmates learn to compose and play in instrumental ensembles. The Chicago Symphony's five-year-old Citizen Musician Initiative seeks to explore the role of musicians in civic life by sending musicians, including Music Director Riccardo Muti and creative consultant Yo-Yo Ma, into schools, ethnic neighborhoods, jails, shelters, and hospitals. The Houston Symphony is piloting a team of "community-embedded musicians" whose full-time work is in K–12 schools, social service organizations, and adult education programs, exploring how to bring what they know as musicians to the needs of their community. In London, the Southbank Centre and the Barbican partner with a number of community organizations, including a Southbank partnership with the Sistema-inspired In Harmony Lambeth program. Clearly, the purpose of these initiatives is not to sell more tickets but to explore, as a civic service, ways to expand the power of music to matter in people's lives.

In 2011, a small string ensemble of musicians from the Los Angeles Philharmonic performed a community concert in L.A.'s St. Thomas the Apostle Parish Church. There is a tried-and-true format for such events: the players arrive early and set up, the usual (relatively few) attendees show up, the players perform impeccably and add some genial spoken remarks, the audience is politely appreciative, and everyone goes home. This occasion was different. Playing alongside the L.A. Phil chamber group were children from the YOLA at HOLA program, which is located in the neighborhood of the concert. The church was packed with neighborhood families, including many who had never attended a performance of Los Angeles Philharmonic musicians before. Their response was spirited, and the performers responded with new excitement. The kids played some wrong notes but stayed focused.

At the strong final note, as the audience cheered, the L.A. Phil musicians and the kids offered each other high fives. The L.A. Phil musicians said afterward that they recognized that something important had just happened; despite the clunker notes and sometimes iffy intonation of the kids' playing, the music had felt more powerful and more poignant than the impeccable renditions they offer in purely professional concerts. They felt a connection to their community and their audience that was rare in their experience. "It was beautiful in every way," said one of the musicians.

WHAT CIVIC LEADERS CAN LEARN FROM EL SISTEMA

In 2011, Thomas DiNapoli, the New York State comptroller, calculated that the cost of handling a single youth in the criminal justice system of New York is $210,000 per youngster per year. (DiNapoli's figures represent the estimated costs of retaining that child in the criminal justice system over multiple years, which is, unfortunately, the statistically predictable outcome.) DiNapoli wrote in his report, "If, for example, New York spends $500,000 on a crime prevention program, and only one child who would otherwise have become a career criminal is diverted from that path, the program would have generated total present-value benefits of $1.5 million to $2.2 million."[38]

These huge "present value benefits" accrue if only *one* child is kept out of crime—and Sistema programs engage many children,

AN ORCHESTRAL FUTURE LAB

In 2007, the Deutsche Kammerphilharmonie Orchestra of Bremen, Germany, needed a new rehearsal space just at the time that a public secondary school in the indigent, high-crime neighborhood of Tenever had been renovated, with space to spare. At first, the school seemed an unlikely place for this topnotch classical ensemble to call home. But the orchestra has a strong collective sense of social mission, and the musicians decided to make the school its "Future Lab" for exploring "new social perspectives through music." Early in its residency there, the orchestra worked with the school to create a series of projects that would bring musicians and students together.

The result is that students and musicians are together every single school day. Musicians visit classes and talk to pupils; pupils visit rehearsals, sitting not in front of but in between musicians. In the lunchroom, musicians sit and eat with pupils. The musicians and the students write an opera together every year.

For the schoolchildren and their community, the effects have been profound. The school's dropout rate has fallen to less than 1 percent. The academic achievement rate has soared. According to a co-head teacher, Annette Rueggeberg, the atmosphere of the school has been transformed. "There is no more fighting or aggression or graffiti," she said. Students are now proud of their school and more confident about themselves. Families in well-to-do neighborhoods of Bremen who would never have dreamed of coming to the Tenever neighborhood are now competing to send their children to school there.

Eight years into this future lab, the Deutsche Kammerphilharmonie is known throughout Germany for its demonstrated social commitment. In 2009, the minister of culture pronounced it the nationwide model project in the field of cultural education. And the musicians say their orchestra has improved for the better. Cellist Stephan Schrader is quoted as saying, "When the children sit between us at rehearsals, our concentration is better. We can actually see their eyes grow wide with excitement when we play certain chords or play quickly. It reminds us of the reason we make music, which is sometimes easy to forget."[37]

frequently hundreds. For responsible civic leaders trying to spend public dollars most effectively and to cut costs wherever possible, what could be more urgently relevant than the idea that Sistema programs, which cost on average less than $2,000 per child per year, could be the most potent cost savings agent on the current horizon?

Since U.S. Sistema programs don't yet have long-term research data, we can't cite the overall percentage of Sistema students who get into trouble with the law, compared to their non-Sistema peers. But early anecdotal evidence suggests a significantly lower percentage. The data we do have from relatively mature programs, such as Scotland's Big Noise program, Liverpool's In Harmony program, and the YOLA program of the L.A. Phil, shows that children in Sistema programs become more self-confident, more socially competent, more academically successful, and happier. The data also shows no criminal involvement by their students (some of whom are now in their teenage years), a dramatic finding in neighborhoods where crime rates for youth remain high or continue to rise.

Admittedly, there's no guarantee that these happier, more confident, socially connected children will not end up in gangs or in jail. But the likelihood that they won't join gangs is already strong enough that investing civic monies in Sistema programs would be a fiscally sound, though perhaps novel, decision. Consider the fact that in the United States, 45 percent of all high school students in 2010 (*all* schools, not just schools in areas of poverty), and 35 percent of middle school students, said there is gang activity in their schools.[39] Gangs in the U.S. are responsible for between 48 percent and 90 percent of local crime in cities, and gang activity is expanding, becoming more sophisticated, migrating into new areas of criminal activity, and getting more heavily armed.[40]

It's impossible to calculate the social costs of gangs. These costs include troubled and shortened lives, the suffering of the victims of crime and violence, the spread of drug abuse, and the gargantuan costs of the criminal justice system, which is patently failing to solve the gang problem. Gang membership is the foremost gateway into a life of crime, and researchers Mark Cohen and Alex Piquero find that just one criminal multiple offender can cost society between $4.2 million and $7.2 million over a lifetime.[41]

Cohen and Piquero's research indicates that effectively stopping one ten-year-old child from joining a gang costs about $3,000.[42] The vast majority of strong Sistema programs around the world cost less than $3,000 per child per year. It's a powerful argument for civic leaders to attend to. Why not invest in Sistema programs *now*, with the prospect of saving some of those millions per gang member in the future?

When addressing "civic leaders," we're thinking not only of elected officials but also about the leaders of major civic institutions. Social initiatives are often most effective when they are partnerships between government and other organizations; in the United States, "collective impact" has become a generic term to describe an unusual partnering of institutions that commit to achieving a public good together. In a collective impact initiative, local groups and governmental agencies with mutual stakes in an issue create a coalition that works together to achieve a community goal—for example, cleaning up a river basin, or reducing teen pregnancies by 50 percent. When collective impact initiatives are well organized, they tap and channel a great deal of latent power. They often achieve and even exceed their goals.

We can imagine a collective impact effort targeting the reduction of gang membership in a neighborhood, spearheaded by a Sistema program partnering with social service organizations, police, and other civic resources. Combining all the resources and knowledge of the social service sector with the magnetic pull of a vibrant music program could be a social intervention of considerable power.

WHAT INTERNATIONAL ANTIPOVERTY ACTIVISTS CAN LEARN FROM EL SISTEMA

When Jean-Claude Decalonne, the founder-director of Passeurs d'Arts in France, was trying to start his program during the economic recession of 2008–9, he encountered a uniform stance among government officials. "Their attitude was generally, 'People have to eat, people have to have jobs, we can tend to the arts later.'"

He responded by telling them, whenever and however he could, that they had it backward. "I said to them, 'It is precisely because we are in great difficulties that arts and culture are indispensable. This moment, right now, is the moment to have absolute confidence in artists—because we have absolute need of them. All of our young people have to prepare themselves for better futures. And it is only artists, and art, that can guide them in that journey."

Our governmental leaders are not used to thinking about arts education as an effective—Jean-Claude would say a necessary—response to economic crisis. But El Sistema makes a credible case for this idea. If we were to write a letter to the many smart and determined NGO leaders who work to redress the effects of poverty around the world, and to the government leaders who also wish to make a difference, the letter might go something like this:

Dear dedicated activist:

We assume you believe that large-scale poverty remediation in a society can only happen with large-scale change in economic and social policy. We agree with you.

But one essential thing we have learned from El Sistema is that it's possible to offer the children of poverty habits of mind and heart that are radically different from the ones society has offered them before, and that are powerful enough to help many change their lives. These alternative habits of mind and heart have the potential to defy the force of received social expectations and norms, and to guide the hundreds of small choices that, in the aggregate, comprise change in a life trajectory.

There is no shortcut. It takes a lot of time—many hours a week of high-quality attention, over years—to create a new sense of possibility in contexts in which people have never encountered possibility. El Sistema takes that time. That's why it has been able to be effective where shorter-term or less intensive projects have failed.

Intrinsic motivation provides the only path to long-term success. While threats and rewards can make an impression on young people as extrinsic motivators, prioritizing intrinsic motivation provides the only route to fundamental and lasting change. El Sistema creates and fosters intrinsic motivation through a process that provides appealing challenges and personal satisfactions at every stage.

Earlier is better. Education research abounds with studies that illuminate how early the achievement gap begins. Children growing up in poverty start losing learning potential early, and the challenges compound as they grow.

And finally, dear dedicated activist: across the world, people with exactly your goals are implementing El Sistema programs and finding that, slowly and gradually, they are working.

EL SISTEMA'S LEARNING FROM OTHERS

In 2014, as the ten members of the fifth and final class of Sistema Fellows were winding up their immersive four-week trip to Venezuela to study El Sistema, they received a request from Maestro Abreu. "Please let us know what we could be doing better," the Maestro asked the Fellows. "Tell us what you have seen here that you think we could improve upon."

Presenting a critique of El Sistema to José Antonio Abreu didn't feel entirely comfortable to the group of young teaching artists, but they rose to the occasion. Their response was both respectful of the immensity of what El Sistema has achieved and reflective of their own considerable range of experiences in the field of music learning. The Maestro was delighted.

A signature strength of El Sistema has always been the avidity with which its leaders have sought guidance throughout the world, and the effectiveness with which they have acted upon what they learned. El Sistema has always borrowed abundantly from other ped-agogies. During the Sistema's formative years, Maestro Abreu was voracious about seeking out and learning from the masters of instru-mental instruction across the Americas and Europe. His teachers learned and absorbed the methods of a number of pedagogies, including the Orff approach, Dalcroze Eurythmics, and the Kodaly and Suzuki methods; these are traditions of instrumental and choral training that have been practiced and refined over many decades in Western music education.

In recent years, the Venezuelan Sistema has added a focus on creating opportunities for students to learn the skills of improvisation and composition. Former New York Philharmonic bassist Jon Deak has been invited to Venezuela to teach the Very Young Composers (VYC) method. VYC, developed by Deak and supported by the New York Philharmonic Education Department, enables children to com-pose for classical ensembles. Already, the Venezuelan Sistema has launched a new orchestra, La Orquesta Contemporanea "El Paraiso" de Simón Bolívar, to perform the new works that children and young people are creating through this method.

Many Sistema programs in other countries are also seeking ways to incorporate improvisation and composition. One prominent example is the Creative Connections workshops series in Baltimore, led by OrchKids founder-director Dan Trahey, in which teachers learn to create a group composition and performance process for their students.

Similar experiments are occurring in many European programs as well; Sistema Europe leaders say the needs are so different in dif-ferent countries that programs must be creative and flexible in devel-oping appropriate pedagogical approaches. "In some programs, it seems particularly important to focus on structure and respect," said Bruno Campo. "In others, an approach based more on spontaneity, improvisation, and 'thinking outside the box' works well. In still oth-ers, the priority is focusing on enjoyment and on lessening fear of failure." To meet these varying needs, European program leaders have incorporated a number of diverse pedagogies, such as a student-led storytelling process and a group improvisatory method called Sound-painting. "We stay rooted in the philosophy and methodology of Sistema," said Bruno, "and try to combine it with essential aspects of European humanistic pedagogical traditions."

BOTH TRADITION AND SISTEMA

Etienne Abelin, a Swiss violinist deeply trained in the European classical tradition, is a member of the Lucerne Festival Orchestra, one of Europe's iconic exemplars of symphonic greatness. He's also deeply embedded in the international El Sistema movement, as the cofounder of the Swiss Sistema-inspired program Superar Suisse and the codirector of the Sistema Europe Youth Orchestra.

Etienne's particular contribution to El Sistema is his dedication to the goal of finding new ways to revitalize classical music in contemporary life. In his search for new ways to bring people—both listeners and music-makers—into experiencing classical music fully and joyfully, he has created a number of initiatives, including the Apples & Olives Indie Classical Festival Zurich, the Ynight Classical Club Nights, the Music Animation Machine, bachSpace, and Music:Eyes. "The time to reinvent classical music is now," Etienne has said. "Never has its soul been more needed; the raw emotions, the strong stories, its deep connection."

Of special interest to him is the rich potential, for Sistema programs, of the Soundpainting method. This is an invented universal sign language for music, with gestural signs to represent various elements of music—i.e. "whole group"; "long note"; "go!"; etc. Group "compositions" are created on the spot, as a conductor uses these signs to indicate a series of musical gestures, and players respond by improvising within the parameters of each gesture.

Etienne sees Soundpainting as one way to extend the Sistema spirit of group participation to the areas of improvisation and composition. "Everyone is contributing to the spontaneous creation of new music. Spontaneous fun, taking turns, playing music together: doesn't that sound like El Sistema?"

A growing number of Sistema programs in the United States and elsewhere are exploring the field of aesthetic education, especially its emphasis on bringing students into full personal engagement with the beauty and richness of musical works. In the Venezuelan Sistema environment, this dimension of learning is often assumed rather than explicitly taught; it is learned organically, and often by example, in the course of playing and singing beautiful music. In the U.S. and some other countries, a body of philosophy and practice in the growing field of teaching artistry teaches the skills of aesthetic attention, analysis, and reflection. These skills enrich music listening, as well as music-making; they offer a wide range of ways to enter works of art and make personally relevant connections inside them.

Many Sistema-inspired programs are seeking to learn from and incorporate the skills of teaching artistry in order to expand the aesthetic dimension of their students' development. At New Jersey's Paterson Music Project, for example, the curriculum includes regular visits by George Marriner Maull, conductor of the Discovery Orchestra, whose mission is "to teach the listening skills that help people emotionally connect with classical music." We have watched Maestro George, as the students call him, lead them in listening—in a lively, participatory way that sometimes involves the air violin—to a Bach *Brandenburg* Concerto movement. We can imagine El Sistema programs incorporating these habits of mind and heart as a consistent feature of the learning curriculum, to further enrich the aesthetic dimension of their students' experience of music and life.

We believe that a true synergy between Sistema programs and other spheres of arts learning is the only way the Sistema movement can flourish and become sustainable in the long term. The true losers in a fractured music learning ecosystem are the children; the more collaboration can be established between Sistema and non-Sistema ways of learning, the richer the experience of music learning will be for all children.

WHAT YOU CAN DO TO SUPPORT EL SISTEMA

We mentioned earlier that we had big plans for you. We hope you will want to support this movement in some way. We have included an appendix that lists Sistema-inspired programs around the world; please use it. In this fast-moving field, some information will have changed by the time you read it, so if you have initial trouble locating a program near you, please persist!

VISIT A PROGRAM. Contact the program leaders, and you will be welcomed. Few programs around the world are as mind-boggling as Venezuela's núcleos, but anywhere you go, you will see how unusually good the work is, and you will feel the potential in the air.

CONTRIBUTE. Every program around the world is under-funded. And no one in this field earns lavish pay. Most full-time employees make just enough to live on; part-time workers have to juggle other income streams; and all are underpaid for the skills and commitment they bring to the work. So financial contributions to help cover the many expenses of running a program are always gratefully welcomed. There may also be in-kind and pro bono ways you can help, by providing products or services from your company or organization.

VOLUNTEER. If you like the feel of a program, and if the aspirations we have described in this book resonate with you, give the program some of your time and skill. In addition to help with office work and with transportation, programs may need legal help, accounting expertise, or hospitality help. If you feel committed to the outcomes of this work, perhaps you would consider joining a program's board of directors, or helping it raise money, or becoming a community advisor, to help the program build stronger connections with its neighborhood. If you are a musician, there may be ways you can contribute in the work itself as an assistant teacher. Music students in high schools, colleges, and conservatories are frequent volunteers in Sistema programs, and often say they receive as much as they give in terms of learning and inspiration.

HOST OR SPONSOR A PERFORMANCE. Sistema orchestras perform at many kinds of events: conferences, public events, private company celebrations, house concerts, and even weddings. Frequent performance is one of the primary aspirations of program leaders and teachers, so they need opportunities to make their work visible to a wider public.

START A PROGRAM. That may sound like a stretch. But most of the programs around the world have started because one or two inspired individuals decided to bring El Sistema to the children in their area. When we are asked how to start a program, our advice is usually simple. First, find partners who have as much commitment as you do. Then build a stakeholder network of individuals and institutions that will support a program, and enlist community leaders as key stakeholders. Ask people to help you; many will.

Make sure your planning is farsighted but flexible, and make sure to listen to people in the community you will serve. Listen hard and long. Be responsive to their needs, interests, and assets. Make connections within the existing local music education programs, both public and private, so you are seen as a colleague and not a competitor.

Take a few deep breaths in recognition of the size of the work that lies ahead, and jump in.

CHAPTER 15

A Reflection and a Celebration

The Russian novelist Fyodor Dostoevsky said the world would
be redeemed by beauty. I read those words for years and wanted
them to be true, but did not believe in them. Then I met José Antonio
Abreu, and saw how he was using the beauty of music to transform
the lives of the people of Venezuela; and then I thought again.
—RICHARD HOLLOWAY, FOUNDER AND CHAIRMAN
OF SISTEMA SCOTLAND

"This is where my friends are."
"I love the sound."
—CHILDREN IN MANY EL SISTEMA PROGRAMS

O ver and over throughout our El Sistema odyssey, we heard
these two answers to our question, "Why do you come here
so many hours every week?" We return to them now, as a
particularly concise distillation of what El Sistema means to children.
The centrality of friendship is clear in the stories and photos that fill
these pages. The mission of El Sistema programs is to exemplify—*to
be*—the kind of social world that children yearn for and thrive in: a
world of collaborative energy, mutual support, and absorbing play. In
these environments, the natural but chaotic sociability of children
develops, through consistently humane interaction, in the direction
of trust, empathy, and friendship.

But what, exactly, do kids mean when they say they love "the
sound"? Some El Sistema ensembles sound magnificent. Many sound
loud; as we've noted, Sistema ensembles tend to err on the side of

boldness. But in many orchestras and choruses, especially of younger kids in younger programs, the sounds produced are not always mellifluous or harmonious. Even within those ensembles, however, kids tend to love the sound they're surrounded by and the sound they're making, and to find it beautiful.

What's essential, then, is that they are actually learning to experience beauty, in the many ways that beauty can appear. Perhaps this is the final open secret at the heart of the transformative power of El Sistema. It is one essential answer to the question "Why does El Sistema work?" Even—perhaps especially—in environments of destitution and adversity, El Sistema develops the human capacity to *experience* beauty. This capacity is more than merely appreciating the attractiveness of well-made art objects; it is the capacity to hear beauty in a scratchy rendition of "Go Tell Aunt Rhody" on half-sized violins as well as in a full symphony orchestra playing Mahler. Yes, the skills and motivational habits developed in years of El Sistema practice are powerful and transferable to life outside of musical ensemble. But the capacity to enter into the experience of beauty, often and deeply, with friends and with community—perhaps that is the core transformative power of El Sistema.

Consider the four Sistema scenarios we sketched briefly in the introduction to this book. When the Kahnawake Mohawk children in Quebec, Canada, rehearse *Joe Drody's Jig 2*, a fiddling tune beloved in their community, they want to play it again. And again. And they can't wait to take on the next, harder piece; the capacity to experience beauty sparks the impulse to create more.

When the members of the Youth Orchestra Los Angeles play the *William Tell* Overture so well that they experience its beauty, they feel a pride and a connection to one another that transcends their material circumstances. As a result, there's a dimension of their lives that feels like abundance, not scarcity. The capacity to experience beauty opens a place of abundance to them and to their families.

When the children of Hammerkullen, Sweden, sing together in the many languages of their families, they learn that the capacity to experience beauty lives in everyone, and is a universal common ground. When they play their instruments together in the shared language of music, they find their connections to one another in their sound, and they experience that sound as beautiful.

And when teenagers in a Brazilian favela sing and play a Mozart mass, they experience a once-foreign musical tradition as vital, meaningful, and moving. *This piece was written by someone not like me, a dead white guy, but it expresses what I feel in my own life, and new things he has invited me to feel. This piece has been played by generations of people who don't look or live like me, but have felt like me.* Their experience of beauty widens compassionate awareness and empathetic connection.

The distinctive power of El Sistema, then, is that it turns aesthetic experience into a medium for compassion, empathy, and an expanded repertoire for making life choices. Maestro Abreu has said that the greatest accomplishment of El Sistema is that in our time, we can think of music as a form of rendering service to others. Within the world of El Sistema, the practice of creating beauty and the practice of empathic inclusion are inseparable: students and teachers create music together in the service of both beauty and solidarity. We believe it is this fusion of two fundamental realms of human purpose that makes El Sistema so inspiring to people of so many cultures around the world. Striving for ever-better artistry, striving for ever-better community—these can be united as a single endeavor, says El Sistema. It's a message that stirs the hearts and minds of people everywhere.

THE FORTIETH BIRTHDAY CELEBRATION

At a little before eleven o'clock on the morning of February 8, 2015, we found our seats in the fourth row of the cavernous 2,400-seat Teresa Carreño Hall in Caracas, Venezuela. The occasion was the "Big Concert," El Sistema's official celebration of its fortieth birthday. The house was packed, including visitors from El Sistema Sweden,

Sistema Scotland, Batuta in Colombia, Sistema Spain, and other countries, as well as thousands of Venezuelans who have been associated with El Sistema over the years.

Before the concert, two short films were shown on video screens flanking the stage. The films were produced by Fundamusical in honor of the fortieth anniversary, but they didn't glorify El Sistema's flagship touring orchestras or its organizational success. The first honored the great teachers of El Sistema, from Maestro Abreu to famous international conductors to beloved Venezuelan instructors. The second celebrated the 423 núcleos around the country and the generations of young people who have struggled and played together. This film concluded with a map of Sistema programs around the world, and there was an audible gasp from the audience, as if few had realized just how vast the program's reach has become.

Then the concert began. The stage had been extended to football-field proportions to accommodate the ensemble of 1,500 people. (No, that's not a misprint.) The official program consisted of works by two renowned Venezuelan composers, Inocente Carreño, and Antonio Estévez, and the fourth movement of Beethoven's Ninth Symphony. Dudamel conducted without scores, as he almost always does, and the sheer massed sound of that gigantic ensemble was overwhelming, a kind of sonic cathedral.

But the occasion was not only about size and sound. The most striking thing about it was the actual composition of the orchestra—and even the order in which its members came onstage. After several hundred choristers had entered and taken their places on the risers in the back, the orchestra members began to emerge from the wings. The first to appear were tiny, maybe eight or nine years old; their feet swung freely when they sat down. Then the oldest players entered, people in their sixties who were the founders of the original youth orchestra in 1975 and who had worked with Maestro Abreu from the beginning to bring the dream to reality. Each of them sat down next to one of the children.

Then came the players and conductors and directors from the

second and third Sistema generations, of all ages and from across the country, including players from the Simón Bolívar Symphony Orchestra and the other international touring orchestras, filling the chairs in between. Deep in the violin section was Eduardo Méndez, executive director of Fundamusical. Deep in the cello section was Fiorentino Mendoza, a founding member and leading teacher. There was Valdemar Rodríguez, a master teacher and director of El Sistema's Clarinet Academy. There was the peripatetic Sistema ambassador Ron Davis Álvarez. Also in the mix were office workers who have worked in Sistema offices for years but stopped performing long ago. By simply watching the entrances, we witnessed the story of El Sistema unfold across time and space.

During the concert itself, this symbolic messaging continued in the rotation of the concertmasters. The first piece, Glosa Sinfónica *Margariteña*, by the living patriarch of Venezuelan composers, ninety-five-year-old Inocente Carreño, was a rhapsodic orchestral fantasy inspired by Carreño's birthplace, Margarita Island. In the seat of honor, as not only concertmaster but also soloist, was the universally known and eternally hip Frank Di Polo, Maestro Abreu's lifelong colleague in creating El Sistema. Frank was a viola virtuoso in his day, but he has been retired from orchestral playing for decades and has taken on prominent roles as ambassador, teacher, and official photographer. Clearly, however, he was the right concertmaster to open the program, simply by virtue of who he has been, and still is, in the evolution of the Sistema.

The second piece was a choral and orchestral favorite of Sistema orchestras, *Cantata Criolla* by Antonio Estévez, a kind of Latin American secular oratorio depicting a "sing-off" between a Venezuelan plainsman and the Devil; the good guy wins, but not before some dramatic vocal pyrotechnics on each side. In the concertmaster's seat for this turbulent work was Ramón Román, now in his sixties, who was the concertmaster of the very first youth orchestra in 1975.

These first two pieces honored Venezuelan folk music, inflected by folk melodies and dance rhythms deeply familiar to the audience.

The concluding work, the iconic fourth movement of Beethoven's Ninth Symphony that ends with the "Ode to Joy," celebrated the truly international scope of El Sistema today, in its joyous affirmation that "All men are brothers." For this work, Alejandro Carreño, the current concertmaster of the Simón Bolívar Symphony Orchestra, finally assumed his regular seat.

The encores brought the orchestral symbolic messaging to new heights. First, the beloved núcleo director Gregory Carreño appeared—son of Inocente (the composer of the concert's first piece) and father of concertmaster Alejandro. Gregory, a founding member of El Sistema and lifelong friend of Maestro Abreu, is severely disabled due to a car accident decades ago; he was helped to the podium by his son Alejandro and Gustavo Dudamel, and he sat in a high chair to conduct.

To his left, in the first row of violins, was a visually eloquent line-up. In the fifth chair was Frank Di Polo. In the fourth chair was Ramón Román. Alejandro Carreño was in the third chair, and next to him was Gustavo Dudamel. The concertmaster, in the first chair, was twelve-year-old Rayson David Tercera Cumares Sequera.

Gregory proceeded to conduct what must have been the largest orchestra in El Sistema history in the "Hallelujah Chorus" from Handel's *Messiah*. Then—as if the stage weren't full enough—out came fifty additional musicians with traditional Venezuelan instruments, including cuatros, harps, maracas, and guitars, to join in on the folk anthems "Alma Llanera" and "Venezuela." For the final encore, young Rayson put down his violin, climbed onto the podium and conducted the Venezuelan national anthem.

Throughout this concert, it was as though El Sistema was saying, "If you want to know our 'basic principles,' just look how we have put this orchestra together. Every decision we have made is a message about who we are." The clearest message was inclusion: people of all ages, from all regions, playing together, playing different kinds of music, mentoring and helping one another, sustaining lifelong friendships, honoring experience, and celebrating youth.

Before the concert, we had asked Ron Davis Álvarez if he was nervous. "Of course not," he had responded. "Do you get nervous before a party with your friends?" When we saw him afterwards and asked him to describe the experience, he put his hand to his heart as he said, "I looked to my left, and there was the teacher who had placed the first violin in my hands. Then I looked to the right, and there was a student into whose hands I had placed her first violin. It was—like that."

We asked him if there was going to be a party afterward for the performers. "We just *had* our party!" he said. "You were there!"

When Dudamel greeted us backstage, we told him we were thinking we might end our book with the story of this occasion, and he said, "Of course! It was amazing! The whole world is with us today."

∽

THIS BIG CONCERT WASN'T EL SISTEMA's only celebratory birthday gesture. During February 2015, the anniversary month, Sistema leaders aspired to present a million concerts. They figured that if every single child in El Sistema Venezuela participated in six or more concerts, they would reach their goal. Performers were to take a photo of each concert and tweet it to a particular address. Students around the country rose to the challenge, taking a friend to perform in a local health clinic, bringing a choral trio to sing in a home for the elderly, or playing with the orchestra in the village square. By mid-month, the Twitter site was so large it took an hour to download.

No one seems to know whether they actually made their goal of 1 million, and it doesn't seem to matter. What matters is that they shared their music with as many people as they could, as a way of saying thanks.

Imagine this. . . .

On the fiftieth anniversary of El Sistema, a million concerts will be easy. There will be a million students in Venezuela alone, and another million students around the world. You will attend one of those concerts on February 12, 2025. You may see hundreds of young people onstage, from neighborhoods that might be near your home but that you don't often visit. These children and young people will be of many races and ethnicities and from a mixture of family financial backgrounds. They will play a series of pieces that impress you, perhaps make you cry, and finally bring you to your feet, cheering. The young musicians will probably be thinking a little about Venezuela (it's a birthday, after all), a little about their own programs, but mostly about how to play that tricky passage in measure 124 and how good the music sounds. After the concert, they will no doubt party with their friends. But they'll go to school the next day. They will be feeling proud and a little grateful (as much as kids are able to be), and brimming with certainty that they have much to say, in music and in many other ways—and that the world is eager to hear them.

Notes

1. These four snapshots come from El Sistema-inspired programs around the world, in order:
   - Baleeira is a favela in the city of Campos dos Goytacazes, Brazil. It is one mile from Orquestrando a Vida (Orchestrating Life), the first El Sistema-inspired program in Brazil.
   - The Hammarkullen neighborhood of Gothenburg is the home of the first of El Sistema Sweden's thirty program sites.
   - YOLA at EXPO (Youth Orchestra of Los Angeles) is the first of the Los Angeles Philharmonic's three El Sistema-inspired program sites, launched in partnership with the Expo Center and the Harmony Project.
   - The Kahnawake Mohawk Territory is one of the three program sites of Encore! Sistema Quebec in Canada. This program is distinguished by being the only one in the world launched and supported by public school music teachers.
2. Chefi Borzacchini, *Venezuela: The Miracle of Music* (Caracas: Fundación Bancaribe, 2010), p. 77.
3. Ibid., p. 73.
4. Ibid., p. 74.
5. Ibid., p. 80.
6. Ibid., p. 58.
7. Ibid., p. 99.
8. Richard Morrison, "Who Would Win the Orchestral World Cup?" *The Times* (London), September 6, 2008.
9. "Estudio del Banco Interamericano de Desarrollo sobre los beneficios socio-económicos que ha tenido El Sistema en Venezuela realizado en el año 2008," por José Cuesta en el Departamento de Investigación del BID.
10. Gustavo Dudamel, "Why I Don't Talk Venezuelan Politics," *Los Angeles Times* op-ed, September 29, 2015.
11. "Orquestas Sinfónicas Penitenciarias, Technical Report 2007–2011,

Behavioral Impact and Artistic Performance," Fundación Musical Simón Bolívar.

12. Borzacchini, p. 61.

13. Ibid., p. 63.

14. A partial list of international awards and honors given to Maestro Abreu and El Sistema Venezuela: Sweden's Right Livelihood Award; The Harvard School of Public Health's "Q Prize," for extraordinary leadership on behalf of children; Spain's Prince of Asturias Award; Canada's Glenn Gould Prize, the nation's most exclusive arts award; the Latin Grammys' Honoris Causa Award; Sweden's Polar Music Prize; Germany's Frankfurt Music Prize; Holland's Erasmus Prize; Austria's Cross of Honor for Science and Art; the Seoul Peace Prize. And there are many more.

15. Alfred Brendel, *Music, Sense, and Nonsense* (London: Robson, 2015).

16. Gabriella Windsor, *Discipline and Happiness: The Case of "The School of the Body," in Colombia,* doctoral dissertation, Institute of Social and Cultural Anthropology, University of Oxford, May 2012.

17. Roy F. Baumeister and Mark R. Leary, "The Need to Belong: Desire for Interpersonal Attachments as a Fundamental Human Motivation," *Psychological Bulletin* 117, no. 3 (May 1995): 497–529.

18. David Dobbs, quoting Steve Cole (UCLA), in "The Social Life of Genes," *Pacific Standard,* September 3, 2013. http://www.psmag.com/books-and-culture/the-social-life-of-genes-64616.

19. Robert T. Muller, "Poverty, Broken Homes, Violence: The Making of a Gang Member," *Psychology Today,* August 24, 2013. https://www.psychologytoday.com/blog/talking-about-trauma/201308/poverty-broken-homes-violence-the-making-gang-member.

20. David W. Johnson and Roger T. Johnson, *Cooperation and Competition: Theory and Research* (Edina, MN: Interaction Book Company, 1989).

21. Roger Nierenberg's "The Music Paradigm" is the foremost among many initiatives that use the orchestra as a living model of extraordinary communication. Nierenberg works with major corporations in daylong or multiday workshops to illuminate key aspects of communication, strategy, and organizational management. Musicians involved in such initiatives are often surprised to learn that the kind of commu-

nication taken for granted in an instrument section, with the section leader (who faces away from her team) giving instructions with a slight nod or shoulder lift, is revelatory and inspiring to professionals in non-musical fields. Business leaders invariably discover that effective leadership by conductors is far from the stereotype of dictatorial control, and is in fact as profoundly interdependent as is good leadership in their own companies.

22. Suzanne Langer, *Philosophy in a New Key: A Study in the Symbolism of Reason, Rite, and Art* (Cambridge, MA: Harvard University Press, 1942).

23. Bennett Reimer, "Music Education as Aesthetic Education: Past and Present," *Music Educators Journal* 75, no. 6 (February 1989): 25.

24. Margaret S. Osborne et al., "Exploring the Academic and Psychosocial Impact of El Sistema-Inspired Music Programs Within Two Low Socio-Economic Schools," *Music Education Research,* DOI: 10.1080/14613808.2015.1056130.

25. Social Mobility Index 2014, CollegeNET/PayScale.

26. Carol Dweck, *Mindset: The New Psychology of Success* (New York: Random House, 2006).

27. Alvaro Rodas, *A Model for Community Participation in the Performing Arts: Social Action Through Music and the Internationalization of the Venezuela Orchestra System*, M.A. thesis for Teachers College at Columbia University.

28. Glasgow Centre for Population Health, study of Big Noise, Scotland; results released May 2015.

29. José Cuesta, "Music to My Ears: The (Many) Socio-Economic Benefits of Music Training Programs," Inter-American Development Bank, Research Department, July 2008.

30. Anne T. Henderson and Karen L. Mapp, *A New Wave of Evidence: The Impact of School, Family, and Community Connections on Student Achievement, Annual Synthesis 2002* (National Center for Family and Community Connections with Schools).

31. *Music Education in England: A Review by Darren Henley for the Department for Education and the Department for Culture, Media and Sport, 2011.*

32. Osborne et al., op. cit.

33. Correspondence with Rebecca Sigel, social innovation manager, Los Angeles Philharmonic Orchestra Education Department.

34. The Brain and Creativity Institute at University of Southern California, five-year longitudinal research project, "Effects of Early Childhood Musical Training on Brain, Cognitive Emotional, and Social Development" (forthcoming).

35. Stanford University SPARQ: "Social Psychological Answers to Real-World Questions," collaboration with Youth Orchestra Los Angeles.

36. S. J. Holochwost, "Music Education, Academic Achievement, and Executive Functions" (forthcoming).

37. Matt Pickles, "The Orchestra Fine-Tuning the Performance of School Students," BBC.com, April 22, 2015.

38. "Cost-Effective Investments in Children at Risk: February 2011," Office of the State Comptroller, New York, Thomas P. DiNapoli, state comptroller.

39. National Center on Addiction and Substance Abuse at Columbia University cited in Sharon Issurdatt, "Gangs, A Growing Problem in Schools," *Practice Perspectives,* September 2011 (National Association of Social Workers).

40. *National Gang Threat Assessment, 2011* (National Gang Intelligence Center).

41. Mark A. Cohen and Alex R. Piquero, "New Evidence on the Monetary Value of Saving a High Risk Youth," *Journal of Quantitative Criminology* 25 (2009): 25–49; Mark A. Cohen, Alex R. Piquero, and Wesley G. Jennings, "Estimating the Costs of Bad Outcomes for At-Risk Youth and the Benefits of Early Childhood Interventions to Reduce Them," *Criminal Justice Policy Review* 21, no. 4 (2010): 391–434.

42. Cohen and Piquero, op. cit.

Acknowledgments

Heartfelt thanks to all those who hosted and helped us in our research:

Ahmad Sarmast, William Harvey (Afghanistan); Bronwyn Lobb, Christopher Nicholls, Erica Rasmussen (Australia); Ismar Poric, Kenan Glavinić, Riad Music (Bosnia); Fiorella Solares, Vanessa Rodrigues, Jony William, Luis Mauricio Carneiro, Ricardo Castro, Beth Ponte, Obadias Cunha (Brazil); Juan Antonio Cuéllar, María Claudia Parias Durán, Juan Felipe Molano Muñoz, Catherine Surace Arenas, Ana Cecelia Restrepo, Liliana Arboleda, Felipe Martínez, Beatriz Barros Vigna, Raquel Murillo Ariza, Gabriel Jaime Arango, Rebecca Levi (Colombia); Lars-Ole Vestergaard, Bjørg Lindvang, Palle Kjeldgaard, Mette Storgård Jensen (Denmark); Marshall Marcus, Richard Hallam, Nina Kaye, Reynaldo Trombetta, Ian Burton, Beth Noble, Lucy Maguire, Gerry Sterling, Zoë Armfeld, Rod Skipp, Peter Garden (England); Jean-Claude Decalonne, Michèle de Gastyne, Jean-Gabriel and Catherine Mahéo (France); Maria Majno, Roberto Grossi, Diego Ravetti, Ayben Fortuna, Mariana Pinto, Antonello Farulli (Italy); Yutaka Kikugawa, Rumi Naito, Michiko Shimizu, Makiko Haraga, Toru Amijima, Maurice Reyna (Japan); Elizabeth Njoroge, Karis Crawford, Levi Wataka, Benjamin Wamocho, Bob Collymore (Kenya); Armando Torres-Chibrás, Arturo Márquez, Laura Calderón de la Barca, José Antonio Herrera, Véronica Soltero-Alatorre, Óscar Argumedo, Luz de Lourdes Arena de Orozco, Esteban Moctezuma, Julio Saldaña (Mexico); Eldevina Materula (Mozambique); Ros Giffney, Joe Harrop, Fiona Douglas, Samantha Winterton (New Zealand); Ahmad Al'Azzeh, Fabienne van Eck, Katja Eckardt (Palestine); Jovianney Emmanuel Cruz, Tinky Cabanatan Cruz, Federico "Piki" Lopez, Monina Lopez, Olivier Ochanine and the OFY members, Lianne Sala (The Philippines); António Wagner Diniz (Portugal); Elana Andrews (Romania); Richard Holloway, Nicola Killean, Alison Gornall (Scotland); Robert Brooks, Adeyemi Oladiran (South Africa); Ms. Park, Hyo-young Lee, Mi-Ryoung Song, Ja-Yeong Lim, Eunsuk Chae, Jeehye Suh (South Korea); Angelika Lošek, Irena Klissenbauer, Gerald

Wirth (Superar); Etienne Abelin, Marco Castellini (Switzerland); Malin Aghed, Petra Kloo Vik, Camilla Sarner, Johanna Ericsson (Sweden); Yeliz Baki, Mehmet Baki, Samuel Matus, Aysel Kızıltan, Serap Gökdeniz, Ömür Bozkurt, Ulvi Içil, Berker Ünsal (Turkey).

Deep thanks to our colleagues at Fundamusical in Venezuela: Executive Director Eduardo Méndez, the always helpful and delightful Patricia Abdelnour, Ron Davis Álvarez, Ulyses Ascanio, David Ascanio, Frank Di Polo, Rafael Elster, Fiorentino Mendoza, Romina Noviello, Valdemar Rodríguez, Roberto Zambrano, and Nohely Oliveros. Thanks also to Rodrigo Guerrero (now working at the Massachusetts Cultural Council) and to Norma Núñez Loaiza (now leading a Sistema program in Allentown, Pennsylvania) for their hospitality and insights during our first visits to Venezuela. We are grateful to have known the late Bolivia Bottome, Maestro Abreu's devoted and close colleague for many years.

Thanks to friends and colleagues in the U.S. and Canadian Sistema movement who helped us with this book about the global movement: Dani Bedoni, Daniel Berkowitz, Jamie Bernstein, Leni Boorstin, Graciela Briceno, Tina Fedeski, José Luis Hernández-Estrada, Erik Holmgren, Adam Johnston, Ken MacLeod, Heath Marlow, Mika Miller, Juan Felipe Molano Muñoz, Daniel Mora-Brito, Gretchen Nielsen, Diogo Pereira, Rebecca Sigel, Keane Southard, Dalouge Smith, Theodora Stathopoulos, Dan Trahey, David Visintin, Karen Zorn. For helping defray research expenses, special thanks to Andrew McDermott, whose generosity also supports the Valley Vibes Sistema program in Sonoma, California.

Thanks also to our Spanish transcript translator, Shayna Gleason; our Danish hosts and friends, Berit Eika and Jørgen Frøkiær; our travel agent, Jeff Himmel; our photographer, Scott Gries. Special thanks to all the astute readers who helped us in the process of writing this book: our agent Richard Balkin, our editor Maribeth Payne, assistant editor Grant Phelps, copy editor Fred Wiemer, and our volunteer readers Amy Miller, Dalouge Smith, and Adam Johnston. Finally, thanks to Tricia's patient and supportive piano students and their families.

APPENDIX I

Directory of El Sistema-Inspired Programs

NOTE: This is the first organized listing of its kind. Because the international movement is young and neither effectively networked nor strictly defined by membership criteria, we know this listing is imperfect. There is certain to be outdated information. There are also programs whose inclusion some might question and some we have missed altogether. We apologize for any errors in our efforts to provide a useful listing of Sistema-inspired and Sistema-like programs around the world. We thank Sistema Global, Sistema Europe, and El Sistema USA for sharing their compiled lists as foundations for this directory.

Country	City/State	Name of Program	Web Link
Angola	various	Orquestra Sinfónica Kaposoka	www.facebook.com/Kaposoka-221343564588446
Argentina	Santa Fe	Fundación Allegro Argentina	www.facebook.com/fundacion.allegroargentina.1
Argentina	San Juan	Fundación Orquesta Escuela San Juan	es-la.facebook.com/orquestaescuela.sanjuan
Argentina	various	Sistema Orquestas Infantiles y Juveniles Argentina	www.sistemadeorquestas.org.ar
Argentina	Córdoba	Orquesta-Escuela Mediterranea	www.proartecordoba.org/category/orquesta
Argentina	Jujuy	Sistema de Orquestas Juveniles e Infantiles de Jujuy	es-es.facebook.com/SOJ.OFICIAL
Armenia	Yerevan	Sistema Armenia	www.sistemaarmenia.com
Australia	various	Sistema Australia, Crashendo!	sistemaaustralia.com.au

Country	City/State	Name of Program	Web Link
Australia	Melbourne	The Pizzicato Effect	www.mso.com.au/education/the-pizzicato-effect
Austria	various	Superar Austria	www.superar.eu
Bolivia	Santa Cruz	La Asociación Pro Arte y Cultura (APAC) de Bolivia	festivalesapac.com
Bolivia	various	Associazione Amici Popolo Guarani	www.amicidelpopologuarani.org
Bolivia	various	Sistema de Coros y Orquestas (SICOR)	www.facebook.com/sicor.bolivia?fref=ts&ref=br_tf
Bosnia & Herzegovina	Srebrenica	Superar Bosnia	bosnia.superar.eu
Brazil	São Paulo	Instituto Baccarelli	institutobaccarelli.org.br/quem-principios
Brazil	Campos dos Goytacazes	Orquestrando a Vida (ONG)	orquestrandoavida.com.br
Brazil	Curitiba	Projeto Cidadão Musical	cidadaomusical.wordpress.com
Brazil	various	Projeto Guri	www.projetoguri.org.br
Brazil	Rio de Janeiro	Ação Social pela Música	www.contrastepropaganda.com.br/aspm
Brazil	Rio de Janeiro	Brazil Strings	brazilstrings.org
Brazil	Bahia	NEOJIBA	neojiba.org
Brazil	Paraíba	Programa de Inclusão Através da Música e das Artes	www.primaparaiba.com
Canada	British Columbia	Bakerview Music Academy	www.bakerviewmusic.ca
Canada	Ontario	Brio Music	www.briomusic.org
Canada	Alberta	Calgary Multicultural Orchestra	www.iaacc.ca/CMO.php
Canada	Ontario	El Sistema Aeolian	www.aeolianhall.ca/el-sistema-aeolian
Canada	Ontario	El Sistema South London	elsistemasouthlondon.ca
Canada	Ontario	Sistema Mississauga	www.sistemamississauga.com
Canada	Quebec	Encore! Sistema Quebec	www.encoresistema.org
Canada	Nova Scotia	Halifax Music Co-op	musicnovascotia.ca/halifaxmusiccoop
Canada	Quebec	Le Garage à Musique	www.garageamusique.org

Country	City/State	Name of Program	Web Link
Canada	Ontario	OrKidstra	leadingnotefoundation.org
Canada	Quebec	Partageons l'Espoir (Share the Warmth)	sharethewarmth.ca
Canada	British Columbia	Saint James Music Academy	sjma.ca
Canada	Ontario	Sistema Huronia	www.sistemahuronia.com
Canada	New Brunswick	Sistema New Brunswick	sistemanb.ca
Canada	British Columbia	Sistema Prince George	sistemapg.com
Canada	Saskatchewan	Sistema Saskatoon	www.sistemasaskatoon.ca
Canada	Ontario	Sistema Toronto	www.sistema-toronto.ca
Canada	Manitoba	Sistema Winnipeg	wso.ca/sistema
Canada	Ontario	Sounds of the Next Generation (SONG)	songprogram.org
Canada	Alberta	Youth Orchestra of Northern Alberta (YONA)	www.yona-sistema.com
Chile	Concepción	Acción Social por la Música Chile	www.accionsocialpor lamusicachile.com
Chile	Santiago	Fundación Orquestas Juveniles e Infantiles de Chile	www.orquestajuvenilchile .com/fundacion
China	Hong Kong	Music for the Growing Mind	http://hk.asiatatler.com/ arts-culture/arts/music-for-the-growing-mind
Colombia	various	Fundación Nacional Batuta	www.fundacionbatuta.org
Colombia	Bogotá	Integración Sistema Musical	http://www.integracionsm .com
Colombia	Medellín	Red de Escuelas de Música de Medellín	www.redmusicamedellin.org
Colombia	Cali	Notas de Paz	http://www.notasdepaz.com
Colombia	Cali	Escuela de Musica Desepaz	https://www.facebook.com/ EscuelaMusicaDesepaz
Costa Rica	various	Sistema Nacional de Educación Musical (SINEM) Costa Rica	www.sinem.go.cr
Croatia	various	So Do, El Sistema Croatia	www.so-do.hr
Czech Republic	Prague	Nadační fond Harmonie	www.nfharmonie.cz
Denmark	various	El Sistema Danmark	elsistema.dk

Country	City/State	Name of Program	Web Link
Denmark	Aarhus	MusikUnik	www.aarhusmusikskole.dk/da/Projekter/Kopi-af-MusikUnik-El-Sistema.aspx
Dominican Republic	Santo Domingo	Fundación Orquesta Sinfónica Juvenil	www.facebook.com/Fundación-Orquesta-Sinfónica-Juvenil-414569461937782
Ecuador	various	Fundación Orquesta Sinfónica Juvenil del Ecuador	www.fosje.org.ec
Ecuador	Cuenca	Fundación Manos Solidarias	fundacion-manos-solidarias.weebly.com
El Salvador	San Salvador	El Sistema El Salvador	www.facebook.com/El-Sistema-El-Salvador-655366794490127
Finland	Helsinki	Sistema Finland	sistemafinland.blogspot.com
France	Gorges	El Sistema France	www.elsistema-france.org
France	Sèvres	Les Petites Mains Symphoniques	www.petitesmains symphoniques.com
France	Paris	Passeurs d'Arts	www.passeursdarts.org
France	Roubaix	Orchestres en Choeur	imaginationforpeople.org/fr/project/orchestres-en-choeur
Greenland	Uummannaq	Uummannaq Music	www.upi.gl/Uummannaq Music.htm
Guatemala	Ciudad de Guatemala	Sistema de Orquestas de Guatemala	soggt.weebly.com
Haiti	Jacmel	École de Musique Dessaix-Baptiste	www.ecolemusiquejacmel-haiti.com
Haiti	Port-au-Prince	École de Musique Sainte Trinité	www.saintetrinitemusique.com
Honduras	Tegucigalpa	Fundación Artes Educativas Coros y Orquestas de Honduras	www.farecoh.org
Hungary	Budapest	Szimfónia Program	http://szimfoniaprogram.hu
India	Goa	Child's Play India Foundation	www.childsplayindia.org
India	New Delhi	Shubendra and Saskia Rao Foundation/Music 4 All	www.music4all.org
Iran	Tehran	Iranian Youth Orchestra	www.nojavanorchestra.org
Ireland	Munster	Sing Out with Strings	www.irishchamberorchestra.com/community-engagement/sing-out-with-strings

Country	City/State	Name of Program	Web Link
Ireland	Dublin	Cherry Orchard Performing Arts Club	www.copac.co.nf
Israel	various	Sulamot	www.ipo.co.il/eng/articles ,304.aspx
Italy	National	Sistema delle Orchestre e dei Cori Giovanili e Infantili in Italia Onlus	www.sistemainitalia.com
Italy, Rome	various	Sistema delle Orchestre e dei Cori Giovanili e Infantili in Italia Onlus	www.sistemainitalia.com
Italy, Abruzzo	Penne	Associazione Musicale "G.Verdi"	www.scuolamusicaverdi.it
Italy, Abruzzo	San Salvo	Associazione Dum Tek	www.sistemainitalia.com
Italy, Abruzzo	Avezzano	Orchestra Giovanile della Diocesi dei Marsi	www.orchestramarsi.it/web/index.php?option=com_content&view=article&id=54&Itemid=60
Italy, Abruzzo	Avezzano	Orchestra Giovanile I Flauti di Toscanini di Avezzano	www.iflautiditoscanini.com/web/tag/flauti-di-toscanini
Italy, Basilicata	Matera	L.A.M.S. Matera	www.lamsmatera.it
Italy, Basilicata	Pietragalla	Concerto Bandistico Giuseppe Pafundi	bandagpafundi.blogspot.it
Italy, Basilicata	Rionero In Vulture	Istituto Comprensivo M. Granata	www.icgranata.gov.it
Italy, Basilicata	Rende (Cosenza)	Piccolo Coro del Rendano	www.piccolocororendano.it
Italy, Calabria	Reggio Calabria	Orchestra Giovanile dello Stretto "Vincenzo Leotta"	www.orchestragiovaniledellostretto.it
Italy, Calabria	Borgia (Catanzaro)	Magna Graecia Flute Choir	www.facebook.com/events/444281019007327/
Italy, Campania	Naples	Progetto Sonora Networking & Performing Arts	progettosonora.it
Italy, Campania	Naples	Associazione Alessandro Scarlatti	www.federculture.it/sistema-delle-orchestre-e-cori-giovanili
Italy, Campania	Naples	Orchestra Giovanile Sanitansamble	www.federculture.it/sistema-delle-orchestre-e-cori-giovanili
Italy, Campania	San Marzano sul Sarno	Orkextra	www.federculture.it/sistema-delle-orchestre-e-cori-giovanili

Country	City/State	Name of Program	Web Link
Italy, Emilia	Reggio Emilia	Comune di Reggio Emilia	www.municipio.re.it/ retecivica/urp/pes.nsf/web/ Hmttl?opendocument
Italy, Emilia	Modena	Progetto "Musica e Società"	www.teatrocomunale modena.it
Italy, Emilia	Parma	Associazione Do Re Miusic	www.doremiusic.com
Italy, Emilia	Casalgrande (Reggio Emilia)	Comune di Casalgrande	www.comune.casalgrande .re.it
Italy, Emilia	Novellara (Reggio Emilia)	Associazione di Promozione Sociale "Lo Schiaccianoci"	www.schiaccianoci.org
Italy, Emilia	Carpi (Modena)	Unione Terre d'Argine	www.sistemainitalia.com
Italy, Emilia	Piacenza	Direzione Didattica IV Circolo	www.cavaquartocircolo.gov.it
Italy, Friuli	San Vito al Tagliamento	Amici Coro Manos Blancas Onlus	www.manosblancasdelfriuli.it
Italy, Lazio	Rome	Scuola Popolare di Musica di Testaccio	www.scuolamusicatestaccio .it
Italy, Lazio	Rome	Istituto Comprensivo Daniele Manin	www.sistemainitalia.com
Italy, Lazio	Pontinia	Istituto "Don Milani"	www.icdonmilani.gov.it
Italy, Lazio	Latina	Collegium Musicum	nuke.collegium-musicum.it
Italy, Lazio	Montefiascone	Associazione Musicale Enarmonia	www.associazioneenarmonia .com
Italy, Lazio	Rome	Associazione Genitori Scuola Di Donato—Piccolo Coro di Piazza Vittorio	www.sistemainitalia.com
Italy, Lazio	Rome	Associazione Culturale Orchestra Giovanile di Roma	www.orchestragiovanile diroma.it/associazione.html
Italy, Liguria	Genoa–La Spezia	Progetto Sviluppo Liguria	www.prosviliguria.org/home
Italy, Liguria	Genoa–La Spezia	Casa della Musica di Genova	www.casadellamusica.ge.it
Italy, Liguria	San Remo (Imperia)	Mappamondo Onlus	www.sistemainitalia.com
Italy, Liguria	La Spezia	GOSP Giovane Orchestra Spezzina	www.fondazionecarispezia.it/ gosp-giovane-orchestra-spezzina-in-concerto-il-28-gennaio-al-teatro-civico-della-spezia/#.VivJU-mvOSI

Country	City/State	Name of Program	Web Link
Italy	Lombardy	Sistema in Lombardia	www.sistemalombardia.eu
Italy, Lombardy	Suzzara	Fondazione Scuola di Arti e Mestieri "F. Bertazzoni"	www.orchestragiovanile pigna.it
Italy, Lombardy	Milan	Associazione l'Albero della Musica (Mani Bianche)	www.alberodellamusica.com
Italy, Lombardy	Milan	Progetto "PEPITA"	www.childrenincrisis.it/italia/ progetto-pepita
Italy, Lombardy	Milan	Associazione Musicale ICM	www.insiemeconlamusica .com
Italy, Lombardy	Tradate	Orchestra Giovanile Lago Maggiore	http://www.oglm.it/
Italy, Lombardy	Milan	I Piccoli Pomeriggi Musicali	http://www. ipiccolipomeriggi.it
Italy, Lombardy	Milan	Allegromoderato Onlus	www.allegromoderato.it
Italy, Lombardy	Milan	Associazione ImmaginArte	http://www. associazioneimmaginarte.it
Italy, Lombardy	Milan	L'Altramusica	http://www.laltramusica.com/
Italy, Marche	Macerata	Scuola di Musica "Liviabella"	www.scuolaliviabella.org
Italy, Marche	Ascoli Piceno	Centro Studi Musica Moderna	www.centrostudimusica moderna.it
Italy, Piedmont	Turin	Teatro Baretti—Scuola Popolare di Musica	www.cineteatrobaretti.it
Italy, Piedmont	Turin	Associazione "Cantabile"	blog.cantabile.it
Italy, Piedmont	Turin	Associazione Culturale "Orme"	www.sistemainitalia.com
Italy, Piedmont	Turin	Manincanto—L'Incanto delle Mani in Canto	www.sistemainitalia.com
Italy, Piedmont	Novara	Scuola di Musica "Dedalo"	www.scuoladimusicadedalo .it/index.php?lang=en
Italy, Puglia	Bari	Musica in Gioco	www.musicaingioco.net
Italy, Puglia	San Severo	Art Village	artvillagesansevero .wordpress.com
Italy, Puglia	Trani	Circolo A.C.L.I. Trani	www.aclitrani.it
Italy, Puglia	Taranto	Comune di Taranto	www.comune.taranto.it
Italy, Puglia	Corigliano d'Otranto	Istituto Comprensivo Corigliano d'Otranto	www.iccorigliano.it
Italy, Sicily	Palermo	Associazione Onlus Talità Kum	www.onlustalitakum.it/serciv .php

Country	City/State	Name of Program	Web Link
Italy, Sicily	Palermo	Coro e Orchestra Giovanile di Brancaccio	orchestracorogiovanile brancaccio.blogspot.it
Italy, Sicily	Catania	Musica Insieme a Librino	www.rotarycatania.it/pages .php?spid=12
Italy, Sicily	Catania	Associazione Musicale Alkantàra	www.facebook.com/ Associazione-musicale-Alkantàra-Piccole-note-sulle-orme-di-Abreu-30528 6789540065/
Italy, Tuscany	Florence	Progetto "Le Piagge"	www.scuolamusicafiesole.it/ it/didattica/corsi-di-base-e-pre-accademici/progetto-piagge
Italy, Veneto	Campolongo Maggiore	Orchestra Diego Valeri	www.facebook.com/ Orchestra-Giovanile-Diego-Valeri-105487072489/
Italy, Veneto	Montebelluna (Treviso)	MusikDrama	www.rejouissance.it/Home .html
Italy, Veneto	Piazzola sul Brenta	I.C.S. Luca Belludi [EX Rete Musicale "Over Tour," Abano]	www.sistemainitalia.com
Italy, Veneto	San Fior (Treviso)	Associazione Culturale "Suono in Orchestra"	www.facebook.com/ Associazione-culturale-Suono-in-Orchestra-San-Fior-254368834717713/
Italy, Veneto	Castelfranco Veneto	Associazione Culturale "Sei per la Musica"	www.seiperlamusica.it
Italy, Veneto	Padua	Portello in Festa	www.facebook.com/ portelloinfesta
Jamaica	Kingston	The National Youth Orchestra of Jamaica	nyoj.org
Japan	Otsuchi	Otsuchi Children's Orchestra	www.elsistemajapan.org
Japan	Soma	Soma Children's Orchestra and Chorus	www.elsistemajapan.org
Kenya	Nairobi	El Sistema Kenya	www.elsistemakenya.org
Kenya	Nairobi	Ghetto Classics	www.artofmusic.co.ke/ ghetto-classics
Liechtenstein	Vaduz	Superar Liechtenstein	superar.eu
Luxembourg	various	El Sistema Luxembourg	www.sistemaluxembourg.lu
Mexico	Monterrey	El Sistema México	www.elsistema.mx
Mexico	Guadalajara	Elevare A.C.	www.elevare.org

Country	City/State	Name of Program	Web Link
Mexico	various	Esperanza Azteca	www.esperanzaazteca.com.mx
Mexico	Morelos	Serenissima Tepozteca	serenissimatepozteca.com
Mexico	various	Sistema Nacional de Fomento Musical	snfm.cultura.gob.mx
Mozambique	Maputo	Xiquitsi	www.xiquitsi.org.mz
Netherlands	Beuningen	El Sistema Nederland	www.elsistema.nl
Netherlands	North Holland	Leerorkest	www.leerorkest.nl/nl/home
New Zealand	Wellington	Arohanui Strings–Sistema Hutt Valley	arohanuistrings.org
New Zealand	Wellington	Kotuku Music Academy	sites.google.com/site/kotukubackup
New Zealand	Auckland	Sistema Aotearoa	apo.co.nz/sistema-aotearoa
New Zealand	Waikato	Sistema Waikato	www.hccm.ac.nz/sistema-waikato
New Zealand	Whangarei	Sistema Whangarei–Toi Akorangi	www.sistemawhangarei.org.nz
New Zealand	Nelson	Nelson Regional Youth Orchestra	
Nicaragua	Managua	Orquesta Sinfónica Juvenil Rubén Darío	www.facebook.com/osjrdnic/info
Norway	Oslo	TØYEN Orchestra (El Sistema Norge)	toyenorkesteret.com
Palestine	Bethlehem	Sounds of Palestine	www.soundsofpalestine.org
Panama	various	El Sistema de Orquestas y Coros Infantiles y Juveniles de Panama	
Paraguay	Ciudad del Este	Organizacion por el Arte y la Cultura Ha Che Valle	www.sanjuan.com.py/valle
Paraguay	various	Sonidos de la Tierra	www.sonidosdelatierra.org.py
Peru	Lima	Orquesta Sinfónica Juvenil del Perú	www.facebook.com/orquestasinfonicanacionaljuvenilperu
Peru	Huacho	Portal Norteño Music Perú	portalnortmusicperu.blogspot.ca
Peru	Trujillo	Arpegio Perú	www.arpegioperu.org
Peru	Lima	Sinfonía por el Perú	www.sinfoniaporelperu.org
Philippines	Manila	Ang Misyon Sistema for the Filipino Youth	www.angmisyon.com

Country	City/State	Name of Program	Web Link
Philippines	Cebu	NPO Seven Spirit	seven-spirit.or.jp
Philippines	Cebu	Sistemang Pilipino	http://sistemangpilipino.org
Portugal	Lisbon	Orquestra Juvenil Geração	www.orquestra.geracao.aml.pt
Puerto Rico	San Juan	Fundación Música y País	www.facebook.com/Fundación-Música-y-Pa%C3%ADs-610791512332383
Puerto Rico	San Juan	Música 100x35 (El Sistema Puerto Rico)	www.facebook.com/musica100x35
Romania	various	Superar Romania	romania.superar.eu
Rwanda	Kigali	Oakdale Kigali Music School	www.facebook.com/KigaliMusicSchool
Saint Lucia	Castries	Saint Lucia School of Music	www.facebook.com/SaintLuciaSchoolofMusic
Serbia	Belgrade	Music Art Project (El Sistema Serbia)	musicartpro.rs
Slovakia	Banská Štiavnica	Superar Slovakia	slovakia.superar.eu
Slovakia	various	The Virtuoso Project	www.virtuoso.sk/en/tlacova-sprava/national-youth-orchestra-established-slovakia
South Africa	Soweto	African Youth Ensemble	www.facebook.com/africanyouthensemble
South Africa	Soweto	Johannesburg Youth Orchestra Company	orchestracompany.org.za
South Africa	Free State	Mangaung Strings Programme	mangaungstringprogr1.wix.com/msp
South Africa	Soweto	Music Is a Great Investment (MIAGI)	www.miagi.co.za
South Africa	Johannesburg	Music Enslightenment Project	www.musicenlightenmentproject.co.za
South Africa	Cape Town	Umculo	umculo.org
South Korea	Seoul	Neighborhood Art School	www.seoulphil.or.kr/en/educate/orchestra/info.do
South Korea	various	Orchestra of Dreams (El Sistema Korea)	www.orchestrakids.or.kr/main/eng01.do
Spain	Madrid	Fundación para la Acción Social por la Música	http://accionsocialporlamusica.es
Spain	Burgos	Jóvenes Arcos de Belorado	sites.google.com/site/jovenesarcosdebelorado

Country	City/State	Name of Program	Web Link
Spain	Barcelona	Voces y Música para la Integración	www.facebook.com/ vocesymusicaparala integracion
Spain	Córdoba	Orquesta-Escuela Mediterranea	www.proartecordoba.org/ category/orquesta
Sri Lanka	various	Music Project Sri Lanka	www.musicprojectsl.com
Sweden	Borlänge	El Sistema Borlänge	http://www.elsistema .se/?page_id=3425
Sweden	Eskilstuna	El Sistema Eskilstuna	http://www.elsistema .se/?page_id=719
Sweden	Gävle	El Sistema i Gävle	http://www.elsistema .se/?page_id=3429
Sweden	Gothenburg	El Sistema i Göteborg	http://www.elsistema .se/?page_id=724
Sweden	Gothenburg	El Sistema Hammarkullen	http://www.elsistema .se/?page_id=16
Sweden	Gothenburg	Kulturskolan Askim-Frölunda-Högsbo	http://www.elsistema .se/?page_id=728
Sweden	Gothenburg	Kulturskolan Centrum	http://www.elsistema .se/?page_id=730
Sweden	Gothenburg	Lundby	http://www.elsistema .se/?page_id=726
Sweden	Gothenburg	Kulturskolan Majorna-Linné	http://www.elsistema .se/?page_id=3021
Sweden	Gothenburg	Norra Hisingen	http://www.elsistema .se/?page_id=3077
Sweden	Gothenburg	Västra Göteborg	http://www.elsistema .se/?page_id=2021
Sweden	Gothenburg	Västra Hisingen	http://www.elsistema .se/?page_id=3082
Sweden	Gothenburg	Örgryte / Härlanda	http://www.elsistema .se/?page_id=734
Sweden	Gothenburg	Östra Göteborg	http://www.elsistema .se/?page_id=722
Sweden	Karlskoga	El Sistema Karlskoga	http://www.elsistema .se/?page_id=3417
Sweden	Malmö	El Sistema Malmö	http://www.elsistema .se/?page_id=732
Sweden	Motala	El Sistema i Motala	http://www.elsistema .se/?page_id=3234
Sweden	Stockholm	El Sistema Stockholm	http://www.elsistema .se/?page_id=1529

Country	City/State	Name of Program	Web Link
Sweden	Södertälje	El Sistema Södertälje	http://www.elsistema .se/?page_id=18
Sweden	Örnsköldsvik	El Sistema Örnsköldsvik	http://www.elsistema .se/?page_id=3406
Sweden	Umeå	El Sistema i Umeå	http://www.elsistema .se/?page_id=1030
Sweden	Vara	Vara Kulturskola	http://www.elsistema .se/?page_id=3413
Sweden	Vänersborg	El Sistema Vänersborg	http://www.elsistema .se/?page_id=3411
Sweden	Åtvidaberg	El Sistema Åtvidaberg	http://www.elsistema .se/?page_id=3415
Sweden	Örebro	El Sistema Örebro	http://www.elsistema .se/?page_id=3409
Switzerland	Lucerne	BaBel Strings	www.babelquartier.ch/detail .php?id=78
Switzerland	Zurich	Superar Suisse	www.superarsuisse.org
Taiwan	Taiwan	El Sistema Taiwan	www.sistemataiwan.org
Thailand	various	Music Alters Everything Foundation	www.maefoundation.org.uk
Turkey	Bursa	Ankara CAKA	www.ankaracaka.com
Turkey	Istanbul	Barış İçin Müzik (Music for Peace)	www.barisicinmuzik.org
Turkey	Ayvalık	Zeytin Çekirdekleri (Olive Seeds)	www.facebook.com/ Zeytin-Çekirdekleri-29570 0360616143
Uganda	Mbale	Elgon Youth Development Centre Uganda	www.facebook.com/ Elgon-Youth-Development- Centre-Uganda- 202063063155925
United Kingdom	various	Sistema England	www.sistemaengland.org.uk
United Kingdom	England	Music First	www.musicfirst.org.uk
United Kingdom	Wales	Sistema Cymru—Codi'r To	www.codirto.com
United Kingdom	Scotland	Sistema Scotland, Big Noise	makeabignoise.org.uk/ sistema-scotland
United Kingdom	England	In Harmony Opera North (Leeds)	www.operanorth.co.uk/ education/in-harmony
United Kingdom	London	In Harmony Lambeth	www.sistemaengland.org.uk/ in-harmony-lambeth

Country	City/State	Name of Program	Web Link
United Kingdom	Liverpool	In Harmony Liverpool	www.liverpoolphil.com/193/in-harmony-liverpool/social-action-through-music.html
United Kingdom	Newcastle	In Harmony Newcastle Gateshead	www.sagegateshead.com/about-us/in-harmony
United Kingdom	Telford and Stoke-on-Trent	In Harmony Telford and Stoke-on-Trent	www.inharmonytelfordstoke.org
United Kingdom	Norwich	Sistema in Norwich	www.sistemanorwich.org.uk
United Kingdom	London	The Nucleo Project	www.sistemaengland.org.uk/sistema-in-norwich
United Kingdom	England	National Orchestra for All	www.nofa.org.uk/index.html
United States	Alabama	Community, Opportunity, and Generosity Through Music Education	cogme.wordpress.com
United States	Alabama	Montgomery Music Project	www.montgomerymusicproject.org
United States	Alabama	Scrollworks	www.facebook.com/Scrollworks
United States	Alaska	Juneau, Alaska Music Matters	juneaumusicmatters.blogspot.ca
United States	California	Alameda Music Proyect	www.alamedamusicproject.org
United States	California	Angelica Center for Arts and Music	www.acamcenter.org
United States	California	Boyle Heights Community Youth Orchestra	www.boyleheightsyouthorchestra.org
United States	California	Caesura Youth Orchestra	www.mycyo.org
United States	California	San Diego Youth Orchestra, Community Opus Project	www.sdys.org/community-opus-project
United States	California	El Sistema Santa Cruz	santacruzeducationfoundation.org/programs/el-sistema-santa-cruz
United States	California	Enriching Lives Through Music	www.elmprogram.org
United States	California	Fortissimo: Orchestra Music Program	www.elmprogram.org
United States	California	Harmony Project	www.harmony-project.org
United States	California	Harmony Stockton	www.harmonystockton.org

Country	City/State	Name of Program	Web Link
United States	California	Incredible Children's Art Network	www.icansbc.org
United States	California	Music Team	www.musicteamsf.org
United States	California	MUSICA!	makingmusica.weebly.com
United States	California	Pacific Chorale Academy	www.pacificchorale.org/concerts_and_events/season_concerts_and_tickets.php?id=139
United States	California	Planet Orchestra	www.planetorch.org
United States	California	Progressions	sanjosejazz.org/education/progressions
United States	California	Renaissance Arts Academy	www.renarts.org
United States	California	Santa Ana Strings	www.pacificsymphony.org/education/santa_ana_strings
United States	California	Santa Rosa Symphony, Simply Strings	santarosasymphony.com/Education-Community/Music-For-Our-Schools/Simply-Strings
United States	California	California Symphony, Sound Minds	www.californiasymphony.org/sound-minds
United States	California	Valley Vibes Orchestras	www.facebook.com/ValleyVibesOrchestras
United States	California	Youth Orchestra Los Angeles	www.laphil.com/education/yola
United States	California	Youth Orchestra Salinas	yosal.org
United States	Colorado	El Sistema Colorado	www.elsistemacolorado.org
United States	Colorado	STEMusic	sites.google.com/a/stemhigh.org/stem-high-academy/teaching-and-learning/music/stemusic
United States	Connecticut	Bravo Waterbury!	www.bravowaterbury.org
United States	Connecticut	Music Haven	musichavenct.org
United States	Connecticut	Project Music	projectmusic.org
United States	District of Columbia	DC Youth Orchestra Program, Children's Orchestra	www.dcyop.org/programs/schoolpartnerships
United States	Florida	Gulfshore Opera Harmony Choir	www.gulfshoreopera.org/outreach/harmony-choir
United States	Florida	Miami Choral Academy	www.seraphicfire.org/miami-choral-academy
United States	Florida	Miami Music Project	www.miamimusicproject.org

Country	City/State	Name of Program	Web Link
United States	Florida	Conservatory School at North Palm Beach Elementary	www.theconservatoryschool.org
United States	Georgia	Atlanta Music Project	www.atlantamusicproject.org
United States	Hawaii	Kalikolehua - El Sistema Hawai'i	www.kalikolehua.com/ Kalikolehua_-_El_Sistema_ Hawaii/Home.html
United States	Illinois	Shift: Englewood	www.shiftyouth.org
United States	Illinois	Sistema Ravinia	ravinia.org/Page/RTP_Play
United States	Illinois	The People's Music School, Youth Orchestras	www.peoplesmusicschool.org/programs/youth-orchestras
United States	Kentucky	North Limestone Musicworks	musicworksckyo.org
United States	Louisianna	Kids' Orchestra	kidsorchestra.org
United States	Louisianna	Make Music NOLA	makemusicnola.org
United States	Maryland	OrchKids	www.bsomusic.org/orchkids
United States	Massachusetts	Bridge Boston Charter School	bridgebostoncs.org/music
United States	Massachusetts	Conservatory Lab Charter School	conservatorylab.org
United States	Massachusetts	El Sistema Somerville	www.facebook.com/El-Sistema-Somerville-2950390 43897144
United States	Massachusetts	Josiah Quincy Orchestra Program	http://www.jqop.org
United States	Massachusetts	Kids 4 Harmony	berkshirechildren.org/ about-kids-4-harmony
United States	Massachusetts	Margarita Muñiz Academy	munizacademy.org
United States	Massachusetts	musiConnects	www.musiconnects.org
United States	Massachusetts	Open Access to Music Education for Children	yofes.org/music-programs
United States	Massachusetts	Revolution of Hope	www.revolutionofhope.org
United States	Michgan	Crescendo Detroit	www.crescendodetroit.org
United States	Michigan	El Sistema at Mitchell	thirdcentury.umich.edu/ el-sistema
United States	Michigan	Kalamazoo Kids in Tune	www.kalamazoosymphony.com/education-community/ community-partnerships/ kids-tune
United States	Minnesota	ComMUSICation	www.commusicationmn.org

Country	City/State	Name of Program	Web Link
United States	Minnesota	El Sistema Minnesota	www.elsistemamn.org
United States	Missouri	Orchestrating Diversity, El Sistema Saint Louis	orchestra.lemp-arts.org
United States	Nevada	Foundation to Assist Young Musicians	thefaym.org
United States	New Jersey	El Sistema Trenton	www.trentoncommunity music.org
United States	New Jersey	New Jersey Symphony Orchestra CHAMPS	www.njsymphony.org/ education-community/ for-educators-students/ njso-champs
United States	New Jersey	Paterson Music Project	whartonmusiccenter.org/ about-pmp/mission
United States	New Jersey	Union City Music Project	www.ucmusicproject.org
United States	New Jersey	Sonic Explorations: Sharing Sounds of Oakwood	http://www.orange.k12.nj.us/ Page/10448
United States	New Mexico	Young Musician Initiative	youngmusicianinitiative.com
United States	New York	Corona Youth Music Project	www.nucleocorona.org
United States	New York	Empire State Youth Orchestra, CHIME	esyo.org/about-us/chime
United States	New York	D'Addario/Harmony Free Lesson Program	www.daddariofoundation .org/post/what-is-the- daddarioharmony-free- lesson-program
United States	New York	Harmony Program	harmonyprogram.org
United States	New York	Imagine Syracuse	imaginesyracuse.blogspot .com
United States	New York	Youth Orchestra of St. Luke's	www.oslmusic.org/ community-education/yosl
United States	New York	Eastman School of Music, ROCMusic	www.esm.rochester.edu/ rocmusic
United States	New York	UpBeat NYC	upbeatnyc.org
United States	New York	Washington Heights (WHIN) Music Project	www.whinmusicproject.org/ home
United States	North Carolina	Kidznotes	www.kidznotes.org
United States	North Carolina	Music Works!	www.musicworksasheville .org
United States	North Carolina	MusicalMinds NC	www.musicalmindsnc.org
United States	North Carolina	Young Musicians of Alamance	www.ymofa.org

Country	City/State	Name of Program	Web Link
United States	Ohio	Cincinnati Choral Academy	
United States	Ohio	CityMusicKidz Youth Orchestra	www.citymusiccleveland.org/Education/about-citymusickidz-youth.php
United States	Ohio	COR Music Project	thecormusicproject.org
United States	Ohio	El Sistema @ Rainey	www.raineyinstitute.org/?project=el-sistema
United States	Ohio	Music for Youth in Cincinnati	www.mycincinnatiorchestra.org
United States	Ohio	Q the Music	www.qthemusic.org
United States	Oklahoma	El Sistema Oklahoma	www.elsistemaok.org
United States	Oklahoma	Sistema Tulsa	sistematulsa.org
United States	Oregon	BRAVO Youth Orchestras	oregonbravo.org
United States	Pennsylvania	El Sistema Lehigh Valley	asaeducation.weebly.com/el-sistema-lehigh-valley.html
United States	Pennsylvania	El Sistema Pittsburgh	elsistemapittsburgh.org
United States	Pennsylvania	Play On, Philly!	www.playonphilly.org
United States	Pennsylvania	Johnstown Symphony Orchestra, Share-the-Music	www.johnstownsymphony.org/index.php?page=education
United States	Pennsylvania/New Jersey	Sister Cities Girlchoir	www.sistercitiesgirlchoir.org
United States	Pennsylvania	Tune Up Philly	pyos.org/ensembles/tup
United States	South Carolina	Kidzymphony Orchestra Program	www.charlestonmusic.org/kidzymphony-orchestra-program.htm
United States	South Dakota	Harmony South Dakota	www.harmonysouthdakota.org
United States	Tennessee	Music City Youth Orchestra, Harmony Project	musiccityyo.org/about.html
United States	Texas	Austin Soundwaves	www.hispanicallianceaustin.org/asw
United States	Texas	B Sharp Youth Music	bsharpkids.org
United States	Texas	Houston Youth Symphony, Coda Music Program	www.houstonyouthsymphony.com/comm/CodaComm.html
United States	Texas	Youth Orchestras of San Antonio	www.yosa.org
United States	Texas	Tocando Community Music Project	www.tocandomusicproject.org

Country	City/State	Name of Program	Web Link
United States	Utah	GraceNotes @ Salty Cricket	saltycricket.org/grace notessalty-cricket/grace notes-am-homeschool-options
United States	Utah	Sistema Utah	www.facebook.com/SistemaUtah
United States	Virginia	BRIDGES: Harmony Through Music	www.bridgesharmony.com
United States	Virginia	Alexandria Symphony Orchestra, Sympatico	www.alexsym.org/education/elsistema
United States	Virginia	Soundscapes	www.soundscapes.org
United States	Washington	Kids in Concert	www.kidsinconcert.org
United States	Washington	Yakima Music en Acción	www.yamamusic.org
United States	Wisconsin	El Sistema Greater Milwaukee	www.elsistema-milwaukee.org
Uruguay	various	Fundación de Orquestas Infantiles y Juveniles de Uruguay	www.orquestas.com.uy/sistema.html
Uruguay	Montevideo	Sembrando Talentos Uruguay	sembrandotalentosuruguay.weebly.com
Venezuela	various	El Sistema/Fundación Musical Simón Bolívar	http://fundamusical.org.ve/
Vietnam	Hanoi	Miracle Choir and Orchestra	www.miraclevietnam.org
Vietnam	various	The Bamboo School	www.thebambooschool.org

A Short List of Recommended Useful Resources

NOTE: Web addresses change and disappear (which is why we do not include them in the text of this book), so we cannot guarantee that these addresses will be active by the time you read this book.

Key Moments

2016 José Antonio Abreu Over Forty Years—a compilation (in Spanish) of highlights from Maestro Abreu's speeches, beginning with the first orchestra rehearsal in 1975: https://youtu.be/9GvygLTLIpA.

2016 The orchestra of the Nucleo Project in London plays a famous Venezuelan folk song as a tribute to El Sistema Venezuela: https://www.youtube.com/watch?v=9IoYpHYlSGU.

2015 Sistema Europe Youth Orchestra in Milan, Italy: https://www.youtube.com/watch?v=zwH7dt-wJzw.

2014 Superar Orchestra and Chorus: students of Sistema programs in central and Eastern Europe performing "Love People," a song written by students of Superar Bosnia: https://vimeo.com/156555498.

2014 Ghetto Classics, a Sistema-inspired program in the Korogosho slum of Nairobi, Kenya: http://www.dw.com/en/kenya-ghetto-classics/a-18742091.

2013 Ensembles of Afghanistan National Institute of Music at the Kennedy Center, Washington, D.C.: https://www.youtube.com/watch?v=cqmduDgvNEc&list=PLNsq6-vcOM3EYHCgBUWirT7mYQpKXlk_3.

2013 White Hands Choir from Venezuela in Salzburg, Austria: https://www.youtube.com/watch?v=DuELOI1uYls.

2013 Sistema Europe Youth Orchestra in Salzburg, Austria: https://www.youtube.com/watch?v=E58s_bOwU_I.

2012 The children of Sistema Scotland performing with the Simón Bolívar Orchestra of Venezuela: https://www.youtube.com/watch?v=BANtDugVaHw.

2010 Simón Bolívar Youth Orchestra performing in the barrio La Vega, Caracas: https://www.youtube.com/watch?v=C50yq3TncxU.

2010 Gustavo Dudamel conducting the youngest national El Sistema orchestra in Venezuela, rehearsing Mahler: https://www.youtube .com/watch?v=fZJGps1Kx00.

2009 José Antonio Abreu TED Talk: https://www.ted.com/talks/José_ abreu_on_kids_transformed_by_music?language=en.

2008 *60 Minutes* television show segment: http://www.cbsnews.com/vid eos/el-sistema.

2007 Simón Bolívar Youth Orchestra of Venezuela performing "Mambo" at the BBC Proms, London: https://www.youtube.com/watch?v=xlAa iBNCYU4.

Internet Sites

El Sistema Venezuela/Fundamusical: http://fundamusical.org.ve; http:// fundamusical.org.ve/el-sistema.

El Sistema USA: https://www.elsistemausa.org.

League of American Orchestras: El Sistema: http://www.americanorches tras.org/youth-education-community/el-sistema.html.

Sistema Europe: http://www.sistemaeurope.org.

Sistema Fellows Program: http://necmusic.edu/sistema-resources.

Sistema Global: http://sistemaglobal.org.

Sistema Global: Rep + Resource: http://sistemaglobal.org/resources.

Take a Stand: http://www.take-a-stand.org/.

Tricia Tunstall website, El Sistema page: http://http://www.changinglives elsistema.com/?page_id=7.

YOLA Resource Library: http://www.laphil.com/education/yola/resource -library.

Films

Crescendo: The Power of Music (2015): http://www.crescendofilmdoc.com; https://hemmingshouse.wordpress.com/2012/05/23/sistema-revolution -national-cbc-broadcast-premiere/.

Side by Side: El Sistema Sweden (2013): http://www.youtube.com/watch? v=PzeVhribHyM.

Beyond the Music: Soundscapes, El Sistema and the Proven Power of Music

(by Joe Hamm): (2013) https://www.youtube.com/watch?v=8_3PtSu Kjzk.

Sistema Revolution (2012, Canada): https://hemmingshouse.wordpress .com/2012/05/23/sistema-revolution-national-cbc-broadcast-premiere.

Dudamel: Let the Children Play: (2010) http://dudamel.net/sponsors.

El Sistema (2008): https://www.youtube.com/watch?v=276oR_tEmbs.

The Promise of Music (2007): http://www.imdb.com/title/tt1223885.

Tocar y Luchar (2006): http://www.imdb.com/title/tt0810049.

Books

Borzacchini, Chefi. *Venezuela: The Miracle of Music* (Caracas: Fundación Bancaribe, 2010).

Hernández-Estrada, José Luis. *Aesthetics of Generosity: El Sistema, Music Education, and Social Change, 2012.*

Kaufmann, Michael, and Stefan Piendl. *Das Wunder von Caracas* (in German) (Munich: Irisiana, 2011).

Tierney, William G., ed. *Rethinking Education and Poverty* (Baltimore: Johns Hopkins University Press, 2015). In particular, Shirley Brice Heath's essay "Museums, Theaters, and Youth Orchestras: Advancing Creative Arts and Sciences Within Underresourced Communities" includes a thoughtful discussion of El Sistema and the multiple advantages of musical ensemble learning.

Tunstall, Tricia. *Changing Lives: Gustavo Dudamel, El Sistema, and the Transformative Power of Music* (New York: W. W. Norton, 2012; paperback, 2013).

Witkowski, Christine, ed. *El Sistema: Music for Social Change* (London: Omnibus Press, 2016). A collection of essays about El Sistema history, principles, pedagogy, and practice across the world.

Research Currently Available Online

"A National Collaborative Evaluation of Sistema-inspired Music Education," WolfBrown/Longy School (2015–16, ongoing): http://wolfbrown .com/news/a-national-collaborative-evaluation-of-sistema-inspired-mu sic-education.

"Exploring the Academic and Psychosocial Impact of El Sistema–Inspired Music Programs Within Two Low Socio-Economic Schools" (about

Pizzicato Effect program, Melbourne): http://dx.doi.org/10.1080/14613
808.2015.1056130 (published online September 1, 2015).

Evaluating Sistema Scotland: Initial Findings Report (2015): http://www
.gcph.co.uk/assets/0000/5059/Sistema_summary_updated.pdf [also
see "Evaluation of Big Noise, Sistema Scotland (2011): www.gov.scot/
Resource/Doc/345409/0114922.pdf].

Sistema Global Literature Review, Andrea Creech and Patricia Gonzalez-
Moreno, Lisa Lorenzino, Grace Waitman (2013): http://sistemaglobal
.org/literature-review.

"A National Sistema Network in Canada: Feasibility Study and Strategic
Plan," Inga Petri (2013): http://www4.nac-cna.ca/pdf/corporate/Sistema
Canada_FeasibilityReport_en.pdf.

"Globalizing El Sistema," Lauren Silberman, M.A. thesis, University of
Oregon (2013): https://globalizingelsistema.wordpress.com/.

"Between Social Harmony and Political Dissonance: The Institutional
and Policy-Based Intricacies of the Venezuelan System of Children
and Youth Orchestras," Daniel Mora-Brito, M.A. thesis, University of
Texas, Austin (2011): https://repositories.lib.utexas.edu/bitstream/han
dle/2152/ETD-UT-2011-08-4155/MORA-BRITO-THESIS.pdf.

"Music to My Ears: The (Many) Socio-Economic Benefits of Music
Training Programs," José Cuesta (Washington D.C.: InterAmerican
Development Bank 2008): http://www.laphil.com/sites/default/files/
media/pdfs/shared/education/yola/iadb-research.pdf.

"Orchestrating 'An Affluence of Spirit': Addressing Self-Esteem in
Impoverished Venezuelan Children Through Music Education," Jen-
nifer Diana Mei-lyn Chang (B.A. thesis, Harvard University, 2007):
https://books.google.com/books/about/Orchestrating_an_affluence_
of_Spirit.html?id=_UQ8QwAACAAJ.

"A Model for Community Participation in the Performing Arts: Social
Action Through Music and the Internationalization of the Venezuela
Orchestra System," Alvaro Rodas, M.A. thesis, Columbia University
(2006): http://bibliotecaamauryveray.cmpr.edu/docs/bib/tesis/Rodas
MastersEssay.pdf.

Newsletters

The Ensemble (covering the U.S. and Canada): Contact theensemblenl@
  gmail.com or theensemblenewsletters.com.

The World Ensemble (in English and Spanish): Contact theworldensem
  ble@gmail.com or theensemblenewsletters.com.

Blogs

Sistema Fellows: http://sistemafellows.typepad.com/my-blog.

Marshall Marcus: http://necmusic.edu/sistema-fellows/blog.

Jonathan Govias: http://jonathangovias.com.

Defining an El Sistema-Inspired Program

As we gathered contact information from all programs around the world for the first time to launch the newsletter *The World Ensemble*, we had to address the issue of organizations that are not really Sistema-inspired using the name to advance their work. The issue is delicate because El Sistema is not a club that explicitly includes and excludes members according to established criteria, and no one in this movement dedicated to inclusivity wants to be in the business of excluding well-intentioned colleagues. However, when clearly non-Sistema-like programs use the name, it weakens the identity and potency of the movement. We have tried to walk the fine line of determining which programs' news *The World Ensemble* will publish (although happily distributing it to everyone) by clarifying which would be considered "El Sistema" programs and which would be considered friends and colleagues. Perhaps these guidelines might be useful to readers as well.

What Is an El Sistema-Inspired Program? What Isn't?

Programs that are El Sistema-inspired (ES-i) use these six core principles and practices to guide their current programs and continuing development. A program that uses all these principles and practices, or that is growing into implementation of them, is an El Sistema-inspired program.

Social Goals

The primary goal of ES-i programs is the social development of young people and their communities. The musical processes and accomplishments are the main means of achieving these social goals, but they are the means, not the end. ES-i programs primarily determine their success by looking at the social outcomes of their students.

Inclusiveness

ES-i programs do not audition students for selection based on ability. They predominantly serve students without ready access to intensive music instruction, and all who want to attend the program are welcome, without cost as a barrier to participation.

Learning in Ensemble

The primary vehicle for musical learning in ES-i programs is the ensemble, as soon as and as often as possible. While one-on-one instruction is usually included, it is secondary in priority because ES-i programs rely on the social development that comes with group learning.

Intensiveness

While musical learning happens in many ways, social development through music requires a commitment of intensive, rigorous, consistent engagement over multiple years. ES-i programs are not content with a few hours of study per week for a year or two, but require, or are moving toward requiring, a significant commitment of hours each week over multiple years.

Mentoring and Peer Learning

Teachers and more experienced students act as mentors to students in ES-i programs, and programs nurture and rely on peer-to-peer instruction.

Learning Environment

ES-i programs strive to create a safe, positive, joyful, hardworking, and high-aspiring home base for all students. Faculty and program leaders continually invest themselves in finding additional ways to make the environment more motivating and positive. ES-i programs have active connections to families and community and always seek their greater involvement. Via performance and partnerships, student experiences extend to new settings within and outside their neighborhoods, expanding their sense of place, belonging, and opportunity.

WE WOULD SUGGEST that whatever its stated values, a program that does not actually run according to these six principles and practices may admire El Sistema, and may be a valuable friend and colleague to the El Sistema movement, but it is not an El Sistema-inspired program.

This distinction is not intended to exclude colleagues, but rather to help the El Sistema-inspired movement grow by clarifying its identity and its central practices. ES-i programs welcome friendships and partnerships with programs that share their aspirations; we have much to learn from them, and hope that we have much to share.

Index

Note: Page numbers in italics indicate illustrations.